METHODOLOGIES OF LEGA

Until quite recently questions about methodology in legal research have been largely confined to understanding the role of doctrinal research as a scholarly discipline. In turn this has involved asking questions not only about coverage but, fundamentally, questions about the identity of the discipline. Is it (mainly) descriptive, hermeneutical, or normative? Should it also be explanatory? Legal scholarship has been torn between, on the one hand, grasping the expanding reality of law and its context, and, on the other, reducing this complex whole to manageable proportions. The purely internal analysis of a legal system, isolated from any societal context, remains an option, and is still seen in the approach of the French academy, but as law aims at ordering society and influencing human behaviour, this approach is felt by many scholars to be insufficient.

Consequently many attempts have been made to conceive legal research differently. Social scientific and comparative approaches have proven fruitful. However, does the introduction of other approaches leave merely a residue of 'legal doctrine', to which pockets of social sciences can be added, or should legal doctrine be merged with the social sciences? What would such a broad interdisciplinary field look like and what would its methods be? This book is an attempt to answer some of these questions.

European Academy of Legal Theory Series: Volume 9

EUROPEAN ACADEMY OF LEGAL THEORY MONOGRAPH SERIES

General Editors
Professor Mark Van Hoecke
Professor François Ost

Titles in this Series

Moral Conflict and Legal Reasoning
Scott Veitch

The Harmonisation of European Private Law
edited by Mark Van Hoecke & Francois Ost

On Law and Legal Reasoning
Fernando Atria

Law as Communication
Mark Van Hoecke

Legisprudence
edited by Luc Wintgens

Epistemology and Methodology of Comparative Law
edited by Mark Van Hoecke

Making the Law Explicit
The Normativity of Legal Argumentation
Matthias Klatt

The Policy of Law
A Legal Theoretical Framework
Mauro Zamboni

Methodologies of Legal Research
Which Kind of Method for What Kind of Discipline?
edited by Mark Van Hoecke

Objectivity in Law and Legal Reasoning
edited by Jaakko Husa and Mark Van Hoecke

Methodologies of Legal Research

Which Kind of Method for What Kind of Discipline?

Edited by

Mark Van Hoecke

·HART·
PUBLISHING

OXFORD AND PORTLAND, OREGON
2013

Published in the United Kingdom by Hart Publishing Ltd
16C Worcester Place, Oxford, OX1 2JW
Telephone: +44 (0)1865 517530
Fax: +44 (0)1865 510710
E-mail: mail@hartpub.co.uk
Website: http://www.hartpub.co.uk

Published in North America (US and Canada) by
Hart Publishing
c/o International Specialized Book Services
920 NE 58th Avenue, Suite 300
Portland, OR 97213-3786
USA
Tel: +1 503 287 3093 or toll-free: (1) 800 944 6190
Fax: +1 503 280 8832
E-mail: orders@isbs.com
Website: http://www.isbs.com

© The editors and contributors severally 2011
First published in 2011. Reprinted in paperback in 2013

The editors and contributors have asserted their right under the Copyright,
Designs and Patents Act 1988, to be identified as the authors of this work.

All rights reserved. No part of this publication may be reproduced, stored in a retrieval system, or transmitted, in any form or by any means, without the prior permission of Hart Publishing, or as expressly permitted by law or under the terms agreed with the appropriate reprographic rights organisation. Enquiries concerning reproduction which may not be covered by the above should be addressed to Hart Publishing Ltd at the address above.

British Library Cataloguing in Publication Data

Data Available

ISBN: 978-1-84946-170-2 (hardback)
ISBN: 978-1-84946-499-4 (paperback)

Typeset by Hope Services Ltd, Abingdon
Printed and bound in Great Britain by
CPI Group (UK) Ltd, Croydon, CR0 4YY

Preface to the Paperback Edition

Legal research is still in the process of establishing an adequate methodology or at least a set of adequate methods. The publication of this book was evidence of this process. Indeed, as the subtitle of the book suggests (*Which Kind of Method for What Kind of Discipline?*), there is still no agreement on the aims of legal research. Anne Ruth Mackor has further developed her paper in this book in an article, published in 2012, entitled 'Legal doctrine as a non-normative discipline: a refinement of Niiniluoto's and Aarnio's distinction between norm-descriptions, norm-contentions and norm–recommendations'.[1] In contrast, another Dutch scholar, Jan Smits, has defended the opposite view in a book published around the same time[2].

In continental Europe, with its longstanding tradition of legal doctrine, typical objects of legal research have been, and largely still are, the searching for solutions for legal problems within a given legal system at the same time as keeping that system coherent. It transpires from a recent report of the German Scientific Council (*Wissenschaftsrat*) that this view remains the underlying purpose of legal scholarship in Germany. In other words the German Scientific Council and its advisors are supporting a rather narrow conception of *Rechtswissenschaft*, although with some suggestions for more Europeanisation, internationalisation and interdisciplinarity[3]. However, the theoretical framework within which such research, transcending the borders of the national legal system, should be carried out remains unclear in the report. Some chapters in our book may thus be useful for finding an answer to this lack of clarity.

Somewhat opposed to the German view on legal scholarship, which is representative for most countries in continental Europe, is the British one. Susan Bartie noted that

> In the past 20 or so years the intellectual coherence of law as an academic discipline has increasingly been called into question. . . . Now legal academics work in many specialised areas, study diverse topics and adopt a variety of methods and perspectives.[4]

The "understanding and internal coherence of legal concepts and legal reasoning" is only one of the research agendas[5] and so, for example, Christopher McCrudden distinguishes three more:

---

[1] Published in the Dutch journal 2 *Recht & Methode*, 2012, 22-45.
[2] Jan Smits, *The Mind and Method of the Legal Academic*, (Cheltenham, Edward Elgar, 2012).
[3] Wissenschaftsrat, *Perspektiven der Rechtswissenschaft in Deutschland. Situation, Analysen, Empfehlungen*, Hamburg 9 November 2012; www.wissenschaftsrat.de/download/archiv/2558-12.pdf
[4] Susan Bartie, 'The Lingering Core of Legal Scholarship', 30 *Legal Studies 2010*, 345-369, 345.
[5] Christopher McCrudden, 'Legal Research and the Social Sciences', 122 *Law Quarterly Review*, 2006, 632-650, 632.

vi   *Preface to the Paperback Edition*

> Secondly, the meaning and validity of law: the examination of what makes law different from, or similar to, other normative systems. . . .
> Thirdly, the ethical and political acceptability of public policy delivered through legal instruments. . . .
> Fourthly, the effect of law.[6]

In practice, there is a certain pressure from research funding bodies and research assessment panels in the UK to focus on the latter, that is to say on more social science oriented research agendas.[7] In fact an important part of what the German Scientific Counsel defines as genuine legal scholarship would simply not count in a British research assessment exercise. Consequently, for those who regard legal scholarship as a form of social science, some chapters in our book may help them to see how other forms of legal scholarship are not only conceivable but also perfectly legitimate, even when such research has little utility for legal practice.

A more structured map of legal research has been offered by one of the authors of this book. Mathias Siems, in a recent paper with Daithí Mac Síthigh on 'Mapping Legal Research', distinguishes between three (ideal) types of legal research: 'law as a practical discipline' (applying), 'law as humanities'[8] (understanding) and 'law as social sciences' (explaining). By splitting up the interdisciplinary approaches to law into two groups, 'humanities' and 'social sciences', the more familiar link of legal research with social science methodology is complemented with the less obvious link between, on the one hand, legal interpretation and, on the other hand, the methodology of interpretation used in other disciplines. The authors also show how a tension between legal practice and law as humanities was already present, both in England and Scotland, at the very origins of law faculties[9], whilst the tension with 'law as social sciences' developed later. Not only are the different types of legal research present in all law faculties (all over the world), but in practice:

> legal academics often tend to mix approaches. For instance, it is not uncommon that a legal researcher starts with an historical introduction, then turns to an analysis of the relevant case law and finally engages with socio-political considerations.[10]

In all this, methodology is often largely absent or at least not made explicit. Today legal research in most countries is moving in the American direction where there is, more than in the UK, a tendency to abandon the link with the legal profession and to move towards interdisciplinary studies.[11]

---

[6] ibid
[7] See, eg: Fiona Cownie, 'The Death of the Textbook Tradition', 3 *European Journal of Legal Education* 2006, 79
[8] "This view relates this approach to legal scholarship to interpretative disciplines such as history, philosophy, theology and literature which are generally recognised as having a primary affiliation with the humanities." (Mathias M Siems & Daithí Mac Síthigh, 'Mapping Legal Research', 71 *Cambridge Law Journal*, 2012, 651-676, 654)
[9] ibid 660
[10] ibid 668
[11] ibid 673 and 671. See also the book *Law and Method*, edited by Bart van Klink and Sanne Taekema (Tübingen, Mohr Siebeck, 2011), which focuses on interdisciplinary research, pointing in the Foreword to "the increasing interdisciplinary character of legal research" (p.V)

Different research agendas imply different methods. That is why we used a plural in the title of our book (*Methodologies* . . .). Even at the level of methodology, however, there is no shared view among legal scholars. In his already mentioned and interesting book, Jan Smits takes a rather sceptical attitude towards methods in legal research. He says that:

> knowledge is acquired in another way that is not strictly prescribed by research methods: the legal discipline is primarily a practice, in which the community of academic colleagues (the forum) decides on what is to be seen as reliable knowledge."[12]

Of course the scientific forum is the ultimate touchstone for scholarship in any discipline. For deciding "what is to be seen as reliable knowledge" one does not rely on subjective personal views or feelings of the members of this group; one relies on a generally accepted paradigmatical framework in the discipline concerned and on a shared methodology. Legal scholarship must, then, make explicit and elaborate its paradigm and methodology, rather than falling back on the view that it is not a scientific activity. In a recently published volume on *Practice and Theory in Comparative Law*, one of the contributors to our book complained that

> . . . much of the most influential work on method remains at the level of pure theory, omitting any sustained testing of its critiques and recommendations in practice, while at the same time much interesting 'substantive' comparative work does not make its methodological choices sufficiently clear.[13]

Such a discrepancy is still not to be found with the methodology of legal research within one single legal system, simply because no theories have yet been developed as in comparative research, which would not fit with legal practice. On the other hand, legal research is still too often carried out without any explicit methodology, if not without any idea of what methodology could be about or even an explicit rejection of any need for methodology in legal research.

However, the idea that '*ius est ars aequi et boni*'[14] is no longer adequate in itself. This book aims to contribute to the elaboration of such a methodology, or rather methodolog*ies*.

Mark Van Hoecke
2 March 2013

---

[12] Jan Smits, *The Mind and Method of the Legal Academic* (Cheltenham, Edward Elgar, 2012) 112-113
[13] Maurice Adams and Jacco Bomhoff, 'Comparing law: practice and theory', ch.1 in: M.Adams and J.Bomhoff (eds), *Practice and Theory in Comparative Law* (Cambridge, Cambridge University Press, 2012) 1
[14] It is, indeed, not accidental that a new journal '*Recht en Methode*' has been created in The Netherlands in 2011. Its focus is on methodology in legal research and in legal education.

Preface

In order to develop a suitable methodology of comparative law, one needs a better view on the methodology of legal scholarship within domestic legal systems. Also, within the context of the current debate on the scientific status of legal scholarship, the question arises as to what kind of discipline legal doctrine is (or should be) and which kind of scientific methodology is most appropriate for what kind of legal research. Here, we are faced with diverging traditions of legal scholarship (eg United Kingdom versus Continental Europe) and diverging underlying theories of 'legal science' in the course of history: a 'positive moral science' (natural law tradition), a discipline aiming at discovering the will of the (historical) legislator (exegetic school), an interdisciplinary discipline (law in context), a social science (legal scholarship as an empirical discipline), a conceptual structure (Begriffsjurisprudenz), a normative 'imputation discipline', clearly distinguishing 'is' and 'ought' (Kelsen), etc. All this could lead to the following questions:

In general:
(a) linking specific approaches and specific methods, on the basis of the various types of research and other distinctions mentioned hereafter;
(b) or scrutinising more deeply one of these approaches or methods, as applied to legal research in a domestic or comparative context.

(1) Types of research

- explanatory (explaining the law, for instance by diverging historical backgrounds in comparative research);
- empirical (identification of the valid law; determining the best legal means for reaching a certain goal – the 'best solution' in comparative law);
- hermeneutic (interpretation, argumentation);
- exploring (looking for new, possibly fruitful paths in legal research);
- logical (coherence, structuring concepts, rules, principles, etc – eg the use of the Hohfeldian analysis of the concept of right in domestic legal doctrine or for the purpose of comparing legal systems);
- instrumental (concept-building);
- evaluative (testing whether rules work in practice, or whether they are in accordance with desirable moral, political, economical aims, or, in comparative law, whether a certain harmonisation proposal could work, taking into account other important divergences in the legal systems concerned).

(2) Use of supporting disciplines

- legal history;
- legal sociology;
- legal anthropology;
- legal psychology;
- law and biology; and
- law and economics.

(3) Levels of comparison

- conceptual framework of legal doctrine;
- principles;
- rules; and
- cases.

(4) Levels of research

- description (interpretation); and
- systematisation (theory building).

(5) Schemes of intelligibility[15]

- causal;
- functional;
- structural;
- hermeneutical;
- actional; and
- dialectical.

(6) Ideological perspectives

- individualistic versus communitarian;
- nationalistic versus international;
- positivist versus morally, politically oriented;
- monistic (order) versus multi-layered (pluralistic, disorder); and
- nature versus culture.

Doctrinal legal research ranges between straightforward descriptions of (new) laws, with some incidental interpretative comments, on the one hand, and innovative theory building (systematisation), on the other. The more 'simple' versions of that research are necessary building blocks for the more sophisticated ones. Inevitably, the more descriptive types of research will be, by far, more numerous. Comparative law usually remains at the level of description, combined with some comparison (but mostly at the 'tourist' level). In attempts of (European) harmonisation, however, a clear level of systematisation (theory building) has been established.

---

[15] See on this J-M Berthelot, L'intelligence du social (Paris, Presses Universitaires de France, 1990) 62–85 and, for an application to legal research, see G Samuel, 'Taking Methods Seriously (Part One)' (2007) 2 Journal of Comparative Law 94, 105ff.

Preface xi

All scientific research, including legal research, starts from assumptions. Most of these assumptions are paradigmatic. This means that they are the generally recognised assumptions ('truths') of legal scholarship within that legal system, or the common assumptions of all the compared legal systems in comparative research. They constitute the paradigmatic framework, which tends not to be debated as such within the discipline itself. Apart from this, researchers may also start from assumptions which are less obvious. In those cases, they have to be made explicit, but not necessarily justified. In some of these cases, the outcome of the research will only be useful to the extent that one accepts its underlying assumptions. Alternatively, a given approach may prove to be more fruitful than research, which (partly) starts from other assumptions. A typical example is the recognised 'legal sources', which are not a matter of discussion within a given legal system (legal scholarship). Sometimes new legal sources (eg 'unwritten general principles of law') or principles (eg priority of European law over domestic law) are accepted as assumptions, as they seem to be more fruitful, eg for keeping law more coherent. A study on such assumptions (and their limits) in domestic legal doctrine and/or in comparative research is another possible topic for research.

The questions and suggestions above were proposed to a number of scholars when inviting them to lecture at a workshop organised, in October 2009, by the Research Group for Methodology of Law and Legal Research at Tilburg University. The current book contains the revised papers presented at that workshop, together with two papers by members of the Tilburg Methodology research group, which are partly a result of the discussions during the workshop and a comment on one or more papers presented there. Other members of the Tilburg Methodology research group who commented during the Conference have been Jan Smits and Koen Van Aeken.

As an introduction to the contributions in this book, some conclusions of the workshop are to be found hereafter.

Legal scholarship is torn between grasping as much as possible the expanding reality of law and its context, on the one hand, and reducing this complex whole to manageable proportions, on the other. In the latter case, a purely internal analysis of the legal system involved, isolated from any societal context, is an option, most notably visible in French legal doctrine.[16] In such an approach, law is largely cut loose from its context, and societal problems are exclusively worded as 'legal' problems, that should be 'solved' without taking into account anything that is not 'law'. Moreover, law in this view means only, for instance, *French state law*, or even more narrowly *French official private law*. Here, 'legal reality' is confined to legislation and case law. There seems to be no other relevant reality for lawyers. In this way, an artificial world is created, in which (sometimes artificial) problems are worded and solved, without any necessary connection to some societal reality. As law aims at ordering society, at influencing human

---

[16] See Horatia Muir-Watt's chapter, 'The Epistemological Function of "la Doctrine"' (ch seven).

behaviour,[17] such an approach is felt to be largely insufficient by many scholars. More specifically, the failure of doctrinal legal research to build, to structure, to interpret and to apply the law in such a way that it fulfils its obvious function in society, together with a complete lack of any methodology, has led an increasing number of scholars to question its scientific status. In chapter four, Mathias Siems argues that teaching and a low profile 'legal doctrine' may very well be carried out by legal practitioners (as was actually the case in England until about half a century ago). So, 'a world without law professors' would indeed be possible in practice.

As a reaction, many attempts have been made, from the nineteenth century onwards, to broaden legal doctrine, or to conceive it differently. Adding a social science dimension[18] or a comparative dimension[19] has proven fruitful. However, the question then becomes one of demarcating the borders of legal science: is there still some kind of 'legal doctrine' left, to which pockets of social sciences have been added? Or will legal doctrine have to be merged with social sciences? If so, which disciplines should be favoured: just traditional legal sociology, or also law and economics and/or legal history and/or legal psychology and/or legal anthropology, or even more exotic disciplines such as 'behavioural economics'[20] and/or 'evolutionary analysis in law'.[21] How would such a broad interdisciplinary discipline look like? Which methods should it use? How can we educate competent scholars who will be able to carry out such a broad research programme or even parts of it?

The demarcation of 'legal doctrine' is not only a matter of fields to be covered, it is also, and even in the first place, a question of the identity of the discipline. Is it (mainly) descriptive? Or rather hermeneutical? Or perhaps normative? Or should it be explanatory? This question is discussed at length in several papers.[22] The main conclusion to be drawn is that several approaches fit with legal doctrine and that all those approaches can be defended to some extent, as long as one keeps a pluralist approach. Under the heading of 'legal doctrine' or, if one prefers, 'legal science', many types of research may be carried out: descriptive, exploratory, explanatory, wording and/or testing hypotheses and/or theories, or just supporting legal practice (and, in that sense, it becomes normative).

Each of those types of research will involve its own methods and each research question will imply the use of the appropriate method(s) for that kind of research.[23] Maybe this variety of possible approaches and methods explains the confusion in the terminology used. Although Jaap Hage ('Truly normative legal

[17] See Julie De Coninck's chapter, 'Behavioural Economics and Legal Research' (ch 14).
[18] See the chapters by Julie De Coninck (ch 14) and by Bart Du Laing (ch 13).
[19] See the chapters by John Bell (ch nine), by Geoffrey Samuel (ch 10) and by Jaakko Husa (ch 11), and Maurice Adams' comments (ch 12).
[20] See Julie De Coninck's chapter 14.
[21] See Bart Du Laing's chapter 13.
[22] See the chapters by Mark Van Hoecke (ch one), Jaap Hage (ch two), Anne Ruth Mackor (ch three), Pauline Westerman (ch five), Jan Vranken (ch six) and Bert van Roermund (ch 15).
[23] See Jaap Hage's chapter two.

science') and Anne Ruth Mackor ('Explanatory non-normative legal doctrine') use seemingly contradictory titles, they nevertheless appear to largely agree in their view on legal doctrine. Roger Brownsword also points to this implicitly, when asking himself 'what am I doing as a legal scholar in contract law?'

Should we try to implement some ideal type of 'legal science', bearing the risk of being cut loose not only from legal practice but from the large majority of legal academics as well? Or should we rather, pragmatically, aim at adjusting legal doctrine's centuries-old research tradition? In the latter case, legal doctrine could develop as 'law in context', while still emphasising the internal perspective on law. Elements of social sciences could be used more systematically for underpinning doctrinal research, instead of trying to realise the ambition of developing an interdisciplinary super-science, which would integrate everything there is to know about law. Legal doctrine should use those disciplines, but not try to integrate them. Such integration raises problems of epistemology, of methodology and of research skills. It would be very difficult, if not impossible, to demarcate a common epistemological framework, within which common methodologies could be worked out for quite diverging research purposes. Moreover, such methods should be so diverse that it would be extremely difficult to combine all the research skills needed, even in a coherent research team. In practice, the adequate research activities will rather be multi-layered, such as legal doctrine using elements of behavioural economics which, in turn, uses elements of evolutionary analysis in law (see the chapters by De Coninck and by Du Laing).

Four papers in this book have focused on comparative law (Samuel, Husa, Bell and Adams), but with a clear connection to legal doctrine. Indeed, Geoffrey Samuel argues that developing methods in comparative law could be a road to developing the methodology of domestic legal doctrine. Bart Du Laing for his part shows how the evolutionary analysis of law could be helpful in developing the methodology of comparative law: varying adaptation of cultures to local conditions as an element for developing a theory of 'legal families'.

Finally, I would like to thank Caroline Laske for checking the English language for part of the papers, and Dr Antal Szerletics for his help in preparing the manuscript for publication, and Mustapha El Karouni for taking care of indexing the book.

Mark Van Hoecke
11 January 2010

Contents

Preface to the Paperback Edition	v
Preface	ix
List of Contributors	xix

1. Legal Doctrine: Which Method(s) for What Kind of Discipline?   1
   Mark Van Hoecke

I.	Historical Developments	1
II.	What Kind of Discipline is Legal Doctrine?	4
III.	Which Methodology for Legal Research?	11
IV.	Conclusion	17

2. The Method of a Truly Normative Legal Science   19
   Jaap Hage

I.	Preliminaries	20
II.	The Possibility of a Normative Science	28
III.	The Method of a Truly Normative Legal Science	40
IV.	Conclusion	43

3. Explanatory Non-Normative Legal Doctrine. Taking the Distinction between Theoretical and Practical Reason Seriously   45
   Anne Ruth Mackor

I.	Introduction	45
II.	Theoretical and Practical Reason	46
III.	Explanatory Legal Doctrine	48
IV.	Normative Legal Doctrine	58
V.	Conclusion	69

4. A World without Law Professors   71
   Mathias M Siems

I.	Introduction	71
II.	Legal Training and Education	72
III.	Legal Research and Writing	78
IV.	Analysis: What Next ?	85

5. Open or Autonomous? The Debate on Legal Methodology as a Reflection of the Debate on Law   87
   Pauline C Westerman

I.	Introduction	87
II.	The Problem of the Lacking Third	88
III.	Legal System as Theoretical Framework	90

	IV.	Legal Doctrine and Legal Science	94
	V.	The Quest for Ongoing Abstraction	95
	VI.	Empty Autonomy	97
	VII.	Revenge of Reality	101
	VIII.	The Need for an Empirical Orientation	105
	IX.	An Empirical Legal Doctrine?	108

6. Methodology of Legal Doctrinal Research: A Comment on Westerman   111
   Jan Vranken

   I. Introduction   111
   II. The Identity of Subject and Theoretical Framework: Four Objections   114
   III. Methodological Consequences   118

7. The Epistemological Function of 'la Doctrine'   123
   Horatia Muir Watt

   I. On the Choice, as a Topic, of the Epistemological Function Played Out in French Legal Tradition by 'la Doctrine'   123
   II. The Current Debates over the Existence and Future of 'la Doctrine' and why they are Significant   125
   III. How the Emergence of 'la Doctrine' is Linked to the Decline of the Code and the Massification of 'la Jurisprudence'   126
   IV. How the Changing Relationship between Law and the other Social Sciences is Relevant to the Rise of 'la Doctrine' and to the Subsequent Shaping of Legal Knowledge   128
   V. Why 'la Doctrine' is Threatened Today in its Interpretative Function   129
   VI. Why the Current Crisis may be for the Better – and may be Good for Comparative Legal Research   131

8. Maps, Methodologies and Critiques: Confessions of a Contract Lawyer   133
   Roger Brownsword

   I. Introduction   133
   II. An Ideological Understanding of Adjudication and of Contract Law   135
   III. The Rationality of Contract Law   137
   IV. The Underlying Ethic of Contract Law   139
   V. The Fit between Doctrine and Business Organisation   143
   VI. The Consent-Based Nature of Contractual Obligation   145
   VII. The Mission of Protecting Reasonable Expectations   146
   VIII. Contract and the Larger Regulatory Environment   148
   IX. Conclusion   152

9. Legal Research and the Distinctiveness of Comparative Law 155
   John Bell

   I. Introduction: Legal Research as a Normative Social Science 155
   II. Hermeneutic Approach to Legal Research 158
   III. The Institutional Character of Law 161
   IV. The Interpretative Character of Law 164
   V. Implications for Comparative Law 167
   VI. Conclusion 175

10. Does One Need an Understanding of Methodology in Law Before One Can Understand Methodology in Comparative Law? 177
    Geoffrey Samuel

    I. The Problem of Interdisciplinarity 178
    II. Methodology and the Status of Comparative Law 182
    III. Methodology and Epistemology in the Social Sciences 188
    IV. Methodology and Epistemology in Law 192
    V. Positivism (Causality) Versus Hermeneutics 194
    VI. Positivism (Causality) Versus Dialectics 198
    VII. Positivism versus Actionalism and Objectification 200
    VIII. Paradigm Authoritarianism Versus Comparative Studies 205

11. Comparative Law, Legal Linguistics and Methodology of Legal Doctrine 209
    Jaakko Husa

    I. Introduction 209
    II. Background of Functionalism 212
    III. From Rabel to Zweigert and Kötz 215
    IV. Legal Languages and Functionalism 223
    V. Conclusion 227

12. Doing What Doesn't Come Naturally. On the Distinctiveness of Comparative Law 229
    Maurice Adams

    I. 'Doing' Law is Immutably Comparative 229
    II. ... 'And Yet it Moves!' 230
    III. Explanatory Comparative Law and Interdisciplinarity 235
    IV. To Conclude 239

13. Promises and Pitfalls of Interdisciplinary Legal Research: The Case of Evolutionary Analysis in Law 241
    Bart Du Laing

    I. Introduction 241
    II. Contemporary Evolutionary Approaches to Human Behaviour and Evolutionary Analysis in Law 244
    III. Taxonomising Evolutionary Analyses in Law: Three Questions 248

14. Behavioural Economics and Legal Research 257
    Julie De Coninck

    I. Introduction 257
    II. Behavioural Economics 258
    III. Behavioural Law and Economics 262
    IV. Closing Remarks 275

15. Theory and Object in Law: the Case for Legal Scholarship as Indirect Speech 277
    Bert Van Roermund

    I. Legal Scholarship Pre-Determined by the Law it Investigates? 278
    II. Theoretical Language as Meta-Language? 282
    III. Some Implications 284

Index 287

List of Contributors

Maurice ADAMS is Professor of General Jurisprudence at Tilburg University and part-time Professor of Comparative Law at Antwerp University.
m.adams@uvt.nl

John BELL is Professor of Law at the University of Cambridge.
jsb48@cam.ac.uk

Roger BROWNSWORD is Professor of Law and Director of TELOS at King's College London, and Honorary Professor in Law at the University of Sheffield.
roger.brownsword@kcl.ac.uk

Julie DE CONINCK was until 2011 Postdoctoral Fellow of the Research Foundation – Flanders (FWO) at the Catholic University of Leuven (KU Leuven), Lecturer at the University of Antwerp, Substitute Lecturer in Comparative Law at KU Leuven (Research Master in Law in cooperation with Tilburg University). Currently she works in legal practice.
de.coninck.julie@gmail.com

Bart DU LAING was until 2011 Postdoctoral Fellow of the Research Foundation – Flanders (FWO) at the University of Ghent, Department of Legal Theory and Legal History. He is now working in legal practice.
bart.dulaing@gmail.com

Jaap HAGE is Professor of Jurisprudence at the University of Maastricht and Professor of Law at the University of Hasselt.
jaap.hage@maastrichtuniversity.nl

Jaakko HUSA is Professor of Legal Culture and Legal Linguistics at the University of Lapland. He is also an Adjunct Professor of Comparative Legal Science at the University of Helsinki and a Member of the International Academy of Comparative Law.
jaakko.husa@ulapland.fi

Anne Ruth MACKOR is Professor of Professional Ethics at the University of Groningen.
a.r.mackor@rug.nl

xx *List of Contributors*

Horatia MUIR-WATT is Professor of Law at the Law School, Sciences-po, Paris.
hmuirwatt@aol.com

Geoffrey SAMUEL is Professor of Law at Kent Law School, University of Kent, at Canterbury.
g.h.samuel@kent.ac.uk

Mathias SIEMS is Professor of Commercial Law at Durham University, UK.
siems@fulbrightmail.org

Mark VAN HOECKE is Research Professor for Legal Theory and Comparative Law at the University of Ghent. From 2008 till 2011 he also held the position of Research Professor for the Methodology of Comparative Law at the University of Tilburg. He is co-director of the European Academy of Legal Theory.
Mark.VanHoecke@ugent.be

Bert VAN ROERMUND is Professor of Philosophy and former Chairholder in the Philosophy of Law at Tilburg University.
g.c.g.j.vanroermund@uvt.nl

Jan VRANKEN is Professor of Methodology of Private Law at Tilburg University.
j.b.m.vranken@uvt.nl

Pauline WESTERMAN is Professor of Legal Philosophy at the University of Groningen, as well as member of staff of the Academy for Legislation in The Hague.
p.c.westerman@rug.nl

1

Legal Doctrine: Which Method(s) for What Kind of Discipline?

MARK VAN HOECKE

I. HISTORICAL DEVELOPMENTS

ROMAN LEGAL DOCTRINE developed since the second century before Christ, and reached a very high level as from the third century after Christ. Its rediscovery and renewed study in Bologna in the eleventh century was the start for the creation of universities. During the whole of the Middle-Ages, legal doctrine was highly thought of and considered as a 'scientific discipline', as in those times 'authoritative interpretation', not 'empirical research', was the main criterion for the scientific status of a discipline. Slowly as from the seventeenth century, but mainly as from the nineteenth century, this changed dramatically. The success of the positive sciences altered the conception of 'science' in western societies. Physics became the model. Hence, a combination of empirical data, mathematics, testing of hypotheses, developing theories with a general validity and without geographical limitations, became the ideal for any 'scholarly discipline'. However, where in legal scholarship do we study 'empirical data', handle them with mathematical models, check 'hypotheses' or construe 'theories'? For sure, law and legal doctrine clearly have their geographical limitations, so that there is no claim to 'general validity' outside the geographical borders of the legal system concerned.

As from the mid-nineteenth century, those conclusions have repeatedly led to the statement that 'legal doctrine' misses basic characteristics in order to be considered a 'legal science', whereas until then legal doctrine had largely been seen to be the model 'science'.[1] More recently, it is particularly the research assessment

---

[1] In 1859, the American legal scholar David Dudley Finn wrote about legal doctrine: 'Compare this science with any of the other sciences; with those which are esteemed the greatest in extent, and the most exalted in subject. Take even astronomy, that noble science which weighs the sun and the planets, measures their distances, traces their orbits, and penetrates the secrets of that great law which governs their motions. Sublime as this science is, it is but the science of inanimate matter, and a few natural laws; while the science which is the subject of our discourse governs the action of human beings, intelligent and immortal, penetrates into the secrets of their souls, subdues their wills, and adapts itself to the endless variety of their wants, motives and conditions.' See DD Finn

procedures and the repartition of public money among 'scientists' that have put this topic into the centre of the scholarly debate. Lawyers have reacted in different ways to this pressure. A large majority of them have pointed to the practical utility, and even necessity, of their publications for legal practice and emphasised the importance of law in society, or they have benignly ignored that criticism. Others have accepted the criticism, taking over the narrow empiricist view on 'science' and tried to make legal scholarship fit that model.[2] In the nineteenth century, this kind of reaction gave birth to 'legal theory' in the sense of a 'positive science of law', a kind of empirical 'natural law', a search for legal concepts, legal rules and legal principles that the whole of mankind would share.[3] There has been some research in legal anthropology (Maine, Post),[4] but largely this remained at the stage of a research programme, which has been forgotten as from the First World War. Somewhat similar to this reaction, we have seen, as from the end of the nineteenth century, and mainly in the course of the twentieth century, the birth and development of other social sciences focusing on law: legal sociology, legal psychology, law and economics. All of those disciplines offer empirical research and theory building in legal matters. However, they never aimed at replacing legal doctrine, but just wanted to supply legal scholars, legal practitioners and policymakers with useful information on legal reality. Unfortunately, their impact has remained quite limited. So, today, there is a somewhat schizophrenic situation in which one discipline, legal doctrine, is basically studying law as a normative system, limiting its 'empirical data' to legal texts and court decisions, whereas other disciplines study legal reality, law as it is. The outcomes of these two strands of disciplines are not

---

'Magnitude and Importance of Legal Science' (1859) in SB Presser and JS Zainaldin (eds), Law and Jurisprudence in American History, 3rd edn (St Paul, Minnesota, West Publishing C°, 1995) 712. From a different perspective, Ivanhoe Tebaldeschi could, in 1979, argue that legal doctrine is the most complete discipline, and, hence, the model science, as it combines deductive reasoning with inductive reasoning and value thinking: I Tebaldeschi, Rechtswissenschaft als Modellwissenschaft (Vienna, Springer Verlag, 1979) 156.

[2] 'Welcher Abstand zeigt sich hier für die Jurisprudenz gegen die Naturwissenschaften' in J von Kirchmann, Die Werthlosigkeit der Jurisprudenz als Wissenschaft (Berlin, Julius Springer, 1848) 14; S van Houten, Das Causalitätsgesetz in der Socialwissenschaft (Haarlem, HD Tjeenk Willink and Leipzig, FA Brockhaus, 1888), arguing in favour of the use of the methods of physics in legal scholarship, mainly by focusing on causal relations: 'Der Grundstein der Socialwissenschaft, wie überhaupt aller Wissenschaft, ist die volle, unbedingte Anerkennung des Causalitätsgesetzes' (p 5). See also: AV Lundstedt, Die Unwissenschaftlichkeit der Rechtswissenschaft (Berlin-Grunewald, W Rothschild, 1932) vol 1; T Mulder, Ik beschuldig de rechtsgeleerde faculteit van onwetenschappelijkheid (Leiden, 1937); G de Geest, 'Hoe maken we van de rechtswetenschap een volwaardige wetenschap?' (2004) Nederlands Juristenblad 58–66.

[3] AH Post, Einleitung in eine Naturwissenschaft des Rechts (Oldenburg, Verlag der Schulzchen Buchhandlung, 1872). For a short introduction to Post and to his legal anthropological research, see: A Lyall, 'Early German Legal Anthropology: Albert Hermann Post and His Questionnaire (2008) 52 Journal of African Law 114–24 (with the questionnaire as an appendix on pages 124–38).

[4] GA Wilken, De vrucht van de beoefening der ethnologie voor de vergelijkende rechtswetenschap, inaugural lecture Rijksuniversiteit Leiden (Leiden, EJ Brill, 1885); SR Steinmetz, Ethnologische Studien zur ersten Entwicklung der Strafe, 2nd edn, 2 vols (Groningen, P Noordhoff, 1928) (1st edn, Leiden 1894); SR Steinmetz, Rechtsverhältnisse von eingeborenen Völkern in Afrika und Ozeanien. Beantwortungen des Fragebogens der Internationalen Vereinigung für vergleichende Rechtswissenschaft und Volkswirtschaftslehre zu Berlin (Berlin, Julius Springer, 1903).

brought together in any systematic way, nor are they combined or integrated at the level of legal scholarship.

Today, in different countries, research assessment and the financial means connected with it have made the empiricist view on science even more influential. This has been to such an extent that it has made lawyers and policymakers in universities think that legal doctrine can only become 'scientific' if it turns into an empirical social science (de Geest). In other words, the aim is to put an end to a tradition of more than two millennia and to imitate the empirical sciences that have a different goal. Instead of concluding that the monist view on science, based on physics, is wrong, 'falsified' in their terminology, because it does not fit with disciplines such as legal doctrine, some have concluded that legal doctrine is (completely) wrong, and has always been so. This is a dangerous development, which, starting from false assumptions (unity and similarity of all scientific disciplines) is jeopardising the future of human sciences in general and legal doctrine in particular.

Of course, the criticism of legal doctrine is partly founded: it is often too descriptive, too autopoietic, without taking the context of the law sufficiently into account; it lacks a clear methodology and the methods of legal doctrine seem to be identical to those of legal practice; it is too parochial, limited to very small scientific communities, because of specialisation and geographical limits; there is not much difference between publications of legal practitioners and of legal scholars. All this may be correct, but as such it does not disqualify legal doctrine as a discipline in its own right, with its own, appropriate, methods.

In this chapter, I will define legal doctrine as an 'empirical-hermeneutical discipline'. Indeed, it has empirical aspects, which make it perfectly comparable with all empirical disciplines, but the core business of legal doctrine is interpretation, which it has also in common with some other disciplines (theology, study of literature).

How can we describe the methodology of legal doctrine in a terminology which is largely used in the scientific community, without narrowing it in such a way that we lose essential characteristics of this discipline?

Legal doctrine has, in the course of history, been practised and conceived in varying ways, emphasising, and sometimes overemphasising, diverging characteristics of this discipline. Below, we will discuss the different angles from which legal doctrine has been presented and the extent to which they give a true picture of this discipline. It will be followed by an analysis of the methodology of legal research in terms of hypotheses and theory building.

II. WHAT KIND OF DISCIPLINE IS LEGAL DOCTRINE?

A. A Hermeneutic Discipline

It can hardly be denied that legal scholars are often interpreting texts and arguing about a choice among diverging interpretations. In this way, legal doctrine is a *hermeneutic discipline*, in the same way as is, for example, the study of literature, or to a somewhat lesser extent, history. Interpreting texts has been the core business of legal doctrine since it started in the Roman Empire.[5]

In a hermeneutic discipline, texts and documents are the main research object and their interpretation, according to standard methods, is the main activity of the researcher. This is clearly the case with legal doctrine.

Often legal scholarship has been presented as another type of 'science', in which the hermeneutic dimension is minimised, or at least made less important. This was done, for instance, when scholars tried to distinguish legal scholarship from legal practice, or to separate the description of the law more clearly from its evaluation, or when legal scholarship was modelled along the lines of the methodology of other disciplines and more specifically of the positive sciences.

B. An Argumentative Discipline

Close to the conception of legal doctrine as a hermeneutic discipline is the conception of an *argumentative discipline*. Here, it is the argumentation to support some legal interpretation or solution that is emphasised, rather than the interpretation as such.[6] The argumentative view has the advantage of putting things into a broader perspective. It allows us to take a step back from the interpreted text or any other document. A concrete legal question can be answered, or a case solved, on the basis of generally accepted, or at least acceptable, views.

---

[5] 'L'oeuvre doctrinale, dans la tradition historique française et, plus largement, européenne, est au premier chef d'interprétation de « lois » écrites . . . Et à cela ne s'est pas borné son rôle. Face à des sources diverses et hétérogènes, elle s'est trouvé aussi pour fonction d'unifier, de créer un ordre juridique cohérent et même, à partir du XVIème siècle, systématique, préparant ainsi les voies de la codification.' See J-L Thireau, 'La doctrine civiliste avant le Code civil' in Y Poirmeur et al, *La doctrine juridique* (Paris, Presses Universitaires de France, 1993) 13–51, 16f.

[6] Argumentation theory has always been at the core of jurisprudential writings. That is why the conception of legal scholarship as an argumentative discipline often acts as an implicit background (see eg Ch Perelman, *Logique juridique. Nouvelle rhétorique* (Paris, Dalloz, 1976); R Alexy, *A Theory of Legal Argumentation*, translated by R Adler and N MacCormick (Oxford, Clarendon Press, 1989); R Dworkin, *Law's Empire* (London, Fontana Press, 1986) 1314, where this is said rather explicitly). Sometimes this conception of legal doctrine as an argumentative discipline is argued for explicitly: J Smits, 'Redefining Normative Legal Science: Towards an Argumentative Discipline' in F Grünfeld et al and F Coomans (eds), *Methods of Human Rights Research* (Antwerp, Intersentia 2009); C Smith et al, 'Criteria voor goed rechtswetenschappelijk onderzoek' (2008) *Nederlands Juristenblad* 685–90 at 690, where, following Ronald Dworkin, the work of the legal scholar and of the judge are rather called an 'argumentative practice' than a 'normative discipline'.

In traditional argumentation theory they are called 'topoi'[7]. In many cases the argumentation will support some interpretation of one or more texts, but in other cases the argumentation may only loosely be related to such texts, eg when based on unwritten legal principles, or when filling gaps in the law, or when a text is simply put aside in favour of an interest or value that is considered to be more important.

From the Middle-Ages until the seventeenth century legal doctrine has developed as an argumentative discipline, which determined what kind of arguments were acceptable in which cases, with whole catalogues of arguments.[8] Actually, interpretation and argumentation cannot be separated from each other, both in legal doctrine and in legal practice. Each text interpretation needs arguments when diverging interpretations could reasonably be sustained, and a legal argumentation will almost always be based on interpreted texts. So, legal doctrine and legal practice are both hermeneutic and argumentative, but interpretation and argumentation appear to be roughly two sides of the same activity, in which interpretation is the goal and argumentation the means for sustaining that interpretation. Hence, if one has to choose it would seem more appropriate to label legal doctrine a 'hermeneutic discipline' rather than an argumentative one.

C. An Empirical Discipline

As already mentioned above, since the nineteenth century and under the influence of the success of the positive sciences, attempts have been made to develop legal scholarship as an empirical discipline.[9] This has been quite explicitly worded by Alf Ross:

> The interpretation of the doctrinal study of law presented in this book rests upon the postulate that the principle of verification must apply also to this field of cognition – that the doctrinal study of law must be recognised as an empirical social science.[10]

According to Ross, this empirical verification takes place by checking statements in legal doctrine against judicial practice: 'Our interpretation, based on the preceding analysis, is that the real content of doctrinal propositions refers to the actions of the courts under certain conditions.'[11]

---

[7] T Viehweg, *Topik und Jurisprudenz: ein Beitrag zur Rechtswissenschaftlichen Grundlagenforschung*, 5th ed (München, Beck Vergag 1974); G Struck, *Topische Jurisprudenz*, (Frankfurt, Athenäum Verlag 1971).

[8] GCCJ van den Bergh, *Geleerd recht. Een geschiedenis van de Europese rechtswetenschap in vogelvlucht,* 2nd edn (Deventer, Kluwer, 1985) 6.

[9] And not only legal scholarship: 'Occasionally, scholars in the "lower" disciplines aspiring to the status of natural scientists have attempted to import an empirical or "scientific" method into their work. In the nineteenth century, for example, such efforts redefined many of the social science disciplines and gave them many of their distinguishing characteristics today.' See DW Vick, 'Interdisciplinarity and the Discipline of Law' (2004) 31 *Journal of Law and Society* 163–93, 172.

[10] A Ross, *On Law and Justice* (London, Stevens & Sons, 1958) 40. This view is explicitly rejected in G Samuel, 'Is Law Really a Social Science? A View from Comparative Law' (2008) 67 *Cambridge Law Journal* 288–321, among others at 319.

[11] ibid.

This view is typical for the realist movements. Ross was the last important representative of Scandinavian realism, but here Ross comes quite close to American realism: 'The prophecies of what courts will do in fact, and nothing more pretentious, are what I mean by the law', in the well known wording by Oliver Wendell Holmes.[12] Ross' conception of legal doctrine as an empirical discipline only fits in such a 'realistic' approach. Today, this realistic movement is not very popular in Europe, not even in Scandinavia. Hence, this conception of legal doctrine cannot be considered to be a workable model as such.

Others have argued that the phenomena which are observed and studied by legal scholars are in fact their empirical data and amount to 'legal rules'.[13] It is, however, to be questioned whether 'legal rules' can be observed empirically. If not, where and how do we find them? For Gerrit De Geest they are found through the reading of published judicial decisions. This view suggests that those rules only 'exist' to the extent that they have been applied by judges. In this way, De Geest is following Alf Ross and American realism. However, De Geest partly contradicts himself when defining the 'empirical truth' in interpreting the law as 'what the legislator or judge really meant'.[14] As methods used in this context, he mentions:

(a) text analysis;
(b) logic (eg syllogism);
(c) field research (including interviews);
(d) statistics; and
(e) methods of historical research.[15]

It is interesting to note that no psychological methods are mentioned as a possible means to discover what a judge or legislator 'really meant'. Without further discussing De Geest's position here, it is obvious that his label 'empirical research' covers a large variety of elements, which show (also according to De Geest) that legal doctrine is partly a hermeneutic discipline (text analysis), an axiomatic discipline (logic) and a historical discipline. Indeed, legal doctrine cannot be reduced to one single type of discipline, but is a combination of several of them. Of course, some may be considered to be more important, or decisive, or typical than others, but, unlike some other disciplines, such as mathematics, it is not one-dimensional.

In Hans Albert's view, the object of an empirical legal doctrine is broader than just legal rules. It also includes the influence of those rules on the members of the society in question.[16] This means a combination of traditional legal doctrine with legal sociology. There are good reasons for such an approach, but putting

---

[12] OW Holmes, 'The Path of the Law' (1897) 10 *Harvard Law Review* 457–78, 461.
[13] G De Geest, 'Hoe maken we van de rechtswetenschap een volwaardige wetenschap?' (2004) *Nederlands Juristenblad* 58–66, 59.
[14] ibid 59.
[15] ibid 61.
[16] H Albert, 'Kennis en Recht' in FD Heyt (ed), *Rationaliteit in wetenschap en samenleving* (Alphen aan de Rijn, Samsom, 1976) 183.

it into practice seems to be very difficult in most cases. Moreover, one may also have to include other disciplines, such as economics, psychology and the like. However, including all this in legal doctrine raises even more questions as to its feasibility.

For the Historical School in nineteenth century Germany[17] and a somewhat comparable movement in the United States in the same period,[18] historical elements constituted the most important empirical data:

> Man is to be studied in every period of his social existence, from the savage to the civilized state, in order to perceive the great truth, that in every condition of freedom, of intelligence, of commerce, and of wealth, his habits, his virtues, his vices, the objects of his desires, and hence the laws necessary for his government, are essentially the same.[19]

This approach clearly represents a belief in a kind of 'natural law' which could be retrieved empirically. This idea used to be quite popular in Europe and in the United States in the nineteenth century, but seems to have almost completely disappeared today.

For others, the object of the empirical research is sociological, economical or socio-psychological data, or more generally 'human behaviour'.[20]

Empirical research is most notably useful in disciplines such as physics, where a reality is studied which exists independently of this discipline. In disciplines such as mathematics or theology, empirical research does not seem to be quite relevant. Mathematical models and theological views create their own reality, which, by definition, cannot be checked empirically. The same is largely true for legal doctrine as well. Whether a certain law 'exists' may be checked 'empirically', but what legal doctrine is mainly about is the *interpretation* of that law or its balancing with other laws or legal principles.

Interpretations are underpinned with arguments and these arguments may partly refer to an 'objective' reality. To this extent the correctness of arguments may be checked empirically. However, most arguments in legal reasoning are not 'true' or 'false' but more or less convincing. They do not qualify for an empirical verification.

---

[17] See A Brockmöller, *Die Entstehung der Rechtstheorie im 19. Jahrhundert in Deutschland* (Baden-Baden, Nomos Verlag, 1997) especially 64 ff (Hugo) and 83 ff (Savigny).
[18] See H Schweber, 'Law and the Natural Sciences in Nineteenth-Century American Universities' in SS Silbey (ed), *Law and Science*, The International Library of Essays in Law and Society (Aldershot, Ashgate, 2008) 3–23.
[19] S Greenleaf, *A Discourse Pronounced at the Inauguration of the Author as Royall Professor of Law in Harvard University* (Cambridge, Massachusetts, James Munroe, 1834) 14.
[20] MA Loth, 'Regel-geleid gedrag; over het object van empirische rechtswetenschap' (1983) 3 *Rechtsfilosofie & Rechtstheorie. Netherlands Journal for Legal Philosophy and Jurisprudence* 213–28, 213.

D. An Explanatory Discipline

A fourth conception of legal doctrine considers it to be an *explanatory discipline*. According to this view, legal doctrine explains why a rule is a valid legal rule in a given society. This explanation may be historical, sociological, psychological, economical and the like, but it may also be based on an internal logic. In this approach, the existence of a rule will be 'explained' by the existence of a higher norm, from which that rule is derived,[21] or the existence of underlying values or principles, or of a larger network of legal rules and principles.

The first kind of explanation reduces legal doctrine to one or more of the social sciences involved. The second, internal, 'explanation' largely reduces this concept to something which is not even a main part of legal scholarly activity, and which does not really fit into our common understanding of what it means to 'explain' something. As Aleksander Peczenik wrote, we are rather faced with a veiled strategy in which presenting legal doctrine as an 'explanatory' discipline would allow us to consider it an 'objective science', and to conceal the legitimation of a rule behind a façade of 'explanation'.[22] In fact, nothing is 'explained' here, rather values or principles are postulated, or some interpretation of a higher rule is posited, which should legitimate the rule one derives from them.

Another view considers it the aim of legal scholarship to explain rule-determined behaviour,[23] in interaction with other actors.[24] However, this is rather the aim of legal sociology than of legal doctrine. Legal scholarship, in this approach, becomes a social technology.[25]

Explaining the whys and wherefores of legal concepts, rules, principles and constructions is indeed not an unimportant part of legal doctrinal research as it is necessary for interpreting them correctly. However, explanation is not the main content of research in legal doctrine, except maybe during some time following large-scale codifications. The hermeneutical and explanatory research activities are closely linked to each other, but explanation is at the service of interpretation, not the other way around. Hence, legal doctrine is not mainly an explanatory discipline.

---

[21] M Van Quickenborne, 'Rechtsstudie als wetenschap' in *Actori incumbit probatio* (Antwerp, Kluwer 1975) 223.

[22] A Peczenik, *Scientia Juris. Legal Doctrine as Knowledge of Law and as a Source of Law* in E Pattaro (ed), *A Treatise of Legal Philosophy and General Jurisprudence* (Dordrecht, Springer 2005) vol 4, 4.

[23] H Albert, *Traktat über rationale Praxis* (Tübingen, JCB Mohr, 1978) 79–80: 'Wer den *Sinn* des Gesetzes bestimmen möchte, muss sich *eo ipso* Gedanken über die mit ihm intendierten *Wirkungen* und die damit angestrebte *Ordnung* machen. Solche Überlegungen machen die Verwendung *nomologischen Wissens* erforderlich, denn die *Steuerungswirkungen* von Gesetzen und Auslegungen sind nicht einfach *logische Konsequenzen* der betreffenden Aussagen.'

[24] MA Loth, 'Regel-geleid gedrag; over het object van empirische rechtswetenschap' (1983) 3 *Rechtsfilosofie & Rechtstheorie. Netherlands Journal for Legal Philosophy and Jurisprudence* 221.

[25] ibid 215.

E. An Axiomatic Discipline

Legal doctrine has sometimes been seen in continental Europe as an *axiomatic discipline*, like mathematics. Gustav Hugo, one of the founders of the Historical School in nineteenth century Germany, worded it as follows:

> Jurisprudenz und Mathematik grenzen auch näher an einander als mancher, der weder Jurist noch Mathematiker ist, weiss. . . . Auch die Jurisprudenz beruht in der Theorie auf einer Art von Construction und auch die Jurisprudenz ist in der Theorie eine exacte Wissenschaft.[26]

For Hugo, legal doctrine was an applied exact science, with also some empirical dimension. This approach to legal doctrine culminated in Germany at the end of the nineteenth century in the '*Begriffsjurisprudenz*' movement, which saw law as an algebra of legal concepts.

In the second half of the twentieth century, this approach to legal doctrine had a revival, which, however, did not last long. Some optimists hoped to encompass the whole of law in a formal logic and/or in computer programmes which, up to now, did not prove to be very successful.

F. A Logical Discipline

The view on legal doctrine as a *logical discipline* is a somewhat more moderate version of the pure axiomatic model:

> In der *Rechtsordnung* spielt das Logische nur eine sekundäre Rolle neben den alogischen Momenten. In der *Rechtsanwendung* spielen diese alogische Momente die sekundäre Rolle neben dem Logischen. In der *Rechtswissenschaft* endlich herrschen ausschliesslich die logische Funktionen: die Jurisprudenz dient mit logischen Mitteln dem logischen Zwecke der Systematisierung.[27]

So, even if law is not always logical in practice, for Julius Moór legal doctrine should be exclusively logical in view of systematising the law. Most scholars with other views on legal doctrine as a discipline have also emphasised the importance of logic in legal reasoning and in the scientific structuring of legal data. However, (the contents of) legal data are too indefinite to enable us to conceive legal doctrine as a purely logical discipline. Too much depends on the interpretation of legal principles, rules and concepts. Hence, even if logic is quite important in law and in legal research, interpretation is even more important. Anyway, logical coherence is a characteristic of scientific research in any discipline and not just typical for the legal sciences.

[26] G Hugo, *Lehrbuch eines civilistischen Cursus, Philosophische Encyclopedie für Juristen* (Berlin, 1799) vol 5, 10 §8.
[27] J Moór, 'Das Logische im Recht' (1927–28) *Revue Internationale de la Théorie du Droit / Internationale Zeitschrift für Theorie des Rechts*, 157–203 at 203. See also, be it less explicitly: R Kranenburg, *De Grondslagen der Rechtswetenschap. Juridische kennisleer en methodologie*, 5th edn (Haarlem, HD Tjeenk Willink, 1955) 30f.

G. A Normative Discipline

Legal doctrine is often called a *normative discipline*, which is not only describing and systematising norms (a discipline *about* norms), but also and to a large extent, a discipline which takes normative positions and makes choices among values and interests. This, indeed, is inevitable when, for example, some interpretation is preferred over alternative ones. Ultimately this choice will be determined by giving more weight to some values or interests than to competing ones. For some, legal doctrine is primarily looking for 'better law'.[28] This refers to elements which are external to law and to legal doctrine: philosophy, morals, history, sociology, economy and politics. Hence, looking for 'better law' may require empirical research, especially when 'better' means better from an economic or sociological point of view, or when reference is made to the 'prevailing moral (or political) convictions'.

This normative approach bears the risk of subjectivity, when a legal scholar is trying to present very personal views and convictions as 'the law'. It should be obvious that such a normative approach can only have a scientific status if it looks for an intersubjective consensus, for the prevailing opinion among legal scholars or among lawyers in general (especially judges and academics who made their views public through judicial decisions or other types of publications). It can be checked empirically as to whether an opinion is (largely) prevailing among those professionals or in society.

For Hans Kelsen, legal doctrine as a normative discipline is a matter of internal logic, not linked to some external criterion for making the law 'better'. He considered the distinction between 'descriptive disciplines' and 'normative disciplines' to be the basic division among sciences. Descriptive disciplines, such as the exact sciences, look for causal relations, whereas normative sciences, such as legal doctrine and ethics, use 'imputation' as a method.[29] 'Imputation' means determining the existence of some obligation (in its broadest sense) and/or a breach of it. This obligation will be derived, through an internal legal logic, from elements of the legal system. Kelsen strongly underestimated the importance of interpretation in law and the influence of non-legal elements through such interpretation. The main reason for this unrealistic view is Kelsen's theory of 'meaning', which he limits to the psychological sender-meaning, that is to the intention of those having issued a rule or a command.[30] By this assumption

---

[28] JAI Wendt, *De methode der rechtswetenschap vanuit kritisch-rationeel perspectief* (Zutphen, Paris, 2008) 141.

[29] H Kelsen, *General Theory of Norms* (Oxford, Clarendon Press, 1991) 22–25.

[30] 'Someone who issues a command *intends* something. He expects the other person to *understand* this something. By his command he intends that the other person is to behave in a certain way. That is the *meaning* of his act or will.' (ibid 32). Hence, according to Kelsen, 'it is more correct to say "a norm *is* a meaning" than "a norm *has* a meaning"' (ibid 26). This view is completely untenable. See my comments on this issue in M Van Hoecke, *Law as Communication* (Oxford, Hart Publishing, 2002) 128–30.

he can minimise the hermeneutic element in legal research and emphasise the normative characteristic of law.

III. WHICH METHODOLOGY FOR LEGAL RESEARCH?

It will be obvious that varying conceptions of legal doctrine imply quite different methodologies. If we accept that legal doctrine is mainly a hermeneutical discipline, which fits best in any case with the way legal doctrine has been conceived most of the time in most legal systems, we may describe its methodology as follows.

Legal scholars collect empirical data (statutes, cases, etc), word hypotheses on their meaning and scope, which they test, using the classic canons of interpretation. In a next stage, they build theories (eg the direct binding force of European Union (EU) law), which they test and from which they derive new hypotheses (eg on the validity, meaning or scope of a domestic rule which conflicts with EU law). Described in this way, doctrinal legal scholarship fits perfectly with the methodology of other disciplines: 'Scientific inquiry, seen in a very broad perspective, may be said to present two main aspects. One is the ascertaining and discovery of facts, the other the construction of hypotheses and theories.'[31]

A. Empirical Data Used in Legal Doctrine

In a first stage, legal doctrine collects all relevant material, notably:

(a) normative sources, such as statutory texts, treaties, general principles of law, customary law, binding precedents, and the like; and
(b) authoritative sources, such as case law, if they are not binding precedents, and scholarly legal writings.

The last category has a somewhat ambivalent position, as it is not external to legal doctrine, even if it will generally be external to the individual researcher. Here, we are faced with a mixture of scholarly legal writings as an authoritative source of law, on the one hand, and legal doctrine as the scientific community which discusses, accepts or rejects positions taken by colleagues and the theories they propose on the other.

In general, the discussion about legal sources will be one of *relevance*. If, for instance, a statutory text has been declared unconstitutional by the Constitutional Court, it will become an irrelevant part of the empirical data on which the legal researcher will build his or her hypotheses or theories. A binding precedent will be more relevant than a non binding one. A (non binding) decision of the Supreme Court will be more relevant than one taken by a lower court.

---

[31] GH von Wright, *Explanation and Understanding* (Ithaca, Cornell University Press, 1971) 1.

A publication by a law professor who is generally considered to be an authority in his or her field will have more weight than the first publication of a young academic. A well underpinned argumentation will be more relevant than just positing the same position, without further argument.

For normative sources, the relevance will be a matter of *validity* in the first instance: is this rule currently part of our legal system or not? This is a binary choice between validity and non-validity.

At the level of *interpretation*, however, it may become a matter of degree: when weighing and balancing the normative force of equally valid rules and principles, one of them may be considered to be more relevant than the other one, even if this higher relevance may be limited to the very case in question.

The relevance of authoritative sources will always be a matter of degree. Even the most famous professor may have a weak moment and the very first publication of a promising young scholar may be brilliant. Sometimes decisions of a supreme court are widely rejected by lower judges and by legal doctrine and, hence, lose a large part of their relevance. Decisions taken, for instance by the American Supreme Court, with a majority of five to four, will be less authoritative than unanimous decisions.

Anyway, all those sources have at least some relevance and the researcher will have to take them into account in her or his research.

A delicate point is the representativeness of the published case law. Actual publication of judicial decisions represents only small percentage of all decisions made (in Belgium one or two per cent). However, a higher percentage has been made accessible through the internet. It is well known that anecdotic motives sometimes play a stronger role than scientific ones when deciding whether to publish.[32] Controversial decisions will be published more easily than those which simply confirm earlier ones. Even the supreme courts' decisions are not all published. Adequate electronic storage of all judicial decisions and appropriate computer programmes and databases should allow a systematic study of all judicial decisions taken in some field or on some legal problem, including statistical analyses. However, up to now this is still not operational in many legal systems.

B. Wording and Checking Research Hypotheses

Every type of scientific research starts from a problem, from some question or series of questions. Sometimes a simple observation of facts leads rather spontaneously to a research question. For example, when there are two conflicting views within case law and legal doctrine, or between higher and lower judges, or between case law on the one hand and legal doctrine on the other, the researcher

---

[32] For example, a claim to obtaining the right to visit one's dog after divorce, when the animal stayed with the ex-partner.

will automatically look for an explanation for these diverging positions and look for arguments which would allow a decisive choice in favour of one of them or that would rather lead to a more convincing third alternative.

In other cases, the research question will be worded on the basis of prior observation in another context, and the empirical data will consciously be selected in view of the research question. This is not specific to law, but common to all disciplines: 'It is therefore clear that facts must be selected on the basis of assumptions as to which ones are *relevant* for resolving a given problem.'[33]

If one wants, for instance, to inquire to what extent some legal fields in private law, in some continental European legal system, could be rearranged, inspired by the English concept of 'trust', one will probably collect data around adoption and bankruptcy law but not from all areas of private law.

Anyway, scientific 'observation' is not a neutral perception of facts that would present themselves spontaneously. We are always faced with a specific reading of selected facts, steered by the research question. The reading of a purely descriptive overview of case law in a certain field and period may lead to the formulation of a legal problem, in view of which additional material will be collected.

As in all disciplines, the observation of empirical data is theory-guided. A problem is formulated within some theoretical framework. Apart from the aim of solving that problem, the outcome of the research will also confirm, refine or falsify those theoretical assumptions. The selection of relevant legal data will be based on a theory of legal sources: which legal sources are relevant in this legal system today, and what are their hierarchical relations? This may, of course, lead to a research question such as, for example: does European law have priority over the national constitutional order?

Neither the selection of empirical data nor their descriptions are neutral activities. When the American Law Institute started, in 1923, the 'Restatements' of the American Common Law, it presented it as a neutral, apolitical activity. The Institute was strongly criticised because it implicitly started from the false assumptions 'that it is possible to describe the law as it is in neutral terms' (pointing to the intertwinement of description and interpretation), 'that it is possible to make meaningful statements of legal rules without references to their rationales' (the aim of the law as interpretation context), or 'without reference to the practical context of their operation' (concrete application as interpretation context).[34]

Indeed, when wording legal rules, as they appear from the valid legal sources, the texts in question are *interpreted*. Often, there is no interpretation problem, as there is an implicit consensus on the precise meaning of the text, but in other cases we are faced with diverging readings of the same text, or the researcher has to determine the exact meaning and scope of a newly enacted statute or a recent

---

[33] E Nagel, 'The Nature and Aim of Science' in S Morgenbesser (ed), *Philosophy of Science Today* (New York, Basic Books, 1967) 3–13, 10.
[34] See on this: W Twining, *Blackstone's Tower: The English Law School* (London, Sweet & Maxwell, 1994) 134.

court decision. In these cases it appears clear that the legal scholar is *wording a hypothesis as to the validity and the precise meaning of a legally relevant text* (relevant within the given legal system at the time of the research).[35] In other words, interpretation is at the core of the whole activity of legal scholarship. Research questions in legal doctrine are, indeed, very often linked to the precise meaning and scope of legal concepts, legal rules, legal principles and/or legal constructions.

Every description of the law includes a whole series of interpretations and offers, in this way, just as many hypotheses about the meaning and scope of legal concepts, rules, principles and the like, that may be confirmed or falsified through scientific research. Explicit interpretation questions are not a marginal phenomenon in law. They arise when texts are unclear, but also when the result of a literal interpretation leads to unreasonable, inequitable or even absurd results. The confrontation of this result with the meaning given to the text, in a way, 'falsifies' the implicit, prima facie meaning of the text. This will then lead to the wording of a new hypothesis about the meaning of a text, which will be checked with a more conscious, methodological interpretation by the researcher.

A hypothesis about the exact meaning of a legal concept, rule, principle and the like, does not only refer to finding out what their authors had in mind. The normative context today and the socially desirable result also co-determine that meaning. Hence, this meaning is evolving and may change in the course of the years, without any change in the texts. A unanimity today as to the meaning of a legal text does not prevent scholars in the future wording new hypotheses as to a slightly or even completely different meaning.

The wording of research questions is free. There are no rules which would limit them. Of course, they should make sense and fit with the paradigmatic theories that act as a framework for the legal doctrinal research in the legal system concerned (the theory of legal sources, for instance, or the theory about the acceptable interpretation methods), unless the researcher aims at questioning this paradigmatic framework as such.

C. Theory Building in Legal Doctrine

A scientific 'theory' is defined as 'a system of coherent, notably non contradictory assertions, views and concepts concerning some area of reality, which are worded in such a way that it is possible to deduct testable hypotheses from them.'[36]

---

[35] See, eg: A André, 'Was heisst rechtswissenschaftliche Forschung?' (1970) *Juristenzeitung* 396–401, 400; H Albert, *Traktat über rationale Praxis* (Tübingen, JCB Mohr, 1978) 80; A Aarnio, *Philosophical Perspectives in Jurisprudence*, Acta Philosophica Fennica no 36 (Helsinki, Academic Bookstore, 1983) 163–84 (On the Truth and Validity of Interpretative Statements in Legal Dogmatics). Compare: 'Seen in the perspective of time all statements of the law, whether by the legislature, or by judges, or by jurists, are no more than working hypotheses.' Lord Goff of Chieveley, 'Judge, Jurist and Legislature' (1987) 2 *Denning Law Journal* 79–95, 80.

[36] AD De Groot, *Methodologie,* 3rd edn (The Hague, Mouton, 1966) 42.

In legal doctrine this would mean:

'A theory in law is a system of coherent, non contradictory assertions, views and concepts concerning some legal system or part of it, which are worded in such a way that it is possible to deduct from them testable hypotheses about the existence (validity) and interpretation of legal concepts, rules or principles.'

For instance, from the theory of direct effect of EU law one may deduct hypotheses about the (in)validity and (re)interpretation of legislative rules in one's own domestic legal system within the EU.

Such theories are, in their turn, based on generally accepted assumptions that create the paradigmatic framework of legal doctrine. These shared assumptions include: a shared understanding of what 'law' is and of its role in society; a theory of valid legal sources and their hierarchy; a methodology of law; an argumentation theory; a legitimation theory and a shared world view (common basic values and norms). Within legal doctrine these are 'meta theories', for which the definition of 'theory' given above is also valid. Such paradigmatic assumptions are deeply rooted in tradition, but may evolve, and sometimes also revolve. Examples are, within the theory of legal sources: the acceptance of the priority of European Union law over domestic law, or the acceptance of 'unwritten general principles of law' as a valid source of law; within the methodology of law: the acceptance of a more active role for the judge in interpreting the law; as to the shared world view: changed views on marriage, family, homosexuality, abortion, euthanasia. In each period, the paradigmatic assumptions of that time are to constitute the framework within which more concrete theories about law may be elaborated, tested, and discussed within the scientific community of legal scholars.

The strength of scientific theories lies in their capacity to cover a domain as large as possible, with a simple framework of concepts, rules and principles and with a capacity to generate a large amount of testable hypotheses. For explanatory disciplines, the explanatory capacity of a theory is another element for judging its strength.

In a first stage, concepts are construed for ordering reality. This implies abstraction, logical coherence and, as far as possible, simplicity. One may, for instance, assume that in primitive societies animals were originally classified according to their size and colour and/or according to their capacity to fly, to swim or to run. Later on, however, when more advanced theoretical knowledge became available, the classification was based on other divisions: mammals/non mammals or similarities and differences as to their DNA structure. In the same way, the development of law and legal doctrine shows an increasing level of abstraction. As, in more primitive societies, rules developed on the basis of concrete cases, there were originally different rules, for instance, for the theft of a horse, a cow or a sheep. In a later stage, a more abstract concept of (theft of) 'cattle' was introduced. In a next stage of abstraction this became (theft of) 'movables'. Concepts like 'cow', 'sheep' or 'horse' directly refer to visible objects in reality, whereas a concept like 'cattle' is an abstraction based on the utility of certain types of animals for men, just like 'pets' or 'deer' which have another type of utility for human beings, and as opposed to 'vermin', which is considered as having no utility for mankind. The very general division between 'movables' and 'immovables' uses in turn, as a decisive criterion, the mobility and hence negotiability of objects. By introducing the distinction between 'corporeal' and 'incorporeal' matters, the 'goods' as tangible objects are broadened with 'rights' and other abstractions, that may only be classified as 'goods' within a developed legal system. All those divisions may seem to be 'natural' to most of us, as we have grown up with them and can hardly imagine a legal system built on other divisions, such as a division between 'rats' and 'non-rats', which used to be the main division in the law of the Kapauku tribe in Papua.[37]

In other words, behind such concepts and divisions, there is some underlying world view and choice of values, interests and principles, which explain the theories these concepts and divisions encompass. Reality is described, understood and ordered, and actually partly created through such concepts and clusters of concepts, which translate an underlying world view. Concepts, indeed, are not neutral tools, they are theory driven. Concept formation and theory building are closely intertwined in each discipline. As Hempel noted, they are in reality two sides of the same activity.[38] Concepts translate divisions of reality that are considered to be more important or more relevant than other divisions. In biology, nowadays, the way of procreation of animals (mammals or not) is considered to be more important than their biotope (water, air or land). In Roman law, the distinction 'movable'/'immovable' was at the core of civil law and not, for instance, the distinction between living creatures and non living things. The underlying criterion is the different economic importance of those categories: Real estate, 'immovable' goods, constituted the main part of every fortune in Europe until the nineteenth century. Movables generally had much less value. Today, however, the economic importance of this legal division has largely been undermined by the birth and development of partnerships. Companies have become the owners of important real estate, whereas the shares in that company are considered to be movable goods. In this way, through the legal construction of companies and firms, 'immovables' changed into 'movables', which made this division largely lose its economic importance. In the 1804 Code Napoléon, the distinction between 'movables' and 'immovables' determined which goods, in the statutory marriage settlement, became 'common' (movables) to both spouses, and which remained the property of one spouse only (immovables).[39] When (thoroughly) changing the law on marriage settlements in 1976, the Belgian legisla-

---

[37] As recorded by L Pospisil, *Anthropology of Law. A Comparative Theory* (New York, Joanna Cotler Books, 1971) 274–302.
[38] CG Hempel, *Fundamentals of Concept Formation in Empirical Science* (Chicago, The University of Chicago Press, 1952) 1f.
[39] This means the movables and immovables the spouses possessed on the day of their wedding (arts 1401 and 1404 of the 1804 Code Napoléon, which remained unchanged for almost two centuries in several countries (in Belgium, for instance, until 1976).

tor dropped this different ruling according to the division movable/immovable and replaced it by the division between the goods that one possessed before the wedding (which remain one's own) and goods acquired during the marriage (which become common).[40] This new division was based on changed views of marriage, including the acceptance of successive marriages and divorces. It is no longer assumed that marriage lasts 'until death separates us', but that successive relationships have become rather the rule than the exception. Hence, nowadays it seems reasonable that spouses would only share what they built up together, during their marriage.

In this way, concepts play an important role in theory building, but at the same time they are, in combination with rules and principles, a result of those theories.

Theory building aims at combining specific interpretations of legal principles, rules and concepts in a (newly) systematised whole.[41] In legal doctrine, systematising means theory building. Re-systematising the law is a continuous activity of legal scholarship due to an inflation of legislation and case law. New legislation, for example in the area of consumer protection, requires some re-systematisation of contract law. New judicial interpretations may necessitate a refinement, or even a radical change, of previous theories. New European rules, which directly affect domestic law, will require a re-systematisation of the affected areas of law in the national legal systems of the Member States.

IV. CONCLUSION

From this short overview of the nature and methodology of legal research it appears that legal doctrine is a scientific discipline in its own right with a methodology that, in its core characteristics, is quite comparable to the methodology used in other disciplines.

However, it also emerged that there is no agreement among legal theorists on the nature of legal doctrine as a discipline, even independently from differences among national traditions of legal scholarship. Starting from the way legal doctrine has been practised in the course of history, since Roman times, in most countries, we may consider it as a mainly hermeneutic discipline, with also empirical, argumentative, logical and normative elements. Description of the law is closely linked to its interpretation and, when describing the law, the legal scholar is wording hypotheses about its existence, validity and meaning. The level of systematisation and concept building is the level of theory building in legal doctrine.

Some aspects which could not be discussed and are open for further research and debate include:

---

[40] Arts 1399, 1405, 1406 and 1408 of the Belgian Civil Code.
[41] See, as to the close intertwinement of interpretation and systematisation in law, eg: J Chevallier, 'Conclusion générale. Les interprètes du droit' in Y Poirmeur, et al, *La doctrine juridique* (Paris, Presses Universitaires de France, 1993) 276.

- The close relationship between legal practice and legal doctrine, including scientific production by (full-time) legal practitioners and scholars active in legal practice, make it difficult sometimes to draw the line between both and to make the distinction between 'scientific' publications and sheer 'vulgarisation', transfer of information on some area of the law.
- Obviously, varying theories of meaning co-determine varying theories on the nature of legal scientific research and its appropriate methodology. It can be doubted if a consensus on such theories of meaning can ever be reached among the international scientific legal community, or even within the community of legal scholars of one single legal system. Hence, it will be even more difficult to reach such a consensus as to the nature and methodology of legal doctrine.
- The problem of 'objectivity' in legal research, as there is no 'objective' reality outside the constructions of legal doctrine. Moreover, legal scholars very regularly take normative positions; posit some choice among values or interests, which is 'subjective' *par excellence*. More than in the exact sciences, the only form of 'objectivity' one may reach is the intersubjective consensus among legal scholars.
- Not all research is about testing hypotheses or construing theories. There are, for instance at a preparatory stage, also 'exploratory inquiries' or purely 'descriptive research' (eg collecting data in view of formulating hypotheses at a later stage, not just vulgarisation).
- It is not because description/interpretation of the law and systematisation/theory building has always been the core business of legal doctrine that one should not consider broadening it, in a more interdisciplinary direction, by putting law more systematically in context and use the appropriate methodologies of other disciplines. The question here is: how far should legal scholars go in that direction and where do they reach their point of incompetence? Conformity with the approach of empirical sciences is not a good reason to do so, but in order to simply understand law and to elaborate theories and concepts in law, one needs this law-in-context approach.[42]

---

[42] See, eg: W Twining, 'Reflections on "Law in Context"' in W Twining, *Law in Context. Enlarging a Discipline* (Oxford, Clarendon Press, 1997) 36–62.

2

The Method of a Truly Normative Legal Science*

JAAP HAGE

THIS CHAPTER CONTAINS an argument to the effect that the proper method for legal science depends on what one takes to be the nature of science, the nature of the law and the kind of questions that are addressed in legal science. It starts from three assumptions, namely that

(a) science is the collaborative pursuit of knowledge;
(b) the law consists of those norms which ought to be enforced by collective means; and
(c) the proper standard to determine what ought to be done is what maximises the long-term happiness of all sentient beings (the H-standard).

On the basis of these assumptions the following positions are argued:

1. Legal science, in the sense of a description of the law, is not impossible for the reason that it is a normative science.
2. In abstract the method of all sciences, including legal science, is to create a coherent set of positions that encompasses 'everything', and therefore also beliefs about the law.
3. The proper method for a normative legal science consists primarily of the methods of sociology, psychology and economics, because the ultimate question to be answered is the collective enforcement of which norms satisfies the H-standard. The more traditional hermeneutic methods only play a role to the extent that they establish positive law that contributes to happiness by providing legal certainty.

---

* The author would like to thank Anne Ruth Mackor, Jan Smits, Michal Araszkiewicz and the other participants of the Tilburg Workshop on the methodology of legal research for useful comments on a draft version of this contribution and discussions on the nature of legal knowledge and science.

I. PRELIMINARIES

In this chapter I will outline a method for a truly normative legal science. With 'truly normative' I mean that this legal science provides the answer to some version of the question 'what should we do?' I will argue that the issue of the method for legal science hangs together with views on the nature of science, on the nature of law, on the justification of alleged knowledge, and – as I will argue – in the end with almost everything. The second section of this chapter will be devoted to an argument that the method for a normative science is essentially the same as that of a science that deals with 'facts'. In this first section I discuss a number of assumptions that are needed to get the argument started. The precise status of these assumptions will be clarified in section III, which deals with the method of normative legal science in particular. Section IV summarises the argument of this chapter.

A. The Nature of Science

If we want to know what the proper method for legal science is, we should at least have some idea of what we mean by 'science'.[1] Science has to do with the pursuit and accumulation of knowledge.[2] Moreover, it aims to systematise this knowledge. How this systematisation takes shape depends on the object of the knowledge. In the case of historical sciences, the system derives from the way in which facts and events explain each other. In the case of physical sciences, the system consists in the laws that are formulated and that are used to explain and predict events and facts, and in the way in which laws are derived from each other. In mathematics, the system consists in the axiomatisation of a subdomain and in the derivation of theorems from these axioms.

A third characteristic of science, which explains other important characteristics, is that science is a social phenomenon. It is impossible to be the only scientist in a field, at least in the long run. Science is a cooperative enterprise aimed at the acquisition, accumulation and systematisation of knowledge. The advantage of science over individual acquisition of knowledge is that scientists can build on the results of their colleagues. To quote Newton: 'If I have seen further it is only by standing on the shoulders of giants.'[3]

---

[1] However, the editor of Blackwell's *A Companion to the Philosophy of Science* (Oxford, Blackwell, 2000), WH Newton-Smith, refused to give a definition in the Introduction of the book, because the prospect to succeed would be bleak.

[2] According to Anne Ruth Mackor, 'Explanatory Non-Normative Legal Doctrine', in chapter three of this volume, an important task of sciences, including legal doctrine, is to explain legal norms. This view is well compatible with the view of science exposed here, because the explanation Mackor is after boils down to the *knowledge* that particular legal norms can be derived from (amongst others) other norms.

[3] In original Latin: 'Pigmaei gigantum humeris impositi plusquam ipsi gigantes vident.' Letter to Robert Hooke of 15 February 1676. See en.wikiquote.org/wiki/Isaac_Newton (last consulted 15 December 2009).

Let us assume that *science is a way in which people collaborate in the pursuit and systematisation of knowledge*. If such collaboration is to be possible, several conditions must be met. First it must be assumed that the aspired knowledge is, at least approximately, the same for everybody involved in the cooperation. If everybody would have his or her own 'truth', it would be impossible for one person to build on the results of other persons.[4] This demand would, in the eyes of many, exclude aesthetics and astrology from the arena of science. Very often the assumption that truth is the same for everybody is made on the basis of another assumption, namely that knowledge describes a world which is mind-independent and therefore the same for everybody (ontological realism). A true description of this independent world would be the same for everybody too. It is possible, however, to assume a truth that is the same for everybody without endorsing ontological realism. Mathematical truth would, according to many, be a case in point.

B. Science and Method

A second precondition for the possibility of cooperative knowledge pursuit is that there exists, at least to a large extent, agreement on what count as good reasons for adopting or rejecting a potential piece of knowledge.[5] Here is where method comes into the picture. For what is a scientific method?

In one sense of the word, it is a way of going about doing science. It is a kind of procedure that is to be followed if the results are to count as 'scientific'.[6] An example of such a procedure would be the empirical cycle as described by De Groot[7] or the Herculean method described by Dworkin in the chapter 'Hard Cases' from *Taking Rights Seriously*.[8]

In another sense, a scientific method indicates what count as good reasons for adopting or rejecting a potential piece of knowledge. Take, for instance, the mathematical thesis known as the Goldbach conjecture,[9] that all even numbers bigger than two can be written as the sum of two prime numbers. One mathematician would count on proof to establish the truth of this thesis, while another mathematician would take a large collection of random even numbers, check whether they can be written as the sum of two primes, and decide from that

---

[4] As Mackor pointed out to me, it is possible that there are several subgroups within a scientific community with different 'truths' in the sense of points of belief convergence. Every such group could theoretically have its own science.

[5] Arguably, there are other preconditions for science in the sense of collaborative knowledge acquisition. One may think in this connection of ways in which scientific results are published, financed, etc. For the present purposes the two mentioned preconditions, a shared knowledge object and a common method, are the most important ones.

[6] Scientific method, even in the sense of a way of going about doing research, is general. This means that a method is *not* an algorithm to be followed in a particular research project.

[7] AD de Groot, *Methodologie* ('s-Gravenhage, Mouton, 1961) chapter 1.

[8] See R Dworkin, *Taking Rights Seriously*, 2nd edn (London, Duckworth, 1978).

[9] See en.wikipedia.org/wiki/Goldbach%27s_conjecture (last consulted 2 November 2009).

sample that the conjecture is almost certainly true. If they consider their own method as the only legitimate one, these two mathematicians cannot cooperate in the pursuit of knowledge on number theory.

The adoption of a particular method in this second sense boils down to agreement on what count as such good reasons. Since such an agreement is a precondition for science as collaborative knowledge acquisition, a shared method is almost by definition a precondition for science.[10]

Reasons in general, and therefore also reasons for accepting or rejecting a particular piece of potential knowledge, are facts that are *relevant* for what they are reasons for or against.[11] The adoption of a method is a choice for what counts as relevant. It is also a choice concerning the kind of data that must be collected in order to argue for or against a potential piece of knowledge. For instance, on a hermeneutic method for legal science, the relevant data for a particular legal conclusion might be that this conclusion is supported by the literal interpretation of a statute, which is adopted as an authoritative text. Therefore, a legal researcher should consult this text, and apply, possibly amongst others, a literal interpretation to it.[12]

The proper way of going about legal research method in the first sense is, to a large extent,[13] determined by method in the second sense of the recognition of particular kinds of data as relevant for the issue at stake. It is this second sense of 'method' that will be at stake in the rest of this chapter. Science in the sense of collaborative knowledge acquisition is practically impossible without such a method.

C. Method and the Object of Knowledge

The idea of a method is often connected to disciplines such as law, physics, mathematics, biology, medicine, history, sociology or psychology. In the following I will continue to write about the methods of a discipline, but this is, in a strict sense, incorrect. Which facts count as reasons for or against a conclusion depends on the type of conclusion and therefore on the research question at issue. One discipline may deal with several kinds of research questions and then different methods are relevant in answering these questions. Legal science is a

---

[10] That science requires a shared method does not exclude that this method is mostly implicit, or that it changes over the course of time. If such a change is drastic, for instance, if physics comes to be based on experiments rather than on interpretation of authoritative texts, the nature of the science also changes.

[11] An extensive discussion of the nature of reasons can be found in JC Hage, *Reasoning with Rules* (Dordrecht, Kluwer, 1997) chapter 2. See also C Redondo, *Reasons for Action and the Law* (Dordrecht, Kluwer, 1999).

[12] It is in this respect that Van Hoecke mentions normative and authoritative sources such as legislation and case law, as empirical data used in legal doctrine. See 'Legal Doctrine: Which Method(s) for What Kind of Discipline?' in chapter one of this volume.

[13] Other factors might be conventions on how results are to be published and restrictions on how research may be financed.

case in point. The question as to what the criminal law of a jurisdiction is – the traditional doctrinal question – differs, for instance, from the question how the contents of the criminal law developed in the course of time – the legal historical question. It is improbable that the same kinds of facts would be relevant to answer these two questions. So, if within a discipline different kinds of research questions are being asked, the issue of method should be focused on a type of research question, rather than on the discipline as a whole.[14] For the following discussion of the method of legal science, I will focus on *the description of the (contents of the) law of a particular jurisdiction at a particular place and time*.[15]

The methods of a scientific discipline are normally chosen because the participants in the discipline assume that these methods lead to the kind of knowledge pursued in their discipline. A good example is formal logic. One of the questions with which formal logic deals is what the theorems of a particular logical system are. Logicians believe that this question has one correct answer. Moreover, each potential theorem either is or is not a theorem of the system at issue. Logicians cooperate in identifying the valid theorems and by giving reasons (proofs) why the proposed theorems are valid. Moreover, the alleged theorems and the accompanying proofs are published, to share the results with other logicians who can build upon them, and who are also enabled to check whether the alleged theorems have been proven. Logicians consider proofs to be relevant because they assume that proofs lead to conclusions which are true, not only for the person who gave the proof, but also for all other logicians. In fact, they even attempt to prove that proofs lead to true results by showing that a particular proof theory is 'sound'. There exists an independent test, in the shape of model theoretic semantics, which determines whether a particular theorem is true, and a particular logical calculus is sound (a recommendable characteristic) if its proofs lead to theorems that are true according to the semantics.[16]

The point of this example is that scientific disciplines tend to assume that there is truth to be had and also that the methods they employ are normally suitable to discover this truth. Formal logicians assume that proofs lead to true theorems; theorists of the physical sciences assume that the cycle of hypothesis formulation, empirical testing of hypotheses, and improving the hypotheses on the basis of the test results, leads to ever better (in the sense of more true) theories,[17] and

---

[14] A consequence of this position is that a researcher should be explicit on the kind of research question that he or she tries to answer, and in particular on the impact which this has for the choice of a method. This is especially true where different questions within one field require different methods. Clarity about the kind of question that is addressed is crucial.

[15] The clause 'of a particular jurisdiction' will be relativised in section III.

[16] More on the nature of logic and in particular the relation between proof theory and (model theoretic) semantics can be found in thorough introductions to formal logic, including S Haack, *Philosophy of Logics* (Cambridge, Cambridge University Press, 1978) and LTF Gamut, *Logic, Language, and Meaning*, 2 vols (Chicago, University of Chicago Press, 1990).

[17] *cf* KR Popper, 'Truth, Rationality, and the Growth of Scientific Knowledge' in KR Popper, *Conjectures and Refutation*, 4th edn (London, Routledge and Kegan Paul, 1972) 215–50. More on the idea of verisimilitude can be found in C Brink, 'Verisimilitude' in Newton-Smith, *Companion to the Philosophy of Science* (Oxford, Blackwell, 2000) 561–63.

moral philosophers assume that mutual adaption of concrete moral intuitions and general moral principles lead to ever better moral theories.[18]

The methods of scientific disciplines are often based on implicit theories concerning the nature of the discipline's objects and the suitability of these methods for obtaining knowledge about objects with that nature. As mathematical theorems are different from physical laws, it takes different data to argue for the truth of theorems than for the existence of physical laws. Changing insights into the nature of a discipline's knowledge object may lead to changes in method. If, for instance, the law is not (anymore) considered to be an answer to the question of what to do, but rather a body of rules, rights and principles that happen to exist at a particular time and place, we might stop arguing about the contents of the law by pointing out the consequences of particular rules, and revert to the study and interpretation of authoritative texts or the behaviour of leading jurists.

A discipline and its methods are part of a wider body of (hypothetical) knowledge, which includes views on the nature of the discipline's knowledge objects and theories on how and why particular data are relevant to establish knowledge about such objects. In connection with the proper method of legal science, this would mean that the view concerning this method hangs together with a view on the nature of the law, and a view on which data are relevant to determine the truth – if there is any to be had – of potential pieces of legal knowledge.

At this point I want to mention the possibility that legal 'science' does not aim at the pursuit of knowledge about something at all. Many lawyers are involved in keeping the law of a particular jurisdiction in good shape. This is done by describing the law as it is, incorporating recent changes caused by, for instance, new legislation and case law, into the body of legal knowledge, by evaluating the existing law and by proposing changes to it, or even – if one is in the position to do so – by bringing about the desired changes.[19] This is an important task of legal 'science', and it is benefited by an academic level of dealing with the law, but it is not science in the sense of the word used here of cooperative knowledge acquisition. It is rather a form of highly qualified *maintenance of the legal system*. There may be some overlap in method with 'real' legal science, but maintenance of the legal system is a different discipline from legal science and I will not deal with it here.

---

[18] The standard reference here is J Rawls, *A Theory of Justice*, 1st edn (Cambridge, Harvard University Press, 1971) section 9. See also N Daniels, 'Reflective Equilibrium', which can be found at www.plato.stanford.edu/entries/reflective-equilibrium (last consulted 11 October 2009). Those moral philosophers who consider themselves as being involved in a normative *scientific* enterprise will also assume that the better theories are closer approximations of a moral 'truth' which should be accepted by everybody, whether they agree or not. Mackor pointed out to me that moral philosophers might, like mathematicians, confine themselves to axiomatising a body of moral rules. That is correct, but then these moral philosophers would not be engaged in a normative enterprise anymore.

[19] See also the description of the practice of the legal discipline by P Westerman, 'Open or Autonomous? The Debate on Legal Methodology as a Reflection on the Debate on Law' in chapter five of this volume.

D. Three Views on the Nature of Law

In most disciplines, a method reflects a view of the discipline's knowledge domain. For instance, in physics it used to be assumed that nature obeys certain 'laws' and that these laws manifest themselves in observable phenomena. Observations can be used to induce hypotheses about the laws and to test the laws through predictions of new observations.[20] The proper method is therefore to use observations to induce laws from (empiricism), or to falsify predictions (critical rationalism). In mathematics the idea is that the domain consists of a set of theorems that somehow 'follow' from the discipline's axioms. The appropriate method is then to deduce the theorems from the axioms (or to prove, if that is possible, that a potential theorem cannot be proven). Similarly, one would expect the method of legal science to reflect a view about the law.[21]

i. Purely Procedural Law

It is possible to distinguish at least three fundamentally different views on the nature of the law. One view is that questions about the contents of the law, even 'easy' questions, have no true answers and that the law consists merely of a set of acceptable argument forms, such as an appeal to legislation, to case law, to legal principles, human rights, legal doctrine, and the standard canons for legal interpretation and legal reasoning. Legal argument is not aimed at finding the contents of the law, because there is no such a thing. It is aimed at convincing one's auditorium of a particular legal position. Some arguments are more authoritative than others[22] and should therefore be more convincing, but what counts in the end is not whether the correct position was defended – because the correct position does not exist – but which argument was most convincing in the sense of being effective. The law would be, to use Rawls' phrase, purely procedural,[23] with the not unimportant clause that the procedures that constitute the law, the acceptable

---

[20] See eg R Harré, *The Philosophies of Science* (Oxford University Press, 1985) chapter 2 and AF Chalmers, *What is this thing called Science?*, 3rd edn (Indianapolis, Hackett, 1999) chapters 4–5.

[21] That is what one should expect, but as yet I know only a few authors writing on legal method, who based their views on a theory about the nature of law. One example is C Smith, 'Het normatieve karakter van de rechtswetenschap. Recht als oordeel' ('The Normative Nature of Legal Doctrine. Law as Judgement'; *Rechtsfilosofie en Rechtstheorie* 2009/ 3, 202–225), who bases himself on the purely procedural view of the law that is described below. Another example is Mackor, 'Explanatory Non-normative Legal Doctrine' in chapter three of this volume, who bases her explanatory account of legal method on the view of law as social fact.

[22] If the authoritativeness of arguments is measured by standards which exist as matter of social fact, the procedural view of the law merges with the view of law as social fact. The 'only' difference between the two would then be that the procedural view of the law focuses on arguments by means of which legal positions can be supported or attacked, while the view of law as social fact focuses on the positions that turn out to be right given the argument forms that are commonly considered to be authoritative. This difference is comparable to that between traditional and dialogical presentations of logical systems. *cf* EM Barth and ECW Krabbe, *From Axiom to Dialogue* (Berlin, Walter de Gruyter, 1982).

[23] Rawls, *A Theory of Justice* (1971) section 14.

argument forms and the materials to which they refer – legislation, treaties, case law and custom – to a large extent constrain the possible outcomes.[24] The law for a concrete case, or for a case type, would be the outcome of a battle of arguments.[25]

Legal science in the sense of collaborative knowledge acquisition requires the possibility of agreement. If the law is purely procedural, this possibility can only exist if the nature of the legal procedure constrains the possible outcomes of a battle of arguments to such an extent that only one outcome is viable.[26] However, then the law is not purely procedural anymore, because most legal discussions would have only one possible outcome if played by the procedural rules, and then the contents of the law are fixed, more or less in the same way as mathematical theorems are fixed by the axioms and the rules of the proof system. If the law is purely procedural, however, that is if the procedural rules in combination with the contents of the legal sources do not determine the outcomes of legal argument battles, there is no basis for agreement on the contents of the law[27] and legal science in the sense of collaborative pursuit of knowledge is impossible.

ii. Law as Social Fact

A second view of the law holds that the law exists as a matter of social fact, independent of what individuals may believe about it, but dependent on what sufficiently many sufficiently important members of a social group think about the contents of the law and think about what others think about it.[28] A special variant of this view is that of law as institutional fact, according to which most of the law exists thanks to rules that specify what counts as law.[29]

This view of law as social fact has two advantages. First, it explains why the law appears to be a matter of fact, independent of what individual persons think

---

[24] These constrained options correspond to the norm-contentions described in Mackor, 'Explanatory Non-normative Legal Doctrine' in chapter three of this volume.

[25] This view is defended by Smith, *Het normatieve karakter van de rechtswetenschap*, by A Soeteman, *Rechtsgeleerde waarheid* (valedictory address at Vrije Universiteit, 19 June 2009) and by J Smits, *Omstreden rechtswetenschap* (Den Haag, Boom Juridische uitgevers, 2009) 93f. The latter author also gives references to other Dutch adherents of the view that the law is purely procedural (discursive). Formal elaborations of the procedural view of the law are discussed in my paper 'Dialectics in Artificial Intelligence and Law' in JC Hage, *Studies in Legal Logic* (Dordrecht, Springer, 2005) 227–64.

[26] Soeteman, *Rechtsgeleerde waarheid* (2009) 15, writes about legal truth, and therefore seems to assume that the law (often) sufficiently constrains legal arguments to make one outcome the right one. Whether this single right answer can be identified easily or authoritatively is a different matter.

[27] There may be agreement on what the law is *not*, however. In that sense, some knowledge is possible even on a purely procedural view of the law.

[28] One version of this view was made popular in HLA Hart, *The Concept of Law*, 2nd edn (Oxford, Oxford University Press, 1994).

[29] This approach is described in, amongst others, N MacCormick and O Weinberger, An Institutional Theory of Law (Dordrecht, Reidel, 1986); E Lagerspetz, The Opposite Mirrors (Dordrecht, Kluwer, 1995); DWP Ruiter, Institutional Legal Facts (Dordrecht, Kluwer, 1993); also DWP Ruiter, Legal Institutions (Dordrecht, Kluwer, 2001) and N MacCormick, Institutions of Law (Oxford, Oxford University Press, 2007). In chapter nine of this volume, the institutional approach is explicitly adopted by J Bell, 'Legal Research and the Distinctiveness of Comparative Law'.

of it, and that the contents of law depend on a particular jurisdiction. Second, it explains why lawyers tend to argue about the law as if it already exists and as if two conflicting legal positions cannot both be true.

The view of law as social fact has also an important disadvantage, namely that there would be less law than seems at first sight. If law exists as a matter of social fact, there cannot be more law than is fixed by social reality. In particular there cannot be law about which knowledgeable lawyers fundamentally disagree.[30] And yet, such disagreements seem to occur frequently. Does this mean that these lawyers do not disagree about the law, but rather about how the law should be expanded to cover the case at issue? If this is the case, why do these lawyers not clearly separate the two discussions, one about the law that actually exists and the other about the most desirable way to create new law? Somehow the arguments about the contents of the law and what would be desirable legal solutions for types of cases seem to conflate. Is this a matter of methodological confusion, of pious deceit, or is something else the case?

iii. The Normative View of the Law

The third view of the law assumes that something else is the case. According to this view, the law is essentially an answer to the question what to do, and more in particular what to do by means of rules[31] which should be enforced collectively, usually by means of state organs.[32] Notice that according to this third view, the law *is*, not what is actually enforced collectively, but what *ought to be* enforced collectively. To state it in an overly simplified way: the law is an ought, not an is.[33] Therefore, I will call this the *normative view* of the law. On this normative view there is principally no difference between the law as it is, and the law as

---

[30] At first sight, this drastic conclusion seems avoidable by allowing arguments of commonly accepted types on the basis of commonly accepted legal sources. But then there are three possibilities:
1. These arguments do not lead to a unique conclusion.
2. There is a unique conclusion, but this is not commonly accepted.
3. There is a unique conclusion, which is commonly accepted.

Only in the last case we can speak of law as social fact. The second case (as the first) would be a variant of the procedural view of law.

[31] The idea that the law consists of the rules that should be enforced collectively does not involve the other idea that this should apply to rules on an individual basis. One might well opt for the version that complete bodies of rules should be judged on whether they should be enforced collectively, with the proviso that many rules belonging to such a body, in particular the procedural rules (*cf* JH Merryman, *The Civil Law Tradition*, 2nd edn (Stanford University Press, Stanford, 1985) 70/1), do not lend themselves well to enforcement.

[32] At least in theory it is possible to have a different normative view of the law, a view according to which the law is an answer to the question what to do, but not the question which rules to enforce by collective means. It might for instance be the question which rules serve the general interest. I will not pursue this alternative normative view of the law here any further.

[33] This is oversimplified because it assumes that an 'ought' is not an 'is'. In 'What is a norm?' in my *Studies in Legal Logic* (2005) 159–202, I have argued why the proper distinction is between rules and facts, and not between is and ought. I take these two distinctions to be quite different from each other.

it should be.[34] Moreover, the law would be a branch of morality, if morality is taken as that set of standards that indicate what would be good and right things to do all things considered and taking the interests of all human (sentient) beings into account.[35]

The obvious advantage of the normative view is that it explains how discussions on the contents of the law often deal with what is desirable. The equally obvious disadvantage is that it seemingly fails to explain how the law is the same for everybody, why law appears to be primarily national law, and how the law is related to such matters of fact as the contents of legislation and of case law, judicial decisions, and social practices such as the canons for interpretation and legal reasoning. This disadvantage does not need to be real, however. The 'positive' law, which exists as a matter of social fact, is an important – in fact by far the most important – factor that determines the law in the sense of rules that should collectively be enforced. It is highly desirable that the law can function properly in regulating human society and for that purpose it needs to be stable, the same for everybody, and easily recognisable.[36] In practice this means that the law must by and large be positive law.[37] The difference with the view of the law as social fact is, however, that positive law is 'real' law ('real law' in the sense of the law that should be enforced by collective means) not because that is the social practice, but because, and to the extent that, the positive law ought to be enforced collectively.

Moreover – and this has immediate implications for the method of legal science – the positive law is only 'real' law to the extent that it contributes to the recognisability of law and to legal certainty. This means that if the 'positive' law can only be established by means of some contestable interpretation, it cannot fulfil its coordinating function anymore and loses its presumptive force as law.

II. THE POSSIBILITY OF A NORMATIVE SCIENCE

In this contribution I intend to outline a method for legal science as a description of existing law,[38] on the assumption that the normative view of the law is correct. Legal science would then be a normative science, aiming at the collective pursuit and systematisation of normative knowledge, in particular knowledge which rules *should* (here and now) be enforced collectively.

This view of legal science has some similarities with, but should nevertheless be distinguished from the view, promoted by Smits, that legal science is nor-

---

[34] For the famous contention otherwise 'The existence of law is one thing; its merit or demerit is another', see J Austin, *The Province of Jurisprudence Determined*, several edns, note to the 5th lecture.
[35] Clearly, other circumscriptions of morality are possible.
[36] For these and other 'internal' demands on the law, see LLH Fuller, *The Morality of Law*, revised edn (New Haven, Yale University Press, 1969) chapter 2.
[37] This position is far from new; it can already be found in Aquinas. See his *Summa Theologica* I-II, Qu 95.
[38] I therefore ignore other kinds of legal science, such as the explanation of existing law, or the comparison of the law from different jurisdictions.

mative in the sense that it deals with the question of what the law should be.[39] Although Smits is not very explicit about the nature of the law,[40] it seems that he considers the law to be a set of rules, etc that exist in social practice. Legal science should, according to Smits, indicate what this practice should be. In my opinion, the 'real' law, as distinguished from the merely positive law, is itself an answer to a normative question and legal science as description of this 'real' law aims at providing this answer. Despite this difference, the view of Smits on the nature of legal science has an important similarity to my view, because we both assume that legal science deals by and large with the question which rules we should have, or should enforce by collective means.

The method that I apply to formulate the proper method for legal science is to argue why the proposed legal method contributes to the pursuit of knowledge about which norms should be enforced collectively. In particular it is *not* an analysis of the method used in contemporary legal doctrine. This method is, as is correctly pointed out by Van Hoecke,[41] essentially hermeneutic. From the fact that a hermeneutic method is in fact used in the development of legal doctrine, it does not follow that this is the proper method, however. In this sense, I am not a methodological naturalist.[42] As I will argue in section II. E., the method that is actually used in doctrinal legal science is no more than a starting point in the process of deciding which methodological positions stand up to critical scrutiny.

A. Why Normative Science Seems Problematic

It is a popular view that normative science is not well possible.[43] The reason is generally some form of non-cognitivism concerning normative (and evaluative) issues. It is customary to distinguish between the realms of is and ought and to be an ontological realist with respect of the realm of the is, and to be a non-realist with respect to the ought. With regards to is-matters, there would be a mind-independent reality which is the same for everybody[44] and which makes

---

[39] Smits, *Omstreden rechtswetenschap* (2009) 70.

[40] However, he does describe the law as a spontaneous order and a product of natural selection (ibid 79, 81).

[41] See Van Hoecke's contribution in chapter one of this volume.

[42] On methodological naturalism in legal theory, see B Leiter, *Naturalizing Jurisprudence* (Oxford, Oxford University Press, 2007) 30–46. More information about methodological naturalism in general can be found in H Kornbluth (ed), *Naturalizing Epistemology*, 2nd edn (Cambridge, MIT Press, 1994).

[43] For the Netherlands, this position was taken by GE Langemeijer, *Inleiding tot de studie van de wijsbegeerte des rechts* (Zwolle, Tjeenk Willink 1956) 296 and G de Geest, 'Hoe maken we van de rechtswetenschap een volwaardige wetenschap' (2004) 2 *Nederlands Juristenblad* 58–66 (implicit). According to Smits a normative legal science is possible, but in his view it is not possible that such a science would lead to consensus (Smits (n 25) 111). Given my characterisation of science, this last view of Smits implies the negation of his first view about the possibility of a normative legal science.

[44] For a discussion of this form of realism, see M Devitt, *Realism and Truth*, 2nd edn (Oxford, Blackwell, 1991) chapter 2.

every factual proposition true or false.[45] With regard to ought-matters, such a mind-independent reality would be lacking. To state it bluntly: whether we agree about it or not, there would be a true answer to every question of fact, while there is no such true answer concerning normative questions. What ought to be done would not be a matter of facts that are the same for everybody, but a matter of taste, or of choice, which may have a different outcome for different persons, even if they are all fully rational. There is no common ground which can function as a foundation for agreement and where there is no ground for agreement, so runs the argument, there is no room for science.

The same issue can also be approached from a logical point of view.[46] To justify an ought-conclusion by means of a deductively valid argument, at least one of the premises must be an ought-sentence too. Moreover, for a successful justification, the premises of the justificatory argument must be either true, if they are factual, or justified. Since presumably normative premises cannot be true, they must be justified, but this justification requires an argument with at least one normative premise, which must be justified . . . etc. However long the justificatory argument chain is made, it never touches solid ground in the form of premises which have all truth values. This line of argument has become so familiar that attempts to base normative conclusions on solely factual premises are discarded without much discussion as committing the 'naturalistic fallacy'.[47] I will argue that this familiar line of argument against the possibility of a normative science either is much weaker than is usually assumed, or hits purely 'factual' science just as hard as it hits normative science. The central piece of my argument is a theory about the nature of justification.

B. Positions

There are many different things which can be justified, such as beliefs, actions, decisions, verdicts, etc. On first impression one might think that these different objects of justification require different forms of justification, but this impression is only correct to a limited degree.

All forms of justification can be reduced to variants on justification of behaviour (including forbearance). This is obvious for actions, and since decisions and verdicts can be brought under the category of actions (*taking* a decision, or

---

[45] For the purpose of this contribution, I will ignore the complications of vague propositions and of sentences with non-denoting terms in referring positions. These issues are to be dealt with by, for instance, respectively fuzzy set theory and fuzzy logic (see en.wikipedia.org/wiki/Fuzzy_logic, last consulted 12 October 2009) and theories on the relation between sentences and the referring expressions in it. See, eg AC Grayling, *An Introduction to Philosophical Logic*, 3rd edn (Oxford, Blackwell, 1997) chapter 4.

[46] For an example, see RM Hare, *The Language of Morals* (Oxford, Oxford University Press, 1952) chapter 2.

[47] The best exposition of this point is to my knowledge still PW Taylor, *Normative Discourse* (Englewood Cliffs, Prentice Hall, 1961) chapter 9.

giving a verdict with this particular content), it should be obvious for decisions and verdicts too. The same counts for using rules.

It is somewhat less obvious for beliefs, but the justification of a belief with a particular content can be interpreted as the justification of *accepting* this belief content. Accepting something can, for justificatory purposes, be treated as a kind of mental action. And just as it is possible to accept belief contents, it is possible to accept goals, values and principles.

It is even possible to continue along this line, by treating the justification of the different forms of actions as the justification of accepting 'that these actions are the ones that should be performed (under the circumstances)'.[48] In this way, all forms of justification can be treated as the justification of accepting 'something'. As a catch-all term for things that can be mentally accepted, I will from now on use the word 'position'.

Building on this definition, I will use the expression 'position set' for the set of all positions accepted by a person.

C. Local and Global Justification

In the literature on legal justification, justification has sometimes been pictured as a deductively valid argument.[49] In such an argument the conclusion (what is justified) must be true given the truth of the premises. The idea behind this kind of justification is that the 'justifiedness' of the premises is transferred to the conclusion, analogous to the way in which the truth of the premises is transferred to the conclusion in more traditionally conceived deductive arguments.

It seems to me that this picture is mistaken in at least two ways. First, because it suggests that 'being justified' is a characteristic of positions that is similar to truth, only somewhat 'weaker'. Second, because it overlooks the essentially global nature of justification. In a deductively valid argument, the conclusion must be true if the premises are true. This means that the truth of the conclusion is guaranteed by the truth of the premises, and that nothing else is relevant for this truth.[50] For instance, if the statements 'All thieves are punishable' and 'Jane is a thief' are both true, the statement 'Jane is punishable' must be true too. Whatever else may be the case, this cannot influence the truth of the statement 'Jane is punishable', unless it has the implication that one of the premises is

---

[48] See Giovanni Sartor, *Legal Reasoning. A Cognitive Approach to the Law* (Dordrecht, Springer, 2005) chapter 3.
[49] See, eg R Alexy, *Theorie der juristischen Argumentation* (Frankfurt, Suhrkamp, 1978) 273–78 (on 'internal' justification); N MacCormick, *Legal Reasoning and Legal Theory* (Oxford, Clarendon Press, 1978) chapter 2 (on 'first order justification').
[50] This should be read as 'irrelevant from an argumentation-technical point of view'. The only thing that is really relevant for the truth of a conclusion is whether this conclusion corresponds with the facts. However, that has nothing to do with the argument from which the conclusion follows.

false after all.[51] For instance, the fact that Jane is only five years old either has no impact on Jane's punishability, because the statement 'All thieves are punishable' is still considered to be true, or – which is more plausible – it has impact, because it makes the statement 'All thieves are punishable' false.

The general point here is that the truth of the conclusion of a sound justificatory argument (deductively valid with true premises) is not influenced by additional information. If the premises of a deductive justificatory argument are true, its conclusion must be true, and then probably also justified, *whatever else is the case*. Therefore, it is not necessary to consider additional information, because this information cannot change the conclusion anymore. Deductive justification is *local* in the sense that it needs only consider the premises and the conclusion of a deductively valid argument.

The reader who thinks this is unrealistic is probably right. Not because deductively valid justification is not local, but because deductively valid justificatory arguments are seldom offered. They are seldom offered, because they require premises the truth of which cannot be established. Take our example about Jane. It requires the premise that *all* thieves are punishable. That premise can only be established if it is already known that Jane is punishable (that would be a necessary condition), or if there is a rule that makes all thieves punishable, without exceptions. The former demand would beg the question, because we need the premise about all thieves to justify a belief about Jane. The second demand is unrealistic, because rules tend to have exceptions, and these exceptions cannot be enumerated.

Real life justification is normally based on premises that support the conclusion without guaranteeing its truth. If Jane is a thief, this is a reason to believe that she is punishable, but there may be other reasons which invalidate this conclusion. One such a reason would be that Jane is only five years old. In general, a position is justified if the reasons pleading for acceptance outweigh the reasons against accepting it to a sufficient degree. However, this means that *all* reasons for or against acceptance must be balanced and that means in turn that justification must be global. A position which is justified in the light of a particular set of other positions need not be justified in the light of an even larger set of other positions, because this larger set may contain additional reasons against adopting it.[52]

In logic there is a technical term for a similar phenomenon: *nonmonotonicity*. A logic is nonmonotonic if a conclusion that follows from a set of premises does not need to follow from a wider set of premises.[53] Analogously we can say that

---

[51] This may be interpreted as a reason why justification on the deductive account of it is global too. However, then the global nature does not lie in the deductively valid argument itself, but in the justification of the premises.

[52] In fact, it is even more complicated, because apart from reasons against a position, there may be reasons why the reasons for adoption are in general not reasons after all, or are excluded in this special case. More details on the 'logic of reasons' in Hage, *Reasoning with Rules* (1997) chapter 4 and Hage (n 25) chapter 3.

[53] See, eg ML Ginsberg (ed), *Readings in Nonmonotonic Reasoning* (Los Altos, Morgan Kaufman, 1987) 1f.

justification is nonmonotonic because a position that is justified in the light of a set of other positions needs not be justified in the light of a still wider set of positions.[54]

Nonmonotonicity and the global nature of justification go hand in hand. The 'normal' justification of a position is always relative to a particular position set. To get rid of this relativity, one needs to idealise and to assume that it is possible to consider a position in the light of *all* other positions. A position would be justified in an absolute sense if it is justified in the light of all positions. Obviously, absolute justification is an unrealistic notion for practical purposes, but it is useful as a tool for thinking about the nature of justification.

D. Integrated Coherentism

Theories of justification are prone to be criticised for suffering under, what Hans Albert has dubbed, the 'Münchhausen-trilemma', after the famous baron who tried to pull himself out of the morass by his hairs.[55] Because the premises of a justificatory argument would need to be justified themselves, there seem to be only three possibilities:

1. Some premises (eg those resulting from sensory perception under ideal circumstances) are dogmatically accepted as true or justified.
2. The need to justify the premises leads to an infinite regress, because the arguments used to justify the premises also use premises which need to be justified, and so on.
3. The premises of a justificatory argument are indirectly justified by the conclusion of the justificatory argument; in other words: the justification would be circular.

Let us assume that Albert's analysis is correct and that these are the only three possibilities. The question then is whether this is problematic. My answer would be that it is not, because all justification is relative to the set of everything one accepts, one's position set. Justification is necessarily circular in the sense that the justification of every position that a person accepts is based on this person's position set. On what else could it be based? Not on reality itself, because our contact with reality is through what we believe about reality.[56]

The global nature of justification forces us to adopt a coherence theory of justification. The idea behind coherentism is that the justification of a position consists in the position being an element of a wider set of positions which

---

[54] A more extensive argument to the same effect can be found in the paper 'Law and Defeasibility' in Hage (n 25) 7–32.
[55] Hans Albert, *Traktat über kritische Vernunft* (Tübingen, Mohr, 1980) section 2.
[56] Perceptive states that lead to beliefs are not relevant for justification, even if they can *explain* some of our beliefs. It is those beliefs (positions) that play a role in justification.

somehow 'cohere' with each other.[57] Coherentism has the advantage over foundationalism, its main competitor in the theories of justification, that it does not require a foundational set of positions which are considered to be justified without further reasons, and which are therefore made immune against criticism.[58]

This advantage comes with at least two seeming disadvantages. One alleged disadvantage is that if justification is considered to exist in a mutual relation between positions only, the connection with the 'world outside' seems to be lost. Haack writes in this connection about the *consistent fairy story objection*, or – even more picturesque – the drunken sailors argument, because the elements of a coherent theory may keep each other upright like drunken sailors who cannot stand by themselves.[59] I will address this seeming disadvantage in the next section.

The second disadvantage is that the notion of coherence is hard to specify. What does it mean if a set of positions is said to cohere? There are very complicated accounts of this notion of coherence,[60] but it seems that a simple account is possible. If coherence is treated as a characteristic of a set of positions that includes not only beliefs, but also all kinds of standards, a set of positions may also contain the standards that are used to determine whether a particular position is justified in the light of a set of other positions. In fact, a comprehensive position set *would* contain such standards. That makes it possible to use the position set in the definition of coherence. A somewhat simplified account would be the following: A position set is coherent if and only if it includes every position that should be accepted in the light of its content (the counterpart of logical closure), and does not include any position that should be rejected according to its own content (the counterpart of consistency). As this notion of coherence refers to standards that are contained in the coherent set itself, I have called it 'integrated coherentism'.[61] When I write about coherence in the rest of this chapter, I mean integrated coherence.

Since a coherent position set includes everything that should be accepted according to itself, such a set will presumably be infinitely large. For realistic justification we will have to work with more limited sets, under the assumption that the limited set is a representative part of a coherent infinite set. I will call this the *soundness assumption*. This soundness assumption is defeasible, in the sense that it may turn out to be incorrect in the light of new information.

Suppose for instance that we are dealing with the belief that Jane is punishable. We know that Jane is a thief and that the rule exists (is valid) that thieves

[57] This is one possible version of coherentism. For a brief overview of several alternatives, see K Lehrer, 'Coherentism' in J Dancy and E Sosa (eds), *A Companion to Epistemology* (Oxford, Blackwell, 1992) 67–70.
[58] If there are reasons for immunising some positions against criticism, these very reasons are the proof that the privileged positions are not privileged at all, but derive their special position in the set of all positions from their relation to other positions in the same set (the reasons). This kind of 'immunisation' is well compatible with coherentism. For details, see Hage (n 25) 42.
[59] S Haack, *Evidence and Inquiry* (Oxford, Blackwell, 1993) 26f.
[60] An example would be the theory defended by Peczenik and Alexy. See R Alexy and A Peczenik, 'The Concept of Coherence and its Significance for Discursive Rationality' (1990) 3 *Ratio Juris* 130.
[61] JC Hage, 'Law and Coherence' (2004) 17 *Ratio Juris* 87. See also Hage (n 25) 58–59.

are punishable. In the light of this limited position set, we should also accept that Jane is punishable, and the position set should be expanded accordingly. The soundness assumption here includes that there are no other reasons relevant for the punishability of Jane.

When the soundness assumption has been shown[62] to be wrong, the finite position set will have to be changed into another set for which the soundness assumption has not been refuted (yet). If it has been shown that Jane is five years old and that minority (in the sense of criminal law) takes one's punishability away, the soundness assumption has been shown to be wrong. The position set must be expanded to make it include that Jane is five years old and that being a minor takes one's punishability away. Given this expansion of the position set, the belief that Jane is punishable will have to be retracted from it.

E. Spontaneous Positions

A familiar objection against coherence theories is that a coherent position set may be isolated from reality. A set of positions may be coherent while all positions contained in it are false. The elements in the set justify each other, but there is no guarantee that the content of the set as a whole somehow reflects reality. This would be problematic, because a position set will normally include beliefs about the 'world outside'. The limited set consisting of the beliefs that Jane is a thief and that Jane is punishable and the rule that thieves are punishable may be coherent, but does it really justify the belief that Jane is punishable? Maybe Jane does not even exist! From the coherence of the set nothing seems to follow about the truth of the beliefs contained in it. Can such an isolated set justify these beliefs?

This is a familiar objection, but on closer inspection it is not very strong. To see why, one needs to consider how a coherency test of justification will operate in practice.[63] One does not come up with a coherent set of positions from scratch. Normally one starts from an already existing set.[64] The contents of a *real position set*, that is a set that is entertained by some real person, will have two kinds of determinants, rational ones and a-rational ones. The rational determinants

---

[62] Notice the procedural nature of this demand. It does not require truth, nor justifiability; it requires an actual change in a position set. The relevancy of this dynamic aspect is discussed in my 'Dialectics in Artificial Intelligence and Law' in Hage (n 25) 227–64.

[63] There is also a very brief refutation of the objection, namely that it confuses truth and justification. That a position is untrue is no objection against a position being justified, or – better – against a person being justified in accepting this position. This would be different if a person knows, or should have known, that a belief is untrue. However, then the problem is not the falsity of the belief, but the acceptance of the belief that an accepted position is false, which amounts to inconsistency of the position set.

[64] Raz writes in this connection about the 'base'. See J Raz, 'The Relevance of Coherence' in J Raz, *Ethics in the Public Domain* (Oxford, Clarendon Press, 1994) 277–325. This base may also include methodological guidelines. In the case of doctrinal law it may, for instance, contain the guideline that legal doctrine is to be developed by means of understanding authoritative texts (the hermeneutical method). If I am right, this guideline should rationally be replaced by a method that better reflects the nature of law and of science.

make that an existing set is corrected – new positions are added and existing ones are removed – because rationality requires this given the rest of the set. (Remember that the demands of rationality are also specified by the position set.) The a-rational determinants cause 'spontaneous' changes to the contents of the set. New positions are added as a consequence – notice the causal terminology – of perception, memory, intuition, or any other factors which cause what a person accepts. A person may, for instance, accept something because he or she mistakenly believes that this is rational in the light of what else he or she believes. Existing positions are removed, because they are forgotten or abandoned for irrational or a-rational reasons.

These irrational or a-rational influences on a position set are relevant because position sets are biased toward the past. Whether a new position should, from the rational perspective, be added or an existing one removed, depends on the present contents of the set. To see why, one should notice that a particular position can have one of three statuses in the light of (the rest of) a position set:

1. It should be adopted (if not already present) because this is rational; the position is *acceptable*.
2. It should be removed (if it is already present) because this is rational; the position is *rejectable*.
3. It is neutral in the sense that it should neither be adopted nor removed; the position is *suspendable*.

As long as a position set is not coherent – that means in practice: always[65] – the judgment whether a particular position should be added or removed should rationally not be made on the basis of a full position set, but only on the basis of the acceptable positions and of the suspendable positions included in the set.[66] Positions that should not be in the set themselves should not play a role in determining what else should be in the set. Moreover, suspendable positions remain in the set, even if there is no reason to adopt them, and codetermine what is acceptable. So, suspendable elements can be justified because they belong to a coherent position set, without being justified by particular reasons in the set. This may, for instance, hold for beliefs caused by perception, or for evaluative judgments caused by 'intuition'. As long as there is no reason to reject them, they will be maintained. Moreover, suspendable elements can also play a role in determining whether other elements can remain in the set and are therefore justified. Finally, since rational modifications can only take place on the basis of an existing position set, the original elements of any realistic position set must have been spontaneous positions, that are suspendable elements. This is one part of the argument why real position sets do not 'hang in the air'. Real sets stem from sets of spontaneous positions, and this is where we should look for the desired 'contact with reality'.

---

[65] A real position set will always remain incoherent, if only because adoption of everything that should rationally be adopted leads to an infinitely large set, while the human mind is finite.

[66] Acceptable elements, which were not actually accepted yet, should also be taken into account.

A particular position is justified *relative to a position set* if it is an element of this set, and if this set is coherent. Moreover, given the important role of spontaneous positions, the position set should be a real one, held by a particular person.[67] So, the relativity of justification does not only concern position sets, but also persons. A position is justified relative to the set of positions held by a particular person. Therefore, it is better to speak of a person being justified in accepting something,[68] than of a position being justified.

F. The Outside World

How can we be sure that spontaneous positions reflect 'the world outside'? We cannot, simply because we cannot compare positions with the world. We can only compare them with what we accept about the world, including spontaneous positions. Somehow, the 'outside world' seems out of reach, and the objection that a coherent theory may have no contact with reality seems on the one hand to be correct, but on the other hand also to be unavoidable.

Yet, this is not the whole story. Of some of our positions we *believe* that they reflect an external world. We believe that there is such an external world to begin with, and we also believe that this world influences our spontaneous positions. It should be noted, however, that these beliefs, like all of our other beliefs, belong to our position set, and can be corrected on the basis of the rest of the set. The existence of an external world is a bit like the existence of so-called 'theoretical entities'. Entities like electrons cannot be perceived, but their existence is derived from other things that we can perceive. With the external world it is a little different: we believe that we can perceive it, but its existence is still theoretical in the sense that we postulate its existence on the basis of perceptual impressions. The world is, so to speak, necessary to explain our perceptions of it.[69]

In this regard, agreement plays an important role. If different persons have the same beliefs, this may be taken as a reason to assume that there exists an independent object of belief that causes the unanimity of the beliefs about this

---

[67] The idea that position sets may be held by collectivities, for instance in the form of the 'body of scientific knowledge', or by a group of experts, is important, but beyond the scope of this chapter. See KR Popper, 'Epistemology Without a Knowing Subject' and 'On the Theory of the Objective Mind' in KR Popper, *Objective Knowledge* (Oxford, Clarendon Press, 1972) 106–90.

[68] This is called 'doxastic justification', which is opposed to the so-called 'propositional justification' (a particular position is justified). See R Neta and D Prichard (eds), *Arguing about Knowledge* (London, Routledge, 2009) 151.

[69] This should not be read as stating that we believe the external world to exist only because that would explain our beliefs about it. Our cognitive apparatus is such that we spontaneously believe that (most of) our perceptive impressions are impressions of the external world. For example, we do not only spontaneously believe that the sun is shining, but also that the sun is shining in the 'outside' world. In fact, the latter assumption is so natural that we automatically take the first belief to be identical to the second. However, we are able to question this spontaneous belief, and if it is questioned a reason for adopting it (again) is that the external world explains both the existence of our spontaneous beliefs about it, and the convergence of (some of) our beliefs about it with the corresponding beliefs of other persons.

object. For instance, the 'objective' existence of a table explains why we all see the table and believe that it is there.

Agreement in beliefs needs not be explained by an objective external world, however. A second type of explanation would be that agreement on a position is the outflow of the functioning of our cognitive apparatus. Think in this connection of mathematics. Mathematicians tend to agree on many results of their science, but only some of them attribute this agreement to an objectively existing world of mathematical objects, such as for instance natural numbers. Another example would be that our moral intuitions are, at least to some extent, innate.[70]

A third possible explanation of agreement is that a position is the result of a procedure that is designed in such a way that it leads to the same outcome for (almost) everybody. A playful example would be the procedure of throwing an unbiased dice 10,000 times, which leads to the outcome of getting a six more than 1000 times for almost everybody. A legally more relevant example would be that legal arguments based on the same rules and cases and using the same canons of interpretation and argumentation lead, in easy cases, to the same outcomes for almost everybody.[71]

From the fact that agreement on a particular position may be a sign that this position reflects an outside world that is the same for everybody, it does not follow that where agreement is lacking a position does not reflect the outside world. For instance, we believe that the position 'There is water on the moon' reflects the outside world, but there was (at the moment of writing the first draft of this chapter) no agreement yet amongst scientists whether this position is true. However, because we assume that the position reflects the outside world, we tend to believe that an increase in relevant knowledge should, in the end, lead to agreement.[72] Where we do not even expect that an increase in knowledge would lead to agreement, we apparently do not assume that the position reflects the outside world.

G. Conclusion Concerning Justification

The arguments of the above subsections lead to the conclusion that there is no principal difference between the justification of positions that are deemed 'factual' and positions that are deemed 'normative'. In both cases a person is absolutely justified in accepting such a position if this position fits in a coherent

---

[70] This position is argued by Hauser. See MD Hauser, *Moral minds: How Nature Designed our Universal Sense of Right and Wrong* (London, Abacus, 2008).

[71] This may even be so by definition, if easy cases are defined as those cases which lead to agreement amongst those who argue by the rules of law. This position is argued in JC Hage, R Leenes and A Lodder, 'Hard Cases: a Procedural Approach' (1994) 2 *Artificial Intelligence and Law* 113.

[72] This comes near to Pierce's circumscription of truth: 'Truth, what can this possibly mean except it be that there is one destined upshot to enquiry with reference to the question in hand.' Quotation taken from RL Kirkham, *Theories of Truth* (Cambridge, MIT Press, 1992) 81. See also Haack, *Philosophy of Logic* (1978) 97–98.

position set held by this person. As no position set held by an actual person will be coherent in the sense defined above, a less absolute notion of justification is needed. In the spirit of the arguments above, this would be that a person is justified in accepting a position if this position is included in the set of positions actually held by this person, under the assumption that this person is not aware of required changes in his or her position that would make him or her reject this position.[73] The same point can also be made differently. A person is justified in accepting a position if this position is included in his or her actual position set and if this position set also includes the metabelief that the set is sound with respect to the first mentioned position. See Figure 1.

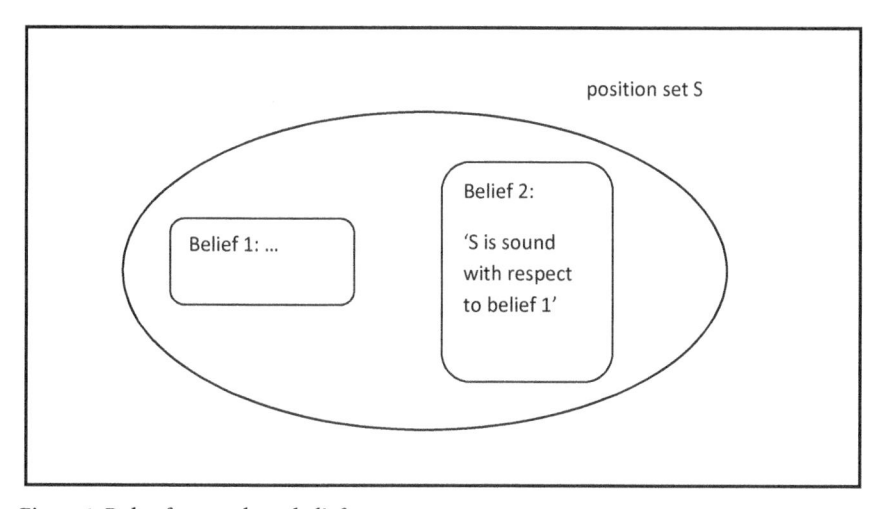

Diagram: A rectangle labeled "position set S" contains an ellipse. Inside the ellipse are two boxes: "Belief 1: ..." and "Belief 2: 'S is sound with respect to belief 1'".

Figure 1: Role of a soundness belief

For the present purposes the most important point is that all three accounts of being justified in accepting a position do not distinguish between 'factual' and 'normative' positions.

The first conclusion that follows from this insight is that the alleged 'gap' between 'is' and 'ought' does not a priori exclude the possibility of a normative science. The reasons mentioned under section II. A., why a normative science would be impossible, turn out not to be very strong.

The second conclusion that follows is that the very abstract method for science 'Develop a coherent set of positions which includes a position concerning the question you want to answer' is the same for all sciences, including normative ones.

---

[73] Additional refinements are possible and in the end necessary, in particular refinements concerning the necessity of making additional inquiries. For instance, a person may believe something because he or she did not make observations that are obviously relevant. Then this person would not be justified in accepting a position if he or she has serious reasons to assume that such observations are both realistically possible and may change his or her beliefs.

At first sight the prospects for a normative science, including a normative legal science, are therefore good. Still, there is a possible problem that has not been dealt with yet, namely that science is only possible when there is a possibility of agreement. Whether a normative science can, in the end, lead to agreement is not an issue that can be dealt with in an a priori fashion. Clearly, agreement and the lack thereof both occur in matters that are traditionally taken to be 'factual' and in matters that tend to be taken as 'normative'. The issue of agreement will therefore be addressed in the next section, in which I will make more detailed proposals for normative legal science and its method.

III. THE METHOD OF A TRULY NORMATIVE LEGAL SCIENCE

The question after the method for legal science can be answered in a very abstract way. There is only one possible reason why a position concerning the contents of the law should be accepted and that is that this position fits in a coherent theory of everything held by the person who is to accept this position. In a sense, this is the only thing which can be said about the method of legal science, or actually any science or method to arrive at justified positions, including knowledge. All other views depend on formulating part of such a coherent position set and are in a sense 'subjective', because any actual position set is a set held by a particular person. This subjectivity indicates the main problem that is to be overcome in the development of a normative legal science or, in fact, any science. The very abstract 'method' for legal science may be illuminating, but because of its high level of abstraction, it is not very attractive. Therefore I will make a proposal for a more concrete method of a truly normative legal science in the following subsections, but not without warning in advance that such a proposal should be taken as part of an all-encompassing theory of everything that aims to be coherent, but will in practice always fall short of this ideal. The method for a truly normative legal science is therefore a hypothesis, comparable to other scientific hypotheses: it is falsifiable by showing that the subset of positions of which it is part is not sound with respect to the method of legal science.

A. Assumptions

At the beginning of this chapter I claimed that the method for a branch of science depends on what one takes science to be, on the object of the science in question, on the questions that one asks about this object, on the view one takes on how answers with regard to such questions can be found, etc. The second section of this chapter put this claim in perspective: scientific method is part of a position set in which it is directly or indirectly linked to many other positions, and the mentioned ones belong to them. In section one I have formulated provisional views concerning these issues, and I will elaborate on some of these views here.

One assumption is that science is a collaborative enterprise aimed at gathering and systematising knowledge. It is therefore *not* aimed at bringing about particular results other than knowledge, although the results of science may be very useful for practical matters. From this assumption follows that science is only possible if there is a possibility of agreement on the object of the science. It also follows that scientists should to a large extent agree on what count as reasons in answering questions about the knowledge object, or – if such agreement is still lacking – about the standards by means of which views about good reasons can be evaluated. So the possibility of a science requires possible agreement in at least two ways: concerning the ultimate results of the science and concerning the methods of the science or the standards for evaluating methodological proposals.

The second assumption, about which I will be brief after the discussion of section I. D., is that the law itself is normative. It is the answer to a normative question and, in particularly, the question 'Which norms should be enforced collectively?' The desirability of enforcement distinguishes the law from morality of aspiration and the collective nature of enforcement distinguishes the law from (some other parts of) morality.[74] That the state was not mentioned as the actor who takes care of the enforcement is because I do not want to limit the existence of law to situations where there is a state.

B. The Standard to Determine What the Law Is

To determine which norms should be enforced collectively we need standards and facts. I take it that the relevancy of the facts is determined by the standards.[75] Any choice for a standard or a set of standards will be controversial. Therefore, I will refrain from formulating such a choice here. It should be emphasised, however, that the adoption of integrated coherentism does not automatically lead to the Dworkinian form of coherentism that goes under the name of law as integrity.[76] Integrated coherentism is well compatible with the acceptance of a plurality of independent values,[77] which need to be balanced in concrete cases, and with multiple standards that govern this balancing. The 'only' demand is that the values and the ways in which they are balanced are coherent in the sense that these positions fit in a coherent theory of 'everything'.[78]

For the purpose of this chapter I will assume that the standard that would be adopted for the determination of which rules should be enforced collectively aims at the promotion of long- term happiness of sentient beings. Let us call it the H-standard.

---

[74] See Fuller, *The Morality of Law* (1969) chapter 1.
[75] Notice that this is an assumption about the 'logic of justification'. This 'logic' is as much part of the position set as the standards and the beliefs about facts, and is therefore amenable to revision too.
[76] See R Dworkin, *Law's Empire* (London, Fontana, 1986) chapters 6 and 7.
[77] With 'independent' I mean in this respect that the values are not ordered in the sense that some of them are merely a means to realise some others.
[78] A more extensive argument to this effect can be found in Hage (n 25) 64–67.

C. Implications for Legal Method

If the H-standard is appropriate to evaluate actions, including the adoption of a position on which norms should be enforced collectively, it is easy to determine what count as relevant facts to determine the contents of the law. Precisely those facts are relevant which concern the consequences for happiness of the collective enforcement of norms. Legal method consists therefore essentially of the methods to determine the consequences of collective behaviour for the long-term happiness of sentient beings. How these consequences can best be determined is an interesting question itself, but the obvious candidates seem to be the methods employed in psychology, (evolutionary) biology, sociology, and possibly economics. Traditional legal methods that work with interpretation of authoritative texts and special forms of legal reasoning are at first sight completely irrelevant.

However, there are some complications. Because the law has, as one of its main tasks, to coordinate human behaviour,[79] it is important, as Fuller has pointed out, that legal rules can easily be known, and that people will usually agree about the contents of the law. In practice this means that most law should be positive law.[80] If that is the case, at least those traditional legal methods that aim at the identification of legal rules that can easily be identified can be part of the method for a truly normative legal science. This probably includes the reading and literal interpretation of traditional legal sources such as legislation, treaties and case law. It certainly does not include the Herculean labour proposed by Dworkin[81] to make a consistent story out of apparently inconsistent legal materials. Positive law, that consists of the rules contained in the traditional legal sources, makes 'real' law, law in the sense of rules that should be enforced by collective means, if and to the extent that it contributes to legal certainty. If the positive law requires an interpretation that is so hard to find that it needs a judge of Herculean powers, it does not contribute to legal certainty. Therefore, such positive law does not make 'real' law.

For the same reason legal method does not include ingenious arguments that produce results which hardly anybody would have expected. It does include, however, the setting aside under circumstances of rules of positive law if these rules literally produce unhappy results in concrete cases.[82]

Apart from legal certainty, there is another reason why law consists by and large of positive law, and that is that positive law often has a democratic legit-

---

[79] I assume that such coordination produces happiness, but this assumption can and should be tested for a full-blown coherent acceptance set.

[80] This is a very short abbreviation of Fuller's argument in chapter 2 of *The Morality of Law* (1969). That argument shows, moreover, that there are more demands than merely that the law is 'positive'.

[81] Dworkin, *Taking Rights Seriously* (1978) chapter 4 and *Law's Empire* (1986) chapters 6ff.

[82] The circumstances in question are by and large that the gain in happiness produced by setting aside the rules outweighs the unhappiness produced by the increased legal uncertainty that follows both from the actual setting aside of the rules and from the expectation that this will happen again in the future.

imation. Not that democracy in itself is a reason to assign positive law the status of law in the sense of collectively enforceable norms. Democracy is important if and to the extent that the adoption of positive law that was brought about in a democratic manner leads to more happiness than law which was not brought about democratically and which was only accepted because of its contents. To the extent that democracy matters, the intention of the democratic legislator may also be relevant for the interpretation of legislation.

D. The Possibility of Agreement

Any science in the sense of the collaborative pursuit of knowledge presupposes that this pursuit can lead to a result in the form of (some degree of) agreement on the investigated issues. Can the method of normative legal science lead to such agreement? In the end, the facts must decide on this question. Will legal scientists in the long run converge on which rules should be enforced collectively? There is reason to be optimistic, however. The very fact that the law must be easily recognisable and that this determines the contents of the law to a large extent, makes it plausible that legal scientists, just like 'normal' users of the law, will agree on the contents of the law. On the assumption that the ultimate standard for what counts as law is the H-standard, it would be very hard to determine whether a particular set rules is in this respect the best if it were not plausible that some set of easily recognisable rules are probably also the rules the collective enforcement of which satisfies this H-standard. This makes the rules that 'happen to exist', the positive law on a plausible interpretation of it, a good candidate to be the law that satisfies the H-standard. This very brief argument about why the positive law is a good candidate for the rules that should be enforced collectively is clearly in need of elaboration. That, however, is a topic for additional research.

IV. CONCLUSION

In this chapter I have argued that the proper method for legal science depends on what one takes to be science, the nature of the law and the kind of questions addressed in legal science. I started from three assumptions, namely that:

(a) Science is the collaborative pursuit of knowledge.
(b) The law consists of those norms which ought to be enforced by collective means.
(c) The H(appiness)-standard provides the proper standard to determine what ought to be done.

On the basis of these assumptions it was argued that:

1. Legal science, in the sense of a description of the law, is not impossible for the reason that it is a normative science.

2. In abstract the method of all sciences, including legal science, is to create a coherent set of positions that encompasses 'everything' (and therefore also beliefs about the law).
3. The proper method for a normative legal science consists primarily of the methods of sociology, psychology and economics, because the ultimate question to be answered is the collective enforcement of which norms satisfies the H-standard; the more traditional hermeneutic methods only play a role to the extent that they establish positive law that contributes to happiness by providing legal certainty.

It may be useful to compare these assumptions and the conclusions that were derived from them to some alternatives mentioned above.

Assumption (a) is not shared by Smits and Smith. This allows them to believe in the possibility of a legal science, while denying that there is a proper knowledge object. They differ on the kind of question to be addressed by legal science, however. According to Smith, the proper question concerns the contents of the law, while according to Smits the question to be answered is what the law should be.

Assumption (b) is widely rejected. Most authors, including Mackor and Smits, (implicitly) assume that the law exists as a matter of social fact. This usually, namely if legal science should answer the question after the contents of the law, leads to the conclusion that the proper method for legal science is hermeneutic. This view has difficulties in explaining the normative and evaluative nature of much legal reasoning, however. These difficulties disappear if one assumes with Smits that legal science answers the question of what the law should be. On this latter view, the role of hermeneutical methods becomes at first sight hard to understand. Why does the understanding of texts help in the determination of the contents of law?

Assumption (c) is only relevant if one takes legal science to be normative. Smts, who takes this view, emphasises that there will be no agreement on the proper standard.

3

Explanatory Non-Normative Legal Doctrine. Taking the Distinction between Theoretical and Practical Reason Seriously

ANNE RUTH MACKOR*

I. INTRODUCTION

IN THIS CHAPTER I will deal with two closely related questions. The first is the question whether legal doctrine is an explanatory discipline, the second whether it is a normative discipline. The dominant view holds that legal doctrine is not explanatory and that, or rather because, it is normative.

With respect to the first topic some legal theorists argue that although it is an aim of legal doctrine to systematise law, the claim that this systematisation is a kind of explanation amounts to a distortion or at least an unhelpful stretching of the notion of explanation. The nature of legal doctrinal systematisation is fundamentally different from the explanations of empirical sciences and therefore it is misleading to use the same term for both. More specifically, or so their argument goes, the systematising activity is not explanatory but rather justificatory in nature. To call legal doctrine explanatory is 'to conceal justification behind a façade of explanation'.[1] This brings us to the second claim.

---

* I thank Mark Van Hoecke for his invitation to the Workshop on Methodology of Legal Research (University of Tilburg, The Netherlands, 30 October 2009). I thank Jaap Hage, Bert van Roermund and Pauline Westerman for their constructive comments.

[1] Aleksander Peczenik, *Scientia Juris. Legal Doctrine as Knowledge of Law and as a Source of Law*, in E Pattaro (ed), *A Treatise of Legal Philosophy and General Jurisprudence* vol 4 (Dordrecht, Springer 2005) 4, as quoted by Mark Van Hoecke, 'Legal Doctrine: Which Method(s) for What Kind of Discipline?' in chapter one of this volume. Peczenik rejects the view that legal doctrine offers explanations. Van Hoecke quotes him approvingly, but later seems to leave some room for explanation.

The second claim many legal scholars and legal theorists make is that legal doctrine is normative in nature.[2] Herewith they do not mean to make the trivial and undisputed claim that the object of legal doctrine is normative. They claim that legal doctrinal statements themselves are normative. In a nutshell, their argument is that legal doctrine is interpretative, that legal interpretation is inherently normative and that therefore legal doctrine is normative. Smith, for example, claims that also the most 'neutral' or 'objective' study of positive law presupposes a normative point of view.[3] Soeteman argues that 'legal answers, in easy cases as well as in hard cases, always presuppose a normative interpretation of the legal sources.'[4]

In this contribution I shall argue against both claims. I shall contend that legal doctrinal systematisation is an explanatory discipline and I shall contend that it is not a normative discipline, at least not in any 'special' or more profound sense than other, more in particular social and so-called practical, sciences might be called normative.

II. THEORETICAL AND PRACTICAL REASON

In this chapter I will argue that much of the confusion about both questions is due to the fact that legal scholars do not take the distinction between theoretical and practical reason seriously (enough). In particular, or so I will argue, some lessons about the distinction between theoretical and practical reason, more specifically about the claim that legal doctrine belongs to the realm of theoretical reason, can be (re-)learned from Hans Kelsen's work.

Observant readers might object that since Kelsen has explicitly argued that practical reason is a self-contradictory concept, I cannot at the same time assentingly refer to Kelsen and also stress the importance of the distinction between theoretical and practical reason.[5] This objection can be rebutted, however. Kelsen only states that reason *on its own* can never be practical, ie that reason alone can never *prescribe* what to do. In Kelsen's own words:

> Reason as a moral legislator is the central concept of Kant's ethics. But for Kant this reason is *practical reason*: . . . it is both thought and will. . . . practical reason would

---

[2] Peczenik, *Scientia Juris. Legal Doctrine as Knowledge of Law and as a Source of Law* (2005), Van Hoecke, chapter one, sections II.D. and II.G. of this volume. See also Carel Smith, 'Het normatieve karakter van de rechtswetenschap: recht als oordeel' ('The Normative Character of Legal Doctrine: Law as Judgement') (2009) 3 *Rechtsfilosofie & Rechtstheorie* 202 and Arend Soeteman, 'Wetenschappelijke rechtsgeleerdheid. Commentaar op het preadvies van Carel Smith' (Scientific Legal Doctrine. Comments on the Preliminary Report of Carel Smith) (2009) 3 *Rechtsfilosofie & Rechtstheorie* 226, especially section 5.

[3] Smith, 'Het normatieve karakter van de rechtswetenschap: recht als oordeel' (2009) 214.

[4] Soeteman, 'Wetenschappelijke rechtsgeleerdheid' (2009) 266.

[5] For example, in *General Theory of Norms* (Oxford, Clarendon Press, 1991) 358, fn 119 Kelsen argues: 'The self-contradictory concept of practical reason rests on a failure to distinguish . . . between a norm and a statement about a norm.' (Emphasis added).

be at once cognition and norm-positing will. But that is impossible.... by our reason, we cannot find the norms prescribing what we are to do.[6]

If we take the capacity to create norms to be the meaning of the term 'practical reason', I, as most other modern philosophers, agree with Kelsen's rejection of it. However, the notion of practical reason is normally taken in a more relaxed sense, viz. as referring only to the *use* of reason in answering the most fundamental practical question 'What ought I to do?'.[7] To *use* reason for purely theoretical purposes is to use it only for the sake of understanding some part or aspect of reality. As the Dutch Nobel Prize winner in physics, Gerard 't Hooft, has stated, 'My research does not result in a new product ... However, it answers a fundamental desire. Human beings want to know how nature around them is structured.'[8]

Most legal scholars do not use reason *only* for the sake of understanding legal reality. They use reason in order to advise legal practitioners what they should do if they want their decisions to be in accordance with the legal system. However, the fact that the *ultimate goal* of legal doctrine is practical rather than theoretical does not imply that what legal scholars do to *achieve* this aim is itself practical, ie prescriptive, rather than theoretical, ie descriptive and explanatory. The ultimate goal of medicine, aerospace engineering and the science of public administration is to cure people, to build planes and to improve public administration respectively. Thus, they are practical sciences too. However, these sciences try to achieve this aim mainly by offering descriptions and explanations rather than justifications or prescriptions. The same holds, or so I will argue in this chapter, for legal doctrine.

Kelsen devotes a chapter of his *General Theory of Norms* to the analysis of the question 'What ought I to do?'.[9] In it he not only agrees that there is nothing self-contradictory about posing this question, he also fully agrees that reason can play a role in answering it. On Kelsen's account reason can offer information both about the question whether there *is* a norm which prescribes what to do, ie

---

[6] Kelsen, *General Theory of Norms* (1991) 6, 183. The term 'find' in this quote is ambiguous. I would argue that on Kelsen's own account reason is able to find, ie *discover* norms and describe them. The only thing that reason cannot do is to *create* or *posit* norms. On Kelsen's account a norm, which tells us what to do, can only be the content of an act of will. It can never be the content of an act of thought. In this contribution I will not discuss Kelsen's claim that norms are the content of acts of will.

[7] See, eg Ota Weinberger, 'Der Streit um die praktische Vernunft. Gegen Scheinargumente in der praktischen Philosophie' in Robert Alexy und Ralf Dreier (eds), *Rechtssystem und Praktische Vernunft,* vol 1 (Stuttgart, Franz Steiner Verlag, 1993) 46: ‚Die praktische Vernunft is keine Quelle praktischen Wissens, sondern bloss ein Instrument der handlungsrelativen Gedankenverarbeitung.' (Italicisation in the original.) Regarding the distinction between the theoretical and the practical use of reason, see Hilary Bok, *Freedom and Responsibility* (Princeton, Princeton University Press, 1998) chapter two. See also Anne Ruth Mackor, 'What can Neurosciences Say about Responsibility? Taking the Distinction between Theoretical and Practical Reason Seriously' in Nicole A. Vincent (ed), *Legal Responsibility and Neuroscience*, Series on Neurosciences and Law (Oxford, Oxford University Press, 2010, under review).

[8] Volkskrant (13 October 1999) quoted in Herman Koningsveld, *Het verschijnsel wetenschap* (Amsterdam, Boom, 2006) 22.

[9] Kelsen (n 5) chapter 47, 182–83.

whether there is a *valid* norm, and about the question what is the *content* of this norm? To Kelsen's claim I would add that reason can also be helpful in answering the preliminary question 'What norm ought I *posit?*' – either as an autonomous moral being to myself or as a legislator to others. In particular, reason can offer information about how to prevent inconsistencies and incoherencies between the existing – be it personal or positive legal – system and the new norm to be created.[10] Next to that reason can also offer information about the content a norm should have if one wants to realise a particular goal or set of goals.[11]

Thus, my stressing the importance of the distinction between theoretical and practical reason, if we understand it as the distinction between *knowing* what is the case and *prescribing* what to do, between discovering norms and creating norms, is not in conflict but rather in accord with Kelsen's view. Although the information about the validity and the content of norms can be *used for* the practical purpose of deciding what to do, the information itself is *offered by* theoretical reason. The central thesis of this contribution is that even though legal doctrine is a practical discipline in that it intends to contribute to answering one version of the question of practical reason, it does so mainly by offering descriptions and explanations.[12]

III. EXPLANATORY LEGAL DOCTRINE

A. Why bother about the Question whether Legal Doctrinal Systematisation is Explanation?

Section III is devoted to the question in what sense we can and should say, pace Peczenik, Van Hoecke and others, that legal doctrine is an explanatory science. Before answering this question, however, we should first briefly go into the question as to why we would want to quarrel about the question whether legal doctrine is explanatory in the first place.

As I have argued elsewhere,[13] our focus should not be restricted to the internal debate among legal scholars and legal theorists, but rather on the question on

---

[10] Those who defend the view that normative claims cannot be (in)consistent or (in)coherent with each other can instead read the weaker terms (in)compatibility and (non-)entailment. See, on the distinction, Ilkka Niiniluoto, 'Truth and Legal Norms' in Aulis Aarnio and D Neil MacCormick (eds), *Legal Reasoning* (New York, New York University Press, 1992) vol 1. 177.

[11] ibid 183, who calls these kinds of norms of the form, 'If you want A, you ought to do X', technical norms.

[12] It mainly aims to answer the question what we should do from a *legal* point of view. Its aim is not to answer the Kantian practical question, ie what we should do *all things considered*. Compare I Kant, *Kritik der praktischen Vernunft* (Hamburg, Felix Meiner Verlag, 1974) 138 (AA 120): '. . . das [Interesse] des praktischen Gebrauchs [der Vernunft besteht] in der Bestimmung des Willens *in Ansehung des letzten und vollständigen Zwecks.*' (Emphasis added.) More on this distinction can be found in section IV. D.

[13] In Anne Ruth Mackor, 'Tegen de methode' (Against Method) (2007) 24 *Nederlands Juristenblad* 1462–65, I have stressed the importance of the external over and above the internal debate about the nature of legal doctrine.

how we can best explicate the nature of legal doctrine to scientists of other disciplines and, more importantly, to organisations like NWO that fund scientific research.[14] If we have the latter focus, the question whether and in what way legal doctrine is an explanatory discipline seems to be important. By showing that and in what sense legal doctrine is explanatory, we can not only make it clear that legal doctrine pursues the same aim as other disciplines, viz *achieving, enlarging and improving knowledge* of some part or aspect of reality, but also that it does so in ways which are relevantly similar to – and therefore *as respectable and as subsidisable as* – the ways in which other sciences do so. As was argued in section II., the mere fact that legal doctrine aims at applying this knowledge to answer the question what to do or decide, *in itself* does not affect the ways in which legal doctrinal knowledge is achieved.

There is no room to give a profound explication of the features which are claimed to make sciences respectable, but a few remarks might be helpful. One way to explicate the nature of scientific knowledge is to contrast it with everyday knowledge. Scientific knowledge is claimed to differ from everyday knowledge, among others, in being more precise, more profound and more systematic than everyday knowledge.[15] Some scientific systematisations are explanations. Thus, when we are unwilling to call (part of) legal doctrinal systematisation explanation we seem to downplay a fundamental and important characteristic that legal doctrine shares with other sciences.

B. Erklären and Verstehen

Some readers might argue that my problem is merely verbal and could easily be resolved if I would not insist on using the term explanation (*Erklären*). When I instead use the term understanding (*Verstehen*) the disagreement would dissolve. Since the nineteenth century, explanation is claimed to be the aim of the natural

---

[14] NWO is the most influential Dutch organisation that subsidises scientific research.

[15] Scientific knowledge is not necessarily a specification of everyday knowledge. On the contrary, it can be radically different from such knowledge. One might think of the revolutionary changes from geo- to heliocentrism and the introduction of different types of non-Euclidian geometry as examples. Since the aim of legal doctrine is, among others, to clarify the content of and to systematise the relations between the norms of a positive legal order, it seems it cannot be as radically different from the everyday knowledge of legal practitioners as, eg, natural scientific and mathematical knowledge. However, as the development of new doctrines shows, legal scholars sometimes invent new ways to systematise our knowledge of the legal order which are not a specification of but quite different from existing legal doctrinal and practical systematisations. An example is the invention, in the period of the sixteenth to eighteenth century, of the concept of 'subjective right' and further classifications thereof. See Boudewijn Bouckaert, *Algemene rechtsleer: functies en bronnen van het recht* (General Theory of Law: Functions and Sources of the Law) (Antwerpen, Maklu, 2005) 222. Both Aulis Aarnio, *Reason and Authority. A Treatise on the Dynamic Paradigm of Legal Dogmatics* (Ashgate, Aldershot, 1997) 259ff and PW Brouwer, 'Systematisering van recht' (Systematization of Law) in PW Brouwer, MM Henket, AM Hol and H Kloosterhuis (eds), *Drie dimensies van het recht. Rechtstheorie, rechtsgeleerdheid, rechtspraktijk* (Den Haag, Boom Juridische Uitgevers, 1999) 225ff offer twentieth century examples of legal doctrinal inventions. Note, however, that it is quite another question whether new systematisations will be accepted and applied by legal practitioners.

sciences, whereas understanding is the aim of the humanities and therefore also of legal doctrine.[16]

One reason, however, why I believe it is unwise to stick to the more generally accepted term '*Verstehen*' is that this notion is often used in ways which (intend to) downplay the systematic or at least the generalising character of scientific knowledge.[17] It is generally argued that the focus of *verstehende* disciplines, such as history, is on understanding concrete and sometimes even 'once-only' states of affairs and events in ways which typically do not allow for generalisation. A *verstehende* approach is thought to focus on the *idiosyncratic* properties of the particular state of affairs at hand.

It is true that a large part of legal doctrine is directed at understanding concrete states of affairs, viz at determining the validity, the content, or both, of specific judicial decisions. It is also true that *hard cases*, ie cases that are characterised by idiosyncratic features that cause disagreement about the nature of their legal consequences, play a central role in legal doctrinal analyses. However, systematisation and generalisation nevertheless are important in legal doctrinal understanding of concrete decisions, even of hard cases. This is so because both the validity and the content of judicial decisions are understood as deriving from general legal norms.[18] In this respect, the legal doctrinal understanding of judicial decisions in terms of general legal norms does not seem radically different from but, on the contrary, very similar to the natural scientific understanding of concrete states of affairs in terms of general laws of nature.

C. The Principles of Causality and Imputation

There have been some attempts to analyse legal doctrine as an explanatory discipline. In particular, there have been attempts to understand the legal doctrinal explanation of judicial decisions in terms of general legal norms as analogous to natural scientific explanation of concrete states of affairs in terms of general laws of nature.[19] The *locus classicus* of the explication of legal doctrine as an

---

[16] See Anne Ruth Mackor, *Meaningful and Rule-guided Behaviour: A Naturalistic Approach* (unpublished PhD thesis, Groningen, 1997) for an analysis of the distinction between natural and social sciences.

[17] Another reason is that many adherents of *verstehen* argue that *verstehen* is inherently normative. I deal with this claim in section IV.

[18] At least, this is claimed to be true of continental law. This chapter is restricted to an analysis of legal doctrinal study of continental law.

[19] Mark Van Hoecke (in chapter one, n 20 of this volume) refers to Marc Van Quickenborne, 'Rechtsstudie als wetenschap' (Legal Study as Science) in M Coene et al (eds), *Actori Incumbit Probatio* (Antwerpen, Kluwer, 1975) who offers such an analysis. Just like Peczenik and Van Hoecke, however, Van Quickenborne (ibid 227) argues that we should rather speak of justification than explanation because, or so Van Quickenborne argues, the explanandum is 'normatively coloured'. More on this 'normative colouring' in section IV.

explanatory discipline is without any doubt Hans Kelsen's work. Therefore, I will start with an exposition of his account.[20]

Kelsen starts from the claim that the aim of science is to make hypothetical judgements which express a functional connection between two different states of affairs, viz between a condition and consequence. According to Kelsen there are two different types of functional connections, namely causation and imputation (*Zurechnung*).[21] Whereas the principle of causation states, 'If A obtains, then B *is* the case', the principle of imputation says 'If A obtains, then B *ought to be* the case'.[22] Thus, for example, the fact that this volume of gas is heated (A) explains the fact that it *expands* (B). Similarly, the fact that x committed a tort towards y (A) explains the fact that x *ought* to pay compensation to y (B).[23]

Accordingly, Kelsen makes a distinction between natural sciences that explain by means of the principle of causality and normative sciences that explain by means of the principle of imputation. Legal doctrine is perhaps the most prominent of the normative sciences, but it is not unique in being guided by the principle of imputation. Ethics and theology are guided by it too.[24]

However, the fact that legal doctrine, ethics and theology are guided by the principle of imputation is not yet an answer to the question as to what extent they are truly scientific. Kelsen argues:

> Die Rechtswissenschaft bleibt innerhalb der Grenzen der Erfahrung, so lange sie nur Normen zum Gegenstand hat, die durch mensliche Akte gesetzt sind und sie sich nicht auf Normen bezieht, die von übermenschlichen, transzendenten Instanzen ausgehen, das heisst, so lange sie jede metaphysische Spekulation ausschliesst.[25]

The same holds for ethics. Ethics is a science if it confines itself to the study of norms of positive morality, ie if it does not postulate or presume the objective existence of non-positive moral norms.[26] Analogously, it seems that Kelsen can only allow for practical theology as a science either if the existence of God as lawgiver could be established empirically or if theology would take religious norms as acts of human will (eg of church officials).

---

[20] See, eg Hans Kelsen, *Reine Rechtslehre* (Wien, Verlag Franz Deuticke, 1960) chapter 3 and Hans Kelsen, 'Wat is de zuivere rechtsleer?' (What is the Pure Theory of Law?) in *Rechtswetenschap en Gerechtigheid* ('s Gravenhage, A Jongbloed & Zoon, 1954).

[21] Kelsen, *Reine Rechtslehre* (1960) 94 mentions two differences between the principle of causality and the principle of imputation. First, whereas a relation of imputation is produced by an act of will whose meaning is a norm, a causal relation is produced independently of human interference. The fact, however, that the relation of cause and effect is independent of human interference does not imply that the coming into existence of concrete causes and effects is independent of human interference. The second difference between causation and imputation is that the chain of cause and effect is infinite in both directions, whereas a relation of imputation is finite.

[22] I will not discuss probabilistic laws in this contribution.

[23] Kelsen calls the general relations of imputation such as 'all x should do y' general norms and concrete relations of imputation such as 'x ought to do y' individual norms.

[24] See, eg Kelsen (n 20) 90, 111.

[25] ibid 82, fn ii.

[26] Note, however, that this positive morality need not be socially shared. Ethics can also study someone's personal morality, *cf* Kelsen (n 5) 183.

According to Kelsen, normative scientists also stay within the boundaries of experience if the existence of a norm and its norm-giver are explicitly taken to be a *fiction* or a *construct*. Kelsen explicates the difference between fictions and constructs as follows: 'A fiction differs from a hypothesis in that it is accompanied by – or ought to be accompanied by – the awareness that reality does not agree with it.'[27] Moreover, fictions 'are not only in contradiction with reality but self-contradictory in themselves ... To be distinguished from them are constructs which only contradict reality as given, or deviate from it, but are not in themselves self-contradictory.'[28] Thus, on Kelsen's account, ethics and theology can even study non-positive legal, moral and religious norms, at least as long as scholars take them to be fictions or constructs.

According to Kelsen's theory, legal doctrine, theology and ethics are normative sciences. Kelsen's term 'normative sciences' is unfortunate, however. Whereas Kelsen only meant to refer to the fact that normative sciences make statements *about* norms, nowadays the term 'normative sciences' is used to express the claim that these sciences *themselves* make normative claims. The latter claim is explicitly rejected by Kelsen. On Kelsen's account normative sciences are called normative sciences because of the normative character of the imputative connection these sciences study. However, for the very reason that they are sciences they can only offer descriptive statements of these connections. Due to the ambiguity of the notion, I shall not follow Kelsen in his use of the term 'normative sciences'.

Kelsen carefully distinguishes between the objects of legal doctrine, legal norms, and the norm-descriptions that legal doctrine offers. In particular, Kelsen stresses that the fact that norms themselves lack truth value does not imply that we cannot make any true or false statements (descriptions and explanations) about them. The legal doctrinal statement that a particular norm is valid has a truth value and the same holds for the legal doctrinal statement that this norm has a particular content. To make the distinction between legal norms – that are valid or invalid – and descriptions of legal norms – that are true or false – more explicit, and probably also to stress the analogy between natural laws on the one hand and legal doctrinal statements about legal norms on the other, Kelsen proposes to use the term 'legal norms' for the objects of legal doctrinal investigation and the term 'legal laws' for the legal doctrinal descriptive statements about these norms.[29]

As we have seen in section II., Kelsen also explicitly argues that it is not the task, or rather not in the power, of legal doctrine to *create* relations of imputation. On the contrary, just as natural sciences can only discover and describe

[27] Kelsen (n 5) 256.
[28] ibid 256, fn 2. The Basic Norm is a fiction, not a construct. It is self-contradictory 'since it represents the empowering of an ultimate moral or legal authority and so emanates from an authority – admittedly, a fictitious authority – even higher than this one.' (ibid 256). In section IV. D. I will discuss the relevance of the legal doctrinal study of non-positive legal norms taken as constructs.
[29] Kelsen (n 5) 23. Kelsen's term 'legal law' (*Rechtsgesetz*) has not been taken up by other legal theorists. Niiniluoto, 'Truth and Legal Norms' (1992) and others call them norm-descriptions. More on norm-descriptions can be found in section IV. D.

causal relations that exist in nature, legal doctrine is to discover and describe the general legal norms which are found in the particular positive legal order that the legal scholar studies.[30] Just as the relation between, for example, the heating of a gas and the expansion of the gas is not created but discovered by natural scientists, legal scholars do not create but discover the relation between, for example, committing a tort and paying compensation.

In a scheme we can summarise the foregoing as follows:

Object-level

	Individual	General
Causality	States of affairs	Causal relations
Imputation	Legal obligations	General legal norms
	Moral obligations	General moral norms
	Religious obligations	General religious norms

Level of science

	Individual	General
Principle of Causality	Facts (that state of affair p obtains)	Natural laws
Principle of Imputation	Facts (that legal obligation q exists)	Legal laws
	Facts (that moral obligation r exists)	Ethical laws
	Facts (that religious obligation s exists)	Theological laws

Many legal theorists do not so much reject, but rather ignore the possibility of the Kelsenian imputative type of explanation. They seem to believe that legal scholars only have two options, viz either to offer causal explanations or to offer normative claims. Soeteman, for example, explicitly states that the question of legal scholars is not 'How can we explain our norms?' but rather 'What should we do?'[31]

Soeteman is right in claiming that the aim of legal doctrine is not to offer *causal* explanations of the validity or the content of legal norms.[32] However,

---

[30] Obviously, the descriptive statements about these relations are not discovered. They are created, and also contested, by natural scientists and legal scholars respectively.

[31] Soeteman (n 2) 227.

[32] If we are looking for a causal explanation *of the fact that* a particular general norm is valid or that it has this particular content, we must refer to all kinds of political and societal factors that have actually influenced the coming into being of this particular norm. However, this kind of explanation does not belong to legal doctrine proper. Legal doctrine is not interested in a causal explanation of the fact that a norm has a certain content. Its focus is only on the question whether and to what extent the content and the validity can be explained by reference to other norms, not on the question

when Soeteman argues that if the task of legal scholars is not to causally explain norms, their task must be to answer the practical question 'What should we do?' He then too hastily concludes that this turns legal doctrine into a non-explanatory and normative discipline. In doing so he overlooks the possibility that the task of legal doctrine is only to answer the *theoretical* question whether and to what extent the validity and the content of a particular legal norm can be explained by reference to other legal norms. In other words, he ignores Kelsen's claim[33] that legal doctrine can *help* to answer the practical question 'What should we do?', not by offering normative claims, but by offering descriptions and explanations.

D. Explanation of Individual and General Legal Norms

We have seen that Kelsen argues that the aim of science is to make hypothetical judgements that express a functional connection between two different states of affairs, viz between a condition and consequence. In this section we will look in more detail at the similarities between causal explanations in the empirical sciences and imputative explanations in legal doctrine.

From the outset it should be noted that the aim of the natural sciences is not only to explain the *individual fact* that a particular state of affairs obtains by means of a general law that describe a general fact, but also and more importantly to explain the *general fact* itself. Kelsen himself has only compared the natural scientific explanation of individual states of affairs to the legal doctrinal explanation of judicial decisions. In this section I shall expand on Kelsen's analysis and argue that not only the explanation of individual states of affairs and judicial decisions is alike, but that the same holds for the explanation of the causal and imputative connections.

In the foregoing sub-section we have seen that the *individual fact* that a particular volume of gas expands (the effect) is explained by reference to both the individual fact that this particular volume of gas is heated (the cause) and the general fact (described by the gas law) that ceteris paribus all gases which are heated expand.

In turn, the *general fact* that the causal relation itself obtains is explained by means of a theory according to which the heating of a gas is nothing but the increase of the mean kinetic energy of molecules in a gas. Thus, the explanation of the general fact that all gases expand when they are heated is that when temperature rises the mean kinetic energy of the molecules in the gases increases, which means that the molecules bump into each other faster and push each other further apart. That is why volumes of gases expand.

whether it can be causally explained by reference to extra-legal factors. The latter is a question for empirical legal sciences.

[33] Kelsen (n 5) chapter 47.

Analogously, legal doctrine can explain both individual and general facts. Kelsen compares judicial decisions, ie individual legal norms, to concrete empirical states of affairs and general legal norms to causal mechanisms. We have seen that both the content and the validity of the individual norm 'x must do B' (eg x must pay compensation to y) are explained by reference to the individual fact that state of affair A (x committed a tort) obtains and the general fact that the general norm with the content 'In case A obtains, all must do B' (eg all who commit a tort to someone else must compensate this person for the damage done) is valid.

Also, just as natural scientists can explain why causal relations obtain, ie why general facts are true, so legal scholars can explain why the general legal norm with that particular content obtains, ie is valid. In order to explain the validity of the general norm, legal doctrine will refer to one or more higher norms which give this particular general norm its validity.[34]

Van Quickenborne, however, objects to the analogy.[35] For one thing he argues that whereas laws of nature have to be discovered by scientists and are a result of experimentation, general legal norms are *pre-given*. In other words, the job that legal scholars do in establishing legal laws which describe legal norms and in applying these laws in explaining judicial decisions is *not as impressive as* the job natural scientists do in establishing natural laws which describe causal relations and which explain the obtaining of individual states of affairs.

Van Quickenborne is right to claim that there is a difference here, but it is too simple to say that legal norms are pre-given. In fact, it is not true at all that legal norms are pre-given. In the case of written law, the linguistic formulation of norms is pre-given, but that does not mean that the norm, being the *content* of the formulation, is pre-given too. On the contrary, it is not always clear that some linguistic formulation is the expression of a valid norm and often its content is not pre-given with the formulation, but needs further scrutinising. Thus, although most norms – unlike causal mechanisms – have an explicit verbal formulation, it does not follow therefore that legal doctrine cannot make discoveries about their validity and their content.

Van Quickenborne downplays the extent to which legal doctrinal statements about general norms too can be the result of respectable scientific activities such as *hypothesising, testing and falsifying*.[36] Moreover, he does not explicate why and to what extent these kinds of scrutinising legal regulations differ from, and are less impressive than, the scrutinising of causal relations.

We can further clarify this point if we compare legal norms to causal mechanisms that are already known to exist, ie that already have a linguistic formulation.

---

[34] In turn we can ask why this higher law holds, ie is valid until we reach, with Kelsen at least, the Basic Norm. In the natural sciences, we can in principle go on asking for deeper explanations. Compare above n 22.

[35] Van Quickenborne (n 19) 227.

[36] Compare eg CH van Rhee, 'Geen rechtsgeleerdheid, maar rechtswetenschap!' (Not Legal Doctrine, but Legal Science!) (2004) 4 *Rechtsgeleerd Magazijn Themis* 196.

For example, when the relation between the heating and the expanding of gases was discovered, further investigations showed that the relation does not hold for very high temperatures. The consequence has not been that natural scientists have completely rejected the gas law. They rather had to reinterpret the causal relation and therewith to reformulate the gas law. The same holds for legal norms. Sometimes the norm turns out to have another content than legal scholars thought it had. Accordingly, legal scholars have to reinterpret the norm and reformulate their description of it.[37]

There is, however, another and much more important difference between explanations of causal relations and those of general norms. Higher general norms, ie rules of recognition, normally do not prescribe the content of lower norms, but only the *procedure* by which lower general norms can be created.[38] Therefore, the explanation of the content of a lower norm in terms of one or more higher norms is quite 'thin'.[39] However, this does not imply that no explanation whatsoever can be given of the content of the lower general norm. In particular, the content of the lower general norm should not conflict with and preferably both entail and be entailed by the content of other legal norms, principles and underlying legal values, at least within the same statute, within the same legal domain and to some extent within the legal order as a whole. Therefore, the content of general legal norms can at least partially be explained in terms of the content of other general norms, principles and values.

E. Explanation or Interpretation?

Again, some readers might want to object to my use of the term 'explanation' for the legal doctrinal systematic analysis of the content and validity of legal norms in terms of coherence and consistency with other legal norms, principles and underlying values. In particular, some readers might want to argue that such an analysis is more aptly called 'interpretation'. In fact, this seems to be one of Van

---

[37] This example also shows that natural sciences, just like legal doctrine, encounter 'hard cases', ie cases in which the cetera turn out not to be para and where the general norm must be reinterpreted in the light of the hard cases. In the example of high temperatures, this happens through refinement. In other cases this may happen through other interpretation methods. For example, the deeper explanation of the heating and expansion of gases seems to offer an argument to apply the gas law analogously to solids, since solids too consist of molecules, the kinetic energy of which increases when temperature rises. In a similar way, legal scholars look for underlying principles that explain to what extent a legal norm can be applied analogously. See Paul Scholten, *Mr C Asser's handleiding tot de beoefening van het Nederlands burgerlijk recht. Algemeen deel* (Mr C Asser's Guide to the Study of Dutch Civil Law) (Zwolle, WEJ Tjeenk Willink, 1974) 60ff on the use of analogy and refinement in legal interpretation. An earlier edition of this book has been translated to French: *Traité de droit civil néerlandais, partie générale* (Zwolle, WEJ Tjeenk Willink, 1954).

[38] See Kelsen (n 20) 92 and Kelsen, *General Theory of Law and State* (Cambridge, Mass, Harvard University Press, 1946) 398–407, app sub II, especially 400, where he explicitly states that higher norms of positive law only determine the procedure and not the content of lower general norms. More on this below in section III. E.

[39] Even so-called framework acts do not prescribe the content of the lower norms in detail.

Hoecke's main objections to Kelsen's view of legal doctrine.[40] He argues that 'Kelsen strongly underestimates the importance of interpretation in law and the influences of non-legal elements through such interpretation.'

Van Hoecke claims 'The main reason for this unrealistic view is Kelsen's theory of "meaning", which he limits to the psychological sender-meaning, to the intention of those having issued a rule or a command.'[41] To substantiate his claim Van Hoecke quotes Kelsen who states that the meaning of an act of will is the intention that some other person is to behave in a certain way.[42] However, Van Hoecke ignores the fact that Kelsen clearly distinguishes between the meaning of the act of will and its content.[43] On Kelsen's account, the *meaning* of a rule or command is the intention of the normgiver so *that* the other understands his or her expression as a command. The *content* of the rule or command, however, refers to *what* the person is to do or to avoid doing.

Kelsen explicitly states that it is a task of legal doctrine not only to investigate the logical structure, but also to interpret the content of legal norms.[44] He argues that

> This unity [of the legal worldview] is not immediately given in the reality of the law; rather it is a problem to be solved by legal doctrine.... The science of law must eliminate these inconsistencies by *means of interpretation*.[45]

In *General Theory of Law and State*, Kelsen argues more extensively that:

> [. . .] the legal materials which have been produced as positive law must be comprehensible as a meaningful whole, they must lend themselves to a rational interpretation. The pure principle of delegation cannot guarantee this. For it bestows validity upon any content, even the most meaningless, provided it has been created in a certain way. [Principles such as] . . . the principle of lex posterior derogat priori, the principle that the lower norm must give way to the higher, the reinterpretation of constitutional clauses concerning the enactment of statutes, the rule concerning two contradictory clauses of the same statute, the declaration that part of the content of a statute may be legally irrelevant, etc. – all of these have no other purpose than to give a meaningful interpretation to the material of positive law. They all do this by applying the principle of contradiction in the normative sphere. For the most part, they are not rules of positive law, . . ., but presuppositions of legal cognition. This means that they are part of the sense of the basic norm, which thus guarantees the unity of norms of positive law as the unity of a system which, if it is not necessarily just, is at least meaningful.[46]

Much more could be said about Kelsen's theory of interpretation, but these quotes should suffice to make clear that Kelsen does not deny that interpretation plays a crucial role in legal doctrine and that in fact his stance is much closer

---

[40] Van Hoecke, chapter one, section II. G. of this volume.
[41] ibid.
[42] ibid n 29; Kelsen (n 5) 32.
[43] Kelsen (n 5) 33.
[44] Kelsen, 'Wat is de zuivere rechtsleer?' (1954) 14–15.
[45] ibid 13–14 (my translation and italicisation, ARM).
[46] Kelsen *General Theory of Law and State* (1946) 402, 406–07.

to 'modern' interpretationalist views than is often assumed. In other words, although Van Hoecke seems to be right in his critique of Kelsen's psychological theory of intention, this critique does not pertain to Kelsen's views of content and interpretation.

My task in the next section will be to investigate the nature of legal doctrinal interpretation. Moreover, in particular, I will investigate whether interpretation is inherently normative as many legal scholars and legal theorists claim.

IV. NORMATIVE LEGAL DOCTRINE?

A. Total versus Local Legal Normativists

At the outset let me state that I do not deny that normative claims play a role in legal doctrine. However, I would argue that several fundamental misunderstandings underlie the view that legal doctrine is normative rather than descriptive and explanatory in nature. First, I will argue that normative claims do not play a special or more profound role in legal doctrine than they do in other sciences, especially in the social sciences. Section IV. B. deals with this claim. My second claim is that normative claims both can and should be distinguished from descriptive statements. Sections IV. C. and IV. D. are devoted to an underpinning of this claim.

Let me first return to the question that I started section III. A. with, viz the question why it is important to call the systematising activities of legal doctrine explanation rather than interpretation and systematisation. In section III., I argued that we should talk about explanation because the fundamental aim of all sciences is to gain a more profound, precise and systematic understanding of the object they study. Furthermore, I have shown that in this respect legal doctrine is fundamentally in accordance with other sciences. Therefore, it is not misleading to call legal doctrinal systematisation explanation. On the contrary, it would be misleading not to call it explanation.

However, as we saw in section I., Peczenik and Van Hoecke state that to present legal doctrine as an explanatory discipline is 'to conceal justification behind a façade of explanation'.[47] They argue for the opposite position, viz that rules are not explained but rather justified by values, principles and (higher) rules which are themselves postulated and thus debatable.[48] Peczenik, however, seems to weaken his claim when he goes on to argue that

> [t]he distinction between *de lege lata* and *de lege ferenda* is not clear-cut. Legal doctrine pursues a knowledge of existing law, yet in many cases it leads to a change of the law ... Thus, legal doctrine appears to be descriptive and normative at the same time.[49]

---

[47] Peczenik (n 1) 4; Van Hoecke, chapter one, section II. D. of this volume.
[48] Van Hoecke, chapter one, section II. D. of this volume.
[49] Peczenik (n 1) 4f.

I do not believe his argument is convincing. The fact that there is not, or at least not always, a clear divide between statements *de lege lata* and statements *de lege ferenda* is not a good argument to ignore or even reject the distinction altogether. To offer a worn-out analogy, the fact that there is no clear dividing line between people who are bald and those who are not is in itself not a good reason to reject that distinction altogether. It is rather a reason to ask what one wants the distinction for and then to discuss how the criteria should be specified in order to make a useful distinction possible. At least, that is what I will try to do in section IV. C. Interestingly, in the end Peczenik does not seem to deny that it is possible in principle to make a distinction between descriptive and normative legal doctrine. He states that 'If the theories are descriptive, the test is in their coherence with the words of the statute and with factual judicial practice. If the theories are normative, the ultimate test lies in the justice and reasonableness.'[50]

Thus, it seems that Peczenik takes a different stance about the normativity of legal doctrine than, for example, Smith and Soeteman who claim that even descriptive legal doctrinal theories presuppose normative interpretation.[51] Thus, it seems that we should distinguish between the claim that *all* legal doctrinal interpretation is normative and the claim that (a or the most important) *part* of legal doctrinal interpretation is normative.

Soeteman makes the threefold claim that legal doctrine is normative (1) in the (unproblematic) sense that the object of legal doctrine is normative, (2) in the sense that both description and evaluation play a role in the finding of legal norms, and (3) in the sense that legal doctrine aims to offer the best interpretation of valid law which should be acknowledged by others.[52] To distinguish claim (2) and claim (3), I will call (2) total legal normativism and (3) local legal normativism.

The argument that *total legal normativists* such as Smith offer for their claim that even 'descriptive' legal doctrine is normative is that the theory-ladenness of natural sciences which study 'brute facts of nature' is fundamentally different from the theory-ladenness of legal doctrine which studies 'institutional facts'.[53] The claim of total legal normativists boils down to the argument that whereas all 'brute facts' are theory-laden, 'institutional and social facts' are on top of that also value-laden.[54] According to total legal normativists, this implies that legal doctrine has a normative character. I deal with total legal normativism in section IV.B. I will argue that the fact that legal doctrine deals with value-laden

---

[50] Peczenik (n 1) 5.
[51] Smith (n 2) and Soeteman (n 2).
[52] Soeteman (n 2) 229.
[53] Smith (n 2), section 2, especially 203–08.
[54] On the nature of and the distinction between 'brute', 'social' and 'institutional' facts see John Searle, The Construction of Social Reality (London, Penguin, 1995). About legal facts as social and institutional facts, see, eg Niiniluoto (n 10), Jaap Hage, 'Recht als sociaal feit en recht als praktische rede' (Law as Social Fact and Law as Practical Reason) (2009) 1 Rechtsfilosofie & Rechtstheorie 38, 27–36 and Jaap Hage, Two Conceptions of Law and their Implications for Legal Truth, available at ssrn.com/abstract=1443278 (last consulted 3 August 2009).

social and institutional facts does not make legal doctrine different from empirical sciences that study social and institutional facts and thus does not make legal doctrine normative in any relevantly distinct sense.

The argument of *local legal normativists* such as Peczenik seems to be that the aim of legal scholars is not only to establish the validity and the content of law as a social or institutional fact. They also, or even primarily, want to offer arguments for the most coherent and just interpretation of law, in particular in cases where a rule is ambiguous or vague and interpretations result in inconsistencies or incoherencies. According to them, these coherent and just interpretations are normative in nature. However, against these legal theorists I will argue that their argument is muddled. To clarify matters, it is not sufficient to distinguish between descriptive and normative claims. We must distinguish between at least three different types of claims that legal doctrine can make, viz norm-descriptions, norm-contentions and norm-recommendations.[55] Section IV. C. is devoted to an underpinning of this claim. In section IV. D., I apply the distinction between norm-descriptions, norm-contentions and norm-recommendations to answer the notorious question whether there is always 'one right answer' in law.

B. Are Norm-descriptions Normative? An Answer to Total Legal Normativists

Does the fact that legal doctrine studies social and more specifically institutional facts imply that legal doctrine is normative? It seems that total legal normativists offer an affirmative answer to this question.

Before tackling this issue, let us begin with the observation that at least since the defeat of logical positivism, all scientists agree that all scientific observations are steered both by the scientific theory and the methods a scientist uses. For example, both the statement that this gas expands and the statement that all gases expand when heated are 'laden' by a theory about what gases are, what expansion is, etc. Just as importantly, both statements are also 'laden' by a theory about how one can reliably measure the rise of temperature and the expansion of gases.

Theory-ladenness results both in normative claims. Theory-ladenness results, for example, in prescriptive claims about how scientists should measure temperature and when they ought to conclude that temperature has risen x degrees. Theory-ladenness also results in evaluative claims, among others about the quality and reliability of the measurement and therewith about the quality of the scientific conclusions.

Moreover, theory-ladenness implies that both the content and the truth conditions of scientific statements are created through consensus among scientists. In other words, all science has a consensual basis. To offer a worn-out example,

---

[55] I take the distinction from Niiniluoto (n 10) 186ff, but I define the distinction between norm-contentions and norm-recommendations in a different manner. See below in section IV. C.

before it was finally decided that whales are mammals, scientists had to discuss what characteristics determine whether an animal is a fish or a mammal. In other words, they had to decide whether the fact that whales live in the water and have fins should determine that they are fish, or whether the fact that they have lungs and are viviparous should determine that they are mammals.

However, these consensual, prescriptive and evaluative aspects of science do not stand in the way of the truth value of the statement 'this concrete animal here and now is a mammal' being a matter of correspondence of the sentence with reality.[56] After scientists have decided upon the criteria, it is 'up to nature' so to speak to say whether a specific statement is true or false. This is important since truth in the sense of correspondence seems to be an important precondition for the objectivity of scientific statements.

Social sciences, however, have to deal with the additional problem that the objects they study are doubly theory-laden. In the first place, they are not only laden by the theories of scientists, but also by the 'theories' of members of the community through which the social facts that scientists study exist in the first place. Second, these social facts are not merely laden by the descriptive 'theories' of the members of the community that social scientists study, but also by their normative, ie evaluative and prescriptive 'theories'. For example, take a sociologist who studies changes in the number of physically violent acts in a particular community over the last 10 years. The sociologist will not only have to take the descriptive, but also the evaluative and prescriptive views of the community into account that determine what counts as (what kind of) violent behaviour. The point is that the views of the community about what counts as what kind of violent behaviour are entangled with their normative views about what behaviour is condemnable and should therefore result in punishment.

Does the fact that descriptive and normative views of the community are intertwined imply that social sciences do not describe and explain? Does it imply that social sciences are inherently normative? The answer to both questions is a firm 'no'. Social scientists can describe and explain changes in the number of violent acts. In doing so, it is not sufficient that they observe behaviour. They will also have to investigate, among others, whether the norms of the community have changed. This is so because an increase of violent behaviour need not be the effect of an increase of aggression, but might also be caused by the fact that nowadays more types of behaviour are considered violent, condemnable and punishable within the community.

Nevertheless, this does not imply that social scientists themselves make evaluative, let alone prescriptive claims when they refer to the social norms of the members of the community they study. They do not themselves state that violent behaviour should be conceptualised in a particular way, let alone that violent behaviour is wrong and should be punished. They only describe the descriptive, evaluative and prescriptive claims of the members of the community.

---

[56] *cf* Niiniluoto (n 10) 174.

Obviously, social scientists have to *interpret* the norms of the community. These interpretations, as any scientific interpretation, can be *contested* by other scientists. However, when social scientists interpret they (are supposed to) refer to the views of members in the community, not to their own views. In doing so, they do *state* their own views about the views in the community. Just like natural scientific statements, the content and the truth conditions of social scientific statements are created through consensus among social scientists. What is special is that this consensus has in part *as its object* the consensus among members in the community about the content of their norms. This fact, however, does not stand in the way of the truth value of social scientific statements being a matter of correspondence of these statements with reality. In this sense, social scientific statements are just as non-normative and objective as natural scientific statements.

Thus, although total legal normativists are right to claim that 'institutional and social facts' are not only theory-laden but also value-laden, this does not imply that either social sciences or legal doctrine are normative in character.

C. Norm-Descriptions, Norm-Contentions and Norm-Recommendations. An Answer to Local Legal Normativists

In section IV. A., I have defined local legal normativism as the view that *part* of legal doctrine offers normative claims. This is so because legal doctrine not only aims to offer descriptions, but also the best interpretation of valid law. In this sub-section I shall argue that confusion about the precise content of this claim is due to the fact that the distinction between descriptive statements and normative claims – just like the distinction between being bald and not bald which I mentioned in section IV. A. – is not precise enough. For our purpose, which is to analyse the nature of legal doctrinal claims about the best interpretation of valid law, we need to distinguish between three types of statements that legal scholars can make, viz norm-descriptions, norm-contentions and norm-recommendations.

I take the terminology from Niiniluoto, but my explication of the terms is different.[57] I agree with Niiniluoto that norm-descriptions are statements about law as a social fact. I disagree, however, with his definition of norm-contentions and norm-recommendations. Niiniluoto claims that norm-contentions are founded on rational grounds, whereas norm-recommendations are not. On my account both norm-contentions and norm-recommendations can have rational grounds. On my view the difference is that norm-contentions are based on *intra-legal* criteria, whereas norm-recommendations are based on *extra-legal* criteria. Norm-contentions stay within the bounds of legal doctrinal theory about positive law, ie they are claims about the sources, values, norms and standards of interpretation that are accepted within the legal community. Norm-recommendations are

---

[57] Niiniluoto (n 10) 186.

partly or wholly based on extra-legal values and norms. Nevertheless, norm-recommendations can be rational too, viz if they derive from a coherent set of norms.

I will now explicate the differences between the three types of statements in more detail.

i. Norm-Descriptions

Norm-descriptions are *descriptive* statements about the validity and the content of positive legal norms. They are supposed to follow from the legal doctrinal theory which states what the sources, the legal norms and the accepted (hierarchy of) standards of interpretation are. In offering norm-descriptions, legal doctrine intends to describe law as a *social fact*. To the extent that descriptions are about law as a social fact, they are like the social scientific statements I discussed in section IV. B. Like social scientific statements, they do not only study the content of legal norms, but also take into account what straightforwardly follows from it.

For this reason we can say, for example, that the legal doctrinal statement that it is a valid norm of the Dutch Termination of Life on Request and Assisted Suicide (Review Procedures) Bill that cases of euthanasia carried out by nurses are to be judged by regional euthanasia review committees is a *false* norm-description since these committees are only authorised to judge euthanasia when carried out by medical doctors.[58] We can say so, even *before* one of the committees has ever received a reporting of a nurse. In the same manner, legal scholars could say, even before there had been a concrete case, that it is a *true* norm-description that these committees are authorised to judge euthanasia carried out on psychiatric patients.[59] Obviously, as soon as committees nevertheless consider themselves authorised to judge a case of euthanasia carried out by a nurse or if they consider themselves unauthorised to consider a case of euthanasia with respect to a mentally competent person who has a psychiatric disorder, law as a social fact changes and so does the truth value of legal doctrinal statements about them. After a first *contra legem* decision we should probably say that law is ambiguous on this point, but when committees stick to the new interpretation without being overruled by the legislator, law as a social fact has changed.

Since norm-descriptions claim to be descriptive statements about law as a social fact, they can be said to be true or false in the 'normal' sense of these words. That is to say, just like natural and social scientific statements, their content and truth conditions are a matter of consensus, but their truth value depends on the question whether the content of the norm-descriptions *corresponds* with the content of the norms of positive law. Again, this claim does not

---

[58] Accordingly, the coroner should not send a report by a nurse to the committee, but to the public prosecutor.
[59] In 2008 there have been, for the first time since the Act came into force in 2002, two reports of euthanasia carried out on a psychiatric patient. See the Annual Report (in Dutch, 2008, 11–15) at www.euthanasiecommissie.nl/Images/jaarverslag%20RTE%202008_definitief_tcm17-9036.pdf

stand in the way of the possibility that scientists contest the truth of particular norm-descriptions. However, as long as the content and the truth conditions are well-specified, truth is a matter of correspondence.

Therefore, Peczenik's claim that the test of descriptive theories is in their coherence with the words of the statute and with factual judicial practice seems to be a mistaken mixing of object-level and doctrinal level.[60] I would argue that the aim of descriptive theories is to achieve *correspondence* of the content of the words and statements of the legal doctrinal theory, with the content of the norms as they are formulated in statutes and as they show in unwritten legal practice. The test as to whether this correspondence is achieved is found in the *consistency and coherence* of the statements on the level of the legal doctrinal theory, ie in the consistency and coherence of the particular norm-description with other legal doctrinal descriptions.[61]

ii. Norm-Contentions

In cases where the formulations of norms are vague or ambiguous, where the norms turn out to be inconsistent or incoherent, or when there are gaps in the law, the only norm-description that legal scholars can offer is the statement that the formulations are vague or ambiguous, or that the law contains a gap, etc. In order to remove the vagueness, ambiguity, inconsistency or incoherency, legal scholars have to make proposals on how law as a social fact has to be changed in order to deal with these deficiencies.

I propose that we call these proposals norm-contentions. Norm-contentions differ from norm-descriptions in that the latter only deal with what is explicit in or straightforwardly follows from the law. Norm-contentions, on the other hand, are intended to fill in gaps and to eliminate – in one way or the other – vagueness and ambiguity.

Whereas norm-descriptions are statements about law as a social fact, norm-contentions are statements about law as an *optimal internally coherent normative system*.[62] The term 'internal' is meant to refer to the fact that only the norms

---

[60] This claim was discussed in section IV. A.

[61] *cf* Niiniluoto (n 10) 187.

[62] My notion of law as an optimal internally coherent normative system is not only inspired by Kelsen's, but also by Weinrib's and (even) by Dworkin's view of legal doctrine. As I have argued in section III. E., it seems that the differences between Kelsen's and hermeneutical views on legal doctrine have been overstated. See Dworkin, especially *Law's Empire* (The Belknap Press, Cambridge, Mass, 1986) chapter 7, where he compares legal interpretation to the work of a chain novelist. Ibid 237 argues that 'You might not find any interpretation that flows through the text, that fits everything the material you have been given treats as important. You must lower your sights . . . by trying to construct an interpretation that fits the bulk of what you take to be artistically most fundamental in the text. More than one interpretation may survive this more relaxed test. To choose among these, you must turn to your background aesthetic convictions, including those you will regard as formal. Possibly no interpretation will survive even the relaxed test. . . . But you cannot know in advance that you will reach that sceptical result. You must try first.' See also Ernest J Weinrib, 'The Jurisprudence of Legal Formalism' (1993) 16 *Harvard Journal of Law & Public Policy* 583, 583: 'Formalism reflects the law's most abiding aspiration: to be an immanently intelligible normative practice.'

Explanatory Non-Normative Legal Doctrine 65

and the standards of argumentation of *positive law* are taken into account.[63] In other words, contentions must take as much as possible of positive law into account. Due to the fact that only legal norms and presuppositions of legal cognition play a role, it is an internal rather than an external critique of positive law. The term 'normative' refers to the fact that norm-contentions do not aim to improve the logical coherence of positive law tout court. Rather, in doing so the fundamental legal values and legal principles must be given more weight than less fundamental legal norms.

Brouwer's distinction between equivalent and non-equivalent systematisations seems closely related to the distinction between norm-descriptions and norm-contentions.[64] Brouwer argues that an equivalent account should cover all legal material, whether coherent or not, whereas a non-equivalent account allows for a trade-off between the demand of completeness and the demand of coherency. Accordingly, on my account, an equivalent systematisation would consist only of norm-descriptions, whereas a non-equivalent systematisation would consist of both norm-descriptions and norm-contentions.

For example, in the Netherlands – and elsewhere in the western world – 'no punishment without guilt' is a fundamental principle of criminal law. Since all legal scholars fully acknowledge that this *is* the principle of Dutch criminal law (*cf* the sentence of the Dutch Supreme Court,[65] the legal doctrinal statement that it is a fundamental principle is a norm-description. Nevertheless, some legal scholars and legal practitioners (eg solicitor-general Jörg in his quite philosophical conclusion to a sentence of the Dutch Supreme Court)[66] argue that the principle should be read as 'punishment proportionate to the amount of guilt'. Jörg seems to claim that there is an incoherency in both stating that proportionality is foundational of criminal law and that the principle of proportionality only applies to those who have no guilt at all, and not to those who are merely a little bit guilty. Thus, this would count as an example of a conflicting norm-description and norm-contention.

In other words, norm-contentions are not claims about what the court or lawgiver actually does or has done, but rather claims about what a court or the lawgiver should do and what they would do if they were thinking rationally or at least reasonably, ie normatively coherently, about positive law.[67]

On my account, norm-contentions can be explicated in two different ways, viz as descriptive statements or as prescriptive statements. To my mind, the fact that both readings are possible is an important cause of the confusion about the question whether legal doctrinal statements are normative. In one reading,

---

[63] However, as Kelsen (n 38) 406f has argued, not all rules of interpretation are rules of positive law, some are rather presuppositions of legal cognition which guarantee the unity of norms of positive law, not necessarily as an 'objectively' just, but as a meaningful system. *cf* section III. E.

[64] Brouwer 'Systematisering van recht' ('Systematization of Law') (1999) 222–24.

[65] Hoge Raad 10 September 1957, (1958) *Nederlandse Jurisprudentie*, 5.

[66] Hoge Raad 22 March 2005, case number (LJN) AS5881.

[67] One could also say that norm-contentions are claims about or rather which follow from our *ratio iuris*.

norm-contentions can be understood to be *normative* claims, viz if they are taken as statements about law as a *social fact*. In this reading, norm-contentions tell what law as a social fact should look like and what legal officials should decide. Since norm-contentions are an important aspect of the scientific activities of legal scholars, legal scholars who take norm-contentions to be normative claims will claim that legal doctrine is normative.

However, we can also understand norm-contentions as *descriptive* statements. Obviously, they are not descriptive statements about law as a social fact. They are descriptive statements about law as *an optimal, internally coherent normative system*. As was said, norm-descriptions of law as a social fact can conflict with norm-contentions about law as an optimal internally coherent normative system.[68] This can be due to the fact that law as a social fact has gaps, but also because law as a social fact has filled these gaps in a way which is less than optimally normatively coherent.

Nevertheless, the aim of norm-contentions is to take into account as much of law as a social fact, especially of the fundamental principles and values and only, if necessary, to revise less fundamental norms. We can understand this restriction on norm-contentions in terms of Lakatos' theory of scientific research programmes.[69] We could say that there is a hard core of legal doctrinal description of law as a social fact which consists of a description of legal norms and legal values that are fundamental to the particular legal system and a description of less fundamental but uncontested lower norms that are coherent with the rest of the legal system.

Following Lakatos' views, we can say that this hard core cannot be changed by any norm-contention. If the hard core is changed, then – by definition – the research programme is changed. The hard core is surrounded by a protective belt of auxiliary hypotheses about the validity and the content of less crucial legal norms. These auxiliary hypotheses suggest particular ways in which the description of the system can be adapted to make it – ie not the theory, but rather the law itself – more coherent. These hypotheses, which I call norm-contentions, suggest ways to take away inconsistencies and incoherencies and result in a description of law as an optimal internally coherent normative system.

The question is whether we are allowed to understand these norm-contentions to be descriptive statements. I believe that we are. In section III. C. we have seen that on Kelsen's account, legal doctrine can not only *scientifically* study (ie offer descriptions of) positive law.[70] It can also offer descriptions of norms which are *fictions* or *constructs*. I would argue that the norms of the ideally coherent normative legal order should be understood as constructs.[71]

[68] Also compare Brouwer (n 15) 222–24.
[69] Imre Lakatos, 'Falsification and the Methodology of Scientific Research Programmes' in Imre Lakatos and Alan Musgrave (eds), *Criticism and the Growth of Knowledge* (Cambridge, Cambridge University Press, 1970) 91–195.
[70] Kelsen (n 5) 256.
[71] They are not fictions since they are not self-contradictory in themselves. They are only in contradiction with social reality. See section III. C. and Kelsen (n 5) 256, fn 2.

As long as the criteria that determine the delineation of the hard core of law, the auxiliary hypotheses and the (hierarchy of) standards of interpretation are sufficiently clear and precise, it seems correct to call norm-contentions descriptions of law as an optimal internally coherent normative system.

iii. Norm-Recommendations

Norm-recommendations do not describe the legal order as a social fact and they do not describe it as an optimal, internally coherent normative system. They rather intend to improve positive law by reference to *extra-legal* (moral, political) norms, values and goals that do not belong to the positive legal system. They are neither explicitly expressed in the legal norms nor shared within the community of legal officials. These extra-legal norms and values might be founded in views about social justice, but they might just as well relate to goals of efficiency and efficacy or any other extra-legal value a legal scholar might find important.

Norm-recommendations can be statements about the reinterpretation of valid norms, about the elimination of valid norms and about the introduction of new norms. They are neither claimed to correspond to law as a social fact (ie they are not norm-descriptions), nor claimed to correspond to law as an optimal, internally coherent normative system (ie they are not norm-contentions).

The most important difference between norm-contentions and norm-recommendations is that whereas norm-contentions need to respect the hard core of positive law, norm-recommendations need not do so. They can subject each and every part of the legal system to critique, ie including the hard core.

For example, someone might argue that the Dutch Termination of Life on Request and Assisted Suicide (Review Procedures) Bill should be abolished because it conflicts with the principle of 'the sanctity of life'. His claim would be a norm-recommendation because this principle is not a principle of Dutch positive law. One might say that whereas norm-contentions (when read as prescriptions) state what we should do if we restrict ourselves to the legal point of view, norm-recommendations tell us what we should do on the Kantian view of practical reason as 'all things considered'.

Earlier I argued that norm-recommendations can be rationally argued for if they derive from a coherent set of norms. Nevertheless, they are subjective to the extent that the criteria on which the norm-recommendations are based are not intersubjectively shared (ie by definition not as intra-legal criteria, but also not as extra-legal criteria) by the legal community.

Since norm-recommendations are *prescriptive* claims both in relation to law as a social fact and in relation to law as an optimal, internally coherent normative system, they seem to have no correspondence theoretical truth value. However, even norm-recommendations might be read as *descriptive* statements, viz about law as an 'absolute' or 'objective' system (eg natural law). However, I would argue that to the extent that the truth conditions are not sufficiently clear and precise, this descriptive reading is to be rejected.

More importantly, the normative reading of norm-recommendations is to be preferred when the nature of legal doctrine is explicated to scientists of other disciplines. An important reason for this is that scientists from other disciplines also make these kinds of recommendations and present these recommendations as normative claims and, in principle, clearly separate them from their scientific, descriptive and explanatory statements.

This is, at the same time, the reason why we should present norm-contentions as descriptive statements. In the explication of the nature of legal doctrine to scientists of other disciplines, it is important to distinguish recommendations as extra-scientific normative claims from norm-contentions which are not extra-scientific claims but which, on the contrary, make up the core of legal doctrine.[72]

D. One Right Answer?

One reason why the normativity of legal doctrine is so hotly debated is that some legal scholars fear that if we deny the normative nature of legal doctrine, it will leave legal practice empty-handed in hard cases. In those cases, the only norm-description that legal scholars can offer states that there is no fact of the matter as to what the outcome in such a case *is*. Moreover, it seems that any statement about what the outcome *should be* can only be presented as a personal and subjective claim.

In other words, the view that legal doctrine is not normative seems to undermine the claim that we can have a rational debate about the outcome of hard cases. At least, this seems to be the driving fear behind Soeteman's claim that

> Smith rightly argues that the study of law has a hermeneutic character. But his interpretation of legal hermeneutics includes the thesis that in hard cases there is no right or true legal decision. This seems to have negative implications for the scholarly character of the study of law: in hard cases any solution goes.[73]

Therefore, Soeteman argues 'that the study of law defends right answers for hard cases.'

However, I would argue against Soeteman that even if a legal scholar cannot offer 'one right answer' – as I think he or she often cannot do – it does not follow that 'anything goes'. In section IV. C., I argued that legal scholars cannot only make objective norm-descriptions and subjective norm-recommendations. They can also make a third kind of statement, viz objective norm-contentions. In most cases legal scholars will minimally be able to make explicit which answers 'definitely do not go', ie which norm-contentions are false as norm-descriptions of the optimal internally coherent normative system and also to formulate a finite number of answers that are possible, given the shared intra-legal criteria.

---

[72] In their focus on coherency, norm-contentions are sufficiently like statements of logic and mathematics. These are also about constructs. Moreover, they are not presented as normative either.
[73] Soeteman (n 2) 266.

In other words, Soeteman is wrong to claim that the fact that there is 'not *one* right answer' excludes the possibility of a rational debate. What a legal scholar can do is to state the range of *possible* contentions about the norm, given the values, principles and rules of the legal system and the shared views about the (hierarchy of) standards of interpretation. Moreover, or so I would argue, this is a completely scientific thing to do. However, legal scholars go astray when they claim that their personally preferred norm-contention is the 'true' *description* of law as an optimal internally coherent normative system. When legal scholars want to present one of their norm-contentions as the 'one and only right answer', they should not present it as a descriptive norm-contention, but as a normative norm-recommendation.

Thus, it seems that there are two types of norm-recommendations. In section IV. C., I have argued that claims about law which are based on extra-legal criteria are norm-recommendations. Here I would add that some claims that are based on intra-legal criteria are also norm-recommendations. In cases where there is not 'one right answer' but only several options, the choice for one specific option should be called a recommendation too.

V. CONCLUSION

In this chapter I have claimed that legal doctrine is one of the practical sciences in that it aims to help answer the legal version of the question 'What ought I do?' I have argued that it is nevertheless an explanatory non-normative discipline. In section III. I argued that legal doctrine is an explanatory discipline since the explanation of the content and the validity of both individual and general norms is in many respects like natural scientific explanations of individual and general facts. In section IV., I argued that legal doctrine is not a normative discipline. That is not to say that legal scholars do not or should not make prescriptive or evaluative claims. It is only to say that they can and should distinguish their descriptive from their normative claims, just like other scientists do.

Against total legal normativists who claim that all legal doctrinal statements are normative, I have argued that legal doctrinal descriptions of institutional facts do not differ from the descriptions of social and institutional facts that social scientists offer and that therefore they are not normative in any interesting sense of the word.

Against local legal normativists who claim that legal statements about the most coherent and just interpretation of law are normative, I have argued that they should not merely distinguish between descriptive and prescriptive statements but that they should distinguish between norm-descriptions, norm-contentions and norm-recommendations. I have argued that whereas norm-descriptions are descriptive statements belonging to the field of theoretical reason and norm-recommendations are prescriptive claims which belong to the domain of practical reason, norm-contentions can be read in two ways.

They can be read as descriptive statements in relation to law as an ideal, internally coherent normative system, but also as prescriptive claims in relation to law as a social fact.

The distinction between norm-descriptions, norm-contentions and norm-recommendations can also help to dissolve some of the unclarities about the question as to whether there is 'one right answer'. I have argued that in hard cases there is, by definition, *no right answer* in relation to law as a social fact, since in such cases law is ambiguous, vague or has gaps. I have also argued that there need not always be *one right answer* in relation to law as an ideal, internally coherent normative system. However, this does not mean, as some legal scholars fear, that in hard cases 'anything goes'. Legal scholars can often show that some answers are downright false and also that a finite number of answers are possible in relation to law as an ideal, internally coherent normative system.

My main point has been that legal scholars should clearly distinguish between norm-contentions that state which interpretations are possible and impossible on the one hand and their norm-recommendations on the other. Norm-recommendations express their personal interpretive preferences, irrespective of the fact whether it is a preference as seen from the legal perspective or a preference from some overarching perspective of 'all things considered'.

I conclude. Legal doctrine is a practical discipline in that its aim is to help answer the question, 'What ought I to do?' However, just like other practical sciences, it does so mainly by offering norm-descriptions and norm-contentions which can both be understood as descriptive in nature. At least that is what I have *contended*. The main *recommendation* of this chapter is that in our explication of legal doctrine to scientists of other disciplines, we should present norm-contentions as descriptive statements and norm-recommendations as normative claims.

4

A World without Law Professors

MATHIAS M SIEMS*

IN HIS INTRODUCTORY chapter, Mark Van Hoecke identified a number of different approaches to legal research.[1] The following chapter uses an alternative starting point in order to discuss the variety of legal research: I wonder what would be lost if law professors disappeared from the world. One purpose of this thought experiment is to identify for which type of legal research we really need legal academics, or whether legal scholarship could also become part of other social sciences or humanities. Moreover, it will be discussed how this relates to legal teaching and education: do we need law professors to train lawyers, or would it be feasible to separate education and research?

I. INTRODUCTION

In his book the *The World Without Us*, Alan Weisman examines how the world would react if humans suddenly vanished.[2] In order to answer this question he starts with a look at the world before us. However, his analysis is not limited to it since the future of a world without us would not perfectly mirror the past. Moreover, he addresses the policy question of his scenario: 'Is it possible that, instead of heaving a huge biological sigh of relief, the world without us would miss us?'[3]

Inspired by Alan Weisman's book, this chapter will study the thought experiment of a world in which we extract not all human beings but 'just' law professors.[4] The term 'law professors' needs further explanation. I will use it for every legal academic who teaches and researches at law schools/faculties in universities. It does not cover practitioners who are engaged in legal teaching and writing, or academics from other disciplines interested in law. Indeed, the

---

* I am grateful to John Armour, Jacob Henriquez, Olivett Ihama, Daithí Mac Sithigh, Larry Ribstein and the participants of the Workshop on Research Methods at the University of Tilburg for helpful comments. The usual disclaimer applies.
 [1] See chapter one in this volume.
 [2] Alan Weisman, *The World Without Us* (New York, Thomas Dunne, 2007).
 [3] ibid 4.
 [4] The examples used in this chapter are mainly from the UK, the US, and Germany; however, most points should also be applicable to other parts of the world.

two main parts of this chapter discuss whether the functions that in the current system are performed by law professors cannot also be performed by other persons or institutions.

The scenario of this chapter is not entirely hypothetical. In the United Kingdom and the United States a number of new law schools have been established in the last few decades,[5] whereas in Germany two universities no longer offer undergraduate law teaching.[6] The scenario of a world without law professors is also a useful hermeneutic tool in order to reflect on the role of law professors in the current system, for instance, the relationship between teaching and research, the delegation of teaching to practitioners, and the changing focus of legal research. These points will be picked up in the final part of the chapter.

II. LEGAL TRAINING AND EDUCATION

A world without law professors could be disastrous for legal training and education, and thus the legal and economic system as a whole. Although it is difficult to establish a causal relationship between law and economic development,[7] the present chapter accepts that we need legal rules as well as lawyers with expertise in these rules.[8] However, one could argue that legal education, or at least legal training, could also be provided by other institutions.

A. Legal Training by Other Institutions

The usefulness of university- or institution-based legal training has often been questioned. In the early twentieth century Thorstein Veblen asserted that 'the law school belongs in the university no more than a school of fencing or dancing'.[9] Also, at the end of the century, Juergen Ostertag compared theoretical legal education to the school of driving which attempted to teach people how to drive by teaching a detailed manual of the car and then allowing trainees to drive in traffic.[10]

---

[5] See William Twining, *Law in Context: Enlarging a Discipline* (Oxford, Clarendon, 1997) 294 (in England the scale of the national system of legal education is 20 times what it was in 1945). Blog posts at www.money-law.blogspot.com/2007/10/advice-for-erwin-chemerinsky.html (for the debate on the new Irvine Law School in the US).

[6] Namely, the University of Rostock and the Dresden University of Technology. See www.jura.uni-rostock.de/ and www.tu-dresden.de/die_tu_dresden/fakultaeten/juristische_fakultaet/.

[7] For the debate, see Mathias Siems and Simon Deakin, 'Comparative Law and Finance: Past, Present and Future Research' (2010) 166 *Journal of Institutional and Theoretical Economics (JITE)* 120.

[8] See also Frederick Pollock, 'Oxford Law Studies' [originally published in 1890] in Michael Hoeflich (ed), *The Gladsome Light of Jurisprudence* (New York, Greenwood Press, 1988) 255 ('that the profession of the law is necessary in a civilised commonwealth and competence therein by no means to be attained without study, is a matter of common knowledge'). For a polemic counterview, see Fred Rodell, *Woe Unto You, Lawyers* (New York, Reynal & Hitchcock, 1939).

[9] Thorstein Veblen, *The Higher Learning in America* (New York, BW Huebsch, 1918) 211.

[10] Juergen Ostertag, 'Legal Education in Germany and the United States – A Structural Comparison' (1993) 26 *Vanderbilt Journal of Transnational Law* 301.

A first counter-model would be that law is (again) to be learned in an apprentice system. In the longer historical context, university-based training is a recent development in Common Law countries.[11] Today, however, most countries 'only' have a vocational stage in addition to an institution-based (usually, university-based) education.[12] This is also part of a wider trend because in many countries universities are now engaged in fields such as nursing or social work which used to be left to vocational training.[13]

At least for legal education, there are good reasons for this development. Due to the growing juridification of society, it cannot easily be assumed that prospective lawyers would learn everything they need to know 'on the job'. Given the complexity of the legal system, an institution-based legal education can ensure that the knowledge and wisdom of the current generation of lawyers can be handed over to the next one.[14] Historically, Frederick Pollock defended university-based legal education since it is a technical study 'which cannot be undertaken here, or not so well here as elsewhere'.[15] Thus, an apprentice system could provide a certain level of legal training but, even in a world without law professors, it would not be chosen as the sole means of transmitting legal knowledge.

Thus, a second, and more realistic, counter-model would be based on legal training in law schools whose teachers are not law professors or other academics. These law teachers would be practitioners who do some part-time teaching, or who teach full-time for a defined period of time. Some may argue that this cannot work. In 1887, the US-American jurist Christopher Columbus Langdell alleged:

> If it [ie law] is not a science, it is a species of handicraft, and may be left by serving an apprenticeship to one who practises it. . . . If printed books are the ultimate sources of all legal knowledge, . . . then a university, and a university alone, can afford every possible facility for teaching and learning law.[16]

This Langedellian view of law as 'law in books only' was, however, already discredited by the US legal realists of the early twentieth century. Jerome Frank also proposed a major reform of teaching law students.[17] Many law schools, he

---

[11] See Thomas Wood, 'Some Thoughts Concerning the Study of the Laws of England in the Two Universities' [originally published in 1708] in Hoeflich (ed), *The Gladsome Light of Jurisprudence* (1988) 34–52 and William Blackstone, 'A Discourse on the Study of Law' [originally published in 1759] in Hoeflich (n 8) 53–73; JH Baker, *The Third University of England: The Inns of Court and the Common-Law Tradition* (London, Selden Society, 1990); Fiona Cownie and Raymond Cocks, *'A Great and Noble Occupation!': The History of the Society of Legal Scholars* (Oxford, Hart Publishing, 2009).

[12] A good overview (in German) can be found at www.europaeische-juristenausbildung.de.

[13] For a comparative overview, see Jane Lethbridge, 'Changing Care Services and Labour Markets' (Working Paper 2007), available at www.psiru.org/reports/2008-3-H-Carepoliciesla-bourmarkets.doc.

[14] See Béla Pokol, *The Concept of Law: The Multi-layered Legal System* (Budapest, Rejtjel Edition, 2000) 121.

[15] Pollock, 'Oxford Law Studies' (1988) 260.

[16] Christopher Columbus Langdell, 'Harvard Celebration Speech' (1887) 9 *The Law Quarterly Review* 123–25, 124.

[17] Jerome Frank, 'Why Not a Clinical Lawyer-School?' (1933) 81 *University of Pennsylvania Law Review* 907–23.

claimed, were not equipped to train lawyers but to graduate men able to become law teachers. Thus, they were not 'lawyer-schools' but 'law-teacher schools'. Instead, he suggested a 'clinical lawyer-school' where a considerable proportion of law teachers should not have less than five to 10 years of varied experience in the actual practice of law.[18]

More recently, the Carnegie Report for the Advancement of Teaching Report on Educating Lawyers followed a similar line of reasoning. The Report criticised that most American law schools 'give only casual attention to teaching students how to use legal thinking in the complexity of actual law practice' and therefore fail 'to complement the focus on skill in legal analyses with effective support for developing ethical and social skills'.[19] Thus, one may applaud the development that in many US law schools, teaching is increasingly delegated to adjunct professors.[20] William Wang goes further and proposes to unbundle the distinct services that the law school offers to students. In particular, he suggests that the impartation of knowledge, skills and values can be performed by tutoring firms and producers, sellers, and renters of books, videos, and computerised instruction.[21]

It may be argued that these suggestions may be working in the United States because, being post-graduate institutions, US law schools already have a vocational focus, whereas in the United Kingdom (and other European countries), law faculties provide general legal education.[22] However, this difference should not be overemphasised. In the United Kingdom too, the main focus of legal education is on teaching students to become practicing lawyers.[23] Moreover, it can be suggested that the United Kingdom is already on the path to a clinical lawyer-school. For the purpose of entry into professional training, it is regarded as equivalent to an LLB degree if a non-law graduate passes a one year Diploma course. Such a course is not only offered by universities but also professional schools, such as the College of Law and the BPP.[24] In addition, the BPP has just started its own LLBs and LLMs programmes, mainly taught by practitioners.[25]

From a continental European perspective it may, however, be objected that the academic nature of the Civil Law tradition would rule out any legal training without the involvement of universities. In the Civil Law world the first law professors emerged in Northern Italy in the 12th century. When the Italian city

---

[18] ibid 914.
[19] William M Sullivan, Anne Colby, Judith Welch Wegner, Lloyd Bond and Lee S Shulman, *Educating Lawyers: Preparation for the Profession of Law* (John Wiley & Sons, Hoboken NJ, 2007) 6.
[20] See prawfsblawg.blogs.com/prawfsblawg/2007/11/will-the-tenure.html.
[21] William KS Wang, 'The Restructuring of Legal Education along Functional Lines' (Working Paper, 2008), available at ssrn.com/abstract=1161305.
[22] John Bell, 'Legal Education' in *Oxford Handbook of Legal Studies* (Oxford, Oxford University Press, 2005) 901–19, 901; Twining, Law in Context (1997) 352.
[23] Though only a minority choose to do so. See Richard Collier, '"We're All Socio-Legal Now?" Legal Education, Scholarship and the "Global Knowledge Economy" – Reflections on the UK Experience' (2004) 26 *The Sydney Law Review* 503.
[24] See www.sra.org.uk/students/conversion-courses/cpe-gdl-providers.page.
[25] See www.bpplawschool.com/programmes/llb/index.htm.

states increased commerce and trade, there was a need to expand and improve the legal system. This was done by way of reception of the Corpus Juris Civilis, which, however, needed law professors to understand and categorise the content of these rules.[26] This academic background can still be felt today. For instance, Pierre Legrand argues that there are major differences between Civil Law and Common Law countries. Whereas the Common Law is said to be inductive, pragmatic, fact-bound, and past-oriented, the Civil Law is deductive, logical and systematic, rule-bound, and future-oriented.[27]

The predominant view is, however, that these differences between Common Law and Civil Law should not be exaggerated.[28] The undergraduate degrees of Continental European universities are also not 'deeper' than the LLB degree of UK universities. For instance, in Germany, as in England, the main focus of undergraduate courses is on the legislation and court decisions of the core areas of law (contract, tort, criminal, constitutional law, etc) and how these rules would apply to hypothetical cases. There is also a similar level of abstraction. For instance, contract law textbooks in both jurisdictions enlist the requirements for the formation of contracts, the validity of contracts, contractual remedies, etc in general terms and provide details on how these requirements are understood by courts and academics. This does not mean that the approaches to teaching law are identical in Germany and in England. However, for present purposes it is decisive that in both jurisdictions the majority of university-based legal training is not very sophisticated from an epistemological perspective but is predominantly knowledge transmission.

Thus, in Civil Law countries too, practitioners would be able to provide legal training equivalent to the current university-based training. In reality, a significant involvement of practitioners in teaching already takes place in many Civil Law countries. In Italy and the Netherlands it is common that law professors also practice as advocates. In Germany it is even the case that 95 per cent of all undergraduate students receive the majority of their undergraduate legal training from practitioners. These persons, called *Repetitoren*, prepare students for the First Juridical Exam. Students use these training courses because university classes are typically very large and German law professors are not able to tutor individual students. Since in many German cities there is an oversupply of practicing lawyers, these lawyers offer tailor-made training courses on a commercial basis.[29]

---

[26] See James G Apple and Robert P Deyling, A Primer on the Civil-Law System (1995), available at www.ripit4me.org/PublishedAuthors/Govt/FJC/CivilLaw.pdf.

[27] See Pierre Legrand, 'European Legal Systems are not Converging' (1996) 45 *International and Comparative Law Quarterly* 53; Pierre Legrand, 'The Impossibility of Legal Transplants' (1997) 4 Maastricht Journal of European and Comparative Law 112.

[28] See already Mathias Siems, 'Legal Origins: Reconciling Law & Finance and Comparative Law' (2007) 52 *McGill Law Journal* 55–81.

[29] Philip Leith, 'Legal Education in Germany: Becoming a Lawyer, Judge, and Professor' (1995) 4 Web JCLI, available at webjcli.ncl.ac.uk/articles4/leith4.rtf.

The overall result is that in a world without law professors 'purely professional law schools' would provide the legal training currently offered by universities. In general, the provision of this training would be similar to the existing one. However, there may also be two differences.

First, this concerns the substance of teaching. Practising lawyers would be less interested in the abstraction of legal rules (or even their 'supercomplexity'[30]) than academic teachers. In contrast to academics, they would also put more emphasis on persuasion than on establishing the 'correct answer' to a particular legal question.[31] This sounds like a shortcoming but it can also be seen in a more positive light. According to Oliver Wendell Holmes, 'the business of a law school is not sufficiently described when you merely say that it is to teach law, or to make lawyers. It is to teach law in the grand manner, and to make great lawyers.'[32] Holmes did not specify these terms in detail. Presumably, he meant that lawyers should not only know the law but also learn how to think and how to perform like a lawyer. In this respect, teaching by practitioners may be advantageous because it can lead to more complete lawyers.[33]

Second, the amount of legal training may change. Currently, the majority of UK undergraduate law students do not go on to practice law.[34] Thus, a market for legal education, where law schools are entirely run by the professions, may reduce legal education. In addition, the present class of practitioners may decide to train fewer lawyers than under the current system in order to be sheltered from competition. However, this outcome is not unavoidable, because the Government (or competition authorities) may step in to prevent a commodification of legal training.[35] For instance, it may decide to establish state-run professional law schools where practitioners are hired to teach law. Furthermore, even without law professors, universities may still provide deep legal education.

B. Deep Legal Education

It is often said that legal education should not only focus on teaching the legal rules to undergraduate students. In substance, legal education should be part of a liberal education. Thus, there should also be a training of 'intelligence and sensibility',[36] of 'moral experience',[37] of understanding law 'marked by method-

[30] Bell, 'Legal Education' (2005) 909.
[31] Anthony T Kronman, *The Lost Lawyer* (Cambridge MA, Belknap, 1993) 128.
[32] Oliver Wendell Holmes, 'The Use of Law Schools' [originally published in 1896] in Hoeflich (n 8) 265–71.
[33] But see also section II. B. below.
[34] Collier, 'We're All Socio-Legal Now?' (2004) 528.
[35] See also *The Competition Authority of the Republic of Ireland, Solicitors & Barristers* (December 2006) chapter 4, available at www.tca.ie/controls/getimage.ashx?image_id=1627.
[36] Anthony Bradney, 'Liberalising Legal Education' in Fiona Cownie (ed), *The Law School – Global Issues, Local Questions* (Darthmouth, Ashgate, 1999) 1–25.
[37] Maksymilian Del Mar, 'Moral Experience and Legal Education' (Working Paper, 2009), available at ssrn.com/abstract=1351547.

ological and epistemological diversity',[38] and of the skills to encourage students 'to think for themselves'.[39] In the UK context, William Twining also suggested that university law schools should adopt a broader and more ambitious role than they have in the past. They should reach

> from legal literacy to judicial training; from different kinds of law or non-lawyers to advanced specialist studies for a variety of consumers; from primary academic and vocational studies to continuing education that ranges across the whole spectrum from 'get-skilled-quick' to 'get-wise-slow'.[40]

This broader role, he argues, can only be fulfilled by a law school which is an academic institution devoted to the advancement of learning about law.[41]

In the scenario of a world without law professors, various points have to be distinguished: first, some of these additional functions can also be fulfilled by purely professional law schools. For instance, these law schools too can teach students 'to think for themselves' (it really depends on how legal topics are taught and not who teaches them). Practitioners would also be very well equipped to provide more general education on the law, may it be to other lawyers as continuing education or to the general public. This can also be shown in the context of transition economies. Lawyers from the West have provided legal education in order to facilitate the transition of former Communist countries to market economies.[42] Academic lawyers, however, may often feel overburdened by the request to suggest rules that will be directly relevant to the practice of an unfamiliar legal system,[43] whereas legal practitioners have more experience in applying the law into different socio-economic contexts.

Second, there are some subjects which cannot easily be taught by practitioners. For instance, many of the old 'legal x' and new 'law and x' topics are part of legal education.[44] However, legal practitioners would usually not have the time or interest to teach topics such as legal philosophy, legal history, legal sociology, law and economics, law and finance, law and religion, etc. In a world without law professors this can be solved by shifting these topics to other schools or faculties of the university. This may require some reallocation of resources; however, it may not be unfeasible because disciplines such as philosophy, history, or economics already have an interest in the role of law in their own disciplinary context.[45] Then, for instance, some of this law-in-context education may

---

[38] Collier (n 23) 518–19. See also Roger Brownsword, 'Law School for Lawyers, Citizens and People' in Cownie, *The Law School* (1999) 26–40.

[39] Fleur Johns, 'On Writing Dangerously' (2004) 26 *The Sydney Law Review* 473, 485.

[40] Twining (n 5) 293. See also William Twining, *Blackstone's Tower: The English Law School* (London, Sweet & Maxwell, 1994).

[41] Twining (n 5) 301.

[42] For instance, one can refer to the Riga Graduate School of Law in Latvia (www.rgsl.edu.lv) and the legal studies department of the Central European University in Hungary (www.ceu.hu/legal/).

[43] Günter Frankenberg, 'Stranger Than Paradise: Identity & Politics in Comparative Law' (1997) *Utah Law Review* 259.

[44] An increased demand for 'law and' training is expected by Larry Ribstein, 'The Death of Big Law' (2010) *Wisconsin Law Review* 74.

[45] See also section III. C. below.

be made a prerequisite for a law degree. Or, in reversal to the current situation, academics from these schools and faculties may be invited to deliver guest lectures at the purely professional law schools.

Third, supporters of the liberal arts view of legal education may still object that purely professional schools and non-law faculties alone would not be able to cover all aspects of a deep legal education. For instance, some topics of jurisprudence, deep-level comparative law or legal research methods may not be sufficiently interesting to either of these two types of institutions.[46] However, in the current system of legal education, these topics only play a marginal role.[47] Thus, from the standpoint of the present system with its focus on learning the legal rules of a particular country, a world without law professors would not leave a considerable gap in legal education.[48]

C. Conclusion

Without academic teachers, legal training would shift back to the legal professions. Purely professional law schools would provide legal training for future lawyers. This is feasible in both Common Law and Civil Law jurisdictions. These professional law schools can also be involved in a more general provision of legal education. In addition, non-law faculties of universities can take responsibility for teaching on law-related subjects. This role of other parts of the university will also become apparent in the following section on legal research.

III. LEGAL RESEARCH AND WRITING

Without law professors, *law* would disappear as a separate academic discipline. Some may applaud such a development. In 1848 Julius von Kirchmann gave a controversial talk at a lawyers' conference in Berlin in which he claimed legal research to be worthless because it did not aim to establish general truths but merely to support the current legal system.[49] A similar criticism can also be found today. For instance, it is said that

> it is not easy to see that law is a discipline in the usual sense. What truths do lawyers come up with? What are the great legal discoveries of the past ten years, or fifty years, or even a hundred? There do not seem to be any.[50]

---

[46] See also William Twining, *General Jurisprudence* (Cambridge, Cambridge University Press, 2009) 19 with reference to Mark Van Hoecke, What is Legal Theory? (Leuven, Akko, 1985) ('general jurisprudence' as a discipline between abstract legal philosophy and legal dogmatics).
[47] For research see section III. C. below.
[48] See section II. A. above.
[49] Julius von Kirchmann, *Die Wertlosigkeit der Jurisprudenz als Wissenschaft* (Heidelberg, Manutius, 1848, reprinted in 1988).
[50] AWB Simpson, *Invitation to Law* (Oxford, Blackwell, 1988) 178.

Likewise, an empirical study into perceptions of different academic disciplines found that 'the predominant notion of academic lawyers is that they are not really academic – one respondent described them as "arcane, distant and alien; an appendage to the university world"'.[51] For present purposes, it is important to distinguish between three types of legal research.

A. Self-interested Research

Self-interested legal research can emerge in two variants. The first one concerns publications which are mainly written for one's own professional advancement.[52] Publication lists matter for any appointment or promotion decision, however, many legal articles hardly have any impact.[53] Second, legal writing can be an act of self-definition, because naturally, 'what we choose to write about, the voice we employ, the points we choose to make, all are important expressions of self'.[54]

Without law professors some persons may still write about law for entirely intrinsic reasons. However, merely self-referential research would disappear. Since in most countries universities are public institutions, public resources would therefore be saved.

B. Doctrinal Research

More complex is the impact on doctrinal legal research. In general terms, the merits of doctrinal work are well described by Richard Posner:

> The messy work product of the judges and legislators requires a good deal of tidying up, of synthesis, analysis, restatement, and critique. These are intellectually demanding tasks, requiring vast knowledge and the ability (not only brains and knowledge and judgment, but also *Sitzfleisch*) to organize dispersed, fragmentary, prolix, and rebarbative materials. These are tasks that lack the theoretical breadth or ambition of scholarship in more typically academic fields. Yet they are of inestimable importance to the legal system and of greater social value than much esoteric interdisciplinary legal scholarship.[55]

Specifically, there are a number of ways in which doctrinal research has an impact on the legal system. Textbooks and casebooks are used to train future

---

[51] Tony Becher, *Academic Tribes and Territories, Intellectual Enquiry and the Cultures of Disciplines* (Milton Keynes, Open University Press, 2001) 30.
[52] Erwin Chemerinsky, 'Why Write?' (2009) 107 *Michigan Law Review* 881, 881f.
[53] See eg the Washington & Lee Ranking of Journals, available at lawlib.wlu.edu/LJ/.
[54] Chemerinsky, 'Why Write?' (2009) 893. For a different view in the context of US law schools, see Alan Watson, *The Shame of American Legal Education* (Lake Mary FL, Vandeplas, 2005) 47 (a reason for becoming a law professor is often the desire to leave legal practice).
[55] Richard A Posner, 'In Memoriam: Bernard D. Meltzer (1914–2007)' (2007) 74 *University of Chicago Law Review* 435–38, 437. See also Mathias Siems, 'Legal Originality' (2008) 28 *Oxford Journal of Legal Studies* 147–64, 153.

generations of lawyers. Commentaries and case notes may influence judges, and academic articles and monographs can assist lawmakers in drafting and implementing legislation.[56] Thus, according to Peter Birks, 'traditional legal research and scholarship which criticises, explains, corrects and directs legal doctrine is still and must remain the heart of the law schools' research'.[57]

Similar to legal education,[58] it may be argued that the role of doctrinal research is more pronounced in the Civil Law than in the Common Law tradition. For Germany in particular, Stefan Vogenauer has shown how legal scholars have had a profound impact on legislative and judicial lawmaking.[59] The Common Law, by contrast, managed to flourish for centuries without law professors.[60] Today, however, here too, there is a 'symbiotic relationship between the senior judiciary and established legal scholars'.[61] With respect to the United Kingdom, one can also refer to the involvement of legal academics in the law commissions whose recommendations for law reform often have a profound practical effect.[62]

Without law professors, doctrinal publications would not disappear because other lawyers would, to some extent, fill the gap. The practitioners who teach at the purely professional law schools would transform their teaching materials into textbooks, making them akin to law professors under the current system.[63] In addition, practitioners themselves would demand doctrinal publications, such as commentaries and handbooks, which explain and consolidate the law. These works can be written by fellow practitioners. Peter Birks objects that

> the sheer size of the modern caseload makes it impossible for those engaged in the day to day business of adjudication to perceive and reflect upon the larger tensions underlying the law which they have to apply and the relative merits and demerits of the different directions in which it might be developed.[64]

However, even today many practitioners are heavily involved in writing books and articles which aim to develop a coherent description of the legal system.[65] In a world without law professors this would be even more pronounced: the

---

[56] William Twining, Ward Farnsworth, Stefan Vogenauer and Fernando Teson, 'The Role of Academics in the Legal System' in *Oxford Handbook of Legal Studies* (2005) 920–49 at 936–37; Chemerinsky (n 52) 883 and 888.

[57] Peter Birks, 'Editor's Preface' in Peter Birks (ed), *What are Law Schools For?* (Oxford, Oxford University Press, 1996) ix. For a similar view see Harry T Edwards, 'The Growing Disjunction between Legal Education and the Legal Profession' (1992) 91 *Michigan Law Review* 34–78.

[58] See section II. A. above.

[59] Stefan Vogenauer, 'An Empire of Light? II: Learning and Lawmaking in Germany Today' (2006) 4 Oxford Journal of Legal Studies 627–63. See also Geoffrey Samuel, *Epistemology and Method in Law* (Aldershot, Ashgate, 2003) 116–19.

[60] Birks, 'Editor's Preface' (1996) vi.

[61] Twining et al, 'The Role of Academics in the Legal System' (2005) 928.

[62] According to www.lawcom.gov.uk. See also www.scotlawcom.gov.uk.

[63] See section II. A. above.

[64] Birks (n 57) vii.

[65] For instance, in Germany in the Commentaries to the Civil Code, such as the Palandt (annually updated), or in the United Kingdom in books such as Harvey McGregor, QC, *McGregor on Damages*, 18th edn (London, Sweet & Maxwell, 2009).

revenues that legal authors receive would rise because in the current system the funding of law professors for doctrinal research leads to a distortion of competition.[66]

Put differently, in today's system law professors often operate as well-paid research assistants for judges and governments. An alternative system in a world without law professors would provide direct funding for such activities. Judges could be provided with research assistants, similar to the clerks at the highest US and German courts.[67] As far as the Government and the legislator have an interest in the doctrinal treatment of a particular field of law, they may create a system in which they pay directly for it. For instance, they may establish permanent advisory institutions, like law commissions, or they may call tenders to support doctrinal research on particular legal questions. The output of such research could then also be made publicly available, thus fostering the debate about the best solution to a particular legal problem.

Overall, doctrinal research would persist. However, market conditions would reduce the amount of doctrinal research because currently we observe an oversupply.[68] This is mainly a result of developments which started in the nineteenth century. According to Gerhard Casper, the core premise of legal thinking of that time was (and often still is) that a scientific specialisation of law is possible, and that therefore law professors should carefully analyse the text of the law in order to extract general legal principles and concepts.[69] This can best be done in comprehensive textbooks. Since the number of law professors has been growing,[70] it is no surprise that today there is an oversupply of textbooks on, say, English contract law, German criminal law, etc.

Moreover, many of these textbooks (and related forms of legal writing) are based on a relatively narrow understanding of the law. For instance, it has been said that 'much conventional scholarship is out of touch with fundamental social problems' and that 'too many debates in leading law reviews are excessively insular and self-referential',[71] that textual interpretation disregards that we 'have learned from social choice theory, public choice theory, and literary theory, that the issues are more complex and less determinate than had been earlier believed',[72] that doctrine's 'strict ideal objectivity is insufficient for legal

---

[66] See also Birks (n 57) vi ('the state, it might be said, pays a massive subsidy to the law publishers. The publishers make their profits from the dissemination of the results of research, passing back in the form of royalties a relatively small thank-you to the author.').

[67] For the US see Todd C Peppers, *Courtiers of the Marble Palace: The Rise And Influence of the Supreme Court Law Clerk* (Stanford CA, Stanford University Press, 2006). For Germany see www.bgh-hiwis.de.

[68] See Richard A Posner, 'The State of Legal Scholarship Today: A Comment on Schlag' (2009) 97 *Georgetown Law Journal* 845, 850 and 853.

[69] Gerhard Casper, 'Two Models of Legal Education' (1973–74) 41 *Tennessee Law Review* 13, 16 and 22.

[70] See section II. A. above.

[71] Deborah L Rhode, 'Legal Scholarship' (2002) 115 *Harvard Law Review* 1327–61, 1342.

[72] Brian H Bix, 'Law as an Autonomous Discipline' in *Oxford Handbook of Legal Studies* (n 22) 975–87, 983.

studies',[73] and that therefore we observe too much hidden advocacy scholarship 'in which political sallies are concealed in formalistic legal discourse'.[74] Thus, the more interesting question is what would happen to deep forms of legal research?

C. Deep Research

Academics often use a negative definition in order to identify deep research. According to Pierre Schlag, 'deep mastery of a subject is not itself scholarship'.[75] Deep legal research also has to go beyond the work of practitioners. As suggested by Jeremy Webber, 'law schools are . . . best conceived as a parallel branch of the profession, with their own standards of excellence and their own purposes'.[76] Moreover, deep research has to transcend research that *could* equally be done by practitioners.[77] Since practitioners can engage in doctrinal legal research (as explained), non-doctrinal original forms of legal research should qualify as deep research. The prime examples are the 'legal x' and 'law and x' fields such as legal philosophy, legal history, legal sociology, law and economics, law and finance, law and religion, etc[78] as well as research on the methods of legal reasoning and deep level comparative law.[79]

It could be unrealistic to assume that all of these forms of legal research would survive in a world in which all law professors suddenly vanished. However, if we modify the initial scenario a little bit, such a survival would be more likely. So, let us not imagine that all law professors suddenly vanished, but that all law professors would have to apply for positions in other faculties or schools of their universities. The scenario is therefore an 'academic dinner party test': law professors have to convince academics from other disciplines that their research is worth pursuing. In principle, deep-research legal academics should be able to pass this test. For instance, legal historians would move to history, legal philosophers to philosophy, and law and economics scholars to economics. Deep comparative legal research may emigrate to comparative politics, comparative economics, or

---

[73] Christoph Engel and Wolfgang Schön, 'Vorwort' in Christoph Engel and Wolfgang Schön (eds), Das Proprium der Rechtswissenschaft (Tübingen, Mohr, 2007) (English version of the preface available at www.coll.mpg.de/book/cii48-proper-task-academic-law).

[74] Richard A Posner, 'The Decline of Law as an Autonomous Discipline: 1962–1987' (1987) 100 *Harvard Law Review* 761, 778.

[75] Pierre Schlag, 'Spam Jurisprudence, Air Law, and the Rank Anxiety of Nothing Happening (A Report on the State of the Art)' (2009) 97 *Georgetown Law Journal* 803, 807, fn 15.

[76] Jeremy Webber, 'Legal Research, the Law Schools and the Profession' (2004) 26 *The Sydney Law Review* 565.

[77] See Twining et al (n 56) 940 ('but if legal scholarship should one day be no longer of a different kind than legal practice, it might easily be asked what it is needed for.').

[78] See section II. B. above.

[79] On the latter see Mark Van Hoecke, 'Deep Level Comparative Law' in Mark Van Hoecke (ed), *Epistemology and Methodology of Comparative Law* (Oxford, Hart Publishing, 2004) 165–95. See also Jan Smits, 'Redefining Normative Legal Science: Towards an Argumentative Discipline' in Fons Coomans, Fred Grünfeld, and Menno Kamminga (eds), *Methods of Human Rights Research* (Antwerp, Intersentia, 2009) 45–58, 52 (value of comparative law to answer normative questions).

development studies. Also, academics who specialise in legal research methods may be able to convince (other) philosophers of science.

How many law professors would find a new home, would naturally depend on the posts available in other disciplines. Moreover, we can distinguish between countries. In the United States, Richard Posner already declared 'the decline of law as an autonomous discipline' more than 20 years ago.[80] Similarly, Jeffrey Lipshaw writes in a recent paper:

> How many legal scholars are still toiling merely in the explication of the self-contained system? Not many, I think. Skim through SSRN for more than a few minutes. To the contrary, almost all of us are bringing law and . . . insights to this discipline.[81]

The UK legal academia is currently in a transitional phase. Although it is still a complaint that the bias towards text in legal research leads to a dislocation from other social sciences,[82] it has also been said that 'legal scholarship today is generally more varied, more lively, more sophisticated, and more self-confident' than fifty years ago.[83] The German situation can be thought of the opposite to the American one. In a book on the proper task of academic law it is stated:

> German legal scholars do not write in English. They do not publish discussion papers. They do not make their texts available online. Their law papers are not subject to peer review. They pay no heed to the impact factor. They do not finance their research from third-party funding. They do not have special research areas (*Sonderforschungsbereiche*). They are epistemologically naïve. They do not draft models. They do not use mathematics. They do not falsify hypotheses. They do not use statistics. They do not carry out interviews. They do not conduct experiments. There are exceptions to each of these statements. But this is a fair description of the large majority of German legal scholarship. In the concert of disciplines, legal studies increasingly seems to be singing out of unison.[84]

If law professors manage to get positions at other schools or faculties, there are some reasons why this could have a beneficial effect on the quality of their research. Such a development could increase the diversity of legal research. Since other faculties and schools would integrate research on law, the current problem of law schools as 'intellectual silos' would be overcome.[85] The non-law faculties or schools may also have better training facilities. For instance, it is a major problem for the emerging field of empirical legal studies in Europe that law faculties have hardly any existing expertise in quantitative research methods. A relocation of such legal research to schools in other social sciences may solve

---

[80] Posner, 'The Decline of Law as an Autonomous Discipline' (1987).
[81] Jeffrey Lipshaw, 'Memo to Lawyers: How Not to Retire And Teach' (2008) 30 *North Carolina Central Law Review* 151.
[82] Maksymilian Del Mar, 'Beyond Text in Legal Education: Art, Ethics and The Carnegie Report' (Working Paper 2008) 32, available at ssrn.com/abstract=1087790. See also Samuel, *Epistemology and Method in Law* (2003) 329.
[83] Twining (n 5) 338f. See also Fiona Cownie, *Legal Academics* (Oxford, Hart Publishing, 2004).
[84] Engel and Schön, 'Vorwort' (2007).
[85] See Dame Hazel Genn, Martin Partington and Sally Wheeler, *Law in the Real World: Improving Our Understanding of How Law Works: Final Report and Recommendation* (2006).

this problem. Finally, the bond with other disciplines may increase the impact of legal research. This can most clearly be seen in the field of comparative law. Insights from traditional comparative law are typically disregarded by courts and legislators, whereas the new quantitative form of comparative law, initiated by financial economists, has had a profound impact on lawmakers all around the world.[86]

Yet, such a re-allocation of legal research would also have its costs. In particular, it could be expected that a dispersion of scholars with interests in legal research into various disciplines would necessarily diminish the engagement between such scholars. This point is, however, not specific about scholars with interests in legal research. Generally, too, research projects may benefit from joined work between, say, historians, sociologists and economists. Such collaboration would then also include legal historians, legal sociologists and law and economics scholars.

The integration of deep legal research into non-law schools and faculties can also lead to frictions. On a general level it could be a problem that other social sciences may just look at law under the aspect of its 'use value'. Knowledge about law would therefore not be regarded as a value in itself but law would merely matter as a 'governance tool'.[87] Moreover, other social scientist would presumably have little interest in 'basic interdisciplinary legal research', ie research which uses the same questions as starting points as traditional legal research but also considers other academic disciplines in order to answer these questions.[88] There can also be problems with more advanced forms of interdisciplinary legal research. For instance, lawyers often look at law and economics in order to escape the narrowness of traditional legal research, but then experience a similar narrowness, namely that according to economists proper research can only consist of modelling or empirics. Empirical approaches to law and economics may also lead to disagreements because economists may treat legal rules as a 'pure datum' whereas lawyers may point out that 'anything but the most banal question is likely to be complex, nuanced, [and] contested'.[89]

D. Conclusion

In a world without law professors only self-referential legal research would disappear. Doctrinal research would persist but it would be done by practitioners and the current oversupply would melt down. At universities, legal research

---

[86] See eg Mathias Siems, 'The End of Comparative Law' (2007) 2/2 *Journal of Comparative Law* 133–50. For a different assessment of the economic analysis of law, see Eric Posner, 'Economic Analysis of Contract Law After Three Decades: Success or Failure?' (2003) 112 *Yale Law Journal* 829.

[87] Engel and Schön (n 73); Collier (n 23) 512.

[88] For this distinction see Mathias Siems, 'The Taxonomy of Interdisciplinary Legal Research: Finding the Way Out of the Desert' (2009) 7 *Journal of Commonwealth Law and Legal Education* 5.

[89] Christopher McCrudden 'Legal Research and Social Sciences' (2006) 122 *Law Quarterly Review* 632, 648.

would continue but it would shift to related fields of social sciences and humanities (politics, economics, philosophy, history, etc). Thus, the threshold would be an 'academic dinner party test': legal research would have to show that it is of interest for other academic disciplines. Most high quality legal research may therefore be able to survive.

IV. ANALYSIS: WHAT NEXT?

It can be concluded that in a world without law professors, legal education and research would not disappear. There would be some changes, but in some respects one could even argue that without law professors the quality of both teaching and research may improve. So does this mean that it would be best to get rid of law professors? Such a conclusion cannot be drawn from this chapter. It was not its purpose to evaluate whether such a scenario would be better than the present system. Moreover, a world without law professors would also have its problems because some forms of teaching and research would fall between the two remaining stools (ie purely professional law schools and law-related activities in other parts of the university).

More generally, it could be objected that the response of this chapter to a world without law professors would lead to a separation between institutions responsible for legal education and legal research. This may be contrary to the very foundations of the university. In the German model, developed by Wilhelm von Humboldt, universities are characterised by the unity of teaching and research.[90] Similarly, many universities in the English-speaking world put emphasis on 'research led teaching'.[91] With respect to law, it is said in the United Kingdom that legal research and teaching are closely linked together: 'if university lawyers were asked which of the two mattered more they would almost all object to the decoupling'.[92] A different picture can be found in the United States, but, here too, it is discussed whether the disjunction between teaching and legal scholarship should be restored.[93]

There is no denying that there can be synergies between teaching and research. However, the scenario of a world without law professors shows that it is possible to separate these two functions. This can also be confirmed by divisions in the current system. On the one hand, there are law teachers without research obligations. In most universities legal practitioners contribute to teaching. Moreover, in the United Kingdom there are universities, such as the former polytechnics and the providers of professional legal education (BPP and College of Law) that

---

[90] For a brief summary in English, see G Hohendorf, 'Wilhelm von Humboldt (1767–1835)' (1993) 23 *Prospects: the Quarterly Review of Comparative Education* 612–23.
[91] For a counterview, see Ian M Kinchin and David B Hay, 'The Myth of the Research-Led Teacher' (2007) 13 *Teachers and Teaching: Theory and Practice* 43–61.
[92] Birks (n 57) vi.
[93] Edward Rubin, 'Should Law Schools Support Faculty Research?' (2009) 17 *The Journal of Contemporary Legal Issues* 139, 162.

provide good legal education but usually do not have research ambitions.[94] On the other hand, there can also be legal research without teaching. Most countries know the status of a research professor. In addition, research councils often finance fellowships that enable professors to focus on research for a substantial period of time.

These considerations already lead to the general conclusions that can be drawn from the foregoing discussion. So what can the scenario of a world without law professors tell us about the current system of legal education and research? First, it is possible to delegate the training of prospective lawyers, and to some extent legal education more generally, to legal practitioners. Second, doctrinal research can also be well done by legal practitioners. Third, in return, law professors should favour deep legal research since we already observe an oversupply of descriptive legal writings. Fourth, since such deep research is often interdisciplinary, there is a need to foster collaboration across disciplines. Fifth and finally, the relationship between teaching and research can be handled in a flexible way. Universities should not prescribe a fixed allocation of time but, if appropriate, let academics specialise in either teaching or research.[95]

---

[94] See also section II. A. above.
[95] For this point, see www.phdcomics.com/comics.php?f=1060.

5

Open or Autonomous? The Debate on Legal Methodology as a Reflection of the Debate on Law

PAULINE C WESTERMAN

I. INTRODUCTION

THE MAIN CONCERN in this collection of essays is to develop a suitable methodology of legal research. That is a normative question. It deals with the methods that *should* be used by legal scholars. Before addressing this question I think it is useful to abandon that normative perspective, and first inquire as to what legal researchers actually do. What kind of questions do they address, which theoretical framework is used? In this article I will argue that the theoretical framework commonly used by scholars who engage in doctrinal analysis is made up from the legal system itself. The legal system is not only the subject of inquiry, but its categories and concepts form, at the same time, the conceptual framework of legal doctrinal research.[1]

If we keep in mind that the legal system performs this double function of both subject-matter and theoretical framework, it is understandable that methodological questions are usually not seen as questions in their own right. They are usually addressed by engaging in reflections on the nature of the legal system itself. Those who maintain that there is a separate methodology for legal doctrinal research which is fundamentally different from the methodology of social sciences, argue that law is an autonomous system, to be differentiated from morals, politics or economics. Those who advocate a kind of legal research that makes room for other perspectives – sociological, philosophical, economical or political – clothe their argument equally in terms of considerations pertaining to the legal system itself, arguing that the legal system is open, responsive or purposive.

In this contribution, I will try to substantiate these claims by paying attention to two rather extreme opposites: the ideal of autonomous law and autonomous

---

[1] Section I. and II. of this contribution are a shorter version of PC Westerman and MJ Wissink, 'Rechtsgeleerdheid als rechtswetenschap' (2008) 440 *Nederlands Juristenblad* 503–507.

legal methodology as expounded by the seventeenth century natural law theorists such as Hugo Grotius and, at the other end of the spectrum, the ideal of purposive law coupled with a critique of traditional doctrinal research as expounded by Von Jhering in the nineteenth century. The two extremes show that the different views on legal methodology are largely informed by the image of law. If that image revolves around the model of corrective justice, it tends to stress legal autonomy. Insofar as that image includes law as emanating from public authority and takes the model of distributive justice as its starting-point, it depicts law as fundamentally open to other systems which leads to the view that legal research also has to include other perspectives as well.

Although much of the debate concerning legal methodology oscillated between both extremes, this does not merely involve a repetition of arguments. New forms of law give rise to new forms of criticism. The article concludes by examining the background of the contemporary uneasiness with law and legal doctrine and the current emphasis on the desirability of an empirical approach to law. It is argued that a single plea for a 'more empirical orientation', although understandable in the light of contemporary legal developments, is in itself not very informative. Even if we decide to substitute legal doctrine for 'empirical' legal science, this involves a choice between different rival – external – theoretical frameworks. Such a choice in itself requires further reflection on the two conflicting images of law that haunted the scene for such a long time.

II. THE PROBLEM OF THE LACKING THIRD

In order to analyse the kind of research that is nowadays commonly carried out at universities in Western Europe, at least in the Netherlands, it is worthwhile to ask what kind of *questions* are usually addressed by such researchers. What are *the kinds* of problems they address and from which theoretical framework do they start?

Now some of us will immediately reply that there are no such questions. They will complain that characteristic for a lot of legal research is the lack of a theoretical framework and the lack of any focused leading questions that will serve as a guideline for inquiry. Most of this research, it is said, consists in pure description of positive law, the existing set of rules, standards, legal arrangements and practices, by an author who does not seem to have any particular question in mind, let alone a theoretical perspective.

Indeed, it should be conceded that an explicit theoretical perspective is often lacking. Most of the time, we can only guess at the questions that drove the legal scholar to writing the lengthy treatises that are produced at law schools. I am myself trained as a philosopher, and I must confess, that initially, in the first years of working at a Law Faculty, I found this lack of theoretical perspective very hard to swallow. How could my new colleagues just sit down to write a piece without knowing what they wanted to know?

My legal colleagues were not disturbed in the least, I found out to my surprise. They seemed to know exactly what they were heading for. Most of them take as a starting-point a certain new legal development, such as a new interpretation of a certain doctrine, or a new piece of European regulation, and just set out to describe how this new development fits in with the area of law they are working in, or, if it does not seem to fit in, how the existing system should be rearranged in order to accommodate for this novelty. So after first depicting what the new development actually consists of, my colleagues commonly address the question of how the new development can be made consistent with the rest of the legal system, in which sense other related concepts are affected and how current distinctions should be adapted and modified. After having described all this, they usually recommend steps in order to accommodate for the new development.

Not only legal developments but also new social developments are studied in this way. Again, existing legal concepts and categories are studied as to their capability to accommodate for these new developments. Recommendations are drawn up in order to fit in these novelties in the legal system in such a way that the integrity and coherence of the legal system is preserved. If new interpretations or new distinctions are proposed, they are commonly justified by reference to the coherence of the legal system as such or by reference to some important underlying legal principles.

The work of my legal colleagues reminded me very much of my mother, who, after having bought a new item for the household, was always busy, for hours it seemed, to find a proper place for it. It commonly brought with it a massive rearrangement of the entire household, cupboards had to be rearranged, but after all that was done our apartment looked as if nothing had happened and as if the order had never been upset.

The comparison with my mother made it clear to me why my colleagues were not disturbed by the lack of a leading theoretical question. Just like my mother, they knew very well what to do. They felt the pressing need to put everything in order. To all concerned there is no doubt as to what the enterprise consists of. That is why legal scholars, in their research proposals, usually confine themselves to pointing out *what* will be investigated (the novel item), rather than *how*. If you ask them about the methods to be employed, most legal scholars retort that this is something that cannot be foreseen or anticipated, but which will be clarified during the process of researching. This again testifies to the appropriateness of the comparison with my mother, who also could not really tell beforehand whether the new item could easily be fitted in or not. This all depends on both the features of the newly bought item and the existing furniture. It does not depend on any third item.

It seems that, indeed, legal doctrinal research is marked by the absence of an independent third, an independent theoretical perspective that enables the researcher to assess the scope and nature of both the new item and the existing order. But how is that possible? How can the legal researcher make sense of these new developments without an independent theoretical point of view? If Popper is right and if all scientific research is necessarily theory-laden,[2] how can the legal researcher do without?

Many people would retort that the lack of a theoretical framework indeed testifies to the fact that the legal researcher is not engaging in any kind of science at all. I do not agree with them. Rather, I think that the *function* of the theory, namely to provide a guideline and a perspective from which the object can be described in a meaningful way, is exercised by the legal system itself. Just as the existing order in the household dictates the work that should be carried out in order to accommodate for the new item, the categories and concepts of the legal system or of the specific area of law dictate the kind and the amount of reconstruction and reinterpretation needed to arrive at the desired end-result. It is with an eye to the existing order that the new item is regarded, interpreted and fitted in. The concepts or categories therefore play a double role. They are elements of the legal system and they are elements of the conceptual or theoretical framework used by the researcher. In legal doctrinal research, object and theoretical framework are identical. The 'how'question is not recognised as a question that is separate from the 'what'-question, for the simple reason that the former collapses into the latter.

III. LEGAL SYSTEM AS THEORETICAL FRAMEWORK

The legal system itself provides the concepts required in order to study a certain legal or social development. That means that the law is not only the object of research, but also the theoretical perspective from which that object is studied. Its concepts and categories are not only concepts used by the officials who make, interpret and apply the law, but are at the same time the conceptual tools to be used by the legal scholar.

If we keep this in mind, some peculiarities of legal doctrinal research can be understood as being essential, in the sense of intrinsically connected to the enterprise itself. The first concerns the practical orientation of legal scholarship; the second refers to the importance of overview and the third concerns the intrinsic normativity of legal doctrinal research.

A. Practical Orientation

As Radbruch remarked,[3] neither legal practitioners nor legal scholars are interested in general propositions. Their primary concern is to deal successfully with a particular case. The judge may handle the case by deciding it; the legislator

---

[2] KR Popper, *Conjectures and Refutations: The Growth of Scientific Knowledge* (Routledge & Kegan Paul, London, 1974).

[3] G Radbruch, *Rechtsphilosophie*, Erik Wolf and Hans-Peter Schneider (eds), (KF Koehler Verlag, Stuttgart, 1973) 217.

may deal with it by drafting a law pertaining to the particular case, and the legal academic may handle it by assigning it a place within the legal system. What all these people actually do when handling the case may vary, but for all of them, legal knowledge is not sought for its own sake but in order to handle the particular case. Furthermore, for *all* these figures, whether practitioner or theorist, the legal system functions as a theoretical framework that selects facts and highlights them as legally relevant ones. That means that the legal doctrinal researcher does not adopt a standpoint vis-à-vis the legal system that is different from the practitioner. The researcher does not set out to understand the legal system, but his or her energy is primarily directed to give sense and to order new cases or developments. The shift from an academic career to a career in the judiciary does not involve a radical change in one's outlook and perspective. It mainly involves a change in what one does with a certain case.

The difference between 'ordering' and 'understanding' is, I think, crucial for grasping the 'point' of doing legal research. Even if Mackor, in her contribution to this volume, would be right in maintaining that legal doctrine is explanatory and non-normative in the same way as other social sciences, the 'point' of doing doctrinal research is still different from those disciplines. One may object to this that disciplines such as economics and medicine are just as practice-oriented. This is certainly true. Yet, in those disciplines it is still assumed that practice is helped by better explanations or a better understanding of the studied object. If we know more about DNA we will be able to cure a certain disease. In legal doctrinal research, however, this seems to be reversed. Legal scholars are not interested in understanding, for instance, the nature of 'duties of care' in the same way as I, as a philosopher, am interested in the nature of these new rules or as political scientists are in explaining their origin and political context. Legal scholars take their existence for granted, it seems, and are primarily interested in the question of how such duties of care can be reconciled with other parts of the system, whether they should be enforced by penal or by administrative sanctions, and so on. This lack of interest is, I think, indicative of the general feeling that an understanding of the phenomenon is not *necessary* for arriving at a coherent order. Whereas in economics and medicine understanding is vital for practical purposes, the purpose of the legal scholar is to 'maintain the system', to use Hage's expression.[4] Since that system also functions as a theoretical framework, legal scholars are often blamed for merely defending their theories – in a dogmatic way – rather than understanding the world. This is the reason why legal scholars can be blamed for being too practice-oriented (maintaining the system as a real workable legal system), as well as for being too academic (maintaining the same system as theoretical framework).

The difference between understanding and ordering also pervades comparative legal research. I think it is helpful to distinguish between comparative

---

[4] Hage's contribution to this book (chapter two) does not explicitly deal with this kind of system-maintenance.

research which aims at increasing one's knowledge about legal systems, their structure or function, and comparative research which is undertaken with the aim of getting some fresh ideas concerning a good and workable order. Whereas the former kind of research may be interdisciplinary in nature, as is maintained in some contributions to this volume, this does not hold for the latter approach to comparative research. There, comparisons serve to arrive in a good order; they are comparable to my mother's frequent allusions as to how the neighbours had arranged their flat.

B. The Importance of Overview

If we keep this in mind, the special features of legal interpretation can be understood. Legal interpretation is not carried out to understand things, but to order matters. However, for such an order, overview is needed. That is why von Savigny wrote that interpretation is only one of three components of legal method. Since interpretation merely deals with laws 'im einzelnen und als einzeln betrachtet', law should also be studied from a systematical viewpoint in which the 'innere Zusammenhang der Begriffe und der Grundsätze' can be reconstructed and finally law should be understood from a historical viewpoint, in which law is seen as a 'successives Ganzes'.[5] Interpretation in itself is not enough. It should be coupled with the systematic effort to see law as integrity and with the historical effort to see law as continuity, ie as indeed the chain novel that appears in Dworkin's writings.[6] That is why 'overview' is thought to be a paramount virtue of the legal scholar. My colleagues do not so much emphasise the virtue of originality, but distinguish between scholars who have and those who lack overview. That is why many legal treatises are written in the form and style of handbooks that give an overview of how a certain legal arrangement has been developed over the ages. It is an expression of the desire to construct the legal system as a whole.

C. Normativity

So, a good legal scholar gives an account of law that maximises both systematic integrity and historical continuity. But these features are not only thought of as virtues of a good theory. Rational reconstruction is not carried out for its own sake, but is a means to a further end. For the judge, that further end consists of reaching good decisions, for the legal researcher the end consists of proposing a

---

[5] Friedrich Carl von Savigny, *Vorlesungen über juristische Methodologie 1802–1842*, edited by A Mazzacane (Vittorio Klostermann, Frankfurt am Main, 1993) 139. See also in the same vein Radbruch, *Einführung in die Rechtswissenschaft*, edited by K Zweigert, (KF Koehler Verlag, Stuttgart, 1952) 242 ff.

[6] R Dworkin, *A Matter of Principle* (Harvard University Press, Cambridge MA, 1985) 158–66.

coherent, meaningful and workable new arrangement. Integrity, coherence and continuity are also, and more importantly, virtues of a good legal system. The criteria for good legal research (good *ordering*) are not separated from the criteria for a good legal system (*order*). What is thought to be good legal research depends on what is thought to be good law. Just as my mother did not regard her ordering activities successful if they did not result in tidy cupboards, the quality of legal research depends on the outcome: the rearrangement that is proposed. The outcome is judged by reference to multiple criteria. Coherence and consistency are such important criteria, as are practicality and effectiveness. Legitimacy or downright fairness may be felt to be as important if not more important than mere coherence.

Many of such criteria are commonly referred to as 'legal principles'[7] and it is good to bear in mind that legal principles also play a double role. They guide legal reasoning by legal officials, but they also serve as points of orientation in doctrinal research. Just like judges and legislators, legal researchers may have different views on the weight of these criteria. In view of the principle or legal equality, one solution may be assessed as better than another, whereas from the viewpoint of justified expectations the reverse may be preferred. Legal principles are theoretical and practical criteria at the same time and are normative and contestable.

Apart from these essential characteristics, that are inherent to the aim of legal research to establish order, we may distinguish a few characteristics that are contingent on the kind of legal system that is studied and which, as I argued, forms the theoretical framework at the same time.

The first of these is the alleged *national* character of legal doctrinal research. The willingness to publish in international journals and to address an international audience is indeed very limited in those areas of law which are mainly relevant within a certain national culture. We have to keep in mind that since the theoretical background is formed by the legal system itself, possibilities of communicating one's findings and solutions in terms that are accessible to foreigners are limited, for they are living in a different legal system. However, the more the national legal order is pervaded by European and international law, the study of law will no doubt internationalise as well. This development is not dependent on the willingness of the scholars themselves, but is simply dictated by the mere identity of object and theoretical framework.

The second contingent feature consists in the degree of *innovation* that is allowed. Contrary to what is often said,[8] legal doctrine is *not* essentially conservative. It can be conservative in times of great social stability. But if a certain legal order is confronted with frequent changes, and if new items should be fitted in regularly, legal research is compelled to be innovative as well. Its aim is not to

---

[7] Note that coherence in itself can rather be seen as a prerequisite for a bundle of legal principles, such as certainty and equality.
[8] See, for instance, the contributions of Brownsword (chapter eight) and Samuel (chapter ten) in this volume.

restore order, but to find a new order, and to rearrange matters in such a way that the new development fits in. In such legal systems reconstructive work is constantly carried out. We have, however, to keep in mind that such a reconstruction is carried out on the basis of the existing network of concepts and categories. If legal scholars are regarded as a conservative lot, that is probably due to the fact that they start from the existing legal order as their theoretical framework. But that does not mean that they are not prepared to propose changes to that order, either piecemeal or drastically if need be.

IV. LEGAL DOCTRINE AND LEGAL SCIENCE

In line with the suggestions of the organisers of the Tilburg conference, I propose to reserve the term 'legal doctrine' for the type of research, sketched above, which draws on the legal system as the main supplier of concepts, categories and criteria. The term 'legal science', although a rather bizarre term in the English speaking world, can then be used in order to denote a mixed bag of other non-legal disciplines that study the law from an independent theoretical framework, which consists of concepts, categories and criteria that are not primarily borrowed from the legal system itself. These may include historical studies, sociological research, philosophy, political theory and economy.

These disciplines, different as they may be, are marked by a more or less independent theoretical perspective and thus do not share the characteristics mentioned above. They *may* be normative – as political theory or philosophy – but they are not necessarily so. In judging and evaluating a certain legal arrangement they *may* be informed by legal principles and other criteria that are generally respected within the legal system, but not necessarily so, and more often than not they go 'beyond' these principles by examining and questioning their status as such. These disciplines may also be practice-oriented, such as economy or sociology, aiming at either enhancing effectiveness or efficiency, but they do not restrict themselves to enquiries concerning the best legal arrangements. They may include other means in order to maximise these virtues. Unlike legal doctrine, the features of legal science are not bound up with the features of the legal system. The degree to which they address an international audience, as well as the degree of innovation are not determined by the degree of internationalisation and innovation by the legal system. These features are determined by the theoretical perspective, which is, in the case of these disciplines, independent from the legal system.

Although I think that this distinction between legal science and legal doctrine is vital for an understanding of what legal scholars do, we should keep in mind, however, that it is not a rigid one. We may differentiate between those who take the legal system as their vantage-point and those who do not, but it is not always easy to decide whether a certain concept belongs to the legal system or whether it is derived from some sort of external theory. How do we draw the line between what is within and what is outside the legal system? Since the distinction between legal doctrine and legal science depends on the question whether the theoretical framework is formed by the legal system or by something else, the distinction depends on how we draw the boundaries between the legal system and its surroundings.

These boundaries are contested. The debate on the proper concept of law is not a mere academic debate concerning the definition of law. It is a debate about the extent to which the legal system *should* be open to political, moral or economical considerations and influences. It is a debate concerning the extent to which law can be considered as autonomous and the extent to which is can be conceived as instrumental to political ends. That means that the debate on the boundaries is a normative debate in itself. So we have a double normativity here. Not only is the task of a legal scholar essentially normative in the sense that the scholar wants to find good solutions, but the scholar's theoretical framework is also normative in the sense that it is dependent on normative assumptions concerning the existence of law as a system in its own right.

What we might expect is that pleas for a legal discipline as a discipline with a proper methodology, distinguishable from other methodologies, are accompanied by claims concerning the autonomy of law. And vice versa, we might expect that as soon as the autonomy of the legal system is questioned or doubted, the legal scholar will inevitably be confronted with the charge that he or she is not only lacking any real subject-matter, but that he or she is also lacking a proper theoretical framework, which is different from the theories of other social sciences. As soon as people start to doubt the possibility and desirability of singling out exclusively 'legal' phenomena, or to capture phenomena by ordering them in exclusively 'legal' categories, thereby differentiating the legal from the non-legal, the question concerning a proper legal methodology will revive in full strength.

V. THE QUEST FOR ONGOING ABSTRACTION

It is time to substantiate these claims and I think that there is no better way to do this than by examining two extreme positions. This is not to suggest that the debate is conducted between extremists of both camps. Rather, most positions can be located at some point between these extremes. However, an analysis of extreme positions will clarify the scope of the playing field. At one end of the continuum we find seventeenth century natural law theorists such as Hugo Grotius, whereas at the other end we hear the radically opposite voice of von Jhering in mid-nineteenth century Germany.

'Let the cobbler stick to his last', Samuel Pufendorf wrote in his foreword to the *De Jure Naturae et Gentium*[9] and do not let 'the theologians and politicians

---

[9] Samuel Pufendorf, '*De Jure Naturae et Gentium libri octo*' (1688), translated by CH and WA Oldfather in *The Classics of International Law* (Clarendon Press, Oxford, 1934).

meddle with business of which they are ignorant'. He is echoing Grotius who, in the prolegomena to his *De Jure Belli*,[10] boasts that before him, no one studied the law 'in a universal and methodological way'. What did Grotius then understand by methodological and universal? He understood that as the systematic effort to deduce *more geometrico*, positive law from the eternal precepts of natural law. In order to describe and to order law in a methodological way, it had, according to the natural lawyers, to be understood as flowing from certain fixed principles, which are universally and eternally valid. The proposal of the natural lawyers can be characterised as the proposal to arrive at ever more abstract foundations, that give sense and unity to what – without such an abstract foundation – would appear scattered rules and regulations.

Obviously, in order to give rise to a true and reliable study of law, these abstract pillars themselves had to be reliable as well. The natural lawyers did not merely understand their quest for ongoing abstraction as a quest for a pure conceptual or rational construction. They did not content themselves with a more or less subjective attribution of purposes in order to give meaning to law. That meaning had to be objective. That means that the abstract foundation from which the body of law was thought to emanate had to be granted objective existence and validity. The precepts of natural law were supposed to be indubitable *axioms* in the mathematical sense of that word.

Although I described this ideal at some length in my book on natural law,[11] I always took this talk about indubitable axioms for granted without realising that in fact, the way these indubitable foundations of law were used is precisely opposite to the way axioms are used in mathematics. Whereas the four Euclidian axioms form the *starting point* for any geometrician, the axioms made up by natural law precepts are end points for the legal scholar. Whereas the former indeed deduce particular propositions from axioms, the latter arrive at the axioms after a long process of abstraction. That is why Radbruch characterised legal interpretation as a 'Zu-Ende-Denken eines Gedachten'. Axioms are the end product of a quest for ever higher purpose.[12]

However, if we are to think of axioms as end points of rational reconstruction, there is something deeply problematical about them. For how can it be guaranteed that others arrive at the same end points? The disturbing possibility arises that what is an axiom for the one will be an arbitrary purpose for the other. The natural lawyers who spoke and wrote with such confidence about indubitable axioms did not see this as a real problem because they thought that

---

[10] Hugo Grotius, '*De Jure Belli ac Pacis Libri Tres*', James Brown Scott (ed), translated by F W Kelsey in *The Classics of International Law* (Clarendon Press, Oxford, 1925) Prol 1.

[11] PC Westerman, *The Disintegration of Natural Law Theory: Aquinas to Finnis* (Brill, Leiden, 1998).

[12] 'Jetzt gilt es, die durch die Konstruktion herausgestellten Zwecke der einzelnen Rechtsinstitute als Mittel zu höheren und immer höheren Zwecken und letzten Endes zu einem höchsten Zwecke alles Rechts zu begreifen und darzustellen. Das unerreichbare Ideal der juristischen Systematik ist die widerspruchlose Konstruktion der gesamten Rechtsordnung aus einem einheitlichen Zweckprinzip heraus und damit die Einheit der Rechtsordnung slechthin.'. G Radbruch, *Einführung in die Rechtswissenschaft*, edited by K Zweigert (KF Koehler Verlag, Stuttgart, 1952) 246.

to everyone in their right mind, endowed with reason, these ultimate truths were self-evident. But even they had to acknowledge that although it is in principle possible to reconstruct rationally and *more geometrico* the fundamental aims and purposes from which all law can be derived and deduced, these aims and purposes are not necessarily the ones that a real legislator has in mind in drafting the law. In other words, despite their rationalist optimism, they had to find a solution to the problem that was so eloquently worded by Radbruch who thought that the ideal of rational abstraction is unattainable, because the quest for ongoing abstraction will inevitably be disturbed by all those actors on the legal scene, in particular the legislator, who have their own purposes, and who use the law as a means to these purposes rather than to the abstract purposes, principles and axioms that the legal scholar has in mind and which form the end point of the scholar's quest for systematic order.

As any librarian knows, any catalogue system is potentially vulnerable to a reality which is much more complex than the tree of catalogue headings. Radbruch calls to mind that there is not one, but two legal systems that are studied by the legal scholar.[13] The first is the systematic unity that results from rational reconstruction; the second is the real 'living' law as an empirical reality. It is not only difficult but impossible to make the two pictures melt into one coherent whole. Empirical reality will always disturb the categories and layers of ongoing abstraction that are brought about by the legal doctrinal scholar.

The seventeenth century theorists, however, did not allow for such duplicity of legal orders. Rather than being resigned to the fact that they inevitably had to take into account the ever changing will of the legislator and the exigencies of everyday life, they kept saying that all these contingencies had to be barred from the law. That is why they insist on drawing a sharp distinction between the fixed and immutable laws of nature on the one hand and the requirements of what they call 'mere expediency' on the other, which are flowing with the changing tide of political life, and are unstable, capricious, and contingent to such a degree that they cannot be the object of a really serious investigation. According to the natural lawyers, the law can only be studied in a methodological and universal way if it *excludes* politics, morals and religion from the law itself. The plea for law as an autonomous discipline is at the same time a plea for law as an autonomous sphere of life. In fact, if we understand legal doctrine as a kind of research in which the legal system itself is both object and theoretical perspective, we are able to understand that the two are insolubly connected.

VI. EMPTY AUTONOMY

The attempt to professionalise legal doctrine was therefore more than just a further application of the Cartesian ideal of mathematical truth. It brought with it

---

[13] In a similar vein, see also the interesting article by James Gordley, 'The State's Private Law and Legal Academia' (2008) 56 *American Journal of Comparative Law* 639–52.

the attempt to carve out a separate realm, autonomous and independent from politics and morals. However, in order to give law such an autonomous existence, its size and scope had to be diminished considerably. If we take Grotius as an exemplary figure – but we might as well have taken Locke or a less well-known figure – its scope is limited by focusing exclusively on the perfect rights between supposedly equal parties in a paradigmatic contractual relationship. These three major limitations will be explained shortly.

A. Law only Deals with Enforcement of Perfect Rights and Duties

A perfect right is defined by Grotius as the right to one's own (*facultas*)[14] and gives rise to perfect obligations in others, such as the duty not to steal or to take someone's life. Such rights and duties are vital for a continued existence of society and are therefore legally enforceable. That is not the case with imperfect rights and duties. The fulfilment of imperfect obligations, for instance the obligation to give alms, to help one's neighbour or to increase the wellbeing of others, may contribute to a pleasant or a good society, but is not indispensable. Society may not be a pleasant one if its members forsake imperfect duties, but is still able to subsist. Imperfect rights; the right to be treated well or the right to assistance and benevolence, are not legally enforceable. One cannot claim a (perfect) 'right' to be treated with benevolence. One can only say that it would be suitable if a man is treated with benevolence in a certain case.[15] In itself the distinction between perfect and imperfect obligations is well-known from Aristotle's work. New is here that Grotius confines the sphere of law to the regulation and enforcement of perfect rights and duties alone.

B. Law only Deals with Corrective Justice

The second move is connected to the first and again makes use of an Aristotelian distinction, namely that between corrective and distributive justice. Although the distinction is well-known, it is still worthwhile to spend a few words on the difference between two types of justice, which are more adequately understood as two types of relationships between people. Corrective justice deals with the relationship between two (private) parties. Rules pertaining to corrective justice are of the type 'If A takes from B, B should be compensated'. Or 'If A misled B, A should pay damage'. In both cases B was injured in his, perfect, right 'to his own' and should be given compensation. According to Grotius, corrective justice 'consists in leaving others in quiet possession of what is already their own'.[16]

---

[14] Hugo Grotius, *De Jure Praedae Commentarius* (1604), James Brown Scott (ed), translated by GL Williams in *The Classics of International Law* (Clarendon Press, Oxford, 1950) I, I, V.

[15] See Westerman *The Disintegration of Natural Law Theory* (1998) 174.

[16] Grotius, '*De Jure Belli* (1925) Prol 10.

What exactly 'his own' consists of, is not a question that can be addressed within the scheme of corrective order. Corrective justice takes a certain state of affairs as its starting point. Even if poor B takes from rich A, B should still compensate A for his or her wrongful act. *Whether* the status quo is justified or *whether* the original relation should be restored at all are questions that fall outside the model of corrective justice.[17]

However, these very questions are addressed, and even unavoidable in the model of distributive justice. Distributive justice pertains to the relationship between one distributor and two or more recipients. The father who has to divide his property among his sons is an often invoked example of distributive justice. The father has to decide the criteria that should determine how his heritage should be distributed. Should he give according to desert, or according to need? Should he give to the obedient, to the handicapped, or to the talented son? And to what end? Here it is not a matter of giving everyone's due, but of deciding what everyone's due *is*.[18]

Grotius asserts that questions pertaining to distributive justice fall outside the scope of law. It is for politicians to decide what everyone's due is. Law confines itself to making sure that people enjoy the 'quiet possession of what is already their own'. The question whether a certain party originally acquired 'his own' in a fair way, is not deemed to be *legally* relevant. Law is exclusively about corrective justice.[19]

C. The Paradigm of Contract

So, the domain of law is restricted by two great moves: the first discards imperfect rights from the legal domain; the second discards questions of distributive justice from law. This does not mean that Grotius confines law to private law. Grotius himself criticises such a simple identification between corrective justice and private law by referring to the example of the father who distributes his property.[20] Nevertheless, we can see that the autonomy of law is preserved and defended by casting legal relations in a form and in a vocabulary which is derived from private law and which pertains to the bipolar relationship between contracting and presumably equal partners.

As we have seen, the principles of natural law, although called 'axioms', are in fact the end point of a process of abstraction. It is no wonder then, that

---

[17] This is why Kelsen criticised these notions of 'eternal justice' as empty shells. See H Kelsen, 'What is Justice?' in H Kelsen, *Essays in Legal and Moral Philosophy*, edited by Ota Weinberger (Reidel, Dordrecht, 1973, orig 1953) 1–26.

[18] For the endless discussion on such criteria, see Chaim Perelman, *Justice, Law and Legal Argument: Essays on Moral and Legal Reasoning* (Reidel, Dordrecht, 1980) and more specifically Ronald Dworkin, *Sovereign Virtue: the Theory and Practice of Equality* (Harvard University Press, Cambridge MA, 2000).

[19] Westerman (n 11) 173–76.

[20] Grotius (n 10) I, VIII, 2.

having discarded from positive law all reference to imperfect rights and duties and all the questions pertaining to distributive justice, the end point of abstraction, the natural laws themselves, are equally devoid from all reference to distributive matters and the allocation of imperfect rights and duties. Like positive law, they are clearly expressed in the bipolar vocabulary of private law. The four precepts of natural law according to Grotius are as follows:

a) To 'abstain from that which is another's and to restore to another of anything of his which we may have'.
b) To fulfil promises.
c) To make good of a loss incurred through our fault.
d) To inflict 'penalties upon men according to their deserts'.[21]

As I pointed out earlier, this formulation of natural law, cast as it is in the framework of corrective justice, undermines its critical potential. These laws may be eternal, universal and immutable, but they fail to tell us how society should look, or how positive law should be designed in order to agree with these immutable precepts. Natural law does not tell us which system or arrangement of property should be established. It only tells us that *if* a certain system of property is introduced, we should abstain from someone else's property. The same applies to c), the precept regarding compensation. Again, what is to be counted as 'loss' has to be decided by positive law. It cannot serve as a standard according to which positive law itself can be evaluated. The precept d) that penalties may be inflicted on transgressors merely points out that one has a right to punish, but it does not inform us on how the right to punish should be executed. So the only natural law that plays a role of any significance here is b) that once we made a promise, we should keep it. In other words, the entire justification of positive law is dependent on the fiction of an original contract.[22]

We see then that Grotius has a certain price to pay for his endeavour to turn law into an autonomous sphere of life. Law has to be disentangled from the intricate dilemma's concerning the proper distribution of goods, nor should it deal with how the specific institutions of society should be designed. Imperfect rights and obligations, aiming for a *good* life rather than for *a* life, fall outside its domain. The role of law thus diminished, it can boast of being erected on immutable and universal grounds. The autonomy of law involves a drastic reduction of what is considered to be legally relevant.

We now understand why Grotius was more optimistic than Radbruch about the possibility of rationalistic legal doctrine. It is by discarding the purposes and aims lawgivers and judicial decision-makers might entertain, that he could cling to the ideal of a rational reconstruction of the entire body of law as emanating from just four eternally and universally valid precepts. The professional doctrinal scholar is only free to attribute the abstract and higher principles if all other – really existing aims and purposes – are banned from the law altogether.

[21] Grotius (n 10) Prol 8.
[22] Westerman (n 11) 161–63.

The paradigm of private law seems to be eminently suited for such an aimless universe. The central assumption is that every citizen should be free to pursue his or her own aim as long as other people are not hindered in the pursuit of their own ends.[23]

VII. REVENGE OF REALITY

Although natural law theory suffered decline, Grotius' proposal for a truly 'methodological approach' was and remained widely followed. Von Savigny's three-staged description of jurisprudence may have been inspired by the *Volksgeist* instead of natural law, but the ideal of legal doctrine as a search for ever 'higher' (or 'deeper') levels of abstraction, remained the same.

The quest for overview and for unifying points of view kept dominating legal discourse; prompting legal doctrinal research in an upward spiral to ever more abstract concepts, principles and values. In fact, one of the great opponents to such a kind of jurisprudence, von Jhering, recognised the underlying ambition of this endeavour when he openly conceded that he had initially fled in the higher world of fixed concepts in order to escape the power of the legislator.[24] Later, von Jhering understood that such a flight was futile. Those who remained in the safe and secure world of legal academia might have avoided all contamination with dirty politics, but the price for that was that legal doctrine became sterile, devoid of contact with the real world, and seemingly unaware of the fact that law had to serve real purposes in the real world, instead of the lofty purposes and ends that are produced by rational construction and which originate in the minds of legal academics.[25]

It is no wonder then, that the criticism that was ventured around the 1850s was mainly directed at the failure of legal research to remain in touch with practical reality. Unlike contemporary criticism, which blames legal doctrine for being unscientific because of its normative and practical orientation, people like von Kirchmann and von Jhering attacked legal doctrine for the opposite reason, namely that it had *severed* the link with reality. Whereas today, legal doctrine is criticised for being more interested in ordering than in understanding, von Jhering and von Kirchmann criticised legal doctrine mainly for the fact that it ordered without having a specific end in view, as the librarian who endlessly arranges and rearranges catalogues and systems without paying attention to the needs of the visitors who come to consult the books. That is why we hear von Kirchmann complaining that legal doctrine always comes too late, running

---

[23] The contribution of Muir-Watt to this volume testifies to the persistence of the private law model also in contemporary attempts to maintain the assumed purity of 'la doctrine' (chapter seven).
[24] 'Ich rettete mich in de höhere Welt der in sich ruhenden Begriffe, an welche die Macht des Gesetzgebers nicht hinanreichte' (R von Jhering, *Scherz und Ernst in der Jurisprudenz: Eine Weihnachtsgabe für das juristische Publikum* (Leipzig 1904) 342.
[25] See Hans Peter Haferkamp, 'The Science of Private Law and the State in Nineteenth Century Germany' (2008) 56 *American Journal of Comparative Law* 667.

behind legal and social developments, dusting concepts that are outdated and no longer in use.[26]

We may be inclined to attribute this criticism to the rapid changes in the social make-up of nineteenth century Germany, but this may be only half of the story. There are good reasons to suppose that Grotius's times were far more turbulent. The important difference is, however, that boundaries began to shift.[27] It was no longer thought possible, nor desirable, to cling to the traditional and neat division of tasks, proposed by the natural lawyers, between law (as maintaining corrective justice) and politics (as taking care of distributive justice), and between law (as the enforcement of perfect rights) and morals (as the enforcements of imperfect rights). In fact, we see that the two great moves by means of which the natural lawyers had tried to ban politics and morals are counteracted in von Jhering's book, *Der Zweck im Recht*,[28] by equally sweeping moves in exactly the opposite direction.

A. Law should Deal with Imperfect Rights and Duties (ie Needs)

In von Jhering's book, *Der Zweck in Recht*, there is no talk of perfect rights and duties, but of needs. Instead of the bipolar model in which the perfect right of the one matches a corresponding perfect obligation of the other, we come across the exemplary model of partnership; the voluntary association of men who join forces in order to pursue a common aim or interest, which consists of the fulfilment of individual and social needs and to provide for social and economic security.

Von Jhering reasons in a direction which is exactly the opposite from the direction taken by the natural lawyers. Instead of stressing the primacy of individual freedom, von Jhering discerns the historical tendency, which he thought to be both inevitable and desirable, towards *de*-privatisation, in which many tasks (eg care for the poor, education), originally entrusted to private parties, are then pursued by first collective associations, and finally by the State itself. With great foresight, von Jhering predicted that the State will, in the end, devour all purposes, and will finally have absorbed the entire society.[29]

It is clear that by 'purposes', von Jhering refers to real aims, to social needs, to safety and security and to material equality rather than just formal equality.[30]

---

[26] JH von Kirchmann, *Die Wertlosigkeit der Jurisprudenz als Wissenschaft,* ein Vortrag gehalten in der juridischen Gesellschaft zu Berlin (Julius Springer Verlag, Berlin, 1846).

[27] I agree here with Chaim Salman, 'Public Law, Private Law, and Legal Science' (2008) 56 *American Journal of Comparative Law* 691–703. Salman points to the link between the dominance of a private law discourse and legal science.

[28] Rudolf von Jhering, *Der Zweck im Recht*, 2nd edn (Breitkopf und Härtel, Leipzig, 1884) vol 1. The entire text can be downloaded or either just read at www.archive.org/stream/derzweckimrecht07jhergoog.

[29] 'Der Staat ist der, der alle Zwecke der Gesellschaft verschlingt, wenn der Schluss von der Vergangenheit auf die Zukunft ein berechtiger ist, so wird er am Ende der Dinge die ganze Gesellschaft in sich aufgenommen haben.' von Jhering, *Der Zweck im Recht* (1884) 304–05.

[30] ibid 354.

They are not the abstract axioms at which the natural lawyers arrive after a long process of reasoning.

B. Law is about Distributive Justice

So instead of confining law to the enforcement of perfect rights alone, it also needs to cover the alleviation of needs. It is not surprising, therefore, that von Jhering also opposes the second great move of the natural lawyers. He does not confine the legal realm to corrective justice. On the contrary, distributive justice is the foundation of the State, and the *raison d'être* of law as primary means of coercion in the service of the State's ends. The main task of the State consists in the fulfilment of needs and to provide for social and economic security.[31] It uses law as a means to that end – hence the title of the book – and much attention is paid to the question on how the State can achieve its ends.

Like Bentham, von Jhering is attracted to the idea that people are most efficiently regulated by the pursuit of their own interests.[32] Punishment is no longer merely a legal reaction to a legal offence, justifiable by the Kantian categorical imperative. Punishment and rewards are seen as the distribution of pain and pleasure,[33] justifiable by practical – governmental – aims. They should be distributed in such a manner that the pursuit of private interests (avoidance of pain; pursuit of pleasure) leads to the pursuit of the collective aims.

C. The Validity of Contracts Dependent on State's Aims

According to von Jhering, law is not confined to the regulation of private interests and aims alone. On the contrary: only the protection of common interests can be called law. The pursuit of private interests alone is *Unrecht*, injustice.[34] It is therefore not surprising that the contract loses its relevance as the model *par excellence* in which all relations are cast. Rather than understanding and legitimising society on the basis of a primordial contractual relation, von Jhering claims that the contract can be understood as a legal arrangement between parties whose wishes are limited by the world surrounding them.[35] Contract law is not a timeless model; instead it is coloured and shaped by a changing environment. If contracts go against the aims pursued by the State or against the

---

[31] Significantly, nineteenth century Germany was far more advanced in drafting social security law than the surrounding democracies (see RC van Caenegem, Geschiedkundige Inleiding tot het recht, vol II Het publiekrecht, 3rd edn (Story-Scientia, Gent, 1994) 175 ff.
[32] He even calls it 'das Wunder der menschlichen Welt, dass eine Kraft die das Kleinste will, das Grösste schaft' (see von Jhering (n 28) 46).
[33] ibid 361.
[34] ibid 292.
[35] ibid 265.

common interest, we should consider them null and void.[36] Autonomy can be limited by state interest.

It is clear then that the second legal system which Radbruch discerned, the empirical, real existing law as emanating from the State and as serving aims pursued by the State, has gained prominence in von Jherings writings. For such a legal system the traditional way of studying legal doctrine was ill-fitted. Its schematisations and categories, its distinctions and concepts and above all its quest for ever higher spheres of abstraction as unifying points of view could not even begin to do justice to the kind of law von Jhering had in mind. His ironical, sometimes even biting comments in *Scherz und Ernst in der Jurisprudenz*[37] reveal the deeply felt inadequacy of legal doctrine to come to terms with a changed reality. It was no longer possible to cut the legal system in two and to throw half of it away as legally irrelevant. It was no longer possible, nor considered desirable, to ban the legislator from the law, just as it was no longer possible to ignore the State's increased tasks and powers.

It is instructive to read Grotius and von Jhering because they represent the two extremes between which the debate concerning the autonomy of law and legal methodology has oscillated. Neither of the two extremes was ever victorious. To this day, the search for unity, continuity and coherence remains to be considered important and indispensable for legal doctrine. They are emphasised not only in the United States, in Dworkin's work, but also in The Netherlands and Germany.[38] The same applies to the dominance of the model of corrective justice as proper to law. Although it has been said that today not even the staunchest liberal dares to venture the opinion that law should exclusively be concerned with corrective justice alone,[39] Grotius's position is still echoed. The only difference is probably that the battleground is for a large part – but not completely – confined to the domain of private law alone. But once we are within that realm, we are informed by someone like Weinrib[40] that distributive justice, as it is largely dependent on the aims the distributor has in mind, is legally irrelevant. Also here, this removal of distributive justice is explicitly linked to the perception of coherence as the ultimate virtue: 'If the law is to be coherent, any given relationship cannot rest on a combination of corrective and distributive justifications.'[41] Therefore: 'the purpose of private law is to be private law'.[42]

[36] ibid 314.
[37] See n 18.
[38] Eloquently phrased by Larenz: 'Sie legt die Gesetze aus, sie bildet dat Recht gemäss den der Rechtsordnung immanenten Wertmassstäben und den in ihr liegenden gedanklichen Möglichkeiten fort und sie sucht immer aufs neue die Fülle des Rechtsstoffs unter einheitlichen Gesichtspunkten zu erfassen, nicht nur um der äusseren Einheit und Übersichtlichkeit willen, sondern auch, um so weit als möglich eine innere Einheit, eine sachliche Übereinstimmung der einzelnen Regeln herbeizuführen.' Karl Larenz, *Ueber die Unentbehrlichkeit der Jurisprudenz als Wissenschaft, Vortrag gehalten vor der Berliner Juristischen Gesellschaft am 20. April* (Walter de Gruyter & Co Berlin, 1966) 12.
[39] Chaim Salman, 'Public Law, Private Law, and Legal Science' (2008) 56 *American Journal of Comparative Law* 697.
[40] EJ Weinrib, *The Idea of Private Law* (Harvard University Press, Cambridge MA, 1995).
[41] ibid 73.
[42] ibid 5.

Choosing between the two pictures of law that Radbruch discerned, Weinrib stresses the idealised, abstract and coherent picture of law with a capital L, at the expense of the other, the empirical concept of law, which is dismissed as a set of regulations issued by politicians, incoherent and arbitrary and therefore not fit to be studied as serious law.

Von Jhering's view has not been defeated either. Although the self-confidence with which Von Jherings advocated a powerful state has, of course, disappeared, we find the purposive nature of law re-emphasised and redefined as a normative ideal in Nonet's and Selznick's plea for a responsive law.[43] And here again, we see that the fiercest struggle is fought within the field of private law. Where someone like Duncan Kennedy[44] points out that the technicalities of contract law are not 'merely technical' but political as well, it seems that the contract has not only been dethroned as primary paradigm for all law, but also lost much of its supposed self-evident neutrality within the confines of private law.

VIII. THE NEED FOR AN EMPIRICAL ORIENTATION

This does not imply that the twentieth century debate is a mere repetition of the nineteenth century dispute. In fact, it seems as if the debate is radicalised. Although von Jhering had stressed that law was instrumental to the realisation of common interests, law was not a '*mere*' means in the sense that it can be substituted by other (non-legal) means as well. For von Jhering, the norm remained central. Law, as the totality of coercive norms, was for him the only conceivable means for the State to exercise authority. The arguments for that view are expounded in his description of the development of norms that proceeded from the simple individual command through the unilaterally binding norm to the bilaterally binding norm. Already the unilaterally binding norm, according to von Jhering, although the product of a despot, bore the nucleus of a just order by its capacity to order in general categories, by means of which at least formal equality could be established. It is here that we see him trying to reconcile the idea of the rule of law as a kind of intrinsically valuable 'Selbstzweck', with the notion of law as coercive order in the pursuit of ends.[45]

In the twentieth century this attempt seems to have been abandoned. Although the importance of formality, of rules and procedures remains to be stressed by the advocates of legal autonomy, it is questioned by those who argue in favour of responsive or purposive law. The value and usefulness of rules have been questioned and criticised in two successive stages. During the first stage the virtues of *precise rules* were questioned; during the second stage the virtues of *rules as such* were questioned.

[43] Ph Nonet and Ph Selznick, *Law and Society in Transition: Toward Responsive Law* (Harper and Row, New York, 1978).
[44] Duncan Kennedy, 'The Political Stakes in "Merely Technical" Issues of Contract Law' (2001) *European Review of Private Law* 7–28.
[45] Von Jhering (n 28) 320–40.

It is not my intention to rehearse the extensive debates concerning merits and demerits of standards or general clauses. It suffices to note that people like Nonet and Selznick, Unger,[46] and Kennedy all seem to welcome the formulation of general clauses, not as an unavoidable evil, but as a way to loosen up the rigidity of the law. General clauses seem to invite rather than to foreclose discussion about their meaning, they even seem indicative of an 'altruistic' attitude[47] and in general they are thought to enable and to facilitate an attitude that tries to see 'beyond' the rule, taking into account the underlying purpose rather than the literal meaning of the rule. It is claimed that law's purposes are better served by flexibility, even at the cost of vagueness.

In the second stage the criticism is more radical than that. Law is not merely thought to be instrumental to underlying purposes, but is seen as *merely* 'a' means, equivalent or sometimes even inferior to other, non-legal means. Instead of von Jhering's acknowledgment of the virtues of norms *as norms* (enabling at least formal equality and some form of order), a fairly dominant view now – for obvious reasons mainly expressed by political scientists and economists[48] rather than by legal scholars – is that rules are ineffective and cumbersome instruments, to be avoided if possible. It is repeatedly pointed out that it costs time and energy to get them adopted and applied, that they invite calculative behaviour and a search for loopholes, and that norm-conformity still does not guarantee the realisation of the desired goals. The more ambitious the regulators are, aiming to cover technically complex issues and socially complex social fields, the less effective the rule seems to be.

Despite increasing scepticism about rules and despite an abundance of experiments with alternative forms of regulating behaviour, rules did not, of course, cease to exist. However, some of them acquired a different form. As I described elsewhere,[49] many rules nowadays prescribe in a fairly direct manner the goals that should be attained. They do that in abstract terms ('employers should further health and safety at work') or in highly concrete terms, in which case they directly prescribe targets to be reached ('by 2015 the global warming effect should be reduced by 10 per cent'). Since rules are increasingly goal-oriented, they may also take the form of benchmarks, which stipulate the *average* performance of

---

[46] RM Unger, *Law in Modern Society: Toward a Criticism of Social Theory* (The Free Press, New York, 1976).

[47] Duncan Kennedy, *A Critique of Adjudication [fin de siècle]* (Harvard University Press, Cambridge MA, 1997).

[48] The well-known book by David Osborne and Ted Gaebler, *Reinventing Government: How the Entrepreneurial Spirit is Transforming the Public Sector* (Addison-Wesley Publishing Company, Reading MA, 1992), set the tone not just for a result-driven form of public management, but also for many complaints about rules, which were identified with inertia, bureaucracy and red tape. The many programmes at the European level, as well as at the level of MemberStates proclaiming 'better regulation', testify to the dominance of this view in legislative circles.

[49] PC Westerman, 'Governing by Goals: Governance as a Legal Style' (2007) *Legisprudence: International Journal for the Study of Legislation* 51–72 and PC Westerman, 'The Emergence of New Types of Norms' in LJ Wintgens (ed), *Legislation in Context: Essays in Legisprudence* (Ashgate, Aldershot, 2007) 117–33.

comparable actors ('the average school produces 15 per cent test-scores of eight and higher').

In all these cases, whether rules are substituted – and complemented – by general clauses, or by non-legal means, or by target-rules and benchmarks, the rule is seen as at best secondary to the achievement of goals. This ongoing instrumentalisation has led to different demands on both legislator and judge. The legislator is required to make an informed choice between legal arrangements and other non-legal means and to evaluate their effectiveness in realising the desired aims. This requirement is, for instance, expressed by the principle of proportionality as it is formulated in the Treaty of Amsterdam,[50] which requires that one should not take any action that exceeds that which is necessary to achieve the desired aim. Since legal rules are generally considered relatively 'heavy' instruments to achieve the desired goals, the principle requires that rule-makers first ask themselves whether the aim justifies such heavy means, or whether lighter, less expensive and more flexible instruments are available and it requires that if the latter are available, they should be awarded priority. For example: if roundabouts can be constructed in such a way that drivers need to limit speed in order to avoid car damage, such a roundabout is deemed more effective than signs specifying the maximum speed allowed, and should therefore be preferred to rule-making.[51] In practice the principle of proportionality requires lawmakers to conduct a so-called Regulatory Impact Assessment (RIA), in order to judge whether legal means are appropriate and, if so, which legal means are most effective, and whether non-legal means are more promising in terms of effectiveness. Not only *ex ante* but also *ex post* evaluations are thought to be desirable.[52]

However, the judge is also confronted with the need for a more empirical outlook. Of course, the judge is not required to choose between different instruments in achieving a certain goal, but he or she has to interpret and apply the rules. General clauses as well as abstract goal-prescriptions should be concretised. Where the judge is confronted with concrete rules such as target-rules or benchmarks, he or she has to make sense of them. The application of such rules requires an assessment of the level of performance that can reasonably be expected. Can we reasonably expect this small chemistry plant to reach the same targets as a large multinational firm? Can we reasonably expect this elderly home to reduce the rate of falling accidents by 10 per cent? In order to answer such questions, empirical and often very technical data is needed, and the judge should at least be able to understand and to interpret that expertise.

---

[50] See the Conclusions of the European Council of Edinburgh, 1992, which were reaffirmed in the Treaty of Amsterdam.
[51] One may wonder whether it is indeed cheaper to build roundabouts than to make and enforce rules.
[52] Regulatory Impact Analysis, a tool for policy coherence, report by the Organisation for Economic Co-operation and Development (OECD), 2009.

IX. AN EMPIRICAL LEGAL DOCTRINE?

The different demands on both legislators and judicial decision-makers lead to different demands on legal scholarship. In a situation in which both legislators and judges feel the need to adopt a more empirical point of view regarding both the content and the effectiveness of rules, it is to be expected that traditional legal doctrine is no longer felt to be adequate or helpful. If we entertain doubts about the merits of rules, what to think then of the activity of analysing, ordering and systematising rules?

It is good to realise once again the difference here with the nineteenth century kind of dissatisfaction with the traditional toolkit of doctrinal analysis: interpretation and construction according to unifying principles. There, the main criticism was that this endless ordering in ever more abstract categories disregarded the use and purpose of the law. Criticism was directed at the librarian who did not keep in mind that his ordered collection of books had in the end to be consulted and used by visitors. Contemporary attacks are more devastating for legal doctrine in the sense that they don't seem to endorse the view anymore that books are valuable or should be consulted at all. In the contemporary debate, the librarian is criticised on the grounds that he or she deals with books without having *investigated their usefulness* and without *understanding their function*. The traditional legal scholar is therefore not only criticised for his lack of practical orientation, as in the nineteenth century, but for his uncritical and above all, unempirical attitude towards rules. The legal scholar is criticised, in other words, for exactly that attitude I referred to above in section III. A., under the heading of 'practical orientation', which seems to indicate that understanding a certain phenomenon is not regarded as a prerequisite for arriving at a good legal order.

This double charge can partly be countered. The *understanding* of rules can easily be improved by adding extra courses to the legal curriculum. Statistics, and courses on methodology of social and natural sciences may provide the modern judicial decision-maker with the necessary tools to interpret the rules as well as the context in which they were established and administered. Consequently, the legal scholar may be required to pay more attention to the context in which legal arrangements are established and in which they operate than is nowadays common. There are good arguments in favour of an approach in which there is no longer a strict separation between law with a capital L and the messy regulations of legislators. There are equally good reasons to ask attention for the way rules are drafted and established, and the various functions they exercise. Phenomena such as multilevel governance should no longer be entrusted to the political scientist alone but should be addressed by the legal scholar as well. If the legal scholar is to engage in the traditional task of constructing a coherent picture of law, he or she is wise to address not only the idealised picture of law but also the empirical one. It is no longer a viable option to discard distributive justice, public authority or the many and complex forms of contemporary rulemaking from the scene. Of course, coherence may in this case be much more difficult to achieve than by mere rational reconstruction, but the attempt is necessary if the legal scholar does not want to end up with only a truncated concept of law that has no connection whatsoever with legal reality.

However, that is only one way of reading the demand for a more empirical orientation. The other way is to read it as the requirement that the legal scholar should abandon his search for internal coherence altogether, should stop with his ordering activities and engage in empirical investigations concerning the usefulness and effectiveness of rules (and possibly to compare them to other means) from an external perspective. Although the subject matter of such a discipline may still be rules and procedures, it adopts a theoretical perspective that is not directly informed by legal categories.[53] Although we have seen that the boundaries between legal doctrine and legal science are contested and dependent on how we regard the legal system, we might plausibly argue that such effectiveness studies have trespassed those boundaries and that here, legal doctrine has definitely been substituted for legal science.

That leaves the fundamental question unanswered whether such a substitution is desirable. Some people would say that it is important to make law 'work' and if this would entail the need for an empirical investigation into the effects and effectiveness of rules, so be it. Why would we deplore the loss of normative legal doctrine, if it is supplanted by a more empirical and more 'scientific' approach?

There are a number of misunderstandings surrounding this claim. The first concerns the confusion around the term 'empirical'. We have seen that indeed, there is a need for a more empirical understanding of law in the sense that its origins, establishment and effectiveness should be investigated instead of discarded as legally irrelevant. But such an empirical outlook does not guarantee objectivity, neutrality or the absence of normativity. Theoretical frameworks that are inspired by sociology of public management are not value-free or nonnormative. The shift towards legal science does not free legal scholarship from its inherent normativity. It merely involves a substitution of one kind of normativity for another.

The second problem is related to this. The term 'empirical' in itself does not say anything about the *kind* of external theoretical framework that should be used. In view of the current emphasis on effectiveness in the pursuit of goals, it is to be expected that the new theoretical framework will be derived from public management studies or economy in which cost-benefit analyses prevail. However, this need not be the only available one. The establishment and working of rules can be studied in lots of other ways, and by the help of vocabularies

---

[53] If we agree with Luhmann to view law as a *Konditionalprogramm* rather than as a *Zweckprogramm*, we may be tempted to think that here legal doctrine stops orienting itself towards this *Konditionalprogramm* and proceeds to study law as if it were a *Zweckprogramm*. *cf* Niklas Luhmann, *Zweckbegriff und Systemrationalität* (Suhrkamp, Frankfurt am Main, 1973, first edn 1968).

that are not necessarily limited to effectiveness alone.[54] The turn towards a more empirical orientation should therefore be seen as *opening up* a whole set of possible lines of theoretical inquiry. One should be cautious not to narrow down one's theoretical perspective to the well-trodden path of studies into effectiveness alone.

The third problem has to do with the double image of law as sketched by Radbruch. As we have seen, it can plausibly be argued that in order to arrive at a coherent picture of law one should not focus on an idealised and necessarily truncated picture of law as based on the model of corrective justice and perfect rights alone. But that does not mean that we should from now on focus entirely on that other half of the legal system: the empirical picture of law as emanating from the will of the legislator and which is pervaded by political decisions about distributive justice. Law does not *cease* to exercise its traditional functions. The modern legal system can still to a large extent be understood as dealing with corrective justice, and as consisting in legal arrangements that aim at facilitating and coordinating actions of citizens who are free to follow their own purposes. Just as it was no good to discard distributive justice as irrelevant to the analysis of law, it is no good to dismiss the requirements of corrective justice as irrelevant to the analysis of law.

To conclude then, even if one maintains that there are no good reasons to separate the legal from the non-legal world, and even if one decides that legal doctrine should melt into legal science, nothing has yet been said on the kind of legal science that should be developed. The rhetorical distinctions that oppose 'normative' legal doctrine to 'descriptive' legal science, or that oppose a closed and narrow-minded legal scholar to the more empirically sensitive scientist, should not mislead us into thinking that once we favour the 'open' and the 'empirical', we are saved from the delusions of the past.[55] On the contrary, the task ahead is to reflect on which issues deserve our attention, and which theoretical tools should be used. Such reflection is largely informed by one's view on the different functions of law itself. That means that once more we have to think critically on the images of law that haunted the scene for such a long time and to inquire into the various and complex ways in which they interact.

---

[54] Eg the 'legal consciousness' movement contributes to the development of such a 'bottom-up' theoretical framework. See, eg MJ Hertogh, *Living Law: Reconsidering Eugen Ehrlich* (Oxford, Oxford University Press, 2009).

[55] I agree here with Hage in his contribution to this volume (chapter two) that empirical social sciences also justify their beliefs against the background of a set of other beliefs.

6

Methodology of Legal Doctrinal Research: A Comment on Westerman

JAN BM VRANKEN

I. INTRODUCTION

THIS CHAPTER HAS been formed as part of a discussion between Pauline Westerman and I. As she stated in footnote 1 of her chapter in this volume, in 2008 she and her colleague Marc Wissink wrote an article in the Dutch *Nederlands Juristenblad* (NJB) on legal scholarship as an academic discipline.[1] She summarised this article in sections I. and II. of her chapter.

I quite disagreed with the article in the *Nederlands Juristenblad* and I criticised it in a paper entitled 'Does Legal Scholarship Benefit from a Broad Floodlight?'[2] The title was inspired by the position Westerman and Wissink took up. They state that in all sciences, the scientific character of the research is determined largely by how and to what extent the data is interpreted within a theoretical framework. This holds true for legal scholarship as well. The only distinction they see is that both the interpretation and the theoretical framework within legal scholarship are viewed differently than in other sciences. They explain these differences through posing two questions: '*What* is being interpreted?' and '*What is the purpose* of the interpretation?'. In answering the first question, the legal scholar differs greatly from, for example, the empirical scientist, but there is much similarity with scholars such as researchers in literature, idea historians or biblical exegetes. The latter scholars devote themselves to texts, just as legal scholars do. The researchers in literature, idea historians or biblical exegetes do this to gain a better understanding of the author or period they are studying. Westerman and Wissink maintain that these categories of scholars may use hypothesis and underlying theory in much the same way as empirical scientists, but only to a certain extent. There is a limit: the text has to be interpreted as a

---

[1] PC Westerman and MJ Wissink, 'Rechtsgeleerdheid als rechtswetenschap'(2008) *Nederlands Juristenblad*, 503. The title is difficult to translate, but I think (hope that) the translation in the text is comprehensible.

[2] JBM Vranken, 'Is de rechtswetenschap gebaat bij een breed strijklicht. Over juridische dogmatiek en methodologie' (Does Legal Scholarship Benefit from a Broad Floodlight? On Legal Doctrinal Research and Methodology) in P Essers, et al (eds), *Met recht. Liber amicorum Theo Raaijmakers* (Deventer, Kluwer juridisch, 2009) 543.

whole as much as possible, which is at odds with strict hypothesis and theories because, they say, '(t)heorizing degenerates into prejudice'. Also, a little further down, applying this to legal scholars: 'The hermeneutical legal scholar benefits more from a broad floodlight.'[3]

I do not object to anything up to this point. On the contrary: it would seem to me that most lawyers wholeheartedly agree that a good legal scholar needs to see the full breadth of the theoretical floodlight, and not only that. They will add that the same is true for practical lawyers, such as judges, barristers, solicitors, company lawyers, notary publics and legislative lawyers. I feel that it can be extended even further, and that all scholars need to meet this demand within their field, if not all professionals. Someone with a broad view is able to think associatively and can be creative and innovative, for example when they make connections that others do not see, or shed new light from an unexpected angle on an existing problem. On the other hand, it is far from impossible for a specialist in a specific area of law or another field to present surprising ideas, especially because they have such a full command of the subject.

My fundamental objection against Westerman and Wissink is, therefore, not that they expected a broad view from legal researchers, but that they consider this broad view incompatible with any other theoretical perspective than 'the' legal system. In their article they posit that in legal scholarship only one floodlight, meaning one hypothesis, one theoretical perspective is valid: the consistency and coherence of the legal system. The legal scholar must interpret the rules and principles of law with the aim of integrating new social or legal issues into the existing legal system.

> But how is this done? The only way is by using certain basic concepts and principles *within the system itself*. . . . This means nothing less than that the legal system, which is the *subject* of the research, is also the *theoretical* framework. In legal scholarship, object and theoretical perspective are the same.[4]

The way I understood their view, is that they fear another hypothesis, another perspective would fail to encompass the full extent of available texts and therefore the fullness of law and the legal system. Westerman and Wissink do not see the system as static, closed or unchanging, as integrating something into the system is also changing the system to fit a reality that is constantly in motion. This means that legal systems are open and continuously developing.

They identified three consequences of the identity of object and theoretical perspective in legal scholarship: first, the tight link between legal scholarship and practice; second, the predominantly national orientation, even though the advancing influence of Europe and the international community will result in a more internationally oriented legal scholarship; and third, that the ability to innovate is important, but not the only virtue of good scholarship, because good legal scholars

[3] Westerman and Wissink, 'Rechtsgeleerdheid als rechtswetenschap'(2008) 504.
[4] Westerman and Wissink (n 1) 504 (italics in original).

must also be ingenious in finding arguments, they must be able to fit these into a logical framework, and above all, they must have a *comprehensive view* of a certain field. A comprehensive view here means that they should be able to encompass the entire breadth of the theoretical floodlight - the legal system -, which enables them to consistently accommodate the various perspectives.[5]

In chapter five of this volume, Pauline Westerman makes crystal clear from the outset that

(a) she does not take up a normative position, but merely inquires as to what legal researchers commonly and actually do, ie conducting legal doctrinal research[6][7];
(b) in section I. and II. of her paper she exclusively confines herself to an analysis and description of what she considers the characteristics of that prevailing type of legal scholarship; and
(c) in accordance with the suggestion of the organisers of the Tilburg Conference, she qualifies other forms of legal scholarship as 'legal science', distinctive from 'legal doctrine'.

The starting point of my comment is that Westerman repeats the key characteristic of legal doctrine she identified in the NJB article several times: legal doctrinal scholars not only use the legal system as their *subject* of inquiry, but also as their *theoretical framework*.[8] In this paper she has embedded her central finding in a new[9] discussion, which concerns the extent to which a legal system can be

---

[5] ibid.
[6] Which is distinguished from various other types of legal scholarship. Without attempting a comprehensive listing, I mention inside out and outside in approaches; descriptive, prescriptive, and normative research; hermeneutic, argumentative, explanatory, axiomatic, logical, designing and normative legal scholarship; legal doctrinal, multi-disciplinary, socio-legal and empirical research. The differences between these variations of legal scholarly research are immense. Some of them partly overlap, for example legal doctrinal and hermeneutic, argumentative, logical or explanatory research. Some others, such as empirical and multi-disciplinary research, are strongly on the rise and are almost fundamentally different from legal doctrinal research, both to nature and method. For references, see n 7.
[7] A short and incomplete selection: R Brownsword, 'An Introduction to Legal Research' (2006) (www.welcome.ac.uk/stellent/groups/corporatesite); EL Rubin, 'Legal Scholarship' (2001) *The International Encyclopedia of the Social and Behavioural Sciences*; RA Posner, 'Legal Scholarship Today' (2001–2002) *Harvard law Review*, 1314; N Duxbury, *'Jurists & Judges, An Essay on Influence'* (Oxford, Hart Publishing, 2001); BH Bix, 'Law as an Autonomous Discipline' in P Cane and M Tushnet (eds), *The Oxford Handbook of Legal Studies* (Oxford, Oxford University Press, 2003) 975; F Cownie, *Legal Academics: Culture and Identities* (Oxford, Hart Publishing, 2004); Chr Crudden, 'Legal Research and the Social Sciences' (2006) *Law Quarterly Review* 632; M Van Hoecke, 'Hoe wetenschappelijk is de rechtswetenschap? (How Academic is Legal Scholarship?)' (Inaugural lecture, Gent, 2009; M Van Hoecke, *'Is de rechtswetenschap een empirische wetenschap?'* (Is Legal Scholarship an Empirical Discipline?, inaugural lecture Tilburg (The Hague, Boom Juridische uitgevers, 2010); Martijn Hesselink, 'A European Legal Method? On European Private Law and Scientific Method' (2009) *European Law Journal* 20.
[8] The consequences Westerman identifies in her paper are slightly, but not fundamentally, different from those in the Nederlands Juristenblad article: practical orientation, the importance of overview as a paramount virtue of a legal scholar, normativity of the legal research (aiming at finding good solutions), national orientation and innovation on the basis of the existing legal system.
[9] New, not in the sense of a discussion on a topic that was not discussed before, but new in the sense that the *Nederlands Juristenblad* article had a different context.

considered as autonomous, and the extent to which the legal system *should* (her italics) be open to political, economical, financial, social and cultural considerations and influences from outside the legal system. She uses her analysis and description of legal doctrinal research and its central finding as one extreme position on legal scholarship, which she compares with other approaches. Her line of argument is, in short, that different views on legal research (what should be done?) lead to different legal methodologies, but that in the end both are reflections on what one considers to be law.

II. THE IDENTITY OF SUBJECT AND THEORETICAL FRAMEWORK: FOUR OBJECTIONS

The *first* objection against the central finding is that it is often far from clear which system shapes the perspective of the researcher, or should shape it. In many cases the researcher first needs to select the appropriate system before they can start. In contract and tort law alone, there are hundreds of systems (and subsystems, but I will ignore that complication).

This can be illustrated with some examples. Rent law, labour law and financial law each constitute their own system. However, they can be connected by general contract and tort law, which would lead to a different systematisation and possibly to different answers to questions. It would also be possible to class them, together with purchasing and misleading advertising, for example, as part of consumer law, an area of law with accents that partly differ from general contract and tort law. Another example is cyber law, a relatively new field. The question is whether it is comparable to offline law, or whether it has its own concepts, rules and principles. For now, this question remains unanswered.[10] So what should be done? The same is true for private law that originated in Europe. Is this a separate system, distinct from national systems, because it is primarily aimed towards the internal market and protecting consumers, while national private law strives to serve a wider range of interests? If one assumes this to be the case, which is the most common opinion, both systems need to be tailored to each other, which means that European private law needs to be integrated in national systems. This is often a painful process, because the two systems are incompatible in many ways. In this approach, researchers remain focused on their own legal system and the orientation is primarily national. A newer, and more difficult, approach is to view private law in Europe as a single, multi-layered system, in which elements of public and private law, procedural law and substantive law, national law and European law, state and non-state law must be forged into a new whole.[11]

[10] Compare, among others, the overview in R Dunne, *Computers and the Law* (Cambridge, Cambridge University Press, 2009). More on contract law alone can be found in, for example, L Trakman, 'The Boundaries of Contract Law in Cyberspace' (2009) *University of New South Wales Law Journal* 159 (http://law.bepress.com/unswwps/flrps09/art13).
[11] Hesselink, 'A European Legal Method?' (2009) 39–43.

In all these examples, the answers to legal questions depend on the system from which the researcher tries to find them, in order: from rent law, general contract and tort law, consumer law, cyber law or European law as a single, multi-layered system. How can they determine their choice, meaning how can they choose what floodlight to use, the system that must be the starting and ending point of all legal doctrinal research as Westerman analysis describes it? It is as clear as day that this choice needs to be made first. This holds true on a micro-level as well. Here, we no longer speak of systems, but rather of doctrines. Does the case fall under the reversal of the burden of proof, or under the duty to provide prima facie evidence? Should the legal question be placed within the framework of dissolution of contracts, or in the wider perspective of remedies (dissolution, cancellation, annulment and adaptation of contracts)? Does it concern kindness among friends without legally binding force, or a binding contract? Should it fall under the rule of unlawful enrichment, contract or tort? Sometimes doctrines disappear, such as acceptance of risk, or new ones develop, such as duties to inform and, of late, duties of care. It would be easy to provide dozens of examples, but my point is made.

The *second* reason why I disagree with the key characteristic of legal doctrinal research Westerman identifies – the identity of subject and theoretical perspective – is that, even when the applicable system is certain or has been chosen, it is often not clear which viewpoints fall within that system and which do not. The congealed weighing of interests that is anchored in legal rules[12] and which results in relevant viewpoints is not set in stone. A system is, as already said, always in development and thus basically open. The validity of viewpoints needs to be tested over and over again, to determine whether their relative worth has changed, and to see whether new viewpoints or factors have arisen. These tests are always necessary, even more so when the question concerns new situations and developments which sometimes require that existing distinctions are amended or expanded, so that a productive new weighing of interests can yield socially useful and improved law. Sometimes, the researcher comes up with a surprising new angle or association and presses for changes in the system. Is this allowed, desirable or perhaps even necessary? I think the answer is an emphatic yes, but in relation to the view that subject and theoretical perspective coincide, the question is how to determine whether the new balancing, new viewpoints, new distinctions or new angles the researcher wants to introduce stay within the limits of the developing system, especially taking into account that changes often have unforeseeable consequences in other parts of the law or for other doctrines. Yet, how do we clarify what a researcher is allowed to do?

In answer to this question I will give some examples. According to the prevailing opinion, codes of conduct, guidelines, and other forms of self-regulation or co-regulation do not play a significant part in contract and tort law at present.

---

[12] For clarity reasons rules are used here as a collective term. They include principles, doctrines, viewpoints, vague standards, judicial decision and so on.

Do researchers step outside the field defined for legal doctrinal scholars when they argue that these factors should be included[13]? Another example is the inflexible stance towards limitation of action periods, which in the past was justified by pointing towards legal certainty. The inflexibility has been significantly softened over the last few years. A whole range of elements that until recently were not acknowledged are now taken into account. The groundwork for this change was laid partly in literature. Did those who argued for more flexibility back then still use the (open) system as their starting and ending point, as is demanded in legal doctrinal research according to the analysis of Westerman? The same is true for those who argue for the acknowledgement of revindicatory claims towards bank accounts in certain situations. Following present standards these claims fail, but would it not be possible for this to change, as happened with other changes that seemed impossible 30 years ago?

The question is the same for all these examples: when and why does a viewpoint or argument remain within the limits of the system, and when and why does it not? Nobody is able to answer this question beforehand and that is not unsurprising, because developing law does not proceed step-by-step, along a predictable route. There is no preconceived aim, no master plan; there is only a debate, in which some dare to go further than others. I welcome that. In the end legal research, as other kinds of academic research, benefits more from creativity, fantasy, an open mind, contrary thinking and paradigmatic change than it would from rigid guarding of the system. Criticisms and new ideas may be discontinuities today, but tomorrow they could grow into established opinions. Whether they do will only become apparent in hindsight, within the debating forums where colleagues meet. This is why I am convinced that the idea of the legal system as both the starting and the ending point of legal scholarly research is untenable in itself. Eventually, the system is what researchers themselves make out of it, and that can vary from strictly delineated to almost boundless openness. One must not be too quick in seeing threats to 'the' system. It has been proven that 'the' system is quite resilient, not only in the long term but in the short-term future as well.[14] I cannot think of a better sound bite and final thought than the title of an article by HCF Schoordijk: 'We should not View the Law as a System, before Systematising it'.[15]

My *third* objection against Westerman's central finding relates to the role of the researcher. What is the driving force behind progress in law? What are the societal and legal developments which the researcher has to understand in order to 'translate' or 'integrate' them into the legal system? According to Westerman's

---

[13] I Giesen, *Alternatieve regelgeving in het privaatrecht* (Alternative Rulemaking in Private Law) (Deventer, Kluwer juridisch, 2007) 68–69 and 98–99.

[14] W Snijders, who drafted the 1992 civil code and civil procedure code in the Netherlands, in an article on irregularities in property, contract and tort law, (2005) *Weekblad voor Privaatrecht en Notariaat* (WPNR) 79 and 94 (passim).

[15] HCF Schoordijk, 'Het recht moeten wij niet denken als een systeem vooraleer wij er systeem in gebracht hebben' (translated to 'We should not View the Law as a System, before Systematising it') (2008) *Nederlands Juristenblad* 1720.

view, the researcher is mainly a follower and I think this is simply not the case. It completely ignores the choices that, in my opinion, researchers always need to make before they can start translating and integrating: what system should be chosen and which (new) viewpoints should be included, and what should be their relative weight? I explained that legitimate choices can be made from completely different perspectives other than just the consistency and coherence of the system. The researcher enjoys a large degree of freedom here, with very few, if any, prior limitations. Whether the chosen perspective yields usable or better law, can only be judged in hindsight. A consequence of this is that the researchers can start their work independently from societal and legal developments. They do not need to wait for an 'assignment' before employing their creativity. They can come up with ideas, posit theories, and apply various approaches off their own bat, without following topical casuistry, if they feel they can advance the law in that way. A good, creative researcher would do so. They are, as I attempted to say previously, people who think outside the box, who ask themselves the question: could this be done differently? They are people who draw inspiration from a wide range of internal and external comparative law, or from insights from other disciplines, and who are willing to push boundaries and, where necessary, break them. Indeed, why should legal scholars always consider themselves bound by current law?

Perhaps one is inclined to answer that the kind of researcher I welcome here is not a legal doctrinal scholar anymore. I do not stick to sharp distinctions. Therefore, to make myself clear and to avoid easy escapes: even if I limit myself to legal doctrinal research, and accept Westerman's analysis and description thereof which exclusively emphasises the legal system as the starting and ending point, the view that the desirable broad theoretical framework of the researcher is incompatible with another floodlight than 'the' system, does not hold water. 'The' system is not only a collection of connected rules,[16] but also a collection of perspectives.[17] Each rule can be approached from a large number of divergent perspectives. The notice of default in the context of failures to comply, for example, can be viewed from the perspectives of the right to be heard before granting legal action, of the need to protect parties against hasty action, of being counterproductive towards amicable settlements, or from the perspective that it does not contribute to harmonising European private law. Meaning and knowledge are always dependent on perspective. I feel it is useless to deny this reality. Would it not be better for the doctrinal researcher to clearly formulate and justify the perspective from which they depart?

This is unusual in law. Legal scholars want to tackle the whole problem at once. However, influenced by the debate on methods and legal methodology, the awareness that a more specified focus might be desirable is gaining ground. It

---

[16] See for the concept of rules, n 12.
[17] M Doorman, *Steeds Mooier. Over de geschiedenis en zin van vooruitgangsideeën in de kunst*, thesis (Amsterdam, Bakker, 1994) (5th edition, 2005) links progress in art to an increasing number of perspectives. I consider this a fruitful idea.

would offer the opportunity to build on the work of others, and from there add something new. This can be achieved with a well-formulated research question in which the legal scholar explains and justifies the choices he or she makes. In his PhD thesis, Tijssen noted that of the 90 dissertations he investigated, which were all defended between March 1999 and June 2006, more than 50 per cent had a clearly formulated research question. Quality remains an issue, but both the percentage and the quality will probably see significant improvements, because meetings with young PhD researchers in Tilburg, Louvain, Ghent and Florence showed that there is a great need for clearly defined, attainable research questions, and much effort is poured into them.[18]

In light of the above, I can be brief in describing my *fourth* objection. Consistency and coherence of the legal system as the only allowable and obvious perspective for legal doctrinal research, is far from evident. Instead, it is based on a normative choice. However, why should a consistent and coherent system be preferable over, for example, social justice, improving the wellbeing of people, the proper functioning of markets, practicality, functionality, effectiveness or Europeanisation and globalisation?[19] If we follow Westerman's analysis and description, we have to conclude that no choice exists between perspectives within legal doctrinal research. As soon as legal researchers choose another framework than consistency and coherence of the legal system, they are no longer conducting legal doctrinal research, but legal science. I strongly disagree because even from a very strict doctrinal approach I hope to have shown that more perspectives than consistency and coherence are possible and desirable, but, again, I do not stick to definitions.

III. METHODOLOGICAL CONSEQUENCES

In my critical review, the central finding of Westerman's analysis and description of doctrinal legal research, that the *subject* and *theoretical framework* of this type of legal scholarship are one and the same, turns out to be untenable for at least four reasons.

First, because there are hundreds of different systems in contract and tort law alone, which are subject to constant change when old ones disappear and new ones arise.

Second, because all systems are open and in a never-ending state of development, it is impossible to say beforehand what new arguments or viewpoints are allowable or not. *Third*, because the researcher is more than someone who just translates and integrates new developments in law and society in one or more of

---

[18] The courses were held by my colleague RAJ van Gestel, who participated in the 2007 founding of the Research Group for Methodology of Law and Legal Research, School of Law, Tilburg University (www.tilburguniversity.nl/faculties/law/research/methodology). A consultation with individual PhD researchers on their intended project was always part of these courses.

[19] I drew inspiration from Hesselink (n 7) 34–36.

the many systems. Researchers also have an independent position in furthering the law. The wide view – the knowledge and the overview that a researcher has or should have – is the essential inspiration for finding new perspectives that can contribute in improving the law. An erudite researcher is better equipped for innovation than a narrow-gauge lawyer.

Fourth, because choosing consistency and coherence of the legal system as the only valid perspective is a normative choice, which without further substantiation is no better or worse than many other perspectives, either in connection with them or substituting them.

The central idea of the above is the inevitability of making choices, not only between the legal doctrinal approach and an external approach, as Westerman points out in her chapter in this volume, but also within the doctrinal approach itself,[20] the four issues I indicated. As soon as a researcher has to make choices, the consequence is that they have to explain or justify them. That is part of what is required in the academic world. This world is based on the assumption that academic scholarship, as Tijssen states,[21] is an open, democratic, and self-reflecting enterprise. It does not accept immunisation against critical assessment. On the contrary, it demands transparency. Why does the researcher choose the perspective of Europeanisation and not, for instance, the consumer perspective? This is a methodological question. In legal doctrinal research, however, methodological questions are quite unusual and, to be frank, they are hardly needed if the idea of the identity of subject and theoretical framework would be correct. Why explain the choice for the perspective of consistency and coherence of the system if this is the only possible one? In that view researchers would merely have to choose whether they prefer to do legal doctrinal research and not, for example, empirical research, but as long as legal doctrinal research strongly prevails in legal scholarship, nobody will ask.

This was the situation until some years ago. Nowadays, we have vehement debates on both the academic nature of the legal discipline – is law an academic discipline? – the various types of legal scholarship which can be distinguished[22] and their methodological consequences. In this comment I only mention this debate without going into the diverse and manifold reasons.[23] I limit myself to

---

[20] The same applies, of course, to the external perspective if the researcher chooses such perspective.

[21] HEB Tijssen, De juridische dissertatie onder de loep. De verantwoording van methodologische keuzes in juridische dissertaties ('Legal Dissertations through a Magnifying Glass. Justification of Methodological Choices in Legal Dissertations') (The Hague, Boom Juridische uitgevers, 2009) 120–22, 137 ff and 183 ff.

[22] See n 6 and n 7.

[23] To give an impression of this diversity, I mention, among others, (a) the increasing contextualising of law, where more than just legal doctrinal elements are considered; (b) the increasing popularity of law and movements, especially law and economics and law and social sciences, as a symptom of a wider movement, in other fields as well, towards more multidisciplinary research, because the problems that need to be solved cannot be reduced to mono-disciplinary limits. The multi-disciplinary evaluating committees of funding institutions in countries and in Europe follow suit and strengthen this trend; (c) the need of primarily regulators and policymakers (and judges as well) for more advanced knowledge regarding the effects and effectiveness of the intended rule (or

the observation that methodological issues in doctrinal research are emerging.[24] The Tilburg Conference, of which the current book is the result, reflects this growing, international attention.

Where multi-disciplinary[25] and empirical[26] researches are concerned, there is no disagreement. Methodological questions are unavoidable. The researcher not only has to gather knowledge on what is required in other disciplines for reliable and valid research, or the demands placed on empirical research, but he or she also has to adapt the research to the peculiarity of legal scholarship. What determines that peculiarity? Answering that question inevitably leads to legal doctrinal research. Some, including myself, maintain that this type of research would benefit from a better methodological justification. One of the underlying reasons is that such a justification would enable putting into operation the generally accepted quality criteria for legal research: originality (innovation), rigour, significance, thoroughness and exploring boundaries.[27] Developments in, among others, Belgium and England, point to the same or similar view.[28] Primarily a well-formulated research question, which I referred to at the end of my third objection, forces scholars to consider the innovative contribution they expect

---

judgments), which requires a lot of knowledge in the fields of social sciences and economic evaluative research; (d) dissatisfaction with the common approach, which unavoidably leads to a certain degree of tunnel vision. The desire to break through that limitation is nothing new and far from limited to legal research (even though it itself tends to lead to a different form of tunnel vision); (e) the worldwide increasing interest developing criteria to assess the quality of legal research, eg on behalf of research assessment exercises, funding institutions or awards committees.

[24] In 2007 we established in Tilburg the Research Group for the Methodology of Law and Legal Research (www.tilburguniversity.nl/faculties/law/research/methodology). The 2009 Tilburg Workshop is one of the research activities of the Group.

[25] Outside of law and economics and law and literature, multi-disciplinarity can be found primarily in what could be described as Law and Social Sciences, which is also called New Legal Realism. See, for example, ThJ Miles and CR Sunstein, 'The New Legal Realism' (2007) (www.law.uchicago.edu); H Erlanger et al, 'Is It Time for a New Legal Realism?'(2005) *Wisconsin Law Review* 335. For the UK, see for example the overview in Crudden, 'Legal Research and the Social Sciences' (2006).

[26] Empirical legal research has a long history in the US, although its track record is far from flawless (for example Heise, Uhlen, Korobkin, Epstein and King, who are among those mentioned in G Mitchell, 'Empirical Legal Scholarship as Scientific Dialogue' (2005) *North Carolina Law Review* 167. Empirical research in the US recently received an enormous boost from Empirical Law Studies (ELS). ELS is developing energetically, partly because of the involvement of a number of top law schools (Cornell, New York, and Austin Texas) which provide money and influence. For now, the conducted research is exclusively quantitative and statistical. The research is large-scale and aimed at developing large databases which will be accessible to everyone. A sympathetically critical evaluation of ELS can be found in E Chambliss,'When Do Thoughts Persuade? Some Thoughts on the Market for Empirical Legal Studies'(www.nyls.edu).

[27] This includes inter- or multi-disciplinary, international, and internal, external or historical comparative legal research.

[28] See for Belgium www.vlir.be/media/docs/Onderzoeksbeleid/ranking_resultaat.pdf, for England refer to www.hero.ac.uk.rae and T Sastry and B Bekhradnia, 'Using Metrics to Allocate Research Funds: A Short Evaluation of Alternatives to the Research Assessment Exercise' (2006) *Oxford Higher Education Policy Institute*; R Johnston, 'On Structuring Subjective Judgements: Originality, Significance and Rigour in RAE 2008' (2008) *Higher Education Quarterly* 120, 132–33; Society of Legal Scholars, AHRB Journal Reference List, 23 January 2005. This can be retrieved from: www.legalscholars.ac.uk/pubdocs/05/joint_letter_ahrb.pdf.

to make, the sources they need to consult, and the methods they need to use to answer the research question.[29]

To avoid misunderstandings, I immediately add that a proper methodological justification is no guarantee for high quality research, as quality always depends on the contents, but it does make it easier to determine when quality is *lacking*. It sets a minimum limit. Not everyone agrees however, far from it. The debate on whether or not a proper methodological justification of legal doctrinal research is desirable or even possible is still raging. However, I applaud the fact that the discussion has started, even though the debate is still in its infancy, as is shown in this comment: we are still struggling with the preliminary issue of determining the main characteristics of legal doctrinal research.

---

[29] RAJ van Gestel and JBM Vranken, 'Legal Scholarly Papers. Towards Criteria for Methodological Justification'. Exploring Three Methodological Quality Criteria for Legal Research (2007) *Nederlands Juristenblad* 1448. An English version of the article is forthcoming; a draft is already available (j.b.m.vranken@uvt.nl).

7

The Epistemological Function of 'la Doctrine'

HORATIA MUIR WATT

I. ON THE CHOICE, AS A TOPIC, OF THE EPISTEMOLOGICAL FUNCTION PLAYED OUT IN THE FRENCH LEGAL TRADITION BY 'LA DOCTRINE'

IN PRESENTING THE research programme for this workshop on legal scholarship, Mark Van Hoecke proposes that 'in order to develop a suitable methodology of comparative law one needs a better view on the methodology of legal scholarship within domestic legal systems'. However, like Geoffrey Samuel,[1] I am not entirely convinced that this is so, at least insofar as it might suggest that any methodology in the field of comparative legal research is in some way the mirror image of its domestic counterparts. On the other hand, it is certainly true that understanding the role assigned to legal scholarship within any given legal tradition may provide considerable insights into the way in which that tradition portrays itself for the benefit of its own actors or beyond, how it functions and evolves, or how it balances the various political forces which play out in the arena of legal power. Students of comparative law are familiar, for instance, with the traditional distrust shown by English courts towards the learned writings of living authors and, at least until recently, the correlatively undeveloped state of speculative academic scholarship, as opposed to the remarkable influence of doctrinal writings on the courts in civilian legal systems.[2] They are told that this difference bears a direct relationship to the composition and hierarchy of the sources of law – or, what is presented, significantly, in the civilian legal vocabulary as a 'theory of sources' – within these different traditions, in which

---

[1] See the author's contribution in chapter 10 of this volume.
[2] An excellent account is to be found in Neil Duxbury's, Jurists and Judges. An Essay on Influence (Oxford, Hart Publishing, 2001); P Birks, 'The Academic and the Practitioner' (1998) 18 *Legal Studies* 397; B Markesinis, 'A Matter of Style' (1994) 110 *Law Quarterly Review* 607; J Bell, 'Sources of Law' in P Birks (ed), English Private Law (Oxford, Oxford University Press, 2000) 43; H Lawson 'Doctrinal Writing: A Foreign Element in English Law?' in E Caemmerer, S Mentschikoff and K Zweigert (eds), *Ius Privatum Gentium, Festschrift für Max Rheinstein zum 70. Geburtstag am 5. Juli 1969* (Tübingen, Mohr, 1969) vol I, 191; A Braun, 'Professors and Judges in Italy: It takes two to Tango' (2006) 26 *Oxford Journal of Legal Studies* 665.

the courts are respectively all-powerful or reduced to the Napoleonic status of automat, and therefore either majestically oblivious to academic guidance or on the contrary subjected to scholarly interpretation of their own case law.

While this received comparative wisdom certainly corresponds to the official judicial and academic 'self-portraits' which have formed the legal mentality in each of these traditions,[3] Mark Van Hoecke's invitation to explore the relationship between domestic legal scholarship and comparative law provides an interesting opportunity to further the exploration of the foundational discourse which, within the civilian tradition, and particularly in France, personifies academic legal scholarship as 'la Doctrine', made flesh through the scholarly community of jurisconsults.[4] At least in its current representation as an 'entity',[5] 'la Doctrine' may indeed be an idiosyncratic feature of the French legal heritage. Although it is clearly akin to the German *Professorenrecht*, it has come to mean both the *droit savant* and the *société savante* which produces it. As the latter, it is represented as exerting influence over the judiciary, whose decisions, increasingly 'massified',[6] it rationalises and orders;[7] by the same token, it holds the keys to the way in which legal knowledge is framed and transmitted within the French legal tradition. From an external perspective, Mitch Lasser's 'Judicial self-portraits' has already suggested that 'la Doctrine' developed essentially as a discursive device secreted within a tradition geared to the muzzling of the judiciary.[8] Attempting to respond, therefore, to Mark Van Hoecke's working proposal, this chapter explores the epistemological function played out in the French legal tradition by 'la Doctrine', and attempts to situate 'la Doctrine' within a cultural matrix made of forms of legal knowledge and methods of reasoning. This in turn may be helpful to grasp the profound changes which are currently taking place.

---

[3] The reference is to Mitchell Lasser's 'Judicial (Self-) Portraits: Judicial Discourse in the French Legal System' (1995) 104 *Yale Law Journal* 1325.

[4] On 'la Doctrine' as an attribute of the civilian legal tradition, see Ph Jestaz, 'Genèse et structure du champ doctrinal' (2005) *Recueil Dalloz* 19.

[5] On 'l'entité doctrinale', see Jestaz and Jamin, 'L'entité doctrinale française' (1997) *Dalloz*, chronique 167ff; Jestaz, 'Déclin de la doctrine?' (1994) *Droits* n°20, 85ff; Jamin 'La rupture de l'Ecole et du Palais dans le mouvement des idées' *Mélanges Moury* (1998) vol 1, 69ff; Ph Jestaz and Ch Jamin, *La doctrine* (Paris, Dalloz, 2004). This book has generated a large number of reactions, including from the inside. See MA Frison-Roche and S Bories, 'La jurisprudence massive' (1993) *Recueil Dalloz* 287; and for example, Patrick Morvan, 'La notion de doctrine' (2005) *Recueil Dalloz* 2421. According to this author, the characteristic of 'la Doctrine' is the written word, 'l'écrit doctrinal'.

[6] Frison-Roche and Bories, 'La jurisprudence massive' (1993).

[7] The interaction between 'doctrine' and 'jurisprudence' has been a topic of fascination for decades: see Ph Jestaz, 'Doctrine et jurisprudence: cent ans après', (2002) *Revue Trimestrielle de Droit civil* 1, referring to an article bearing the same title by Esmein, one century earlier: (1902) *Revue Trimestrielle de Droit civil* 5.

[8] Lasser, 'Judicial (Self-) Portraits' (1995).

II. THE CURRENT DEBATES OVER THE EXISTENCE AND FUTURE OF 'LA DOCTRINE' AND WHY THEY ARE SIGNIFICANT

This exploration draws upon Philippe Jestaz's and Christophe Jamin's excellent critical, historical account of the rise of 'la Doctrine' as an 'entity', which progressively acquired control during the nineteenth century over access to legal knowledge. Their book sparked considerable controversy, generating angry critique from within la Doctrine's own ranks from those members of the academic sub-community who style themselves as free-thinkers and thus not in any way part of an 'entity'.[9] Of course, this very reaction encourages further research on the epistemological function of this community, or at least of its controversial representation, within the legal system as a whole. In its least controversial acception, the idea of an entity refers to the community (or rather, the professional sub-community) of *jurisconsults (les savants juristes)*, described in Christian Atias' leading classic on 'Epistémologie juridique'[10] as sharing distinctive methods of legal reasoning (*savoir-faire*), modes of recruitment (the *concours d'agrégation*) and legal knowledge (*le savoir juridique*).[11] Atias emphasises, however, that the community is epistemological, not ideological, insofar as it shares forms of legal knowledge while remaining potentially divided over substantive solutions or policies. It may well be that the sensitive point is that, as an entity, 'la Doctrine' is to a large extent anonymous,[12] in the sense that it is as it were the collective regulator of a national corpus of legal knowledge, to which each member, even if named, remains to a large extent the servant.[13] 'La Doctrine' thinks or favours this or that, with a citation in a footnote to one or more scholarly writings. This fosters a certain untraceability of new ideas. When launched, these tend to disappear into the corpus to enrich a common intellectual heritage. The downside is conformism, a common form of quasi-plagiarism, and frequent use and abuse of second-hand sources. To say 'la Doctrine says' dispenses with detailed citation and even verification of handed-down ideas.

Atias predicts an underground and invisible march, as far as the French scholarly community of lawyers is concerned, towards the overthrowing of tradition.[14] I would tend to agree, insofar as the decline of traditional forms of legal knowledge seems inevitable in today's changing and interconnected world. However, I am not entirely convinced that this march will necessarily lead, as Atias thinks,

---

[9] L Aynès, P-Y Gautier and F Terré 'Antithèse de 'l'entité': à propos d'une opinion sur la doctrine' (1997) *Dalloz*, chronique 229ff.
[10] C Atias, *Epistémologie juridique*, Précis Dalloz, 1st edn (Paris, Dalloz, 2002).
[11] Atias asserts his own voluntary exile from the academic sub-community by signing his publications as 'avocat' and not as 'professeur des universités'. Significantly, the term 'Doctrine' does not figure in the index of his book.
[12] Anonymous in the same way as the Court, especially the Cour de cassation, and its third-person-singular.
[13] To a large extent, the academic community is the mirror image of the clerics of the Church.
[14] Atias, *Epistémologie juridique* (2002) no 268.

to the dominance of a technocratic, political, rule-based legal approach, which would tend to make law subservient to the State. Basically, the fears voiced by Atias are linked to the risk of loss, through technocratisation of legal knowledge, of the methods of legal reasoning 'specific to private law'. Hence,

> [l]a réforme souterraine de la tradition juridique est en marche; indolore, insoupçonnée, apparemment indélibérée, elle transforme le savoir juridique et ne va pas tarder à donner raison aux maîtres de la philosophie de l'Etat, qui rêvaient de lui asservir le droit. La rencontre fortuite de leurs théories, de la révision des programmes d'enseignement et de la modification des procédures de recrutement aura des conséquences qui seront bientôt présentées comme le résultat d'un mouvement (ou d'un progrès) nécessaire, spontané, irrépressible; nul n'en portera donc la responsabilité.[15]

It is true that the current upheaval within the French system of legal education indisputably involves a decline of the national community of legal scholars. The rise of competing communities fosters changing perspectives on law and alternative modes of creation and transmission of legal knowledge. However, to a large extent, it is precisely those traditional visions and forms which accompanied the rise of 'la Doctrine', which contained the seeds of its own discontent. Building on Jestaz' and Jamin's account, a body of remarkable contemporary introspective literature on 'la Doctrine' by its more critical fringe is no doubt the sign of these underground upheavals,[16] at present still barely perceptible or least largely denied on the surface.

III. HOW THE EMERGENCE OF 'LA DOCTRINE' IS LINKED TO THE DECLINE OF THE CODE AND THE MASSIFICATION OF 'LA JURISPRUDENCE'

Despite the venerable Roman roots of the function of *jurisconsult*, the current epistemological function of 'la Doctrine' seems to be as recent as its appearance as a term – around the middle of the nineteenth century.[17] During the first part of the nineteenth century, legal scholarship was devoted to the exegesis of the Code,[18] so that it is only when the Code was no longer able to deal with changing social and economic conditions that the fragmented and increasingly voluminous body of case law, which then came to be called 'la jurisprudence' – meaning at the same time or variously the corpus of judges, the decided cases themselves, and the implicit underlying principles awaiting doctrinal revelation – became

---

[15] Atias (n 10) no 268.
[16] See in particular, the work of two remarkable young writers, Sébastien Pimont, 'A propos de l'activité doctrinale civiliste. Quelques questions dans l'air du temps' (2006) *Revue Trimestrielle de Droit civil* 707; Vincent Forray, 'Autour des méthodes jusnaturalistes, en droit civil' (2006) *Revue de la Recherche Juridique – Droit prospectif* vol 3; see too,'Les méthodes de la doctrine' (2005) *Journée d'étude*. Their work has inspired much of the thought in this text.
[17] Ph Jestaz, 'Genèse et strucure du champ doctrinal' (2005).
[18] The notion of 'Doctrine' tends to apply above all to the field of private law scholarship. This is no doubt due to the symbolic significance of the Code.

the main object of academic study in the law faculties.[19] It was thus quite naturally that the appearance of 'la jurisprudence massive' heralded the birth of 'la Doctrine' by creating the need for a new interpretative function for academic scholarship.[20] The justification for the latter grew out of the progressive obsolescence of the Code and the perceived need to formulate new principles out of the body of cases, whose motivation remained minimal simply because *la jurisprudence* was still fictionally the mouth-piece of the Code.

At this point, beyond the quarrels over whether 'la jurisprudence' was authentically a 'source' of law or merely an 'authority' (which continue to this day), whether or not it was social custom (Planiol) or a tool of social engineering (Gény), legal scholars recognised it – superseding the Code itself – as a new object of 'legal science'. In turn, 'la Doctrine' represented itself as interpreting and ordering the 'sources' of law. The institution of *la jurisprudence* beside the ageing Code as a source, if not of law, then of interpretation of the law, meant that cases had to be gathered thematically for descriptive or informational purposes (a function which is now taken over by databases and technology) and then provided with a form of overriding rationality, so as to fit within a coherent *système* whose framework was still imputable to the Code. 'La Doctrine' was there to reveal, through the study of the cases, the underlying principles of the law (Esmein), fictionally contained within or at least consistent with the Code, and presumably inaccessible to the judges themselves, too occupied by the trees of day-to-day adjudication to see the wood of legal principle.[21]

Self-proclaimed, self-legitimising, 'la Doctrine' thus used *la jurisprudence* as a means to wield interpretative power.[22] Mere judicial statements lacked real normative relevance unless they were made to fit within a doctrinal construction. In other words, law had come to be seen as legal *science* (or at least, was perceived to correspond to a certain prevailing idea of 'science'); cases, dealing with mere facts, were in need of the intermediation of 'la Doctrine' before they could be considered a 'source' of law – to be offered in turn to the courts as the intellectual basis of their future decisions. Interestingly, however, as Mitch Lasser suggests, the power ploy was not one-way.[23] The judges used doctrinal controversy as a device for displacing hermeneutical difficulties away from, or out of, the Code. Condemned to pay lip-service to the legislator (Montesquieu's '*la bouche de la loi*', Napoléon's '*juge-automate*'), their own creativity cloaked itself in academic debate better to break out of the limits imposed by the black-letter of the Code.[24]

---

[19] See Forray, 'Autour des méthodes jusnaturalistes, en droit civil' (2006).
[20] See Frison-Roche and Bories (n 5).
[21] In addition, curiously, one of the characteristics of 'la doctrine' appears to be the fact that it addresses itself rather than an outside audience. See Forray (n 16).
[22] Ph Jestaz (n 4).
[23] See Lasser (n 3).
[24] Very successfully! However, on the lack of counterweight to this unofficial or unrecognised judicial power, see M Lasser, 'The European Pasteurization of French Law' (2004) 90 *Cornell Law Review* 995.

IV. HOW THE CHANGING RELATIONSHIP BETWEEN LAW AND THE OTHER SOCIAL SCIENCES IS RELEVANT TO THE RISE OF 'LA DOCTRINE' AND TO THE SUBSEQUENT SHAPING OF LEGAL KNOWLEDGE

The fact of representing law henceforth as legal 'science'[25] had the paradoxical function of separating it progressively from the other social sciences. Its supposed scientificity was linked more to deductivism, ideas about the structure of legal norms and the abstract logic represented to be at work in the judicial syllogism, than to empirical discovery of principle. Indeed, according to Jamin, the emergence of 'la Doctrine' as the sole means of access to knowledge of the law was one of the strategies by which the legal field organised its own resistance to the input of sociology, politics or economics.[26] Turning its back on the path taken by legal realism and stifling the seeds planted by Gény, 'la Doctrine' adopted dogmatism (*la dogmatique*) in the name of science. Empiricism, yes, but in order to discover, amid the cases, a 'system' composed of legal theory. Thus, law came to be regarded no longer as '*la science sociale par excellence*', as it had been during the nineteenth century. Exit Durkheim! Legal knowledge and legal reasoning were considered to be epistemologically and methodologically apart from knowledge and reasoning on other fields. Sociology et al were considered unscientific (law was more akin to maths than to ethnology) and a little too much to the left. The *facultés de droit* claimed a new independant status in forming a highly specialised professional elite and thereupon renounced interdisciplinarity.

Indeed, still according to Jamin, the legal realist turn was thus missed when Gény and other social science-minded academic lawyers were pushed aside by the success of the great dogmatic treatises of civil law (and the reassuring myth they carried of the continuity and higher values of civil law).[27] There was no longer any need to look beyond the internal logic of the law since – in a sort of neo-natural law revival – the Civil Code as interpreted by the courts contained all that was necessary to govern civil society. Law appeared as a self-contained, self-referential discipline in the quest for order and internal coherence. Within the great treatises on the civil law, 'la jurisprudence' was represented as an object of study (and, increasingly, an independent source of law), but at the same time largely reduced to illustrations of legal theory as framed by the authors of the textbooks. It thus became very difficult to distinguish between legal doctrines or theories and the description of judicial practice.[28] Having (self-) proclaimed its interpretative role, 'la Doctrine' became essentially passive, 'lying in wait for the next case'.[29]

---

[25] On this much-discussed theme, see Paul Amselek, 'La part de la science dans l'activité des juristes' (1997) *Recueil Dalloz* 337.
[26] Jestaz and Jamin, *La doctrine* (2004) 139ff.
[27] ibid.
[28] Pimont, 'A propos de l'activité doctrinale civiliste' (2006).
[29] ibid.

This turn to dogmatism explains why the epistemological studies going on in other fields of social science have had little impact within the legal field. The fact too that 'la Doctrine' was born in self-defence, from the onslaught of other rising social sciences, meant that the collective unconscious of the academic legal community has always feared invasion or contamination from outside sources and tends to be protective of its monopoly of access to the legal sphere. Typically, any mention of economics in the consecrated field of the civil law is perceived necessarily as an inroad by a neo-liberal market doctrine profoundly feared by the academic clerics in charge. Similarly, the attempts at law and society, once hopefully started by Carbonnier, have practically died along with him.

Moreover, in addition to the lack of contact with other fields of social science, legal dogmatism led to a fragmentation within the legal field, along the public/private, but also along the lines of other categories (civil/commercial/private/international/intellectual property), academic sanctuaries which must not be violated – with the exception perhaps of the law of obligations, the Roman law matrix of all the rest. Within the university, the formation of professors through the *concours d'agrégation* accentuates these divisions, all the while constituting and conforming to the requirements of status, but also method (*le plan en deux parties*) and style (modest and rule-loving, as critically described by Atias[30]) for entry into 'la Doctrine'. The latter thus ultimately appears as a collectivity whose members accept to play by its self-proclaimed principles,[31] including the deep or unspoken rules and categories which govern the acquisition and diffusion of legal knowledge. This includes methods of dogmatic, non inter-active transmission – which is itself attuned to the large number of students in the law faculties – and an emphasis on legal theory and rules rather than on facts and debate.

V. WHY 'LA DOCTRINE' IS THREATENED TODAY IN ITS INTERPRETATIVE FUNCTION

Increasingly, critical undercurrents and obvious changes in sources of legal knowledge induced by Europeanisation and globalisation of the law invite speculation as to where 'la Doctrine' is going today. Can it maintain its political role in favour of professorial power, while other actors and interpreters spring up outside the university? Can it preserve its epistemological function as a means of representing, organising and transmitting an accepted form of legal knowledge in the face of pressure from outside the domestic legal sphere? Will the decline of the university – the unmistakeable consequence of inbreeding and the inward-looking perspective induced by legal dogmatism – and the correlative rise of other, parallel sources of framing and transmitting knowledge of the law

---

[30] Atias (n 10) no 265.
[31] Including its rituals, see Jestaz and Jamin (n 5) 193ff.

– notably, the Grandes Ecoles, whose faculty have not gone through the traditional 'rites de passage' linked to the *agrégation de droit* – lead, as Atias appears to think, to the supremacy of a rule-based, technocratic version of the law? This of course may be so. However, there are other ways of looking both at the crisis and the possible outcome.

The crisis in the condition of the corpus of academic lawyers – diminishing prestige (lesser incentive for the best students to join their ranks), lower standard of living (inducing flight to the law firms), increased numbers of students (discouraging creative teaching), burdensome administrative chores (distracting time and energy from research) – is also of course a crisis in the life of 'la Doctrine', whose task in ordering and theorising the law is already made increasingly hard by the diversification of the materials (now also linguistically diverse), in a field which is increasingly Europeanised and globalised. How indeed can 'la Doctrine', isolated for so long from the other social sciences, engage in debate fuelled elsewhere in the world by interdisciplinarity? How can it engage in a transnational dialogue with a global focus after having avoided (in all but its critical fringe) all contact with religion, psychoanalysis or anthropology? How can it assess the contribution of other cultures when the *concours d'agrégation* and its long preparation discourage any distraction through stays abroad and then close the ranks of the legal community to foreign researchers?

One response, rightly identified by Atias, has been the development of parallel means of access to legal knowledge through introduction of integrated legal teaching within the Grandes Ecoles. Outside the university – often outside the *concours d'agrégation*, outside standard publications in legal reviews, outside the French language, outside the standard academic curriculum and outside the strict borders of disciplinary fields – these parallel communities are not an accepted part of 'la Doctrine'. Is Bruno Latour's 'La fabrique du droit'[32] part of academic legal culture? No, surely not. The author is a philosopher-sociologist-anthropologist-ethnologist – anything but a lawyer – and his work is too interdisciplinary to be considered as 'law' or legal science. Yet, on the French educational scene, it is work in this vein rather than law-faculty-taught legal positivism which is used to form tomorrow's elites. Does this promise the rise of legal technocrats, as Atias fears? Not necessarily. Indeed, the reverse may be true. Of course, access to legal knowledge is no longer (exclusively) mediated by the publications of 'la Doctrine', in the style and according to the methods transmitted through the law faculties. But practically, this turn from the law schools may herald a new turn towards interdisciplinarity. To link up with the topic of this workshop, it may also open the way to greater comparative law input.

---

[32] In actual fact, his book on the workings of the *Conseil d'Etat*, is entitled in English 'The Making of the Law' (Cambridge, Polity Press, 2009).

VI. WHY THE CURRENT CRISIS MAY BE FOR THE BETTER – AND MAY BE GOOD FOR COMPARATIVE LEGAL RESEARCH

Indeed, if there has been, all along, a critical perspective on law in France, it is to be found in philosophy, literature and psychoanalysis, or the social sciences.[33] It often contains a strong comparative component, which might well go to confirm the relationship, explored by Geoffrey Samuel, between comparative law and the accession of law to the status of social science.[34] If law is to be taken seriously as a social science, he says, there is an urgent need to foster the external perspectives and epistemological contribution of legal comparison.

However, the reverse is equally true. Serious research in comparative law has to come through the re-linking of law and the other social sciences. This is why the most interesting – critical and imaginative – comparative legal research has for some time been taking place outside the law schools – generating very little interest, indeed, from the lawyers themselves.[35] But the time for a break with dogmatism may have come. If students of law are provided with interdisciplinary tools and linguistic skills which allow them to participate in a wider debate within the social sciences, legal reasoning might, to a certain extent, be 'demystified'.[36] This is not to deny the epistemological specificity of legal knowledge; it is merely to say that it seems to me to be a good thing that access to such knowledge does not remain imprisoned within the dogmatic canons laid down by 'la Doctrine'.

---

[33] There is highly respected legal scholarship going on today in France elsewhere, ie outside the law faculties and often within the other social sciences. Beyond interdisciplinarity, it often has a strongly comparative or 'open' component. Take the *Collège de France*, for instance. Today, there is (for the first time) a chair in comparative legal studies, occupied by the law professor Mireille Delmas-Marty. Also, significantly, if one looks at some of Foucault's great courses, such as 'Naissance de la biopolitique' (1978–1979) which attempts to give a historical, philosophical and economic explanation of the difference between political and economic liberalism and neo-liberalism, one can see that it is full not only of a critical external perspective on the law, but also of perfectly well-informed comparative legal knowledge. Similarly, if one turns to the Institut des Hautes Etudes en sciences sociales (IHESS), much of the contemporary research, from bioethics to identity, has a strong, even dominant, legal comparative component. Very recently, the legal philosopher Alain Supiot created a Social Science Research Institute in Nantes, in which lawyers are invited to interact with social scientists from the world over, on issues of method and epistemology, more or less spurned by the law schools.

[34] G Samuel, 'Is Law really a Social Science? A View from Comparative Law' (2008) 67 *Cambridge Law Journal* 288.

[35] Who, in the law faculties, beyond the fringe (apart from the comparatists Geoffrey Samuel or Pierre Legrand) reads Berthelot or indeed Derrida?

[36] L Alexander and F Sherwin, *Demystifying Legal Reasoning* (Cambridge, Cambridge University Press, 2006).

8

Maps, Methodologies, and Critiques: Confessions of a Contract Lawyer

ROGER BROWNSWORD[*]

I. INTRODUCTION

A COUPLE OF years ago, I agreed to act as the editor of a long-established contract law casebook.[1] The brief was very clear: the last edition of the casebook had been published in 2000; there had been some major case law developments since then; and the casebook was in urgent need of updating. Stated bluntly, my job was to make sure that readers at least got securely to first base. However, in most of my writing about contract law, I see myself as trying to do something rather different; to be sure, we need to get to first base, but if we are to deepen our understanding of contract law we need to get to second, third, and fourth base. Yet, what is it precisely that is implicated in this deeper (theoretical) understanding of the law?

I confess that I am not sure how to answer the question that I have just posed. Quite plausibly, we might say that the purpose of our theoretical inquiries is to improve our understanding of how contract doctrine is generated and then how it plays out in practice; in other words, theory helps to explain how contract law is made and then how it works. Or, we might say that the purpose of theory is to offer us a critical vantage point from which we can assess the appropriateness of the standards and values that are embodied in particular regimes of contract law. Or, we might say that theory can assist us with both our explanatory and our evaluative inquiries.[2] However, an answer along any of these lines will take us into the contested terrain of sociology and philosophy. As Karl Llewellyn

---

[*] An earlier version of this contribution was presented at the workshop on 'Methodology of Legal Research', held at the University of Tilburg on 30–31 October 2009. I am grateful to those who participated at the workshop for their comments. Needless to say, however, the usual disclaimers apply: this is my confession and mine alone.

[1] Roger Brownsword (ed), *Smith and Thomas: A Casebook on Contract,* 12th edn (London, Sweet and Maxwell, 2009).

[2] Compare Mark Van Hoecke, 'Legal Doctrine: Which Method for What Kind of Discipline?' (in this volume, chapter one); and, in general, Christopher McCrudden, 'Legal Research and the Social Sciences' (2006) 122 *Law Quarterly Review* 632.

warns in his classic introduction, *The Bramble Bush*,[3] to go beyond first base is not risk-free; it can be confusing.

In my 'jurisprudential' writing, together with Deryck Beyleveld, I have staked out a legal idealist position (the 'Sheffield school of natural law', as some now term it)[4] that conceives of law (including the law of contract) as an essentially moral enterprise and that argues for a Gewirthian rights ethic as the governing standard.[5] Occasionally, I have worked quite explicitly from this (or a similar rights-based) perspective to address a particular doctrinal issue in the law of contract.[6] However, even though the methodology associated with this kind of exercise is very clear, there are two difficulties: one is that the starting point is deeply controversial; and the other is that there is a long-drop from high theory to doctrinal detail.[7] For the most part, although I am conscious that this general theoretical view is in the background, my attention is on more foreground matters – and the question is, what precisely is it that we are doing when we theorise intuitively in these foreground ways?

In the foreground, as for all commentators on contract law, there have been a number of doctrinal issues that have captured my attention – particularly, doctrines that relate to unfair terms, to third party rights, and to good faith. However, I can see that, as I have addressed these doctrinal issues, I have been making a number of seemingly rather different essays in my attempt to take the discussion beyond first base. The terms in which I now characterise these essays are not necessarily the terms that I would have used had I been asked at the time of writing to explain what I was doing. This contribution, as I have said, is a confession of uncertainty – and, even with the benefit of the opportunity to retrace one's steps, I am not at all sure that I can give a wholly satisfactory account of my research activities as a contract lawyer.

Stated shortly, the essays to which I have referred focus on the following matters: the internal coherence of contract doctrine;[8] the ideologies that drive adjudicative practice and the substantive ideologies of contract law;[9] the rationality

---

[3] Karl N Llewellyn, *The Bramble Bush* (New York, Oceana, 1930).
[4] See (2006) 19:2 *Ratio Juris* 127–244, a special issue on the Sheffield School.
[5] The root of this work is Deryck Beyleveld and Roger Brownsword, *Law as a Moral Judgment* (London, Sweet and Maxwell, 1986; reprinted by Sheffield Academic Press, 1994). Most recently, see Roger Brownsword, 'Friends, Romans, Countrymen: Is there a Universal Right to Identity?' (2009) 1 *Law, Innovation and Technology* 223.
[6] One example is Roger Brownsword, 'Liberalism and the Law of Contract' in R Bellamy (ed), *Liberalism and Recent Legal and Social Philosophy* ARSP Beiheft 36 (Stuttgart, Franz Steiner, 1989) 86.
[7] Compare Charles Fried, 'Rights and the Common Law' in RG Frey (ed), *Utility and Rights* (Oxford, Basil Blackwell, 1985) 215 at 231: 'The picture I have . . . is of philosophy proposing an elaborate structure of arguments and considerations that descend from on high but stop some twenty feet above the ground. It is the peculiar task of law to complete this structure of ideals and values, to bring it down to earth . . .'.
[8] See, eg Roger Brownsword, 'Remedy-Stipulation in the English Law of Contract: Freedom or Paternalism?' (1977) 9 *Ottawa Law Review* 95 – this kind of inquiry evidently being typical of the period; see McCrudden, 'Legal Research and the Social Sciences' (2006).
[9] See, eg John N Adams and Roger Brownsword, *Understanding Contract Law* (originally London, Fontana, 1987); and 'The Ideologies of Contract' (1987) 7 *Legal Studies* 205; and Roger

of contract doctrine (and its judicial administration);[10] the underlying ethic of contract law;[11] the fit between doctrine and business organisation and practice;[12] the nature of consent-based contractual obligation;[13] the mission of protecting reasonable expectations;[14] and contract law in a larger regulatory environment.[15] If we treat the first of these essays as taking up a particular aspect of the rationality of contract doctrine, then we have seven pathways to consider, each leading us on beyond first base and each claiming to illuminate our understanding of contract law.

Enough of these introductory remarks. In what follows, I will sketch the scenery as we follow each of these pathways, commenting on how we might think that our understanding of contract law is improved, and concluding with some short overarching remarks about methodology (about how we theorise contract law) and about the significance of our theoretical products.

II. AN IDEOLOGICAL UNDERSTANDING OF ADJUDICATION AND OF CONTRACT LAW

In the 1970s, John Griffith published *The Politics of the Judiciary*, one of the few law books in Fontana's list. The book sold well, going rapidly through a number of new editions, and Fontana was persuaded that it should publish a series of titles on the core law subjects (the 'Understanding Law' series as it was to become). When I was commissioned (with John Adams) to write the contract

---

Brownsword, 'Static and Dynamic Market Individualism' in Roger Halson (ed), *Exploring the Boundaries of Contract* (Aldershot, Dartmouth, 1996) 48; and 'Contract Law, Co-operation, and Good Faith: the Movement from Static to Dynamic Market-Individualism' in Simon Deakin and Jonathan Michie (eds), *Contracts, Co-operation and Competition* (Oxford, Oxford University Press, 1997) 255.

[10] See especially, Roger Brownsword, 'Towards a Rational Law of Contract' in Thomas Wilhelmsson (ed), *Perspectives of Critical Contract Law* (Aldershot, Dartmouth, 1993) 241.

[11] See, eg Roger Brownsword, 'From Co-operative Contracting to a Contract of Co-operation' in David Campbell and Peter Vincent-Jones (eds), *Contract and Economic Organisation* (Aldershot, Dartmouth, 1996) 14; '"Good Faith in Contracts" Revisited' in M Freeman (ed), (1996) 49 *Current Legal Problems* 111; and 'Individualism, Co-operativism and an Ethic for European Contract Law' (2001) 64 *Modern Law Review* 628.

[12] See, eg Roger Brownsword, 'Network Contracts Revisited' in Marc Amstutz and Gunther Teubner (eds), *Networks: Legal Issues of Multilateral Contracts* (Oxford, Hart Publishing, 2009) 31; and 'Contracts with Network Effects – For Competitors, For Consumers, For Commerce?' (forthcoming).

[13] See, eg Roger Brownsword, 'Contract, Consent, and Civil Society: Private Governance and Public Imposition' in Peter Odell and Chris Willett (eds), *Civil Society* (Oxford, Hart Publishing, 2008) 5.

[14] See especially, Roger Brownsword, 'After *Investors*: Interpretation, Expectation and the Implicit Dimension of the "New Contextualism"' in David Campbell, Hugh Collins, and John Wightman (eds), *The Implicit Dimensions of Contract* (Oxford, Hart Publishing, 2003) 103; and *Contract Law: Themes for the Twenty-First Century* (Oxford, Oxford University Press, 2006).

[15] See, eg Roger Brownsword, 'Regulating Transactions: Good Faith and Fair Dealing' in Geraint Howells and Reiner Schulze (eds), *Modernising and Harmonising Consumer Contract Law* (Munich, Sellier, 2009) 87.

law title, in the spirit of *Politics*, I took the brief to be to expose the underlying values of the law. Quite how the ideologies of contract law – the ideologies of adjudicative formalism and realism, together with the substantive ideologies of market-individualism and consumer-welfarism – emerged in the writing is too long a story to tell. Suffice it to say that we viewed it as a fairly primitive map that would help readers to understand the configuration of some of the key values that lie below the doctrinal surface in this area of the law.

In what ways might it be claimed that an ideological map of this kind advances our understanding of contract law? It seems to me that two claims might be made: one is that the map reveals a pattern in both doctrine and the reasoning of judicial decision-makers that enables us to see more clearly where we are; and the other is that the pattern so disclosed might generate some hypotheses about how judicial decisions are actually made. The latter claim, that there might be some explanatory potential in the ideological mapping, is fairly weak, leaving it open whether the potential can be realised; but, if there is no such explanatory assistance, then any improvement in our understanding rests entirely on the former claim.

How solid is the former claim? In retrospect, it seems to me that the claim is reasonably robust and enduring insofar as it asserts the significance of the formalist/realist axis in relation to the adjudicative enterprise. For, any account of the Rule of Law surely will specify the extent to which judges are required to follow the principles established in the case law, as well as setting the limits to judicial result-orientation. Accordingly, to map the position of particular adjudications relative to these indicators is to take one's bearings from some markers which, to put it at its weakest, are generally recognised to be fundamental to notions of legality.

By contrast, the claim as it relates to the axis of market-individualism and consumer-welfarism seems to be, if not ephemeral, at any rate less enduring. The map sketched in *Understanding Contract Law* was primitive. Any doctrinal feature or any decision that did not fit with classical market-individualist thinking was treated as a manifestation of consumer-welfarism. At the time, because so many of the key cases were consumer disputes, this did not seem to be a serious objection. However, during the last 20 years, there has been a reworking of the commercial law of contract that invites a fresh drawing of the ideological lines. In the light of these doctrinal developments, we can now see that the critical question is: how far should the law of contract be understood as having the function of rigidly prescribing the rules for the market as against responding flexibly to the practices that give particular markets their distinctive normative identity?[16] Meanwhile, on the consumer wing, the law retains strong

---

[16] See Roger Brownsword, 'Static and Dynamic Market Individualism' in Roger Halson (ed), *Exploring the Boundaries of Contract* (Aldershot, Dartmouth, 1996) 48; and Roger Brownsword, *Contract Law: Themes for the Twenty-First Century* (Oxford, Oxford University Press, 2006) chapter 7.

protective welfarist instincts.[17] However, the imposed 'welfarism' that protects consumers is rather different to the welfarist co-operativism that the law – shaking off its attachment to a strict individualist view – is now ready to recognise in some commercial relationships and business contexts. To facilitate a mapping that does justice to (i) the different assumptions about the function of contract law and (ii) the complexity of the transactional ethics that underlies this part of the ideological framework, some considerable regrinding of the lens is required. Still, this is not necessarily a fatal blow to this kind of understanding – it is simply accepting that the lens might need to be adjusted if the pattern is to be brought clearly into focus.

That said, it would be a mistake to assume that, provided we are willing to adjust the ideological frame, this kind of approach is immune to objection. Far from it, for it remains vulnerable to 'relativists' who maintain that the preferred ideological matrix is simply one of many available perspectives; the idea that the pattern yielded by the frame corresponds to some immanent pattern in doctrine or decision-making is a mistake; and the idea that there is some Archimedean vantage point that tells us what the key variables are for the construction of the ideological frame is also a mistake. All that we have, on this view, are so many perspectives, so many maps, each yielding its own picture and patterns. Equally, particular ideological framings are vulnerable to those who take a non-relativist line (as I do in my jurisprudential writings); for these critics will insist that the ideological frame must flow from and be coherent with the background theory rather than one's intuitive sense of what is going on in practice.[18] Accordingly, even if we are vigilant in adjusting our ideological lens, we are still not in the clear.

III. THE RATIONALITY OF CONTRACT LAW

A promising starting point for moving beyond first base is the widely shared idea that the law aspires to be a rational enterprise. This offers three attractive, and seemingly straightforward, critical angles on the law and its administration; and a fourth that is far more problematic. Let me start with the three (apparently) easier critical angles.

---

[17] Sometimes, the instinct is 'procedural', ensuring that consumers are in a position to make their own free and informed choices; at other times, the instinct is more 'substantive', immunising consumers against transactional features that are judged to be unfair or unreasonable. In the controversial Supreme Court decision in *The Office of Fair Trading v Abbey National Plc* [2009] UKSC 6, concerning the interpretation of Regulation 6(2) of the Unfair Terms in Consumer Contracts Regulations 1999 SI 1999/2083, there are many passing references to this distinction, albeit expressed as a compromise between classical notions of freedom of contract (the procedural instinct) and the recognition of consumer rights (the substantive instinct). See eg Lord Walker [44].

[18] I tried to operate in this way in Roger Brownsword, 'The Philosophy of Welfarism and its Emergence in the Modern English Law of Contract' in Roger Brownsword, Geraint Howells, and Thomas Wilhelmsson (eds), *Welfarism in Contract Law* (Aldershot, Dartmouth, 1994) 21.

If the law is to be rational, this surely implies that:

(i) there should not be any contradictions within the body of doctrine;
(ii) the law should be applied and administered as it is declared – as Lon Fuller famously put it, that there should be a congruence in the administration of the law;[19] and
(iii) the law should be effective in achieving its intended purpose.

On closer inspection, however, each of these easy angles is more difficult than it seems. The first needs to be able to distinguish between flat contradiction and a tension between competing principles; while examples of the former are relatively rare, examples of the latter are legion – but not so obviously irrational. With regard to the second, although the casebook of modern contract law is littered with examples of courts bending the law and violating the requirement of congruence, some would defend this in the name of the interests that the courts have sought to protect (particularly the interests of more vulnerable parties). So, to cash this critique, we need to have some way of measuring the rationality of bending the law for well-intended purposes. The third critical angle asks whether the law is instrumentally effective (relative to its intended purposes). While, as I will argue in due course, the modern law of consumer protection is highly regulatory and comes with a clear declaration of intent, it is far from clear what the general body of contract law is designed to achieve. To ask the innocent question, 'What precisely is contract law for?' is not so stupid.[20]

This brings us to the fourth possible rationality critique. Here, the question is whether the law of contract has the content that it is rationally required to have. In my case, armed with my background jurisprudential convictions, I would ask whether it has a suitable agent-respecting content. However, this kind of critical project, as I have indicated already, takes us into deep water. Moreover, there are many who simply reject the idea that the law is rationally required to have any particular content – instrumental rationality is as far as we can go.

Having said all of this, it seems to me that an interrogation of the rationality of the law remains one of the more attractive options for getting beyond first base. If we are committed to the idea that the law should aspire to be a rational enterprise, we need to be clear about what this aspiration means and just how far the law of contract lives up to the ideal.

---

[19] Lon L Fuller, *The Morality of Law* (New Haven, Yale University Press, 1969).
[20] Compare Roger Brownsword, *Contract Law: Themes for the Twenty-First Century* (Oxford, Oxford University Press, 2006) chapter 1. See, too, the pointed introductory remarks in Willem H van Boom, *Efficacious Enforcement in Contract and Tort* (Erasmus Law Lectures 5) (The Hague, Boom Juridische Uitgevers, 2006) – for example, at 9: 'Ask ten scholars what the aim is of the right to terminate a contract after the counterpart has not performed in conformity with the contract, or what the goals of tortious liability for accidental injury are. You will probably end up with more than ten possible answers and less than one straight answer.'

IV. THE UNDERLYING ETHIC OF CONTRACT LAW

Another common denominator in our thinking about contract law is that it sets the rules for marketplace dealing. However, we might ask, 'How do people relate to one another in the marketplace? Is their attitude adversarial and self-interested or co-operative and other-regarding?' and 'What assumptions does contract law make about the implicit ethic of marketplace dealing?' If the ethic presupposed by the law of contract is out of line either with how contractors relate to one another or with how they ought to relate to one another, then it seems to be set up in the wrong way. Again, a critical angle on the law seems possible.

Notoriously, the classical common law of contract embeds an ethic of self-interested dealing. In one of the great cases of the last century, that of the *Suisse Atlantique Societe d'Armement SA v NV Rotterdamsche Kolen Centrale*,[21] we see just how powerful this underlying ethic is.[22] There, the claimants, the Swiss owners of the motor vessel, *General Guisen*, argued that they had not received the performance that they reasonably expected from the defendant charters, a Dutch company. The charter in question, a two-year consecutive voyage charter-party, had been entered into in December 1956. It was accepted by the defendants that, in breach of contract, they had taken considerably more time than the charter permitted for loading and discharging the vessel in port. However, the charter provided that, in these circumstances, the charterers should pay damages at an agreed rate of $1,000 per day to the owners; and these demurrage payments (in total some $150,000) had been made and duly accepted by the owners. Effectively, so far as Mocatta J and the judges in the Court of Appeal were concerned, that was that – there were a number of breaches of the express terms of the charter, the damages agreed under the contract had been paid, and the owners had been properly compensated.

There was, however, rather more than this to the owners' claim that they had not received the performance that they reasonably expected under the charter. It was the owners' contention that the charterers had deliberately taken their time with loading and discharging the vessel because it made economic sense for them to pay demurrage at the agreed rate rather than pay the freight rates set by the contract. It was not altogether clear why the charterers found themselves in this position; but a plausible view is that this reflected the way freight rates had moved at that time, first moving up when the charter was entered into (because of the closure of the Suez canal in the previous month) and then down (once the Suez canal reopened in April 1957). At all events, the claimants argued that this

---

[21] *Suisse Atlantique Societe d'Armement SA v NV Rotterdamsche Kolen Centrale* [1965] 1 Lloyd's Rep 166 (Mocatta J), [1965] 1 Lloyd's Rep 533 (CA), [1967] 1 AC 361 (HL).

[22] Here, I am drawing on Roger Brownsword, '*Suisse Atlantique* Revisited' in Paul Mitchell and Charles Mitchell (eds), *Landmark Cases in the Law of Contract* (Oxford, Hart Publishing, 2008) 299.

strategic conduct by the charterers meant that, instead of some 14–17 voyages that might reasonably have been expected, there were only eight transatlantic voyages during the period of the charter. This, they argued, was in breach of an implied term for cooperation and was worth some $580,000 (if 14 voyages) – $875,000 (if 17 voyages) in damages.

Even if the courts had been prepared to embrace the idea of an implied duty of cooperation, which would not have been unprecedented,[23] the owners actually pitched their claim for implicit cooperation very steeply in their own favour. Quite how much cooperation a commercial contractor might reasonably expect where its economic interests are in conflict with the economic interests of a co-contractor is moot – and the idea of a reasonable expectation itself is one to which I will return in a later part of the chapter. However, if the owners' objection in *Suisse Atlantique* was that the charterers had not taken account of their (the owners') legitimate interests, the charterers surely could have met this complaint without having entirely to subordinate their own economic interests to those of the owners – which, seemingly, was what the owners were arguing for by way of cooperation. At all events, as I have said, the owners' argument received no support from either Mocatta J or the Court of Appeal; and the owners suffered the same fate when they appealed to the House of Lords. So, for example, Viscount Dilhorne saw the matter as entirely straightforward, saying:

> In my opinion, no such contractual right [to a certain number of voyages or to co-operative efforts to make the maximum number of voyages] is to be implied either on the construction of the charterparty or by operation of law. The charterparty might have provided that not less than a certain number of voyages should be accomplished. It did not do so.[24]

As represented before their Lordships, although the breach was now upgraded as possibly repudiatory and fundamental, the claim was still essentially that the self-serving conduct of the charterers breached the implicit cooperative norms of the contractual relationship. As Lord Reid remarked:

> [The owners'] allegation would appear to cover a case where the charterers decided that it would pay them better to delay loading and discharge and paying the resulting demurrage at the relatively low agreed rate, rather than load and discharge more speedily and then have to buy more coal and pay the relatively high agreed freight on the additional voyages which would then be possible.[25]

So, even though the claim was now dressed up in different doctrinal language, in substance it was the same; the Law Lords were fully aware of the essential nature of the complaint; and like the courts below, they did not see any merit

---

[23] See JF Burrows, 'Contractual Co-operation and the Implied Term' (1968) 31 MLR 390; and, in the modern case law, see, eg *Scally v Southern Health and Social Services Board* [1992] 1 AC 294; *Philips Electronique Grand Public SA v British Sky Broadcasting Ltd* [1995] EMLR 472; *Philips International BV v British Satellite Broadcasting Ltd* [1995] EMLR 472; and *Timeload v British Telecommunications Plc* [1995] EMLR 459.

[24] *Suisse Atlantique* [1967] 1 AC 361 (HL)389.

[25] *Suisse Atlantique* [1967] AC 361 (HL) 397.

in it. For the Law Lords in the mid-1960s, it was perfectly natural to assume an ethic of self-reliance as the default position for contract law.

Surely, though, there is nothing new in this? Is it not a relatively consistent thread of English contract law – or, at any rate, the commercial law of contract – that contractors are permitted (although, of course, not required) to conduct themselves in an entirely self-interested fashion? Indeed, it is and this is so much the culture of the last century that the judges at all levels in *Suisse Atlantique* do not even pause to give the matter a second thought. Nevertheless, it is important to see just how powerful this culture is.

Before the parties have entered into a contractual relationship, the classical view is that they are *permitted* to deal with their cards close to their chests. Again, it should be emphasised that nothing in the classical law *requires* parties to deal in this manner. Hence, the substantial empirical evidence that highlights a cooperative approach to contracting in many business communities does not of itself point to a defect in the classical law. To the extent that the classical law is prescriptive, it is merely in the default ethic that it assumes. Nevertheless, that default position is potentially very significant. So, for example, in *Smith v Hughes*,[26] Lord Cockburn CJ famously said:

> The question is not what a man of scrupulous morality or nice honour would do under such circumstances. The case put of the purchase of an estate, in which there is a mine under the surface, but the fact is unknown to the seller, is one in which a man of tender conscience or high honour would be unwilling to take advantage of the ignorance of the seller; but there can be no doubt that the contract for the sale of the estate would be binding.[27]

Then, in *Walford v Miles*,[28] it was Lord Ackner's turn to emphasise that, in the negotiating stage (covered by an adversarial ethic), neither side owes anything to the other. A duty to negotiate in good faith, Lord Ackner asserted, would be 'inherently repugnant to the adversarial position of the parties'.[29] Notice, though, Lord Ackner is not saying that adversarial dealing is inherent to the very idea of contract; it is simply that this is the legal default position for the regulation of negotiations.

Once parties are in a legal relationship with one another, we might expect the default position to change somewhat; the parties, after all, are no longer 'strangers'. However, if one side is in breach, it is perhaps understandable that the extra-contractual default should be restored. At all events, the classical view is that, where one party is in breach of contract, then the innocent party may legitimately take up any of the legally available options irrespective of whether this is for self-serving economic advantage – in other words, self-reliance is once again

---

[26] *Smith v Hughes* [1871] LR 6 QB 597.
[27] ibid 603–04.
[28] *Walford v Miles* [1992] 2 AC 128.
[29] ibid 138. Similarly, see eg, Slade LJ in *Banque Financière de la Cité SA v Westgate Insurance Co Ltd* [1989] 2 All ER 952, 1013; and May LJ in *Bank of Nova Scotia v Hellenic Mutual War Risks Association (Bermuda) Ltd, The Good Luck* [1989] 3 All ER 628, 667.

the default ethic. One of the clearest examples of this approach is *Arcos Ltd v EA Ronaasen and Son*[30] where the Law Lords unanimously ruled that sellers who failed to deliver goods corresponding precisely to the contractual description had no cause for complaint if, on a falling market, buyers then rejected the goods purely for their own economic advantage. According to Lord Atkin:

> If a condition is not performed the buyer has a right to reject. I do not myself think that there is any difference between business men and lawyers on this matter. No doubt, in business, men often find it unnecessary or inexpedient to insist on their strict legal rights. In a normal market if they get something substantially like the specified goods they may take them with or without grumbling and a claim for an allowance. But in a falling market I find the buyers are often as eager to insist on their legal rights as courts of law are to maintain them. No doubt at all times sellers are prepared to take a liberal view as to the rigidity of their own obligations, and possibly buyers who in turn are sellers may dislike too much precision. But buyers are not, so far as my experience goes, inclined to think that the rights defined in the code [i.e. the Sale of Goods Act] are in excess of business needs.[31]

Hence, the uncompromising view is seen (accurately or otherwise) as being congruent with business practice and expectation.

This brings us back to the *Suisse Atlantique* case itself. Now, on the facts, this is different from the negotiation cases because the parties are in a contractual relationship; and it is different from cases like *Arcos* because the complaint is made, not by the party in breach, but by the innocent party. If we think that a plea for cooperation is much less attractive when made by a party in breach (albeit a costless and trivial breach), then cases such as *Arcos* will seem to make some sense. However, where the plea comes from exactly the opposite direction, it is not so obvious that the classical default makes sense. On the face of it, what is so striking about the Law Lords' position in *Suisse Atlantique* is that, without hesitation, they default to upholding the right of a contract-breaker to act in a self-serving manner in just the way that they would resort to the same default in contractual negotiations or where it is the innocent party who exercises its remedial options. Neglecting co-operativism, the Law Lords saw no problem in the defendant charterers playing the contract to their own economic advantage, seemingly treating the payment of agreed damages as an option on the same par as performance. So it is that their Lordships presuppose a particularly aggressive and one-sided version of efficient breach theory.[32]

Having made this extended detour into a case that has long been closed, what should we infer about the assumption of self-reliance? First, if the critical point is whether the law, with its underlying assumption of self-reliant dealing, maps well onto the actual dealings between parties, we need to undertake the kind

---

[30] *Arcos Ltd v EA Ronaasen and Son* [1933] AC 470.
[31] ibid 480.
[32] Compare the general line of critique in Daniel Friedmann, 'The Efficient Breach Fallacy' (1989) 18 *Journal of Legal Studies* 1.

of empirical inquiries that were pioneered by Stewart Macaulay.[33] In addition, if it turns out that the attitudes of contractors vary from one marketplace to another, from one time to another (for example, depending upon the background economic conditions), and from one relationship to another, then we need to consider whether the law should be geared to respond flexibly to these factors. Second, however, if the issue is not whether the law maps accurately onto practice but whether the ethic that the law effectively prescribes is appropriate, then we need to have a background position that enables us to defend one ethic rather than another.[34]

V. THE FIT BETWEEN DOCTRINE AND BUSINESS ORGANISATION

There is another way in which we might explore whether doctrine fits with business practice. Here, the question is not so much whether contracting parties relate to one another in a spirit of competition or cooperation, but how businesses are organised. Classical contract assumes that businesses are organised in such a way that they meet their requirements either by going into the market or by dealing with the matter in-house. In the former case, contract law governs; in the latter, company law applies. However, this dichotomy, market or firm, makes no allowance for the possibility of the networked or connected kind of organisation that we find in franchising, consortia, and alliances, and the like.[35]

Consider, for example, the way in which business is now organised to service a consumer credit-supported market. In the important case of *OFT v Lloyds TSB Bank Plc*[36] (where the House of Lords held that the protection given to credit card holders by section 75(1) of the Consumer Credit Act 1974 extends to more complex modern credit networks, as well as to transactions made with overseas suppliers[37]), Lord Mance sketched the changing networked character of the credit infrastructure in the following way:

> Large-scale consolidation has led to card issuers becoming members of one of the two main international credit card networks, VISA and MasterCard. Under the rules of these networks, certain card issuers are authorised to act as 'merchant acquirers'. . . . They

---

[33] Seminally, see Stewart Macaulay, 'Non-Contractual Relations in Business' (1963) 28 *American Sociological Review* 55; and 'Elegant Models, Empirical Patterns, and the Complexities of Contract' (1977) 11 *Law and Society Review* 507.

[34] Compare Roger Brownsword, 'Contract Law, Co-operation, and Good Faith: the Movement from Static to Dynamic Market-Individualism' in Simon Deakin and Jonathan Michie (eds), *Contracts, Co-operation and Competition* (Oxford, Oxford University Press, 1997) 255.

[35] Generally, compare Gunther Teubner, '*Coincidentia Oppositorum*: Hybrid Networks Beyond Contract and Organization' (Storrs Lectures, 2003–04, Yale Law School).

[36] *OFT v Lloyds TSB Bank Plc* [2007] UKHL 48.

[37] Under the provisions of section 75(1), a creditor who is party to a debtor-creditor-supplier agreement is jointly and severally liable with the supplier for the latter's misrepresentation or breach of contract in relation to a transaction (with the creditor) that is financed by the credit arrangement. Section 75(3) of the Act disapplies the protection afforded by section 75(1), inter alia, where the cash price is under £100 or over £30,000.

contract with suppliers . . . to process all such supply transactions made with cards of the relevant network. . . . Suppliers do not become members of the network, but contract with merchant acquirers to honour the cards of the network. . . . Where the merchant acquirer is itself the issuer of the card used in a particular transaction, the transaction is tripartite. . . . But in the more common (and in the case of a foreign transaction inevitable) case of use of a card issued by a card issuer other than the merchant acquirer who acquired the particular supplier, the network operates as a clearing system, through which the merchant acquirer is reimbursed by the card issuer. . . .[38]

At all levels, however, the courts were clear that the fact that 1970s-style three-party networks have been overtaken by four-party networks, did not derail the legislative intention that consumers should be given the protection envisaged by section 75(1).[39]

Despite these encouraging signs of judicial sensitivity to the way that business actually organises itself, imagine that section 75(1) had never been enacted. Imagine, then, a case such as *David Boyack v The Royal Bank of Scotland (RBS)*[40] – a case alluded to by Lord Hope in the *Lloyds TSB* case – where Mr Boyack, having used a credit card (issued by RBS) to buy a clock in Dubai, now alleged that the contract was induced by misrepresentations made by the seller, and contended that RBS (qua card issuer) should be treated as jointly and severally liable for the supplier's misrepresentation. Without the support of section 75(1), Mr Boyack would need to claim that

(i) the law of contract should apply special rules to networks;
(ii) debtor-creditor-supplier arrangements (whether three or four-party schemes) should be treated as networks; and
(iii) one of the network effects is to increase the responsibility of credit card issuers in relation to their card-holders, specifically by securing the rights of card-holders arising from any card-facilitated sale (whether at home or overseas).

This would be a tall order. Having identified a potential blind spot in contract law, what precisely is our point? Is our point that contract maps onto the market and that this is simply its limit; or is the point that the transactions made between and with connected contractors need to be specifically regulated and that it falls to contract law to do the job (for the assistance of claimants such as Mr Boyack)? In other words, are we trying to improve our understanding by observing that networks fall beyond the range of contract law; or is the point the critical one that contract law needs to be moulded so that it can engage squarely with networked contracts?

In my own writing about this issue, at first, I was unsure whether the law should specify the existence conditions for a network (with its own network

---

[38] *OFT v Lloyds TSB Bank Plc* [2007] UKHL 48 [23].
[39] ibid [24].
[40] At the time of *OFT v Lloyds TSB*, pending in the Sheriff Court at Kirkcaldy: see [2007] UKHL 48 [10]–[11] (Lord Hope).

rules), or whether it should be for the contracting parties (and only for the contracting parties) expressly to adopt network rules. More recently, however, I have backed both possibilities, suggesting that the idea of a contract with 'network effects' might be introduced as a regulatory measure (where the specified effects assist the regulatory objectives) or by allowing contractors to opt-in for such effects. However, to appreciate the significance of this suggestion – which might be thought to be trying to have both one's cake and to eat it – we need to understand the way in which the modern law of contract operates in two quite different regulatory modes (imposed command and control regulation for the consumer marketplace and co-regulation for the commercial sector) – and that is something that I will comment on in section VII.

VI. THE CONSENT-BASED NATURE OF CONTRACTUAL OBLIGATION

An assumption that is shared in both common law and civilian thinking is that contract is founded on consent, that contractual obligations are voluntarily assumed, and that the consensual basis of contract is defeated where obligations are taken on in a context coloured by fraud or coercion.[41] However, in my writing about consent in general, I have presented it as a particular kind of procedural, private, and personal justification, quite different to standard justificatory arguments or reasons;[42] and I have applied this to our understanding of consent-based contractual obligation.[43] Here, I have argued that the way in which we understand contractual obligation as consent-based fluctuates between two rather different things. Sometimes our focus is on the contractors' consensual choice of a particular body of rules to govern their dealings; at other times (and more often than not I think), our focus is on the parties' consent to the terms of a particular transaction and not, as such, to the rule framework that regulates the making and performance of that transaction. In other words, we look sometimes for consensual engagement of a particular body of rules; but, at other times, we are looking for a consensus ad idem in relation to a particular exchange. Whereas the former relies on consent to justify applying the body of rules so engaged, the latter relies on consent to bind a party to a particular transaction. Whereas the former is prior to, and external to, the law of contract as such, the latter is an exercise within the law of contract.

Once we are sensitised to this distinction, it becomes apparent that we need an auxiliary jurisprudence, a consent-clearing body of law that is external to, and

---

[41] See, eg Hein Kötz and Axel Flessner, *European Contract Law: Volume One* (Oxford, Clarendon Press, 1998).
[42] See Deryck Beyleveld and Roger Brownsword, *Consent in the Law* (Oxford, Hart, 2007); Roger Brownsword, 'Informed Consent: To Whom it May Concern' (2007) 15 *Jahrbuch für Recht und Ethik* 267; and *Rights, Regulation and the Technological Revolution* (Oxford, Oxford University Press, 2008) chapter 3.
[43] See Roger Brownsword, *Contract Law: Themes for the Twenty-First Century* (Oxford, Oxford University Press, 2006) chapter 12; and 'Contract, Consent, and Civil Society: Private Governance and Public Imposition' in Peter Odell and Chris Willett (eds), *Civil Society* (Oxford, Hart, 2008) 5.

antecedent to, the law of contract. It also becomes apparent that a great deal of transactional activity, especially that in the consumer marketplace, is regulated by a body of imposed law (that is, by a background law of transactions); that obligations so imposed cannot be accounted for by a consent-based theory; and, that insofar as contractual obligations are taken to be consent-based, these obligations (ostensibly obligations of contract law) should not be characterised as contractual. Instead, these are obligations that look much more like the imposed obligations of tort or restitution.

Such an appreciation of the justifying force of consent transforms the way in which we view the law. We now have, as Hans Micklitz puts it, a 'double-theory of consent' and the application of this theory takes an axe to what we assume to be the sphere of the contractual. Of all the theoretical incursions so far considered, this is perhaps the most radical – not that we should assume that the more radical we are, the more we understand the nature of contracts.

VII. THE MISSION OF PROTECTING REASONABLE EXPECTATIONS

Another idea that seems to be widely accepted at first base is that the mission of the modern law of contract is to protect the reasonable expectations of contracting parties.[44] Indeed, as we have seen already in our earlier discussion of the *Suisse Atlantique* case, a recurrent question is whether the owners' expectation (with regard to the performance of the charterers) was reasonable. However, what precisely is it that transforms a mere expectation into a reasonable (legally-to-be protected) expectation? We can try to tighten up our understanding of this idea by identifying four different reference points for the reasonableness of an expectation. These are as follows:

- The rules of contract law.
- The signals, express and implicit, given by one's co-contractor.
- The norms that are recognised in the particular setting or sector in which one is contracting.
- Those principles of fair dealing that, even if not registered in legislation or recognised in practice, nevertheless set the standard of reasonableness.

In other words, a party might argue that its expectation (of performance, of cooperation, of limited liability, etc) is 'reasonable' because it is supported by the formal law of contract, by the signals given by the other party, by the norms of the local marketplace, or by some a priori (substantively rational) standard.[45]

---

[44] Compare eg John N Adams and Roger Brownsword, 'More in Expectation than Hope: The Blackpool Airport Case' (1991) 54 *Modern Law Review* 301; and John N Adams and Roger Brownsword, *Key Issues in Contract* (London, Butterworths, 1995) passim.

[45] Compare Lord Walker's concluding remarks in *The Office of Fair Trading v Abbey National Plc* [2009] UKSC 6 [52]: '[The outcome of the appeal] may cause great disappointment and indeed dismay to a very large number of bank customers who feel that they have been subjected to unfairly high charges in respect of unauthorised overdrafts. But this decision is not the end of the matter

What we can say about this is that contract law enters into uncertain territory once it allows that expectations can be reasonable for reasons other than that they are supported by law or by the express terms of the contract; for, not only is there room for argument about what is implicit or what is reasonable a priori, but also it invites a tension between the various reference points.[46]

This kind of analysis might be thought to be helpful in more than one way. For example, it cautions against the assumption that this mission is easily delivered; and it flags up particular moves in the courts as especially significant. So, for example, in a rush of valedictory decisions, and in particular in the *Transfield Shipping* case,[47] Lord Hoffmann has prioritised the 'context' in which commercial contractors transact and this has set a new frame for the determination of reasonable expectations.

It is worth pausing over what his Lordship says in *Transfield Shipping*, where the basic question was whether the traditional rule concerning remoteness of damage should apply to regulate a claim for consequential loss. According to his Lordship:

> The case therefore raises a fundamental point of principle in the law of contractual damages: is the rule that a party may recover losses which were foreseeable ('not unlikely') an external rule of law, imposed upon the parties to every contract in default of express provision to the contrary, or is it a prima facie assumption about what the parties may be taken to have intended, no doubt applicable in the great majority of cases but capable of rebuttal in cases in which the context, surrounding circumstances or general understanding in the relevant market shows that a party would not reasonably have been regarded as assuming responsibility for such losses?[48]

Favouring the latter view, Lord Hoffmann held that, relative to background market expectations in the shipping sector, 'it is clear that [the parties] would have considered losses [of the type claimed, a matter] for which the charterer was not assuming responsibility'.[49]

To link this up to another of our lines of inquiry, we might ask how this kind of patterning in the law relates to the patterns detected by the ideological approach. Quite simply, whereas the classical law aimed to establish the ground rules for trade, the modern law of commercial contracts aims to endorse the ground rules that are embedded in particular markets; in the classical law, the law led, but now it is practice that leads. With this shift in emphasis (a shift from static to dynamic market-individualist thinking) we find, correlatively, a changing approach to the benchmarks of reasonableness. Practice-based expectations are now in head-to-head competition with legal rule-based expectations.

. . .'. That is to say, the customers might try some other way of pleading the reasonableness of their expectations (and, concomitantly, the unreasonableness of the banks' terms) or press for legislative recognition of, and protection, for their expectations.

[46] We might anticipate this point if we reflect again on the 'conservative' approach of the courts in the *Suisse Atlantique* case (discussed above in section IV).
[47] *Transfield Shipping* [2008] UKHL 48.
[48] ibid [9].
[49] ibid [23].

On the other hand, in consumer contracting, the benchmark for reasonableness is largely set by the law – that is, by legal provisions that are markedly protective of consumer interests. Here, the reason for sticking with the law as the benchmark is not so much for the sake of calculability and predictability (as was the case with the classical law) but because these rules are thought to reflect a fair accommodation of the interests of suppliers and consumers.

VIII. CONTRACT AND THE LARGER REGULATORY ENVIRONMENT

Most recently, I have suggested that we need to review the formal law of contract in the larger regulatory environment. At first base, there tends to be little consideration of whether the law makes any difference in transactional practice and, if so, what difference this is. However, anyone who pauses to think about the matter will recognise that the impact of the law is an important question. So, insofar as we seek to understand how the law impacts on transactions, it seems to me that attending to the larger regulatory environment is a move in the right direction.

To be more specific about the characteristics of a regulatory (or regulated) environment is not entirely straightforward because, whilst some environments are regulated in a top-down fashion (with regulators clearly distinguishable from regulatees), others are more bottom-up (in the sense that they are self-regulatory); and, whilst some are reasonably stable, others are unstable (and conflictual), and so on – indeed, the multi-level regulatory environment represented by the European Union combines many, if not all of these, different characteristics. This complexity and variation notwithstanding, by way of an initial attempt to specify the characteristics of a regulatory environment, we can highlight the following three matters: namely, the intentionality that underlies the regulatory environment (the purposive nature of the environment); the bearing of the environment on the practical reason of regulatees; and the variety of coding instrumentalities (or modalities).

First, a regulatory environment is not the product of unintentional design. To the contrary, an environment that is coded for action is only a regulatory environment in our sense where regulators have self-consciously put in place a range of coding signals that are intended to direct or channel behaviour in a particular way. In this sense, the regulatory environment is purposively produced. So, for example, if we find ourselves in a room that has just one door through which we can enter or exit, it does not follow that this is a regulatory environment: unless the room has been designed precisely in order to channel entrance and exit through the one and only door, it is not a regulatory environment – our options for entrance and exit might be limited but we are not, as such, regulated.[50] This is not to say that regula-

---

[50] Compare the debate about whether the design of Robert Moses' bridges on the New York parkways was intended to have the (racially discriminatory) effect of making it more difficult for the poor, mainly black, population to reach the beaches on Long Island: see Noëmi Manders-Huits and

tors should take no interest in architectural or design features that operate to channel behaviour in particular ways (even if this is not the intention of the architects or designers). If regulators wish to create an environment that is conducive, say, to health or to privacy, they can adopt regulatory measures that encourage architects and technologists to default to health-promoting or privacy-enhancing designs.[51]

Second, the strategy of regulators – that is, the strategy of regulators in shaping the conduct of their regulatees – is to engage with the practical reason (in the broad and inclusive sense of an agent's reasons for action)[52] of regulatees at one or more of the following three levels:

(i) the coding signals that some act, x, categorically ought or ought not to be done relative to standards of right action – regulators thus signal to regulatees that x is, or is not, the right thing to do; or,
(ii) the coding signals that some act, x, ought or ought not to be done relative to the prudential interests of regulatees – regulators thus signal to regulatees that x is, or is not, in their (regulatees') self-interest; or
(iii) the environment is designed in such a way that some act, x, simply cannot be done – in which case, regulatees reason, not that x ought not to be done, but that x cannot be done.

In traditional criminal law environments, the signals to regulatees are either that certain acts should not be done because this would be immoral or that these acts should not be done because it is not in the interests of regulatees to do them.[53] As the regulatory environment relies more on technological management, the signals to regulatees tend to accentuate that the doing of a particular act is contrary to the interests of regulateees or even that an act is simply not possible.[54]

Jeroen van den Hoven, 'The Need for a Value-Sensitive Design of Communication Infrastructures' in Paul Sollie and Marcus Düwell (eds), *Evaluating New Technologies* (Dordrecht, Springer, 2009) 51, 54.

[51] See, eg Manders-Huits and van den Hoven, 'The Need for a Value-Sensitive Design of Communication Infrastructures' (2009); and Peter-Paul Verbeek, 'The Moral Relevance of Technological Artifacts' in Paul Sollie and Marcus Düwell (eds), *Evaluating New Technologies* (Dordrecht, Springer, 2009) 63.

[52] In this broad sense, 'practical reason' encompasses both moral and non-moral reasons for action: see the third feature of a regulatory environment, in the text below.

[53] Compare Alan Norrie, 'Citizenship, Authoritarianism and the Changing Shape of the Criminal Law' in Bernadette McSherry, Alan Norrie, and Simon Bronitt (eds), *Regulating Deviance* (Oxford, Hart, 2009) 13. Ibid 15, Norrie highlights three broad developments in recent British criminal law and justice, namely: (i) an increasing emphasis on notions of moral right and wrong and, concomitantly, on individual responsibility ('responsibilisation'); (ii) an increasing emphasis on dangerousness and, concomitantly, on the need for exceptional forms of punishment or control ('dangerousness'); and (iii) an increasing reliance on preventative orders and new forms of control ('regulation'). While the first of these developments is in line with the aspirations of moral community, it is the second and the third that such a community needs to monitor with care. In this light, see, in particular, Lucia Zedner, 'Fixing the Future? The Pre-emptive Turn in Criminal Justice' in McSherry, Norrie, and Bronitt (eds), *Regulating Deviance* (Oxford, Hart, 2009) 35.

[54] Compare Bert-Jaap Koops, 'Technology and the Crime Society: Rethinking Legal Protection' (2009) 1 *Law, Innovation and Technology* 93.

Third, the modes of channelling that make up a particular regulatory environment can range from law through to architecture, from the law of trespass (prohibiting entry) to a locked door or a password-protected website. So long as the regulatory modality is intended to shape the conduct of regulatees by engaging some dimension of their practical reason, it is a relevant input.

The case of eBay is an interesting one. At its inception, eBay was perceived by its founder, Pierre Omidyar, as no more than a local 'find and buy' site. It was a facility for the Eagle Bay community who could be expected to deal with one another in a proper way. It was social pressure rather than the law of contract that channelled parties towards fair dealing. Thus, when Omidyar introduced the 'Feedback Forum' in February 1996, he posted a message applauding the honesty of users and encouraging the eBay community to use the feedback (reputational) system to name and chase out the few dishonest or deceptive dealers. Omidyar concluded his message by enjoining users to deal with others in the spirit of the Golden Rule (in other words, to deal with others in the way that you would expect them to deal with you).

Sadly, with the rapid growth of eBay, its users were no longer tied to the local Bay community and it became a locus for online fraud. This was a cue for the utilisation of the criminal law (and cooperation with the FBI) rather than for the law of contract. Ironically, contract law only assumed real significance when the (limited) scope of eBay's liability to its users needed to be formalised. However, it would be rash to assume from this that e-commerce can always flourish without the background support of the law of contract. As Jack Goldsmith and Tim Wu[55] say in relation to the eBay experience:

> [W]hat would eBay look like in the absence of government-enforced contract law? One might think, based on the Feedback Forum . . . that eBay could continue to run much of its ordinary business. In the absence of law, though, eBay would need something to make up the difference that the legal threat now provides. It is true that eBay itself might possibly provide greater security for buyers and sellers. And eBay might guarantee that *it* would make sure that the contracts would be honoured. But, . . . the result wouldn't be eBay as we know it, but rather some very different business – and a much more expensive and less popular business. What has made eBay successful and profitable since day one is its hands-off, self-executing, low-cost nature. That, in turn, depends on a robust system of community norms and, also, underneath that community, the rule of law and government coercion.[56]

In other words, if the benefits and efficiencies of online trading are to be fully realised, we probably need law (both criminal law and contract law) in the regulatory mix; but we constantly need to remind ourselves that what we are after is not just this or that bit of law but an overall regulatory environment that best supports e-commerce.

---

[55] Jack Goldsmith and Tim Wu, *Who Controls the Internet?* (Oxford, Oxford University Press, 2006).
[56] ibid 139.

Again, we might draw on the idea of the regulatory environment to calm or to intensify concerns about some tweaking of the formal law.[57] For example, consider two of the objections to the proposed Directive on Consumer Rights.[58]

One objection, perhaps the most fundamental objection articulated by the community of consumer lawyers, is that the proposal is misguided in putting forward a measure of *maximum* harmonisation. *Minimum* harmonisation, it is conceded, is fine; if Member States wish to adopt a higher legal standard of consumer protection than that set by Brussels, they are free to do so. However, where measures of *maximum* harmonisation are adopted, Member States lose this freedom – which might be contrary to the public interest in protecting consumers as well as detrimental to democracy in taking away the power of local communities to make their own public interest judgments.[59] There is no doubt that this is a serious objection. Nevertheless, viewed through a regulatory lens, a measure of maximum harmonisation will be seen as merely an adjustment to the legal part of the regulatory environment. In principle, in certain environments, the *legal* maximum might be treated as the *regulatory* minimum. While the objectors might well be correct in assuming that, in practice, the setting of such a legal maximum will be antithetical to what is taken to be the legitimate regulatory objective of increasing the level of protection for European consumers, without seeing how regulatees respond, we should not jump too mechanically to this conclusion; for, the setting of a legal ceiling does not preclude the possibility that, within particular sectors or zones, there might be self-regulatory standards that aspire to a higher level of consumer protection, or more demanding requirements of good faith and fair dealing. This is all part of the regulatory environment, even if not underwritten by hard law – and, sometimes, soft law is more effective than hard law in achieving the regulatory objectives.

Another objection to the proposal is that the drafting of the Directive is defective to the extent that it deviates from, or simply ignores, the guidance in the draft Common Frame of Reference (DCFR).[60] Certainly, this deficit invites the charge of, at minimum, regulatory inefficiency. After all, why invest in the drafting of the DCFR only to ignore it? In the larger picture, though, there is no particular reason why the regulation of consumer transactions should adopt the language and conventions of a background document that purports to be about the general law of contract. Indeed, in the larger picture, it is not even obvious that the seemingly haphazard specification of different periods for consumers to have the

---

[57] Here, I am drawing on Roger Brownsword, 'Regulating Transactions: Good Faith and Fair Dealing' in Geraint Howells and Reiner Schulze (eds), *Modernising and Harmonising Consumer Contract Law* (Munich, Sellier, 2009) 87.

[58] Proposal for a Directive on Consumer Rights COM (2008) 614/3, Brussels, 9 October 2008.

[59] For this point about local democracy, I am indebted to Hans Micklitz.

[60] See C von Bar et al (eds), *Principles, Definitions and Model Rules of European Private Law; Draft Common Frame of Reference (DCFR); Interim Outline Edition* (Munich, Sellier, 2008); and *Principles, Definitions and Model Rules of European Private Law; Draft Common Frame of Reference (DCFR);Outline Edition* (Munich, Sellier, 2009).

right to withdraw from certain kinds of transaction is counter-productive. To be sure, such untidiness offends our best instincts as lawyers; but whether such untidiness is counter-productive relative to the regulatory purposes is another question – it probably is, but we should not simply assume that this is so. In other words, when we evaluate the proposal, we need to think about the regulatory environment (not merely the hard law segment of that environment) and we need to focus on the particular regulatory purposes that back the proposal.

Another way of putting all this is as follows: many would say that, to get past first base, we must put the law 'in context'.[61] The problem for contextualists is that they have difficulty in drawing the boundaries of the context, coupled with a lack of clarity about how precisely an appreciation of context is to improve our understanding. Nevertheless, I agree that context matters but it is in the shape of the regulatory environment that we need to set the context for legal interventions and decisions.

IX. CONCLUSION

After a stream of confession, what should we conclude? Should we conclude that this is all theory and no product? That would be a depressing commentary on one's labours, and I think that it is unnecessarily negative. Nevertheless, there is a sense that, as we stand at first base, we are damned if we try to push forward with our understanding and damned if we do not.[62] Let me conclude, then, with two sets of overarching remarks, one set relating to methodology – to how we set about the task of theorising contracts – and the other about the significance of our theoretical endeavours.

To start with methodology: some years ago, Ronald Dworkin helpfully distinguished between 'inside out' and 'outside in' methodologies.[63] In the former case, the methodological approach works from within the law, from doctrine and from near-doctrinal starting points, elaborating a more general theory as it works out. In the latter case, the starting point is a more general one, not necessarily associated with a particular domain of law or indeed law itself; and the methodology then involves trying to apply that theory to the particulars of the law. Neither approach is trouble-free. While the former seems to lack reliable theoretical direction, the latter – no matter which particular theoretical bench-

---

[61] For the most recent elaboration of 'contextualism', and by one of its progenitors, see William Twining, *General Jurisprudence* (Cambridge, Cambridge University Press, 2009).

[62] As Mark Van Hoecke, in chapter one of this volume, says of the latter option:

[Legal doctrine is open to a range of criticisms]: it is often too descriptive, too autopoietic, without taking law's context sufficiently into account; it lacks a clear methodology and the methods of legal doctrine seem to be identical to those of legal practice; it is too parochial . . .; [and] there is not much difference between publications of legal practitioners and of legal scholars.

[63] Ronald Dworkin, *Life's Dominion* (London, Harper Collins, 1993) 29. This should not be confused with the distinction between 'internal' and 'external' inquiries, as drawn by McCrudden (n 2).

mark we adopt – will be contested[64] and will seem to be too remote from the particulars that need to be theorised.

In the foregoing, I have said that, at first base, there are a number of common assumptions that invite further analysis – for example, that contract law aspires to be a rational enterprise, that the mission of contract law is to protect reasonable expectations, that the distinctive basis of contractual obligation is consent, and so on. These look like candidates for an inside-out methodology. I have also said that my background jurisprudence leads me to believe that, out there in the theoretical universe that lies beyond first base, there is a constellation of ideas that offers a defensible starting point. And, if we were to adopt an outside-in methodology, that is where I would recommend that we should start.

This takes me to the other concluding matter, the question of significance. Whether we adopt an inside-out or an outside-in, or some hybrid or twin-track, methodology, what significance does any of this have? In some cases, our various pathways lead to a reframing of the law; in others to critical perspectives; and in others to further questions about how the law actually operates in practice. Yet, what does any of this signify? Are any of our efforts actually bringing about improvements in the law itself or in our understanding of it?

As a young academic, I was struck by the story that the American realist, Underhill Moore, had been seen, late in his career, turning out the contents of his filing cabinets and condemning his work as 'wrong, all wrong.' This seemed like an extremely unkind fate for a hard-working academic. However, at least, Underhill Moore supposed that the paradigm in which he was working was one where theories about law could be right or wrong. How much worse might it have been if he had been overcome by the post-modernist sentiment that his work was no more than a pretty play-thing? What if, with each new theory, we simply give the kaleidoscope another spin – what if we take pleasure in each pretty pattern but that is all that there is to it?

The ultimate confession of a contract lawyer, I suggest, is not to admit that we cannot be confident that an inside-out methodology is superior to an outside-in approach, or vice versa; rather, the ultimate confession is that we cannot be confident that the products of our theorising have any significance other than as play-things, that 'improving our understanding' of contract law is simply indulging in a particular intellectual pastime. For my own part, I still presuppose that our theoretical products can be right or wrong, in the sense that they can be more or less coherent products of our thinking, and that they can make a practical contribution to a more legitimate and effective regulation of transactions – but I cannot rule out the possibility that, like Underhill Moore, I have got this wrong.

---

[64] See, eg Martijn W Hesselink, 'If You Don't Like Our Principles, We Have Others' in Roger Brownsword, Hans W Micklitz, Leone Niglia, and Stephen Weatherill (eds), *The Foundations of European Private Law* (Oxford, Hart Publishing, 2011) (forthcoming).

9

Legal Research and the Distinctiveness of Comparative Law

JOHN BELL

I. INTRODUCTION: LEGAL RESEARCH AS A NORMATIVE SOCIAL SCIENCE

CHRISTOPHER MCCRUDDEN HAS identified a number of questions with which legal research is concerned.[1] His approach shows the way in which law is distinctive in relation to empirical social science. I want to select two of these as of particular importance to legal research methods. The first is 'the understanding and internal coherence of legal concepts and legal reasoning' and the second 'the ethical and political acceptability of public policy delivered through legal instruments'.[2] Lawyers are concerned on the one hand with *analytical questions*, such as how legal concepts are defined and fit together, and the extent to which any general principles can be extracted by legal reasoning that can guide future decisions. They are also concerned with *normative questions* of what the law should be to serve not only internal coherence, but broader issues of justice, as well as other social and political policies. Lawyers are thus interested in both what is the current practice of the law, and what it should be. It is this combination that makes law not just an empirical social science, but also a branch of normative moral and political philosophy. I will argue that research in law presents a distinctive form of normativity, based not on the beliefs of the author, but on the standards of a legal system with which he may or may not agree. Comparing two or more legal systems might appear to be a purely descriptive exercise and one which is difficult to undertake, if one is to understand another system well in addition to one's own. However, I will argue that comparative law is not, in fact, significantly different from other branches of legal research.

---

[1] C McCrudden, 'Legal Research and the Social Sciences' (2006) 122 *Law Quarterly Review* 632.
[2] ibid. The other two questions are 'the meaning and validity of law' (how law is different from other normative systems), and 'the effect of law' (how law operates in practice).

A. Normativity in Legal Research

In her challenging chapter in this collection, Pauline Westerman raises the question of how legal research can be normative.[3] She thinks that legal research should focus on the analytical and descriptive study of what lawyers do. She shares with many a reluctance about making statements on what lawyers ought to do, and she turns apparently normative statements into descriptive accounts of social consensus or a consensus of beliefs among lawyers. I think that the difficulty of coming to agreed statements of what the law ought to be does not prevent us making normative claims. First, rightness does not depend on consensus. A statement about what a person should do according to law is a claim to rightness, but it is a claim made in the knowledge of fallibility. It is an argument not based on the authority of the speaker, but on the genuineness of her reading of what the law requires. Second, when we claim that something is normatively right in law, we are making an argument that is different from an absolute moral claim. Legal rules and principles are situated in a particular context. A claim that English contract law ought to be applied in a particular, controversial way, takes for granted a whole institutional context of practices and other established rules. The argument of a doctrinal author is a kind of situational ethic, rather than an absolute statement of what an ideal contract law is like. There are two dimensions to the claim to rightness in such a context. The first is that a particular interpretation makes the law internally consistent and coherent. The second is that the law achieves its purpose more effectively by being applied or developed in a particular way. In this second area, there is a claim to some form of absolute related to a particular social setting. A concept like 'good faith' illustrates this.[4] Good faith or fairness depends on the legitimate expectations we develop of the conduct of others. Is it good faith not to reveal information which will remove a misapprehension from your fellow contracting party? Well, that will depend in part on the availability of information from other sources. However, it also depends on whether we wish to value transparency between the parties or want to foster a more exploitative society. Here the arguments go beyond what is already accepted and appeal to a higher standard of fair dealing. Such statements from within the legal system are still normative, even if they do not claim any absolute rightness.

In order to be 'scientific' (*wissenschaftlich*), legal research does not have to be simply analytical and essentially descriptive. Such descriptive work is a very important element of legal research. It is exemplified in a wide range of disciplines, such as empirical and socio-legal research, legal history, and much writing in textbooks and case commentaries. However, law is also a practical, applied discipline and, like most such disciplines (eg art, architecture, accounting, man-

---

[3] See Pauline Westerman's chapter five of this volume entitled, 'Open or Autonomous? The Debate on Legal Methodology as a Reflection of the Debate on Law'.
[4] See generally R Zimmermann and S Whittaker, *Good Faith in European Contract Law* (Cambridge, Cambridge University Press, 2000) especially chapter 1.

agement, finance, etc), it includes reflection on what should be the purposes of the law and how those might be achieved. In none of these disciplines can questions about the purposes and the means for achieving them be reduced to technical questions about the mechanics of implementation. The goals of law are not set in such clearly pre-determined ways, so that the legal scientist can focus merely on devising technical means for achieving them. Part of the discipline also includes strategy and theory. It is here that most European languages, but not English, are clear. There is a distinction between *legal theory (Rechtstheorie)* and *legal philosophy (Rechtsphilosophie)*.[5] Legal theory involves the study of the underpinning principles of existing legal systems or branches of those systems, such as the theory of contract. This is the principal approach of legal research. Legal philosophy is more speculative and examines the goals of law, unconstrained by what is actually in force in particular legal systems. Both are part of the research enterprise of law, but legal theory is the predominant aspect of most legal research and will be the focus here. The theory of the current law is shaped by ideas of its purposes and ideals. The current state of the law may, for historical or practical reasons, be less than perfect, but the ideal does not therefore become irrelevant. The role of law as a branch of practical reason is to achieve results in concrete settings. I will therefore follow McCrudden in arguing that, in the area of doctrinal legal writing, there is no bright line between the descriptive and the normative and that both are involved.

McCrudden suggests that the analytical question is *internal* to the legal system; it asks questions from the perspective of the lawyer steeped in the law and trying to make sense of all the details of legal rules and doctrines.[6] The *normative* question, like the question on the effect of law, might be seen as either internal or external: is the outcome consistent with the principles and values of law as a social institution, or does it fit with the social objectives that we would ideally like law to be pursuing? McCrudden argues that these two approaches are typically conflated, because we recognise that law should not be seen as completely autonomous, serving its own purposes, but as related to other ethical and social science perspectives.

B. Comparative Law

Comparative law is a sub-branch of legal research in which the normative ambitions of legal research have been transparent over most of its life. The objective of many comparative lawyers has been to achieve harmonisation if not unification of laws.[7] It has stood in contrast to the focus of lawyers in individual states. The focus on unification of law across nation states provides one answer to the

---

[5] M Van Hoecke, *What is Legal Theory?* (Leuven, ACCO, 1985) 7.
[6] McCrudden, 'Legal Research and the Social Sciences' (2006).
[7] See K Zweigert and H Kötz, *An Introduction to Comparative Law*, 3rd edn (translated by Tony Weir, Oxford, Oxford University Press, 1998) 15–18, 58–62.

normative question of what law should be. For many comparative lawyers, however, the focus of comparative law is to present an analysis of internal dynamics and principles of the existing laws of the countries studied. This may seem predominantly descriptive, particularly when studying a foreign system. How can a foreigner do more than describe what foreign lawyers think their legal rules are? (Hence the popularity of research by means of questionnaires sent out to foreign lawyers.) However, there are normative elements. First, the statements of the foreign law are not simply the description of beliefs or actions of foreign lawyers; as we shall see, they are statements of what the subjects of foreign laws should do from the legal point of view. Second, comparative legal research demonstrates that the goals of law can be achieved by different rules and institutions in different social contexts. The very activity of looking at more than one legal system raises questions about the justifiability of differences and whether they achieve the purposes of the law equally effectively and these are normative questions. While the questions of the justifiability of legal rules or principles and their efficacy in achieving the goals of law are part of the research into any aspect of law, they are more often consciously raised in comparative law research.

C. Outline

The distinctiveness of legal research is its focus on normativity presented from the legal point of view. I will develop this argument first by presenting the importance of the hermeneutical within legal scholarship and second, the role of law as institutional knowledge, rather than abstract facts. The third feature is the interpretative character of law. In brief, legal knowledge (as opposed to other knowledge about law) is distinctively *internal* or *hermeneutical*. That legal knowledge arises out of an institutional setting and of a range of concepts. It is contextualised, institutional knowledge, rather than abstract knowledge. Finally, the knowledge is not fully distinct from the interpreter. Law has to be constructed in the art of interpretation. It seems to me that this latter feature provides a better way forward than the presentation of pure alterity that Legrand suggests,[8] whilst taking on board some of his insights. These will then lead to a discussion of comparative law and how it fits with the presentation of legal research in general.

II. HERMENEUTIC APPROACH TO LEGAL RESEARCH

Legal theory takes for granted the importance of the hermeneutical point of view, as MacCormick termed it.[9] By this he meant that the lawyer (and therefore

[8] P Legrand, *Comparer les droits résolument* (Paris, Presses Universitaires de France, 2009) 240–44.
[9] N MacCormick, HLA Hart (London, Butterworths, 1981) 37–40; HLA Hart, The Concept of Law, 2nd edn (Oxford, Oxford University Press, 1994) 86–91, 242–43.

also the writer on law) tries to explain what the law looks like from the point of view of 'a member of the group which accepts and uses the [legal rules] as a guide to conduct'. That does not mean that the writer accepts this legal point of view to be morally correct, but it is treated as normative from the point of view of the ideal 'law-abiding' citizen. In MacCormick's terms, the lawyer's commitment is 'cognitional' rather than 'volitional' – the lawyer is trying to give the right answer from within the system, but need not be wishing to achieve that result. The hermeneutic point of view preserves the classical scientific, ie objective, approach to the study of law. However, as Hart's contrast with the external point of view suggests, it sets legal inquiry on a different path from, say, anthropological enquiry, which may appear to be much more objective. The difference is that anthropological enquiry seeks to be simply empirical. Cognitional hermeneutic legal research provides a perspective from which normative statements are made. In terms of comparative law, this approach is favoured by people such as Ewald.[10] He argues that we should try to explain the system as it appeared to the participants, even if their views are strange, such as the medieval lawyers who put rats on trial. We do the same, when we make statements on a legal system that is not our own – we try to describe what a law-abiding citizen or a lawyer within that system ought to do.

As Samuel has pointed out,[11] this hermeneutic approach, which takes legal rules and principles as authoritative reasons for action, clashes with the more empirical and relational analyses of other social sciences. The hermeneutic approach is not just reporting facts or beliefs, it sets out normative standards. Empirical facts are not ignored. McCrudden is clear that empirical studies of how law works are a legitimate part of the study of law, and such a contextual understanding is not merely legitimate, but it forms the background, contextual knowledge of the internal point of view. Talking about the concept of integrity in judging, Soeharno has helpfully suggested that in exercising 'intuitive' judicial reasoning, the judge is both consciously attentive to the individual case and reflexively 'mindful' of general knowledge, ideas and beliefs that come from past legal experience and training.[12] This reflexive, but often unconscious mindfulness contains within it a general knowledge of the social purposes of the law. Such knowledge is factual, but has importance as a context for reasons for the judge's actions – the justifications that the judge provides.

This point of view of the lawyer or citizen using the legal rules, principles and institutions as guides to conduct incorporates a rationale – a set of reasons why this is a good thing to do and an awareness of the overall social and moral context in which this takes place. If one is really to flesh out the characteristics of the

[10] W Ewald, 'The Jurisprudential Approach to Comparative Law: A Field Guide to "Rats"' (1998) 46 *American Journal of Comparative Law* 701, 705: 'What comparative law should aim for is an understanding of conscious ideas at work in the foreign legal system; that is, the principles, concepts, beliefs, and reasoning that underlie the foreign legal rules and institutions.'
[11] G Samuel, 'Is Law Really a Social Science? A View from Comparative Law' (2008) 67 *Cambridge Law Journal* 288, 292–96.
[12] J Soeharno, *The Integrity of the Judge. A Philosophical Inquiry* (Aldershot, Ashgate, 2008) 57.

paradigm actor conceptualised in the 'internal point of view', then it is a person who takes the law as an authoritative reason for action but is also committed to the construction of a society based on the rule of law.[13] Taking the law as an authority-reason for action generates, in Raz's view, an exclusionary reason, a reason for ignoring at least some other moral reasons that would otherwise exist for acting. It is not just a particularly weighty reason for acting.[14] So, when a legal researcher makes a statement about the law, the researcher is not making an empirical claim about the beliefs of the majority of lawyers or citizens in a particular legal system. The legal researcher is making a normative claim from a particular point of view, which may well not be his or her own. As Kelsen pointed out, it is possible to be an excellent law professor and yet an anarchist.[15] The skill of the lawyer is to be able to state normative standards plausibly, even if the lawyer does not believe in their rightness.

Whilst Samuel is concerned that the 'authority paradigm' is over-central,[16] I do not think this is a problem. He acknowledges that most works on law will focus on the rules and principles which are intended to guide or direct actions from a legal point of view. The model I have presented is of an individual who seeks to behave lawfully, but who wants coherent and consistent instructions. Samuel rightly compares this with some aspects of religious writing.[17] Both of these disciplines discuss reasons for action based on authoritative sources. Surely this is a characteristic feature of law. To take an example, a prosecutor has to explain the situations in which a prosecution will be brought for assisting suicide. Whatever the prosecutor's personal moral positions or his or her perceptions of what people in society might believe, the prosecutor has to start with the legal text, which says that it is a criminal offence in England to provide assistance to a person to commit suicide and, even more clearly, to act directly to end a person's life, even at their request.[18] There are a variety of ethical and religious discussions of the question of whether one person should be able to help another to die, and they disagree. The distinctiveness of the legal perspective is that there are authoritative sources from which an answer must be constructed. The result is that the answer given by an English lawyer will be different from that of a Dutch lawyer

---

[13] At the very least, this paradigm case is closer to Lon Fuller, *The Morality of Law* (New Haven, Yale University Press, 1964) chapters 2 and 3 than the pathological 'bad man'.

[14] See J Raz, *Practical Reason and Norms* (Oxford, Oxford University Press, 1990) 41–42, 62–65, 190–94. See also Z Bankowski, *Living Lawfully* (Dordrecht, Kluwer, 2001) who restates the requirement of the law: do it, don't think about it. I would not necessarily say that this person will treat the law as an absolute reason for action, since the law-abiding citizen might act as a good citizen in disobeying some of its prescriptions.

[15] H Kelsen, *The Pure Theory of Law* (Berkeley, University of California Press, 1967) 218.

[16] Samuel, 'Is Law Really a Social Science? (2008) 308–13.

[17] See further H-G Gadamer, *Truth and Method* (translated by G Barden and J Cumming, London, Sheed and Ward, 1975) 275–305, where the epistemological similarities between law and religion are explained. Essentially, both involve the practical application of universals derived from authoritative sources to particular situations.

[18] See Director of Public Prosecutions, *A Public Consultation on the DPP's Interim Policy for Prosecutors on Assisted Suicide* (September 2009) www.cps.gov.uk/consultations/as_index.html.

or a Swiss lawyer, because the authoritative sources in those systems contain different provisions. The hermeneutical perspective captures this.

III. THE INSTITUTIONAL CHARACTER OF LAW

The second feature that I want to borrow from Neil MacCormick's account of law is the notion of law as 'institutional fact'.[19] An 'institutional fact' is a fact which we invest with meaning within a particular set of social relations because it performs a particular function. The law is not a set of 'natural facts', but a set of facts that become significant within a legal context. As I have written elsewhere,[20] a visitor to England might observe one person sitting on a raised platform and wearing robes who is talking to another person in a box flanked by two men in uniform. Those are fairly close to 'natural' facts. However, they become scenes from a 'trial' when they are seen as a court process by actors within the legal system. The art of Jonathan Swift's *Gulliver's Travels* or Kafka's *The Trial* is to represent to us those 'natural facts' from the point of view of someone who does not share the institutional and internal point of view. When we conduct legal research, we are interested in facts as they are invested with meaning from within the legal system – we are interested in 'trials', not 'men talking to each other'.

Now the institutional character of law arises from the function of law in reducing complexity in life. Social life is very complex with a multiplicity of issues and concerns. There are lots of things going on in a court room, but we need only to focus on some of them in order to understand the idea of a 'trial'. The institutional character of law not only gives us a perspective which invests meaning on reality, it reduces the number of 'relevant' features. In that setting, formalism plays an important part.[21] Legal routine and structure help to reduce complexity and reduce the number of new things of which a legal actor needs to take account. When I convey my house to another person, I fill out forms that prompt me to certain key questions – do I have title to the house? are there outstanding mortgages to be paid off?, and so on. From the legal point of view, questions such as whether the garden is overgrown or the roof tiles need replacing are irrelevant. No purchaser of a house would ignore them, but they are only *legally* relevant when I have been asked to provide guarantees about the state of the premises or these features of the house have become conditions within the contract to convey – things that I am legally bound to correct before conveyance. The law helps us to cope in a complex world of inter-personal relations by developing structures, institutions, and by promoting routines. Within those

---

[19] N MacCormick and O Weinberger, *An Institutional Theory of Law* (Dordrecht, Kluwer, 1986) chapter 3; this draws on JR Searle, *The Social Construction of Reality* (London, Penguin, 1995) 47.
[20] J Bell, *French Legal Cultures* (London, Butterworths, 2001) 5.
[21] RS Summers, *Form and Function in a Legal System: A General Study* (Oxford, Oxford University Press, 2006).

structures and routines, there are rules which limit the number of relevant features to which the lawyer has to pay attention in coming to the 'just' outcome of a case or transaction. Instead of being viewed at large, within their total complexity, situations are viewed through a limited lens of what is relevant within the constraints of legal institutions.

Because law is an institutional fact, MacCormick is right that legal issues arise within a conceptual framework, a bundle of rights and duties. For example, if a relationship is categorised as delictual, then different rights and duties, procedures and remedies will automatically come into play compared with when the relationship is contractual. Concepts have their own inner logic, but they are also part of a nexus of other concepts and ideas. Samuel has pointed out the distinctive structural way in which issues are constructed.[22] In the Roman private law paradigm, legal relationships are structured around persons, things, and actions. In other branches of law and in other systems the structures may be different, but the point is well made that there are accepted frameworks for thinking about a problem that belong within the law.

The institutional character of law explains the argument of Geoffrey Samuel that facts do not exist independently of legal categories.[23] The legal syllogism almost presupposes that the facts exist independently of the law, and that legal rules are applied to them. However, that is not the case. The legal rule conceptualises reality in certain ways. Law is not a 'fact', but a contested construct. Lawson suggested that 'Law is not just fact. It is thought applied to fact.'[24] To take the ancient Roman instructions to the (lay) iudex: 'If it appears that a golden cup has been stolen from Lucius Titius by Dio son of Hermaeus or by his aid and counsel . . .'[25] The issue is whether the cup was 'stolen', not whether it was taken. For the *actio furti*, we need to construct the actions of Dio son of Hermaeus in the light of the requirements of theft. The natural facts become, in this way, 'facts in law'. The law is only concerned with applying legal rules to 'facts in law'. Our focus of attention is given by the institutional categories of the law and what is needed to satisfy them. The institutional character of the law gives us not only the rules, but also the ways of classifying the facts. This is a feature that is well known to lawyers. Any work on judicial review of administrative action will note that judges will only review the mistakes of law made by officials, not their assessment of facts. However, they will then go on to point out that there is typically dispute about the classification of facts and these decisions on classification may well be treated by the courts as 'errors of law' such that they are reviewable by a court.[26] Classification decisions are *par excellence*

---

[22] Samuel (n 11) 317.
[23] G Samuel, *Epistemology and Method in Law* (Aldershot, Ashgate, 2003) 125–48, 173–91, 196–200.
[24] FH Lawson, *The Comparison – Selected Essay* (Amsterdam, North Holland, 1977) vol II, 75–76.
[25] Gaius, *Institutes*, IV. 37.
[26] See J Beatson, 'The Scope of Judicial Review for Error of Law' (1984) 4 *Oxford Journal of Legal Studies* 22. See more generally, J Bell and G Engle (eds), *Cross on Statutory Interpretation*, 3rd edn (London, Butterworths, 1995) 72–92.

examples of the legal construction of reality. The spectacles with which the legal researcher views reality are given by the law.

However, there is a more profound element to legal thinking that Samuel has pointed out.[27] The lawyer learns first and foremost a 'mental map', a way of seeing the relationships between legal concepts and ideas. The lawyer learns to distinguish 'obligations' from 'property', 'delict' from 'quasi-contract' and so on. This forms a grid for reading reality. However, the mental maps of different legal systems are not the same. For example, leases might be in 'property' in one system and 'contract' in another. So issues of relevance may vary from one legal system to another.

The other and very significant feature about facts in legal research is that the issues and evidence studied arise out of legal processes. Take a simple situation, an accident. A boiler may explode in a factory and someone is injured. The doctor is called and the person taken to hospital. The place is cleared up in order that more work can be undertaken in the factory. By the time the victim has recovered, the site is back in action, the boiler repaired or replaced and the victim will have little way of showing that the boiler was defective and so the employer is liable in law for his or her injuries. Under French legislation of 1865, the factory owner was not permitted to clear up the mess until the inspectors had visited the site and given permission. The inspector's report became the basis on which the accident victim could mount an action.[28] So evidence can, in fact, depend on the existence of legal procedures. Likewise, legal rules may explain whether actions are brought. To take the same example, the victim of a boiler explosion was usually an employee. Under English and German legal rules, the employee victim would find it very difficult to bring an action against his or her employer. As a result, there were almost no actions brought for boiler explosions, even though hundreds of people were killed each year.[29] It is only by understanding the legal procedures by which claims might be brought that we can research the questions with which the law is dealing. Equally, judgments about what is 'just' as an outcome have to take account of the procedures by which it was possible to adduce evidence in the case.

So, one major area for understanding is the procedural character of law. As Llewellyn points out, one of the key functions of law is to establish procedures ('arranging for the say and the manner of the saying').[30] As a result, particular facts or rules only become legally interesting within a procedural setting, when someone is trying to use them. Reading the law is not like reading a novel, but more like reading a theatrical play. The play is meant to be performed and the meaning of what is said depends very much on the way in which the dramatisation occurs. Similarly, statements of the law are procedurally constructed. For

---

[27] Bell, *French Legal Cultures* (2001).
[28] See M Martin-Casals (ed), *The Development of Liability in Relation to Technological Change* (Cambridge, Cambridge University Press, 2010) 107.
[29] ibid 15–16.
[30] K Llewellyn, 'Law Jobs' (1940) 49 *Yale Law Journal* 1355.

example, take a European Human Rights case on the right to life of a foetus, *Vo v France*.[31] However, the case is not directly about the right to life of the foetus, but whether the doctor was guilty of involuntary homicide by being so negligent that the foetus had to be aborted. As the case was actually directly about French homicide law, the Court in Strasbourg was able to avoid giving a straight answer to the question of whether the foetus had a convention right. The Court simply stated that the French courts could refuse to convict the doctor of homicide without breaching the Convention. The rights of the foetus, if any, are left undetermined. This poses problems for the hypothetical fact situation method adopted for comparative law by the Trento project.[32] The answers of different national legal systems to the same fact situations often turn on how the case would be procedurally presented to a court. The *Casebook* cases are less beautifully aligned, but they do reveal the kinds of procedural context in which issues arise.[33] It may not always be the case that the same social problems present themselves to legal resolution, because of the procedural context in which the problems will actually arise. The issues do not arise in a pure form, but as part of a legal process.

My argument in this section has been that legal research is distinctive because the objects of study are essentially embedded within the institutions, routines and procedures of the law and cannot be studied effectively from the outside. The legal facts, the legal concepts and the evidence produced of how the law operates are all embedded within legal constructs. They cannot be taken out of that context and studied. Law is therefore like any human or life science in that we cannot study parts of the law outside their organic context. The objects of study are parts of legal organisms and cannot be detached from them in any meaningful way. Unlike life sciences, law is able to reduce the complexity of its subject. It means that the legal answer is not the whole answer to a situation, but makes sense of a defined part of it.

IV. THE INTERPRETATIVE CHARACTER OF LAW

The interpretative character of law is a significant distinctive feature, when combined with the authority paradigm that Samuel identified. The legal theory of Ronald Dworkin focuses on the constraints within which law as interpretation operates. In *Law's Empire*, he argues that the right answer to a legal question involves constructing a story about the rules and principles laid down by the law that makes it the best it can be from the perspective of the political morality of the law.[34] On the one hand, the story must fit the existing rules of law, but on the

---

[31] *Vo v France* (App no 53924/00) (2004) 40 EHRR 12.
[32] See www.common-core.org (last visited 30 December 2009).
[33] See www.casebooks.eu (last visited 30 December 2009).
[34] R Dworkin, *Law's Empire* (London, Fontana, 1986) 228–38; A Marmor, *Interpretation and Legal Theory*, 2nd edn (Oxford, Hart Publishing, 2005) chapter 2.

other hand, when more than one possible story has met the threshold of these rules, then the choice between them is made on the basis of the political morality that best fits the objectives of the law.

I have already mentioned the importantly interpretative character of facts in law. There is also a major interpretative function in relation to the legal rules and principles. As McCrudden points out among others:

> If legal academic work shows anything, it shows that an applicable legal norm on anything but the most banal question is likely to be complex, nuanced and contested. Law is not a datum; it is in constant evolution, developing in ways that are sometimes startling and endlessly inventive.[35]

Lawyers often talk as if there is a 'text' out there in a canonical form that has just to be interpreted. However, in reality, the words of any classical legal text, a statute or a judicial precedent, cannot be taken on their own. The text is situated as part of the legal system. First of all, a text may be modified by other texts, so it is necessary to compile the correct set of words. Those modifications not only change words, they also bring with them a wider context. The text has to be read in the light of both its original context and of the context of the amending statute. Second, the text is not on its own. It speaks out of a body of law with which it interacts. It will assume certain rules and procedures of law. It may well assume certain definitions. It connects with other legal provisions. The interpreter has to hold all this together in the act of interpretation. That is why the idea of 'the intention of the legislator' as a guide to interpretation is so difficult to apply.[36] Finally, having established a context, the text has to be interpreted. To interpret is to bring the text forward, out of its original context and into the present situation to which it is to be applied.

For all these reasons, the act of interpretation is the art of constructing an appropriate text and its meaning. Now one conclusion that Sacco draws from this is that no statement of the law is complete or fully accurate. He would argue that statutes, judicial decisions, academic treatises and articles are all versions of the law or 'formants' which are then used in an interpretative fashion by the judge or lawyer in coming to a decision or writing an account of the law.[37] The result is that the judicial decision or the academic writing is a creative act. It does something that is new. There are obviously degrees of novelty. All the same, it is clear that a representation of the law can be an act of very distinct scholarship and personal judgment by the scholar.

These features substantiate the important interpretative character of any legal research. In what way is that interpretative feature normative? The answer lies in the test of correctness. I think Dworkin is right that the test for the correctness of a legal solution is whether it makes the law the best it could be. Now there is

---

[35] McCrudden (n 1) 648.
[36] Bell and Engle, *Cross on Statutory Interpretation* (1995) 22–31.
[37] R Sacco, 'Legal Formants: A Dynamic Approach to Comparative Law' (1991) 39 *American Journal of Comparative Law* 1.

an internal perspective on this: what a good lawyer in the system would consider to be a compatible solution. That would be a solution that is predominantly consistent and coherent with the rest of the law.[38] However, where more than one solution is possible, then the approach should be to say that the choice is made according to the value perspective that the interpreter thinks is right within the institutional context of that legal system. This was certainly the view of Portalis when presenting the French Civil Code in 1803:

> the function of statute is to establish through a broad view the general maxims of the law; to establish principles rich in consequences and not to descend into the detail of questions which could arise on every question. It is up to the judge and the jurist, imbued with the general spirit of the laws, to direct their application.[39]

There is a cooperative responsibility here. Imbued by the general spirit means that the interpreter must not stray too far from the legislator's text, but there is sufficient creativity within an internal point of view of the system to come to an interpretation which directs future conduct in a creative manner. Since the product of interpretation (the case rule or the academic statement of the law) is about what people are to do now or should do in the future, then these are normative statements of the law.

The control for the rightness of such a normative answer is not straightforward. As McCrudden pointed out,[40] the presentations that are made by lawyers will be contestable. In a real sense, the right answer is the one that should be seen as convincing by the legal community, or by a significant section of it.[41] Actual consensus is a useful indicator of what should be accepted as right, but is not conclusive. Of course, more than one answer may be plausible or convincing as far as significant sections of the legal community are concerned.

When I argue that these interpretative statements of the law are normative, there are two features. First, the banal feature that the statement of the law is designed to direct conduct from the legal point of view. So when I say that English law does not permit a person to administer a lethal overdose to help another to die, even at that person's request, that is not merely descriptive, it is also normative – it is what a person should do from the English legal point of view. Second, within the hermeneutic point of view, the statement of the law is normative not only in terms of the explicit rules, but also in terms of the more tacit awareness of the purposes of the law. This awareness helps the legal actor to construct the statement of the law that makes it the best it could be. This does not make an account of the law a set of reasons for action *all things considered*. An individual citizen will not only be law-abiding, but may be religious and belong to a particular interest group, all of whose perspectives will come to bear

---

[38] N MacCormick, *Legal Reasoning and Legal Theory* (Oxford, Oxford University Press, 1978).
[39] J-E-M Portalis, *Discours et Rapports sur le Code Civil* (S Goyard-Fabre edn, Centre de philosophie politique et juridique, Caen, 1992) 8.
[40] McCrudden (n 1).
[41] J Bell, 'The Acceptability of Legal Arguments' in N MacCormick and P Birks (eds), The Legal Mind (Oxford, Oxford University Press, 1986) 45–65.

on what is the right thing to do all things considered. However, the statements are normative *from the legal point of view*.

V. IMPLICATIONS FOR COMPARATIVE LAW

Comparative law is one variant form of legal research. It shares a number of characteristics of legal research in general, but with some specificities. It shares the three central characteristics. First, it is hermeneutic – it takes the insider's view on all the legal systems studied. Second, it is institutional in that the knowledge of the law is embedded in the institutional structures of concepts, structures of thinking (especially mental maps) and organisations of the systems in question. Third, it is interpretative – in that the comparative lawyer has to interpret both the target legal system and his or her own. However, presentations of comparative law focus on its descriptive character and to the difficulty of the foreign lawyer being able to understand a system that is not his or her own.

A. Hermeneutics and Comparative Law

If a statement of what the law of a particular jurisdiction is the subject of internal controversy, then comparative lawyers have to be doubly careful. They are faced with 'legal formants',[42] provisions of legal texts, judicial utterances, writings from academics that constitute fragmentary statements of the law that can be used by a lawyer within the system to construct a legal answer. The internal lawyer has to select amongst them to make the law the best it could be. The same is true of the comparative lawyer. When we compare, there is no easy way of stating the content of the national law. The statement of what the law is remains an interpretative question, even for the comparative lawyer. It is a matter of presenting a rational reconstruction of the law, which is justified, but which may not directly reflect what the national lawyer would say about his or her own system. Any of us who undertake a comparison by asking a single national lawyer to produce answers to a questionnaire need to be aware of the frailty of that method.[43] A conscientious respondent will give a contestable interpretation, except on issues where there is a clear *ständige Rechtssprechung*. A comparison will therefore typically require an interpretation, a rational reconstruction, of both the comparative lawyer's own national law and of the foreign system. As a result, I am not sure there is as much difference epistemologically between the law as it is perceived within the system and how an outside lawyer views it. Both are trying to interpret it from the inside, but the purposes may be different. The internal lawyer may be trying to resolve particular problems that present

---

[42] Sacco, 'Legal Formants: A Dynamic Approach to Comparative Law' (1991).
[43] See eg the series of the Institut de droit comparé in Paris. R Rodière, *Les Vices du Consentement* (Paris, LGDJ, 1981).

themselves to clients within the system. The outside lawyer may well be trying to benchmark the solutions reached in his or her own system with those reached in another. These could lead to different ways of presenting the same information.

Goetschalckx argues that the hermeneutics dimension offers us a more appropriate form of objectivity in enquiry than the model of natural science – a perspective that is remote from its objects of study.[44] In commenting on the work of Mitchell Lasser, he argues that a description by an American which conveys the internal point of view of the French legal system can be described as 'objective', even though it is a reconstruction of that internal point of view for a non-French audience. Treating the other legal system with respect allows the comparatist to be the voice of that system, albeit with a non-native accent.

Legrand argues that the foreign legal system will always be 'other' for the comparative lawyer. This feature he identifies as the problem of alterity.[45] The hermeneutic perspective both recognises and transcends this problem of alterity. The comparative lawyer has to present the foreign legal system in a form which is faithful to what it looks like from the inside, even though the comparatist is not his or herself an insider. However, the hermeneutic perspective does not see this externality of the comparatist as a problem. Any writer on a legal system can be content with a detached point of view, because the writer is only describing the institutional perspective. Kelsen's anarchist law professor would be a case in point.[46] The professor can be a good writer on the system, without being in any way committed to its continuance. The commitment of the lawyer is to present the institutional solution, not his or her own personal beliefs. Any proper reading of the system, even from the inside, may be legitimately a detached viewpoint. So the difference between the comparatist's detached perspective and the inside lawyer's detached perspective may not be that great. The key is the quality of the presentation, not the commitment of the writer.

The other aspect of alterity to which Legrand helpfully points is the embeddedness of legal culture within a wider social culture.[47] A lawyer explains the law as a person operating within a particular culture. As Montesquieu put it:

> Les lois politiques et civiles de chaque nation . . . doivent être tellement propres au peuple pour lesquelles elles sont faites, que c'est un grand hazard si celles d'une nation peuvent convenir à une autre.[48]

Any account of a legal system has to reflect this. This makes the presentation more challenging for the comparatist, who has to learn about the society and not

---

[44] In N Huls et al (eds), *The Legitimacy of Highest Courts' Rulings* (The Hague, Asser Press, 2009) 91, 106.
[45] Legrand, *Comparer les droits résolument* (2009); also Legrand, *Fragments on Law-as-Culture* (Deventer, Tjeenk Willink, 1999) chapter 1.
[46] See Kelsen, *The Pure Theory of Law* (1967).
[47] See Legrand, *Fragments on Law-as-Culture* (1999) chapters 1 and 8.
[48] Montesquieu, *De l'Esprit des Lois* (1748), Bk 1, chapter 3. See generally, G Dannemann in M Reimann and R Zimmermann (eds), *The Oxford Handbook of Comparative Law* (Oxford, Oxford University Press, 2006) chapter 11, who points to a large range of other comparative lawyers who have focused in differences between legal systems.

just the legal system, but it does not make it impossible. Of course, in any such analysis, the foreign legal system will remain 'other'.

This otherness does not result in incommensurability. There are important ways in which the systems are similar in their purposes. To take an analogy, *le fooding français* reflects the art of presenting food in a French fashion. English cuisine might appear inelegant by comparison. The two fit into different social conventions. All the same, there are sufficient similarities to make an explanation of differences in the presentation of food intelligible. There are sufficient parameters within which the different legal systems are trying to achieve similar results. There are others which are different and reflect very different social settings as well as rules.[49] However, the hermeneutical perspective allows the writer to hold together both fidelity to the internal perspective and recognition of distance and otherness. Ewald makes this clear in his presentation of comparative law:

> If one's aim is to understand the idea that lie behind the foreign legal system (and I argue at length that this should be the aim of comparative law) then sociological data and rule-books alike are unable to furnish what we want, which is a grasp from the inside, or the conscious reasons and principles and conceptions that are employed by the foreign lawyers – a grasp of the styles of *legal thought*.[50]

B. Institutions and Context

The importance of the institutional features of the law is well acknowledged in comparative law. In particular, the approach of Geoffrey Samuel rightly points to the importance of mental maps, and I would also identify procedure as important determinants of the character of legal material. The location of a topic within the mental map of the national lawyer has important implications for how the law is understood and presented. In public law, there are important ideas of 'public policy' or '*ordre public*' or '*Polizeirecht*' which are not interchangeable. The sources of public power in terms of inherent powers of promoting public policy, public services, the exercise of power over public property and the like shape the way a problem is perceived. It is not just a functional issue; it is a perceptual issue where one needs to hold together what is explicit and what is tacitly understood.

Kahn-Freund argued that comparative lawyers need to look not simply at geography and power structures, but also legal structures in each system:

> The great challenge for comparative lawyers is to probe our legal culture for its sources of resistance, for its implicit judgements about the normal way of doing things, for the

---

[49] F Bruinsma thinks this is the case in relation to legal justification. See F Bruinsma, 'A Socio-Legal Analysis of the Legitimacy of Highest Courts' in Huls, *The Legitimacy of Highest Courts' Rulings* (2009) chapter 4.

[50] Ewald, The Jurisprudential Approach to Comparative Law: A Field Guide to "Rats"' (1998) 705.

way in which our identity is bound up with our practices. An important area for this probing, in my view, is the very language in which we make legal arguments.[51]

The importance of the hermeneutic approach is that it requires the researcher to understand the institutional setting out of which the law arises and is used. The normal national lawyer's institutional approach will typically need to be complemented by a wider social and cultural contextualisation of legal developments in the systems to be compared.

Some comparative lawyers would contest the need for such contextualisation. Watson has argued that the legal professions have a large say in the development of the law.[52] These professions will look out for useful examples of legal solutions in other systems and borrow them. Legal change has often come, therefore, from transplants of legal rules. In Watson's view, this process of borrowing is, at least sometimes, insulated from social and economic change in the recipient legal culture. However, Ewald criticised this thesis as an 'insulation thesis'.[53] He would argue that one needs to provide a broader context to understand the nature of the reception within the legal system and its practices, and one cannot focus simply on the texts and rules that have been incorporated or shared.[54] Whereas Watson's view leaves the possibility that one does not need to look at social context to understand the development of legal rules, Ewald's view makes it necessary at least to research the context, and this is a more dominant view in comparative law. It is often the case that legal rules may appear to be similar, whereas the social context (and therefore the practical importance of law) is different.[55]

In short, comparative lawyers cannot be content to present rules without some reference to the organisational setting, the procedural context and the conceptual structure within which legal problems emerge and the rules are operated. It is in this setting that it is possible to work out the extent of differences or similarities between the systems. This is not necessarily a call for socio-legal or even 'law-in-context' work, but it does require thought at least about the legal embeddedness of the legal problems as they present themselves in the different countries studied.

---

[51] GP Fletcher, 'Comparative Law as a Subversive Discipline' (1998) 46 *American Journal of Comparative Law* 683.
[52] A Watson, *The Evolution of Law* (Oxford, Blackwell, 1985).
[53] W Ewald, 'Comparative Jurisprudence (II): The Logic of Legal Transplants' (1995) 43 *American Journal of Comparative Law* 489, 503.
[54] There is also, however, a contrast with the too broad picture painted by contextualists like Friedman, who threaten to dissolve law into other disciplines. See L Friedman, *A History of American Law*, 2nd edn (New York, Simon and Schuster, 1985).
[55] See Martin-Casals, *The Development of Liability in Relation to Technological Change* (2010). In this book, the authors note the way in which the control over steam boilers liable to cause explosions and injure people was operated not only through planning law, but also through insurance companies and trade associations. The combination of controls and liability law was not the same in the different countries studied, even though the industrial activity and the threat it posed was similar. See especially, ibid chapter 1.

C. Interpretation and Culture

As I have already stated, the legal researcher has to interpret the legal sources or formants from which the researcher is constructing his or her presentation of the law. In comparing two legal systems, a double interpretation is going on – an interpretation of the comparatist's own system and the foreign system he or she is comparing with it. Legrand uses the concept of alterity to question whether such an interpretation is possible. For him,[56] the theme of culture is central. Culture renders, specifically nation, any arrangements and rules that exist in a legal system, even if they originate from some wider transnational source. The foreign system remains fundamentally different, because it speaks out of its own culture. I don't think this applies to all branches of a legal system to the same extent.[57] However, it is not necessary to develop this point here. Legrand's situation of the law within a national culture implies that the internal lawyer is taking a number of things for granted, including language. The comparatist will bear this in mind when undertaking research. Legrand is right to warn of the difficulty of this task, but it would not be right to suggest that it is impossible for a comparative lawyer to interpret a foreign legal system. Following the hermeneutic method, the comparatist's presentation of the foreign law will try to reflect the perspective of the typical internal lawyer, but not to reproduce his or her way of explaining the law. That presentation will be a choice made by the comparative lawyer about the most appropriate way of explaining that national law for a comparative audience. However, I would argue that this will not be necessarily unfaithful to the original. It will simply be different.

The account given by Zweigert and Kötz of the comparative method also warns us that the comparative lawyer is looking at different things from the conventional domestic lawyer. They argued, for example, that 'the comparatist must treat as a source of law whatever moulds or affects the living law in his chosen system'.[58] However, they then seem to treat the rules of the legal system as a given. The interpretative analysis points out, rather, that the rules are constructed by the researcher. The comparative researcher is comparing his or her reconstruction of a foreign legal system with his or her reconstruction of his or her own national system. There is not a fixed form in which these rules are stated. The test of their validity is whether the national lawyer of each of the systems could recognise what is presented as his own law.

---

[56] P Legrand, 'Public Law, Europeanisation and Convergence: Can Comparatists Contribute?' in P Beaumont, C Lyons and N Walker (eds), *Convergence and Divergence in European Public Law* (Oxford, Hart Publishing, 2002) chapter 12.
[57] See Bell, *French Legal Cultures* (2001).
[58] Zweigert and Kötz, *An Introduction to Comparative Law* (1998) 32.

D. Stages of Comparison: Enquiry or Communication

The problem of how a legal researcher can accurately describe and make normative statements about the standards of a foreign legal system acutely raises the limits of the hermeneutic method. Legrand's emphasis on the 'otherness' of a foreign legal system raises questions which are best addressed by distinguishing two different phases within legal research. The attention in the previous sections on the hermeneutic perspective and the institutional context and alterity concentrate on the *methodology of enquiry*. This looks at the attitude and self-awareness of the researcher in setting up and conducting an enquiry. The comparative researcher has to undertake research seeking out the point of view of the representative lawyer or the ideal citizen who takes legal rules as reasons for action. Understanding the law in its institutional context, the comparative lawyer offers a rational reconstruction of the rules of the system such that the representative lawyer would recognise as credible. That may, or may not, highlight significant differences between the legal systems under investigation. However, I want now to turn to the second part of research, the *methodology of communication*. The latter looks at how the results of that enquiry are reported. Now the two are not easily separated, because there is an interplay between the way you express your results and the questions you have asked in the first place. However, the two are still distinct. Legrand's emphasis on alterity, the 'otherness' of the foreign legal system and the need to pay attention to its embeddedness in a broader social culture, has particular force in relation to the methodology of enquiry. We have to be sure that we are faithful to the hermeneutic point of view. However, it has less force when it comes to the methodology of communication, because the focus is then on the target audience.

If the work of the comparative lawyer is to be a serious act of communication, then it has not only to be faithful to the system which it explains, it has to be understandable in the system to which that foreign system is explained. There is an act of communication which is not just a matter of translation. It is a deliberate attempt to relate the preoccupations of one system with the preoccupations of another, by way of drawing attention to similarities or differences. The audience of the author is culturally situated. In the simplest case, it is an audience within a single, particular legal community: for example, when I write on French law for an English law audience. That community has its own language, concepts, institutions and frameworks for meaning. It means that you agonise about how to use particular English words to convey the sense that a German lawyer would understand by a term such as *'Polizeirecht'*: 'public order' is not quite right, but nor is 'public policy' nor 'policing law' nor 'regulatory law'. You can maintain a level of strangeness, but thereby you diminish in some way the level of understanding that your target audience can achieve.

In essence, the communication by comparative lawyers is bound to be significantly different in expression and even in content than the communication by the internal lawyer to an audience within his or her own legal community. Even if many of the steps of the methodology of enquiry are similar between the internal lawyer and the comparative lawyer, in that they are adopting a hermeneutical perspective, the methodology of communication must necessarily be different. Take a good introductory book on English law for a French audience. Leading (Cambridge) academics wrote chapters for a French audience.[59] The order and content of those chapters reflects neither an English way of presenting English law, nor a French way of writing about the same topic. Take the chapter on Tort: it begins its main section on 'negligence' with a discussion of general principles and *'le non-délit d'omission'*, followed by a discussion of pure economic loss, before discussing fault, causation and damage.[60] Now this is pedagogically sound, but it does not represent either the way in which English lawyers classify their subject, nor how a French lawyer would do so. The ethics of comparative law require that there is honesty about differences that are perceived by the comparative lawyer, but also a willingness to enable the reader to gain a genuine understanding of the real extent of difference. The comparative lawyer is a go-between and risks being stranded in the no-man's-land in between the two legal systems. I am not convinced that this is quite an Esperanto (a neutral language) which everyone has to speak and into which they have to translate their own ideas.[61] Rather, it is more a kind of language that a married couple from two linguistic communities might develop: something which remains recognisably English or French, but which has lots of words from the other system untranslated or translated into mutually understood special terms.

Legrand has long insisted on this feature – that the comparatist's account of the law of another system will be different from the account given by a member of that system.[62] Indeed, I would go further to say, as I have shown, that the account by an internal lawyer made for comparative purposes is also likely to be different than the same person's account for purely domestic purposes. It is written knowing that another audience has different agendas from a national audience. Explanations are likely to be couched in language which is more accessible for a lawyer from outside the system, and assumptions are spelt out. All this does not mean that the statements of the foreign lawyer or the accounts given by the internal lawyer for comparative purposes are less valid or accurate. They are simply different. There will be a different selection among the 'formants' in order to provide an answer to the comparative research question.

Legrand implies that the comparatist's accounts of different legal systems are incommensurable. This criticism needs breaking down into the parts of the research method that we are considering. In the area of the methodology of enquiry, we have to ask how far it is plausible that the comparative lawyer is able

---

[59] JA Jolowicz (ed), *Le droit anglais,* 2nd edn (Paris, Dalloz, 1992).
[60] ibid chapter 4 (JA Weir).
[61] See H Beale, 'Principles of European Contract Law - useful or legal Esperanto?' (unpublished talk at the Institute of Advanced Legal Studies, 2001).
[62] See eg 'The same and the different' in P Legrand and R Munday (eds), *Comparative Legal Studies: Traditions and Transitions* (Cambridge, Cambridge University Press, 2003) chapter 9.

to understand the foreign legal system from an internal hermeneutic point of view. Here, Gordley offers a different comment which offers the possibility of a bridge between systems. For him there is no self-contained law which speaks out of a monolithic and closed culture. Gordley argues that, in many circumstances at least,

> [t]here is no such thing as a French law or German law or American law that is an *independent* objective of study apart from the law of other countries. Even where a national legislature has adopted a distinct solution, that solution can only be understood through analysis of the problem it was designed to solve. If the problem is transnational, one has to look outside one's national boundaries to understand it. And sometimes, neither the problem nor the solution are national.[63]

For him, many legal problems are conceptually the same, wherever they arise. Equally, he argues that 'if we can describe our differences, it must be because of what we share. If this is so, then studying the differences will shed light on what we have in common.'[64] The whole endeavour of enquiry becomes possible because of what we share, even if there are also important differences. Even if one does not accept the whole of Gordley's argument, he is making a major point about the potential accessibility of one legal system to a person from outside it. This fits with the general hermeneutic approach of legal research, which presupposes that a person can make normative statements about the legal system from the internal point of view, without being personally committed to its rightness.

In terms of the methodology of enquiry, Legrand wants us to adopt a methodology of difference, aiming to present the foreign legal system coherently in all its distinctiveness.[65] Zweigert and Kötz basically adopt the methodological premise of similarity. These are both *heuristics*, tools of research which will draw out relevant information. I do not see it as necessary to adopt as a heuristic device either the methodology of focusing on difference or the methodology of focusing on similarity.[66] The integrity of the comparative enterprise requires that enquiry is open to both similarity and difference. There is a reflection by the enquirer in the light of the evidence which refines initial hypotheses and adopts new ones. The hypothesis at the end of the enquiry may well be more disposed to dissimilarity than to similarity, but that is surely not an initial heuristic device or methodological premise.[67] In any case, it is not clear what difference arises from the use of the Legrand, rather than the Zweigert and Kötz approach as heuristics. Whereas we have plenty of examples of the method that Zweigert and

---

[63] J Gordley, 'Comparative Legal Research: its Function in the Development of Harmonized Law' (1995) 43 *American Journal of Comparative Law* 555, 566.

[64] J Gordley, 'Is Comparative Law a Distinct Discipline?' (1998) 46 *American Journal of Comparative Law* 607, 615. He also thinks that comparative law may serve to clarify misstatements of our own law (613).

[65] Legrand, 'Public Law, Europeanisation and Convergence: Can Comparatists Contribute?' (2002).

[66] This is also the view of Dannemann, Dannemann in *The Oxford Handbook of Comparative Law* (2006).

[67] See Zweigert and Kötz (n 7) 40; Dannemann (n 48) 395–96.

Kötz propose, we have none from Legrand, and that makes it difficult to comprehend what the *comparative* work would look like if his method were adopted in relation to the communication of legal research. It would be easy to construct individual nation studies, each articulating the viewpoint of the internal lawyer, but no comparison between these representations would be taking place.

When it comes to communicating the results of enquiry, then the communicative power of approximation is greater than a stress on difference. Identifying difference is valuable and important, but enabling the reader to bridge the distance so as to gain a point of access into the other system is an essential task of comparative explanation.

VI. CONCLUSION

This contribution has shown that legal research is not simply an empirical social science. It is creative and normative. It is creative because of the importance of interpretation to the enterprise, even of doctrinal legal research. The researcher as interpreter is putting together the legal formants in a distinctive way, appropriate to the purposes of his or her particular research. The researcher is not reproducing statements of others. To that extent, legal research shares approaches with interpretative social sciences, such as ethnography and political science. However, legal research is also normative. It aims to set out the norms that apply in a particular legal system. The researcher is stating what ought to be done according to the legal point of view within a particular legal system. The researcher is not reproducing the beliefs of lawyers about what ought to be done, but giving his or her best interpretation of the norms of the system, however contested they may be. There are links to moral and political philosophy because, as Dworkin shows, what is normative according to the legal point of view is linked to what morally ought to happen. This is a distinctive form of normativity, because it operates within the context of particular legal institutions, concepts and traditions, rather than at large. The legal researcher differs from the philosopher, because he or she does not state what should be done all things considered.

Although comparing two or more legal systems may appear an essentially descriptive task, the purpose of this contribution has been to shown that, in major respects, comparative law is an instance of the more general form of legal research. The way in which it attempts to reconstruct both the foreign and the researcher's own legal systems is similar to general legal research on either of those systems. That said, there are peculiar challenges in comparative legal research. The first is to understand the full institutional setting out of which the legal issues and solutions arise: the organisation of the legal system, its legal concepts, presuppositions and mental map of the relationships between legal institutions, its legal procedures, and the broader social and cultural context and assumptions. In one's own system, much of this is tacit knowledge. In relation to a foreign system, the researcher needs to acquire more explicit knowledge, and also has to make the tacit knowledge of his or her own system more explicit. Second, the hermeneutic approach requires the comparatist to adopt the internal point of view of the systems compared, but not necessarily to believe either of them is right, fair or just. Third, the comparatist is not reporting an internal point of view that comes as clearly packaged, even if he or she makes use of questionnaires addressed to national lawyers. The comparatist has to interpret the systems to enable a dialogue between them. Each law is something that has to be reconstructed in order to provide intelligible results to people from another legal system. Finally, there is presentation in language and ideas that will be understood by lawyers in the home legal system. At each stage the potential for going wrong is great, not least in the institutional and interpretative features. However, that is why there is strength in the rigour of comparative research.

10
Does One Need an Understanding of Methodology in Law Before One Can Understand Methodology in Comparative Law?

GEOFFREY SAMUEL

'IN ORDER TO develop a suitable methodology of comparative law', writes Professor Mark Van Hoecke, 'one needs a better view on the methodology of legal scholarship within domestic legal systems'.[1] This may seem, at first sight, a perfectly reasonable premise, yet on reflection it raises a number of fundamental questions about law as a discipline, about legal scholarship, about methodology in law and about the relationship between legal scholarship and comparative legal studies. It is the purpose of this contribution to reflect upon these questions in the context of the relationship between methodology in what might be termed ordinary legal scholarship within domestic legal systems and methodology in comparative legal scholarship. However, instead of starting out from the premise that one needs a better view of method in ordinary legal research, this contribution will suggest a different premise. Does one need an understanding of methodology in comparative law scholarship before one can properly understand the methods employed within domestic legal systems?

This is not the only question that will be examined in this chapter. A further question is this. Has law as a discipline anything to contribute to social science methodology and epistemology in general, or is it a discipline that is entirely dependent upon methodological and epistemological insights developed by those outside of law? In attempting to answer this question, the present contribution will focus on the work of the late Jean-Michel Berthelot who, before his untimely death, had been producing pioneering insights into methodology and epistemology in sociology. This work, especially Berthelot's ideas on schemes of intelligibility, has been discussed and analysed in considerable detail elsewhere,[2] but it will be revisited once again for several reasons.

---

[1] M Van Hoecke, Workshop on Methodology of Legal Research, Introductory Notes, August 2009, now included in the Foreword to this volume.
[2] See in particular G Samuel, *Epistemology and Method in Law* (Aldershot, Ashgate, 2003) 295– 334; G Samuel, 'Epistemology and Comparative Law: Contributions from the Sciences and Social

First, it is arguable that Berthelot's work is the only sustained attempt to provide a generalised overview of methodology in the social sciences that rises above a strictly historical and descriptive analysis, aiming therefore to fashion a theorised epistemological understanding of what has been going on in this vast area over the last two (or more) centuries. Secondly, Berthelot's schemes of intelligibility undoubtedly provide enormous insights not just into reasoning in the social sciences but equally into legal reasoning.[3] Thirdly, it is arguable that legal reasoning may, in turn, have a specific contribution to make to Berthelot's schemes. Such an argument, or at least the specific argument set out in this contribution, will, it must be said at the outset, be controversial and might not, in the end, be fully sustainable. Yet it is worth investigation since, if nothing else, the argument should provide insights into legal methodology and epistemology.

I. THE PROBLEM OF INTERDISCIPLINARITY

Comparative legal studies, if it has done nothing else, has provoked a number of fundamental questions about methodology.[4] One such question concerns the dominance of what has been called the functional method in comparative law and this issue is now producing a body of ever more sophisticated literature.[5] Yet this literature on methodology in comparative law is equally provoking questions of a different kind. Do comparatists need to be fluent in interdisciplinary approaches before they can properly call themselves a comparative lawyer? The response of some comparatists has been positive,[6] but others have been rather negative. Thus, one French law professor, Bénédicte Fauvarque-Cosson, after asserting that, for better or worse, the Europeanisation of law is already taking place and that European legal systems are already converging attacks one of the dissenters to this thesis in the following way. When 'Legrand advocates complex cultural and interdisciplinary comparison', she says, 'his approach renders the

---

Sciences' in M Van Hoecke (ed), *Epistemology and Methodology of Comparative Law* (Oxford, Hart Publishing, 2004) 35; G Samuel, 'Taking Methods Seriously (Part One)' (2007) 2 *Journal of Comparative Law* 94 and 'Taking Methods Seriously (Part Two)' (2007) 2 *Journal of Comparative Law* 210; G Samuel, 'Can Legal Reasoning Be Demystified?' (2009) 29 *Legal Studies* 181.

[3] See Samuel, 'Can Legal Reasoning Be Demystified?' (2009).
[4] See, eg P Legrand, 'How to Compare Now' (1996) 16 *Legal Studies* 232.
[5] See, eg K Zweigert and H Kötz, *An Introduction to Comparative Law*, 3rd edn (translated by T Weir, Oxford, Oxford University Press, 1998) 34–35; M Graziadei, 'The Functionalist Heritage' in P Legrand and R Munday (eds), *Comparative Legal Studies: Traditions and Transitions* (Cambridge, Cambridge University Press, 2003) 100; R Michaels, 'The Functional Method of Comparative Law' in M Reimann and R Zimmermann (eds), *The Oxford Handbook of Comparative Law* (Oxford, Oxford University Press, 2006) 339; G Samuel, 'Dépasser le fonctionnalisme' in P Legrand (ed), *Comparer les droits, résolument* (Paris, Presses Universitaires de France, 2009) 405.
[6] See, eg E Grande, 'Development of Comparative Law in Italy' in Reimann and Zimmermann (eds), *The Oxford Handbook of Comparative Law* (Oxford, Oxford University Press, 2006) 107. Pierre Legrand argues, of course, that interdisciplinarity is fundamental to comparative law: P Legrand, *Le droit compare,* 3rd edn (Paris, Presses Universitaires de France, 2009) 47–48.

discipline so complicated that it may well discourage and deter scholars from becoming involved in the first place'. She goes on to say that:

> It should also be noted that this highly exclusive approach to comparative law is in complete opposition to the present needs of French society. . . . Especially in the light of the lingering bias that it is impossible to be both a comparatist and a good French lawyer, it seems not only unrealistic but also counterproductive to insist that French comparatists become interdisciplinary specialists or social scientists.[7]

This observation by Fauvarque-Cosson is not an isolated one, for others have also attacked recent comparative law scholarship.[8] Now the attack itself might, at first sight, seem at best rather trite. Yet it is important (even if unintentionally) for two reasons. First, it indicates the kind of conclusions likely to be achieved by a comparatist working solely within the traditional doctrinal methodology that characterises legal scholarship both in the civilian and the common law world.[9] This methodology has been described and discussed in some detail elsewhere and while there might be discernable differences between legal scholarship in the civil law and common law worlds,[10] one common characteristic is that much legal scholarship – particularly *la doctrine* in France[11] – operates within what has been described elsewhere as the authority paradigm.[12] This paradigm is one where the primary scheme of intelligibility is hermeneutics operating in respect of a text (legislation, court judgment) whose authority is never put into question. Such an orientation allows the researcher to do little more than apply standard inductive and deductive techniques – for even the application of the functional method requires a certain familiarity with social science disciplines – with the result that comparative law becomes associated with one form or another of scientific reductionism.[13] Comparatists operating within this paradigm become preoccupied with common denominators; and, as the object of legal research are only texts, the common denominators are often nothing more than assertions drawn from other (textual) assertions.

[7] B Fauvarque-Cosson, 'Development of Comparative Law in France' in M Reimann and R Zimmermann (eds), *The Oxford Handbook of Comparative Law* (Oxford, Oxford University Press, 2006) 35, 61. But *cf* Grande, 'Development of Comparative Law in Italy' (2006) 107, 125–27.

[8] See, eg B Markesinis, 'Understanding American Law by Looking at It Through Foreign Eyes: Towards a Wider Theory for the Study and Use of Foreign Law' (2006) 81 *Tulane Law Review* 123.

[9] As regards the common law, see DW Vick, 'Interdisciplinarity and the Discipline of Law' (2004) 31 *Journal of Law and Society* 163; see also G Samuel, 'Interdisciplinarity and the Authority Paradigm: Should Law Be Taken Seriously by Scientists and Social Scientists?' (2009) 36 *Journal of Law and Society* 431.

[10] See, eg P Jestaz and C Jamin, *La doctrine* (Paris, Dalloz, 2004); *cf* F Cownie, *Legal Academics* (Oxford, Hart Publishing, 2004); C McCrudden, 'Legal Research and the Social Sciences' (2006) 122 *Law Quarterly Review* 632.

[11] See Jestaz and Jamin, *La doctrine* (2004).

[12] See G Samuel, 'Is Law Really a Social Science? A View from Comparative Law' (2008) 67 *Cambridge Law Journal* 288; G Samuel, 'Interdisciplinarity and the Authority Paradigm' (2009).

[13] Scientific reductionism has been described as an epistemological strategy that puts into operation concepts and methods designed to unify an area of knowledge that has had to be fragmented and diversified in order to understand its objects: J-M Besnier, *Les théories de la connaissance* (Paris, Presses Universitaires de France, 2005) 102.

This in turn tends to result in claims of convergence and harmonisation.[14] In other words comparative law orientates itself towards a presumption of similarity rather than difference. This problem has been recognised in other comparative disciplines and thus, for example, Ute Heidmann observes that the 'recognition of differences between facts or objects to be compared is often neglected or omitted in favour of a too hasty focusing on what appears *similar* and, by extension, *universal*'. Heidmann goes on to assert that in the area of literary studies this research for universal themes still largely dominates the work on myths and this in turn leads to a 'deductive approach which presents the danger of eclipsing whole sections of the objects of comparison that the presumed universal sense does not subsume'. In short, 'the universalisation approach relates cultural facts to an abstract construction (the constitution of a prototype or of a list of myth-themes (*mythèmes*)...).'[15]

The second reason why Professor Fauvarque-Cosson's comment is of interest is that it does reflect a view of law, particularly prevalent in France amongst university law professors, that the primary role of the academic lawyer is to produce doctrinal work. This notion of *la doctrine* is examined by two French authors (both law professors) who point out that it has as its mission only to comment upon the positive law and in the manner that is restricted in its methodological approach.[16] This approach views law uniquely from its interior[17] within which the aim is to analyse and to explain in a coherent and logical manner a legal text or court decision and, continuing in this same methodological mode, to guide the reader towards future outcomes with respect to the positive law under consideration.[18] One studies the law using analysis and synthesis in as strict a manner as the pharmaceutical chemist studies the body.[19] A book on the sociology of law will thus not form part of *la doctrine*.[20] Nor, indeed, would a work on legal history or, if too interdisciplinary, a text on comparative law.

Now whatever one might think about the quality or defects of this approach, not only does it illustrate how law is very much a 'discipline' in all senses of the word, but equally it explains the reluctance of the late Jean-Michel Berthelot, who was one of France's leading social science epistemologists, to include law in his collective work on social science epistemology.[21] The academic lawyer is not engaged in a research exercise whose aim is to increase knowledge about society

---

[14] Thus, one of the dangers with Professor Fauvarque-Cosson's remark that European systems *are* converging is that it might be more an exercise in metaphysical speculation than empirical research, for reductionism can often stray beyond what can be validated empirically: ibid 118.

[15] Ute Heidmann, 'Épistémologie et pratique de la comparaison différentielle' in M Burger and C Calme (eds), *Comparer les comparatismes: Perspectives sur l'histoire et les sciences des religions* (Edidit/Arehè, 2006) 143 ff.

[16] Jestaz and Jamin (n 10) 171–72.

[17] ibid 172.

[18] ibid 231.

[19] ibid 160.

[20] ibid 171.

[21] J-M Berthelot (ed), *Épistémologie des sciences sociales* (Paris, Presses Universitaires de France, 2001). This exclusion of law is discussed in Samuel, 'Is Law Really a Social Science?' (2008).

as a social reality; the lawyer is engaged in a hermeneutical exercise that has as its object a legal text and only a legal text. Of course, the interpretative exercise will bring into play certain conceptions and ideologies that the lawyer has about social reality and this will inform his or her textual commentary.[22] Yet there are real epistemological dangers when this doctrinal method is extended into the area of comparative studies. As Heidmann points out, the 'properly thought through and clearly explained construction of axes of comparison is an essential epistemological requirement of the comparative exercise'. For there is

> epistemological truism that one tends to neglect when one remains inside a homogenous and unique disciplinary field of investigation, that is the fact that all the theories, all the notions and focal points of analysis and all the identities are object constructions.

In other words, the 'epistemological truism is often forgotten in favour of a reification or an *ontologicalisation* of concepts'.[23]

Fauvarque-Cosson's assertion that legal systems *are* converging is a good example of this. Maybe they are or maybe they are not. However, when one examines the arguments for and against they tend to be based on the idea that legal concepts and categories such as 'contract', 'property', 'fault', 'interest' and so on have some kind of 'reality' and that it is these 'realities' which are converging. Yet where is the proof, save in the words of the legal texts themselves and within the narrow domain of the *discipline* of law? If the law professors are, as Fauvarque-Cosson seems to be saying, to be discouraged from entering into interdisciplinary work, then they will never be equipped to avoid the epistemological difficulty noted by Heidmann. Comparative law will become an exercise in which, say, '*contrat*' is assumed to be ontologically similar to 'contract' with the result that there is effectively little serious comparison. Or, put another way, comparison in law will have little or no epistemological value beyond the authority-dominated discipline of law. No doubt some would argue that a functional approach might provide a more solid social ontology.[24] Yet the danger here is that functionalism, as practised by authority-orientated lawyers working strictly in a non-interdisciplinary environment, will be methodologically meaningless. For, as Ralf Michaels points out, there are many different meanings of functionalism and if the method is to be used with any intellectual sophistication, these different meanings must be properly appreciated, requiring in turn of course an interdisciplinary sophistication.[25] In addition, one needs to be aware of the alternatives to functionalism, something those who advocate its use in comparative law seem reluctant to investigate.[26]

If, then, comparatists are unwilling to take method seriously, it is difficult to see how comparative legal studies can progress much further than textual

---

[22] See, eg Jestaz and Jamin (n 10) 241–43.
[23] Heidmann, 'Épistémologie et pratique de la comparaison différentielle' (2006) 146.
[24] See generally Michaels, 'The Functional Method of Comparative Law' (2006).
[25] ibid.
[26] Samuel, 'Dépasser le fonctionnalisme' (2009).

182 *Geoffrey Samuel*

analysis and scientific reductionism. Certainly one could not expect those outside law to take comparative law scholarship seriously and this, in turn, raises a question about the intellectual status of methodology within ordinary legal scholarship. What comparative legal studies reveals is not, therefore, a need better to appreciate methodology within ordinary legal scholarship, for according to Berthelot this is either interdisciplinary and pluralistic or simply a hermeneutical programme 'which is not of [lawyers'] own making'.[27] What is needed is a better understanding by lawyers of methodology in the sciences and social sciences and the starting point for such an appreciation might well be comparative law.

II. METHODOLOGY AND THE STATUS OF COMPARATIVE LAW

The question is, accordingly, whether lawyers like Professor Fauvarque-Cosson reflect the current status of comparative legal studies and the hope is that, in general, she does not.[28] However, to assure the status of comparative law a fundamental condition needs to be fulfilled: the comparative lawyer must free him or herself from the authority orientation. The epistemological orientation of the comparatist cannot be that either of textual authority or of legal science authority since the two forms of authority are incapable of providing answers to the two fundamental questions that comparative law, as an intellectual pursuit, poses. What is 'comparison'? And what is 'law'?[29]

Take first of all the comparison question. What is it to compare and why undertake such an exercise? At one level the answer seems simple: thus Vigour states that to compare is, in the first instance, to bring out some differences and some common points according to a criterion that should be defined at the outset and which orientates the view of the researcher.[30] However, how does one begin to identify 'difference' and 'common point' and how does one equally identify a 'criterion'? Before attempting to answer these questions, it is first important to distinguish, even if the distinction in the end proves elusive, between the *function* and the *methods* of comparison. Of course a complete separation would be meaningless since methodology will be determined and often tested in terms of its functions. Yet failing to distinguish between the two can result in work that is comparative in only a rather shallow sense. Thus, for example, the search for the 'best solution' in the context of European Union law is an exercise that is no

---

[27] See Berthelot, *Épistémologie des sciences sociales* (2001) 12.
[28] On this question see H Muir Watt, 'Why There Is No (Longer) a School of Comparative Legal Studies in (Mainstream) France' (conference paper presented to the British Society of Comparative Law annual seminar, University of Keele, 7 September 2009). See also her contribution to this volume in chapter seven.
[29] See further on these questions G Samuel, 'Form, Structure and Content in Comparative Law: Assessing the Links' in E Cashin Ritainel (ed), *Legal Engineering and Comparative Law* (Genève, Schulthess, 2009) 27–50.
[30] C Vigour, *La comparaison dans les sciences sociales* (Paris, La Découverte, 2005) 7.

doubt valuable,[31] but it is not really any more comparative in its methodological sophistication than legal reasoning in general. Lawyers, or at least judges and professors, usually seek the 'best solution' when they work on a litigation problem, even if the general interests in play are not quite the same in a domestic dispute as compared to a European Union one. Of course one response is to say that every jurist is a comparatist without knowing it.[32] Yet if this is the case then comparative law or comparative legal studies might just as well disappear from the curriculum.[33] Comparative method must go beyond any functionally-driven dialectical process in which the objective is to induce a higher level solution.

A number of methodological starting points need, then, to be identified. The first is the distinction between genealogical and analogical comparison. The former is a comparison between two phenomena (the objects of comparison) that, although now distinct, have a common ancestry. From this viewpoint, says Bubloz, it is a matter of explaining similarities between systems in terms of *real* historical connections and thus any resemblance is interpreted as the sign of a genealogical connection.[34] Analogical comparison, by contrast, is where the two phenomena do not have any genealogical or common ancestry connection and thus it is a matter of comparing, at least in the biological sciences, only structure and form. 'In analogical comparison', notes Bubloz,

> to compare A and B is not then about presenting similarities as intrinsic properties resulting from a common source or differences as the sign of an irreducible singularity; to compare A and B is to establish some ideal relations between one phenomenon and another in the hope of improving the respective intelligibility of each of them.[35]

One is comparing relations and aspects and not the things themselves.[36]

This methodological distinction is of some importance to the European legal harmonisation debate in that there is one school of thought which argues the case for legal convergence between the civil and the common law tradition on the basis that there is a common genealogical connection between the two traditions. There was once, so it is argued, a common legal tradition in Europe.[37]

---

[31] K Lenaerts, 'Le droit comparé dans le travail du juge communautaire' in FR van der Mensbrugghe (ed), *L'utilisation de la méthode comparative en droit européen* (Namur, Presses Universitaires de Namur, 2003) 111.

[32] X Thunis, 'L'empire de la comparaison' in FR van der Mensbrugghe, *L'utilisation de la méthode comparative en droit européen* (2003) fn 5, 11.

[33] See Muir Watt, 'Why There Is No (Longer) a School of Comparative Legal Studies in (Mainstream) France' (2009).

[34] Y Bubloz, 'Augustine et Porphyre sur le salut: Pour une comparaison analogique et non apologétique du Christianisme et du Néoplatonisme' in Burger and Calme, *Comparer les comparatismes: Perspectives sur l'histoire et les sciences des religions* (2006) 113, 115.

[35] ibid 117.

[36] JZ Smith, *Drudgery Divine: On the Comparison of Early Christianities and the Religions of Late Antiquity* (Chicago, University of Chicago Press, 1994) 36–53.

[37] R Zimmermann, 'Roman Law and European Legal Unity' in Hartkamp et al (eds), *Towards a European Civil Code*, 3rd edn (The Hague, Kluwer/Ara Aequi Libri, 2004) 21. See also R Zimmermann, 'Savigny's Legacy: Legal History, Comparative Law, and the Emergence of a European Legal Science' (1996) 112 *Law Quarterly Review* 576.

The difficulty with this approach is that it is biased towards bringing out the common points between the objects of comparison within a criterion that is itself governed by a functional objective, namely the desirability of European harmonisation of private law.[38] Now this may be a worthwhile objective and, if so, the genealogical method is one perfectly respectable means of arguing the case. However, it has to be asked if this is really comparative law, rather than just an exercise in European legal history, since there is as such little or no comparison being employed with the aim of discovering new knowledge. In other words the *method* (genealogical) and the *function* (harmonisation) are conflated in support of a particular argument itself forming part of the function. This is not to say that an analogical approach would necessarily avoid these difficulties, for one could still conflate method (the structure of law) with the function (harmonisation of structures). However, it would certainly help avoid the problem of assuming similarity.[39]

Another methodological starting point concerns taxonomy.[40] What kind of classification categories should be employed by the comparatist? If one looks at the European harmonisation texts being produced at the moment these seem simply to reproduce the Gaian institutional system.[41] The world is still divided into contract, tort (delict), property, public law and so on. This scheme is by no means devoid of social science importance. Indeed quite the opposite, yet several questions arise. The first, of course, concerns the extent to which these traditional legal categories actually relate to the empirical acts, activities and operations that go to make up the social facts that are of interest to lawyers. Do the Principles of European Contract Law (PECL) provide an accurate picture of what business people and consumers actually do? One might note here that from a statistical point of view the great majority of contractual claims started in the English courts in any one year are actions in debt for a specific sum of money, usually the price for goods supplied or services rendered.[42] Given that the same is probably true for most European countries, does this not mean that the common law's medieval categories of debt and trespass were at least as socially accurate as anything to be found in Justinian? To what extent did those jurists who drew up the PECL do serious empirical research into the value of 'contract' as a legal category? This question becomes even more relevant in the light of the fact that debts are not just part of the law of obligations but also forms of intangible property.[43] Why, then, is the category of property any less suitable than contract? Why is there still an implied understanding within the harmonisation projects that the distinction between obligations and property continues to be of episte-

---

[38] See generally Hartkamp et al, *Towards a European Civil Code* (2004).
[39] On which see P Legrand, 'The Same and the Different' in P Legrand and R Munday (eds), *Comparative Legal Studies: Traditions and Transitions* (Cambridge, Cambridge University Press, 2003) 240.
[40] C Atias, *Questions et réponses en droit* (Paris, Presses Universitaires de France, 2009) 105–10.
[41] Gaius, Institutes 1.8.
[42] R Zakrzewski, *Remedies Reclassified* (Oxford, Oxford University Press, 2005) 67.
[43] As Gaius himself recognised: G.2.14.

mological value? Perhaps it does remain of value, but one would have thought that taxonomical assumptions would want to be thoroughly tested, with respect to European societies, before one embarks on grand code projects to harmonise this taxonomical thinking. What seems to be happening is that legal taxonomy is being deemed a matter of authority and not research; the categories cohere as a 'scientific' structure and this seems to be enough to endow it with an epistemological validity analogous to that in the natural sciences.[44]

A second question arises with respect to the relationship between social fact and the way these facts are described by lawyers. At what level of generality are facts being described (for example was the claimant in *Donoghue v Stevenson*[45] injured by a 'bottle of ginger-beer' or by a 'product')? How is time being perceived by the lawyers (does everyone die at the same time when a plane explodes)?[46] Are facts presented in terms of a series of dialectical oppositions (is 'state' of the premises being contrasted with the 'layout' of the premises)?[47] How is the behaviour and comportment of the people involved in a litigation problem being described (is the claimant being seen as 'somewhat hysterical' in not liking cricket)?[48] There is nothing new in these questions since they were first seriously posed (or reposed) by the American Realists. However, to what extent is the work done by these Realists actually used by comparative lawyers today? Could one say that the PECL is a text infused by the Realist scholarship? For example, how valuable is it for the PECL to use expressions such as 'sufficient agreement', 'good faith' and the like without some serious empirical research into the nature of trading and service transactions within European societies?[49]

Thirdly, there is the problem of taxonomy and languages. To what extent do different languages classify objects in different ways? As Legrand pointed out:

> Different languages, because they confront [reality] in different ways, thus offer different accounts of reality. No language can pretend to exhaust reality; no language offers a standpoint from which reality would be wholly visible. Rather, each language represents a choice which conditions the answers to be given by reality. Although they all address reality, languages can never be reduced to a single description of it.

The author goes on to give an example. He says:

> Imagine, for example, a spherical, bouncy object. An anglophone will call it 'ball.' A francophone will call it 'balle,' *but only if it is small*. Otherwise, she will refer to it as a 'ballon.' In other words, there is one spherical, bouncy object and two renditions of it through two languages ('ball' and 'balle'). The descriptions vary to the extent that the

---

[44] G Samuel, 'Can Gaius Really be Compared to Darwin?' (2000) 49 *International and Comparative Law Quarterly* 297; G Samuel, 'English Private Law: Old and New Thinking in the Taxonomy Debate' (2004) 24 *Oxford Journal of Legal Studies* 335.
[45] *Donoghue v Stevenson* [1932] AC 562.
[46] See *Re Rowland* [1963] Ch 1
[47] See *Birmingham CC v Oakley* [2001] 1 AC 617.
[48] See *Miller v Jackson* [1977] QB 966.
[49] See on this point G Teubner, 'Legal Irritants: Good Faith in British Law or How Unifying Law Ends Up in New Divergences' (1998) 61 *Modern Law Review* 11.

word 'balle' connotes the idea of smallness in the way the English 'ball' does not. The illustration shows that the complexity of reality will not always be fully captured by a single language: the notion of size is not rendered by the English 'ball.'[50]

No doubt many jurists involved in harmonisation projects take language translation seriously and recourse to the functional method is one way of attempting to tackle the difficult issue raised by Legrand. However, functionalism is only one methodological approach and possibly one that is seriously defective in some ways.[51] Thus, not only will other methodological schemes such as structuralism, hermeneutics or dialectics produce different confrontations between reality and language,[52] but they may well indicate that assuming similarity at the level of function itself is a more ambiguous process than the authority orientated jurist might think. One needs a language through which to describe 'function' but if these languages are themselves different there is the danger of creating new, and false, universalisms at the level of apparent social function.

Compare for example *culpa in contrahendo* in the civil law with liability for misrepresentation in the common law. Both doctrines have as one function the creation of liabilities in respect of events in the period before the actual formation of a binding contract. Yet, misrepresentation also has the function of limiting parties to a contract from claiming that a contract can be avoided on the grounds of mistake.[53] In other words its functions are complex and these can, in turn, only be understood by recourse to structuralist and dialectical methods in as much as the rules of misrepresentation go far in defining the limits of notions such as 'good faith', or 'reasonableness' and 'mistake'. If there are strictly defined liabilities with respect to words uttered before a contract it would seem to follow as a matter of dialectical logic that if one remains silent there cannot be liability.[54] One function, then, of the rules of misrepresentation is to create a relatively clearly defined area of non-liability, or non-obligation, at the pre-contractual stage. It is much less clear if the rules relating to pre-contractual obligations and (or) liability in the civil law have this function; indeed it would probably be an error for a comparatist to assume that they do. As Legrand says, the complexity of reality will not always be fully captured by a single language.

What the present status of comparative law is achieving, therefore, are insights not just at the non-domestic legal level but equally at the level of domestic legal scholarship. Comparative legal studies can help one to understand, for example, ontological and epistemological issues in domestic legal reasoning.[55] More importantly comparative law, with its emphasis on social science methodology, is permitting the legal scholar to gain new insights into domestic legal systems. Thus Annelise Riles, a legal anthropologist and comparative law specialist, writes:

[50] P Legrand, 'Against a European Civil Code' (1997) 60 *Modern Law Review* 44, 56–57.
[51] Samuel (n 5).
[52] On schemes of intelligibility see further Samuel, Taking Methods Seriously (Part One) and (Part Two) (2007) (hereafter referred to as (2007) (n 2); Samuel (2009) (n 2).
[53] *Bell v Lever Brothers* [1932] AC 161.
[54] At least at common law: *English v Dedham Vale Properties Ltd* [1978] 1 WLR 93.
[55] See, eg Samuel (2009) (n 2).

Another implication of the increasingly obsolete character of the distinction between law and society is that the distinction between 'insider' and 'outsider' perspectives that once defined the difference between comparative lawyers and socio-legal scholars no longer adequately characterizes the disciplinary divide. . . .

And she later continues:

Comparative lawyers and socio-legal scholars increasingly understand that they are both insiders and outsiders, both participants and critics, at once. . . . Although Law and Society scholars have long shown some antipathy towards 'theory' and comparative lawyers have shown some antipathy towards empiricism, there is consensus now that scholarship in both fields needs to be both theoretically informed and empirically grounded – and that different mixes of these two elements should be encouraged and appreciated.[56]

Riles goes on to conclude that this 'focus in turn has engendered a new dialogue between comparative lawyers and socio-legal scholars'.[57]

The importance of these observations by Annelise Riles is twofold. First, she is clearly suggesting that law does have its own particular contribution to make to the social sciences in general and such an observation is important when placed alongside Berthelot's exclusion of the discipline of law from his collective work on social science epistemology. Riles would seemingly be implying that the Berthelot attitude is perhaps misguided.[58] Secondly, Riles' observations are important in that they make it very clear that the comparative lawyer cannot do serious work if located simply within the 'internal', and thus authority-orientation governed, epistemological framework of law. The comparatist must be guided by the spirit of enquiry if any serious work is to emerge from comparative law. What, it may be asked, can be achieved from comparing say two legal texts, each from a different system, if the comparatist brings to bear on these texts a set of methods motivated only by the spirit of authority? The very idea of comparison implies, methodologically, both interdisciplinarity and the spirit of enquiry; and this interdisciplinarity ought not to be a one-way process. Domestic legal scholarship could have its own contribution to make to social science epistemology.

However, in order to appreciate how this interdisciplinary dimension to comparative law might provide insights into methodology in legal scholarship in domestic legal systems, one must first investigate two questions. The first question concerns methodology in the social sciences in general. Can one talk in terms of a unitary methodological regime or are there different methods for different disciplines? Indeed is there a plurality of methods within single disciplines? The second question concerns law as a discipline. Given that social science methodology can provide insights into legal reasoning,[59] why is it that

[56] A Riles, 'Comparative Law and Socio-Legal Studies' in Reimann and Zimmermann, *The Oxford Handbook of Comparative Law* (2006) 775, 801–02.
[57] ibid 809.
[58] *cf* Samuel (n 12).
[59] Samuel (2009) (n 2).

there appears to be a lack of emphasis on methodology and epistemology not just in traditional legal scholarship but equally in legal education?[60] Why, in short, are the questions posed within legal scholarship seemingly so restricted in their scope?[61]

III. METHODOLOGY AND EPISTEMOLOGY IN THE SOCIAL SCIENCES

With respect to the first question, Jean-Michel Berthelot, in one of his last published pieces, reminded one that since the nineteenth century social science knowledge has traditionally been dominated by a single model, that of positivism. This model emphasises the three characteristics of experimentation, objectivism and reductionism, themselves motivated by a desire to escape from metaphysical and theological speculation. Positivism took as its object the facts of the world and in the social sciences this meant that the object of this scientific approach was the human. As Berthelot noted, the gains that flowed from this model were considerable. It incited rigour and methodological innovation and it went far in creating a science of mankind, based not on religion or philosophical speculation but on empirical reality.[62]

However, within positivism there developed a debate about method that is encapsulated in the illuminating example given by Berthelot. There can be found on mountain paths small piles of stones in the form of a pyramid and should one wish to reflect on this phenomenon in terms of a unified scientific model of the type that is dominant in the natural sciences, the scheme of intelligibility that comes into play is that of causality. What caused this phenomenon and what are the physical laws that have given rise to its presence?[63] This causal scheme in its turn brings into play a particular kind of reasoning, that of deduction. Once one knows the physical laws involved in this kind of phenomenon all that is necessary is the syllogism; the physical laws (major premise) are brought into relation with the particular circumstances (pyramid of stones, the minor premise), and the explanation follows as a conclusion. Yet this approach fails to explain that the pile of stones is a sign indicating that the path is a safe one for the traveller. There is more to the pile than a simple pyramid of stones of which the cause might be this or that. There is behind it an intention to signify something and this requires a different scheme of understanding that will reveal its sense or signification.[64]

---

[60] In fact these latter questions are investigated in some depth in Samuel (n 9). They will thus only be treated in outline in this present contribution.

[61] Atias, *Questions et réponses en droit* (2009). On the position in English law see S Hedley, The Shock of the Old: Interpretivism in Obligations, in C Ricketts and R Grantham (eds), *Structure and Justification in Private Law: Essays for Peter Birks* (Oxford, Hart Publishing, 2008) 205.

[62] J-M Berthelot, 'Épistémologie des sciences humaines' in S Mesure and P Savidan (eds), *Le dictionnaire des sciences humaines* (Paris, Presses Universitaires de France, 2006) 378.

[63] ibid 380.

[64] ibid.

As Berthelot went on to point out, this dichotomy was formalised within the German social science tradition by an epistemological approach that asserted that social facts were different from the facts of the physical world. They were cultural, arising from human intentionality, and thus required a scheme of intelligibility that was specific, interpretative and based upon the understanding of their sense. In turn this gave rise to the dichotomy between explanation and understanding[65] or, more famously, between the sciences of nature and the sciences of the spirit (*Geiteswissenschaften*).[66] This formal opposition then broke down into a series of other more fragmented dichotomies, such as the ones between structure and history and causes and reasons.[67] The result is that knowledge turns out to be far more complex than the unitary model of positivism would suggest. The 'opposition between explanation and comprehension', observed Berthelot, 'has not led to the establishment of clearly distinct epistemological regimes'; it has, instead, given rise to epistemological pluralism not just within the social sciences in general but within the various individual disciplines that make up this domain.[68] One cannot, in other words, say that in the natural sciences it is the causal scheme which dominates while in the social sciences it is the hermeneutical approach that is relevant. Within all the individual social science disciplines the two regimes provoke not just methodological and epistemological controversies but equally tend to invalidate each other, something which hardly encourages epistemological clarification. Indeed, the controversy goes much deeper in that it threatens the whole foundation upon which positivism is built; there is, so argue the textualists (and Post-Modernists), no such thing as objective knowledge or objective reality in social science (and indeed in the natural sciences); there are only texts and thus all knowledge is interpretative.[69] All knowledge is hermeneutics.

The conclusion that Berthelot draws from this complexity is, as has been mentioned, that there is no single, or even double, epistemological regime that governs the social sciences. Instead one must think in terms of epistemological pluralism and it is in this context that his work on schemes of intelligibility assumes its pioneering importance. He has asserted, at least in his earlier work,[70] that at the centre of this pluralistic approach are six schemes of intelligibility and while he later argued that these six schemes were not in themselves a transcendental theory of social science – they were fundamental ontological and epistemological points of view on social reality – they nevertheless remain

---

[65] ibid. See also RA Makkreel, 'Expliquer et comprendre' in Mesure and Savidan, *Le dictionnaire des sciences humaines* (2006) 441.

[66] See on this point S Mesure, Dilthey, Wilhelm, 1833–1911, in Mesure and Savidan, *Le dictionnaire des sciences humaines* (2006) 277.

[67] See, eg P Engel, 'Monisme' in Mesure and Savidan, *Le dictionnaire des sciences humaines* (2006) 791.

[68] Berthelot (n 21) 380.

[69] ibid.

[70] See in particular J-M Berthelot, *L'intelligence du social* (Paris, Presses Universitaires de France, 1990) 43–85.

relevant.[71] They are an important part of a more complex set of reasoning methods, paradigms and programmes.[72]

These schemes have been quite exhaustively discussed elsewhere,[73] but several general points need repeating of which the most important is this. The operation of these methodological schemes – the causal, functional, structural, hermeneutical, actional and dialectical[74] – can be understood, as has just been said, only in the more general epistemological context of reasoning methods (induction, deduction and analogy) and paradigm orientations.[75] With regard to the latter, two in particular are central to social science methodology.

The first, the dichotomy between a holistic and an individualist approach which often translates into the level of operation from which the *intellectus* observes (so to speak) the *res*. As one social science theorists puts it, 'social reality cannot be reduced to a single equation'; and so when 'the level of operation changes the reality being observed changes'.[76] Consequently, when one is comparing say a structural approach with an actional, it has to be remembered that the two schemes probably involve two different paradigm orientations. A structural approach tends to function on a macro level, while an actional, which focuses on the individual agent, often suggests a micro level.[77] The historian working on *la longue durée* will not of course see the individuals who have shaped certain events but this does not mean that they do not exist; equally the historian who focuses on certain historical individuals will not see social classes and institutions but, again, this does not mean that they are not there.[78] It is this level problem that helps give statistics their bad name ('lies, damned lies and statistics . . .'). One can predict the number of people that will be killed on the road next year in a particular country and one can predict that the majority of those entering into the universities in some countries will come from middle class families. However, one cannot predict which individual persons will be killed on the road and statistics will not tell one why this or that working class child will not go to university. The sociologist will need to operate at the level of individual families in order to understand the precise reasons why a particular child does not go into higher education.

---

[71] J-M Berthelot, 'Programmes, paradigmes, disciplines: pluralité et unité des sciences sociales' in J-M Berthelot (ed), *Épistémologie des sciences sociales* (Paris, Presses Universitaires de France, 2001) 457.

[72] See Samuel (2007) (n 2).

[73] ibid. See also Samuel, Epistemology and Comparative Law (2004).

[74] '[L]e schème *causal* (si x, alors y ou y = f(x)); le schème *fonctionnel* (S ® X ® S, où un phénomène X est analysé à partir de sa fonction – X ® S – dans un système donné); le schème *structural* (où X résulte d'un système fondé, comme la langue, sur des règles disjonctives, A ou non A); le schème *herméneutique* (où X est le symptôme, l'expression d'une signification sous-jacente à découvrir par interprétation); le schème *actanciel* (où X est la résultante, au sein d'un espace donné, d'actions intentionnelles); le schème *dialectique*, enfin (où X est la résultante nécessaire du développement des contradictions internes à un système)': Berthelot (n 21) 484.

[75] Samuel (2007) (n 2).

[76] D Desjeux, *Les sciences sociales* (Paris, Presses Universitaires de France, 2004) 116.

[77] ibid 107.

[78] ibid 95.

A second paradigm orientation that must be appreciated when investigating schemes of intelligibility is the dichotomy between a naturalist and a culturist approach. Are social phenomena to be considered as a continuity of natural phenomena and thus subject to the same mechanisms? Or are social phenomena to be seen as being a matter of cultural norms and values formed within particular groups or societies which, through the mediation of socialisation, enculturation or inculcation, define the sense of the behaviour patterns or social practices?[79] The naturalist paradigm tends to orientate the researcher towards a causal scheme, although functionalism and structuralism may equally have a role.[80] The culturalist paradigm, in contrast, will regard social patterns and practices as signifiers, or manifestations, of a deeper cultural phenomenon and will therefore seek to understand them in terms of what they signify. Here, the hermeneutical scheme will be central. This is not to say that other schemes of intelligibility will be irrelevant within this latter paradigm and so structuralism and (or) functionalism may well be utilised to aid the understanding of the *mentalité* of the actors making up the group or the society. However, the emphasis will be on social facts as mere signs of a deeper cultural and mentality.

A further general point that needs to be made with respect to schemes of intelligibility is that they appear to transcend the various individual disciplines of social science. Nevertheless, disciplines are not irrelevant in respect of these schemes (and paradigms) because each discipline represents what might be called a horizontal division of social fact according certain general focal points such as quantity (economics), space (geography), time (history), social relations (sociology), cultures (anthropology) and mind (psychology).[81] One needs to ask whether 'causality' or 'function' have the same meaning in different disciplines and, if not, whether such terms are being used appropriately in any particular social analysis. When one talks of cause and effect with respect to time, to space, to social relations, to culture or to the mind, is one really talking about the same thing? The same is true with respect to the actional scheme. Different disciplines construct different 'agents' and so, for example, the *homo œconomicus* is unlikely to transplant his or herself with ease from economics to sociology or to psychology. In addition, then, to the various schemes and paradigms, one must reflect on the nature of disciplines. What are the key methods employed in each discipline? What keeps a discipline together? How are assertions within the discipline validated in an epistemological sense?[82]

These discipline questions require separate treatment and so suffice it to conclude for present purposes that there is a certain fragility when one talks of methodology, particularly at the level of the social (or human) sciences, as

---

[79] J-M Berthelot, 'Les sciences du social' in J-M Berthelot (ed), *Épistémologie des sciences sociales* (2001) 247.
[80] Berthelot, 'Programmes, paradigmes, disciplines' (2001) 498.
[81] Desjeux, *Les sciences sociales* (2004) 101.
[82] See generally on these points J Boutier, J-C Passeron and J Revel (eds), *Qu'est-ce qu'une discipline?* (Éditions de l'École des Hautes Études en Sciences Sociales, 2006).

opposed to when one considers method from an internal position within each discipline (and even within disciplines fragility does not necessarily dissipate). Yet this fragility is not something inherent in the various reasoning processes, schemes of intelligibility and paradigms; it results from the impossibility of the mind to comprehend social reality as a complete and continuous whole. In social science research the results obtained in any research enquiry depend both upon the position of the observer and the categorisation of reality into various levels of appreciation and disciplines and sub-disciplines and upon the scheme of intelligibility, or mixture of schemes, employed. Different models result in different 'realities'. This is why method is so important in the social sciences and this is why it forms such a central part of the education process within disciplines. Reality might be continuous but the observation of it is discontinuous,[83] for knowledge of reality can only be gained in terms of its different dimensions and all the different dimensions cannot be observed at the same time.[84]

IV. METHODOLOGY AND EPISTEMOLOGY IN LAW

Perhaps in contrast to other social science disciplines, within the discipline of law, positivism has, and continues to have, an immense influence. However, its epistemological foundation is subtly different from the model's role in many of the other social sciences (assuming that law is a social science).[85] Outside law, positivism has taken as its strict object social reality – the facts of society – whereas inside law the object of epistemological thinking has been largely focused on rules and norms.[86] This has had one huge methodological advantage in that it has allowed jurists, in the past if not the present, to draw an analogy between law and the natural sciences.[87] If the natural sciences are about the induction of natural 'laws' which, as we have seen with the pyramid of stones example, allows one to arrive at an explanation of a physical phenomenon through deductive reasoning, so legal studies is about social laws which equally allow one to arrive at legal explanations through the use of syllogistic reasoning.[88] Law seems to be a discipline founded on the causal scheme of if p then q.

However, there are difficulties with this thesis. One difficulty facing law, in contrast to many of the natural sciences, is with respect to the question of

---

[83] Desjeux (n 76) 109–10.
[84] ibid 94.
[85] cf Samuel (n 12).
[86] M Troper, *La philosophie du droit* (Paris, Presses Universitaires de France, 2003) 66–83. See also O Pfersmann, 'Norme' in D Alland and S Rials (eds), *Dictionnaire de la culture juridique* (Paris, Presses Universitaires de France, 2003) 1079 ; M Troper, 'Normativisme' in Alland and Rials, *Dictionnaire de la culture juridique* (2003) 1074.
[87] A process that started with the sixteenth century humanist jurists: P Stein, *Roman Law in European History* (Cambridge, Cambridge University Press, 1999) 79–82; J-L Thireau, 'Humaniste (Jurisprudence)' in Alland and Rials, *Dictionnaire de la culture juridique* (2003) 795, 798–99.
[88] P Dubouchet, *Sémiotique juridique: introduction à une science du droit* (Paris, Presses Universitaires de France, 1990) 37–70.

validation. In the natural sciences the positivist model has as its role not just explanation but also prediction and it is this predictive aspect that permits a hypothesis to be validated. A theory about the behaviour of volcanoes or comets can be tested through correspondence with the actual behaviour of volcanoes or comets. A theory about norms or rules cannot be validated in the same way because these objects do not have a physical existence; they are not a *res* existing independently of the *intellectus* (mind). They are indeed creations of the *intellectus* and are thus not easily disentangled from the science that is attempting to explain or theorise the phenomenon.

The response of legal theorists to this difficulty was to abandon the correspondence thesis and to associate the discipline of law with that of mathematics, a science which equally does not have an external *res* as its object.[89] The epistemological validity of law is, according to this approach, to be found in its coherence as a system. The result is that much legal scholarship within the Western tradition has been devoted to the fashioning of ever more coherent systems of law and it is this work that has been largely regarded as the focus of what might be called the history of legal science.[90] Coherence and positivism have been, and to some extent continue to be, a highly successful combination when applied to the object of legal science, namely rules and (or) norms. Indeed it is even possible to construct an epistemology of law on a causal scheme of intelligibility.

Thus, in order to determine if a particular rule or norm is a *legal* norm, it has been proposed by Hans Kelsen that it depends upon whether the norm has been validated by a higher legal norm. In turn this higher norm must itself be validated by an even higher norm, thus giving rise to a 'causal' chain that regresses all the way back to a fundamental norm.[91] Cause, here, is not of course factual, but one can still talk in terms of a causal analysis in that one is asking the following question. *Why* is this rule or norm a valid legal norm? It is valid because it is *dependent* upon the higher norm? Again, of course, this causal scheme can apply only if knowledge of law is regarded as knowledge of norms and that these norms themselves are divisible into independent phenomena (norm A dependent upon norm B itself dependent upon norm C and so on). Perhaps one of the most difficult aspects of this causal hierarchy is the location of the ultimate cause in the *Grundnorm*. Herbert Hart tried to avoid this difficulty by moving from the normative to the empirical and to replace norms and the *Grundnorm* with rules and what he called the 'rule of recognition'. This 'rule of recognition is not a valid rule of the system, because there is no higher rule from which it can derive its authority: we have to say, simply, that the rule inheres in

---

[89] See, eg M-F Renoux-Zagamé, Domat, Jean, in P Arabeyre, J-L Halpérin and J Krynen (eds), *Dictionnaire historique des juristes français XIIe-XXe* (Paris, Presses Universitaires de France, 2007) 254, 255. This *mos geometricus* point is developed in Samuel (n 9).
[90] See generally JW Jones, *Historical Introduction to the Theory of Law* (Oxford, Oxford University Press, 1940).
[91] H Kelsen, *The Pure Theory of Law,* translated by M Knight (Berkeley, University of California Press, 1967).

the practices of officials'.⁹² However, as Lacey goes on to point out, 'this fundamental difference should not disguise the structural similarity between Herbert's and Kelsen's theories'. Both positivists were in effect trying 'to specify the limits of law' in a 'causal' or dependence sense 'rather than to pretend that there is a legal or constitutional solution to every problem'.⁹³ Positivism, in other words, is to an extent a theory that sees law in terms of rules or norms governed by a scheme of intelligibility that is, in emphasising dependence within the system all the way back to a valid source, essentially causal.

V. POSITIVISM (CAUSALITY) VERSUS HERMENEUTICS

Whatever the value of such theories, they leave unanswered questions and these unanswered questions are at the heart of a second difficulty with respect to positivism and law. The rule or norm thesis of legal knowledge does not, as Christian Atias has recently indicated, explain the complexities of legal reasoning.⁹⁴ The essence of law is not to be found in the rule or in the norm; law is also about argumentation, rhetoric and the categorisation of the social world, of social facts. As with the other social sciences, causality is simply one approach to legal knowledge which proves to be inadequate when questions arise as to the meaning and sense of a normative proposition or a rule.⁹⁵ Solutions cannot result purely through the use of deduction. In addition therefore to the causal scheme, the jurist often needs to have recourse to an interpretative or hermeneutical approach.

In fact, hermeneutics is not entirely confined to the arts and does have a more scientific side, especially when it incorporates into the sign (*signans*) and meaning (*signatum*) structure a causal approach. Thus, as one Italian philosopher writing on method perceptively points out, the methods of Sherlock Holmes, Freud, art historians, archaeologists, medical autopsy experts and so on are all indulging in a form of hermeneutics. They focus upon signs – sometimes seemingly insignificant signs – in order to tease out of them some deeper information.⁹⁶ This is why the art expert is comparable to the detective: they both are preoccupied with the small, secondary details neglected by the great majority of people who see only a bit of mud on a walking stick or, in the gallery, never interest themselves in how Titian might paint finger nails and ear lobes.⁹⁷

Interestingly, the Italian philosopher goes on to argue that it is in the sphere of law that the hermeneutical method finds its greatest expression. The term *judex*

---

⁹² N Lacey, *A Life of H.L.A. Hart: The Nightmare and the Noble Dream* (Oxford, Oxford University Press, 2004) 250.
⁹³ ibid.
⁹⁴ See generally Atias (n 40) 90–105. See also Samuel (2009) (n 2).
⁹⁵ ibid.
⁹⁶ G Agamben, *Signatura rerum: Sur la méthode* (J Vrin, 2008; translated by J Gayraud) 77–80.
⁹⁷ ibid 77–78.

(judge) designates one who 'says' (*dico*) the law.[98] He is the figure who 'signifies' something much deeper within society. This is a point developed by Ronald Dworkin who has famously drawn on the law and literature movement to suggest that legal reasoning is analogous to writing a 'chain novel'. According to this model, the act of interpretation – that is to say the hermeneutical scheme – is more than just a method; it is at the very heart of the definition of law. Indeed, this is exactly Dworkin's point.[99] In taking as the object of his theory the judge, Dworkin both incorporates a particular schematic method into legal knowledge itself and elevates it to the level of theory so that hermeneutics becomes the means by which law is defined.[100] Like the filmmaker, then, the lawmaker is the communicator of 'something deeper than the surface of life',[101] in the case of law the surface being a legislative text or the report of a case.[102] What is deeper are, as will be seen, the *rights* of the citizens.

The hermeneutical scheme as legal theory might not of course be acceptable to the whole legal community, but there is no denying that interpretation is one scheme of intelligibility that does hold a central place not just in legal method but in legal knowledge in general.[103] Accordingly, in addition to its place in legal theory, the hermeneutical scheme is of central importance in other areas of law. Thus, in a course on introduction to law, the common law student learns the three foundational rules of statutory interpretation – namely the literal, golden and mischief rules[104] – and these are of course nothing more than an axis between a structural (code and dictionary) scheme (literal rule) at one pole and a functional approach (mischief rule) at the other pole. The statutory text can be seen as a signifier of what Parliament intended and much statutory interpretation discussion has focused upon what is permitted to the judge in the search for the signified. Is it permitted, for example, to look at the Parliamentary debates, reports and the like?[105] Interestingly, this search for the signified often leads one back to other schemes of intelligibility such as the structural approach: an ambiguous word or phrase is to be interpreted only by reference to the structure of the statute as a whole or in relation to meanings gleaned from other parts of the same statute.[106] One is not entitled to look beyond the 'code' itself

---

[98] ibid 84–85.
[99] R Dworkin, *Law's Empire* (London, Fontana, 1986) 228–38.
[100] ibid 410–13.
[101] R Durgnat, *Films and Feelings* (London, Faber and Faber, 1967) 33.
[102] Note the importance of methodology in understanding cinema: 'Realism is a means, not an end. . . . An end to what? To showing, surely, something deeper than the surface of life, whether it be the subjective experiences of the characters of the story, or a clarification of social processes, or the artist's feelings about these things. All these are invisible to the camera-eye . . . These "invisible" realities can, must, be reached through diverse methods, or by different methods in various combinations.' Durgnat, ibid.
[103] P Goodrich, *Reading the Law* (Blackwell, 1986).
[104] See, eg C Elliott and F Quinn, *English Legal System,* 10th edn (Pearson Longman, 2009) 51–56.
[105] *Pepper v Hart* [1993] AC 593.
[106] See further Samuel (2009) (n 2).

which explains why the dichotomy is between hermeneutical structuralism and hermeneutical functionalism.[107]

This hermeneutical analysis is not confined to the words of the legislative text, for the idea of interpreting facts is also of relevance when it comes to the role of the judge. This role has been said by Ivanier to be 'a hermeneutical process aiming to discover unknown facts from the known facts of every cause'.[108] This thesis, advanced by a French judge drawing upon his own experience of judging, is of particular importance in as much as it emphasises how facts do not arrive simply as a given. They are processed and refined in a number of ways. This was a point recognised earlier by the American Realists, a section of whom belonged to a group known as 'fact skeptics'. Fact skeptics were those who regarded certainty in law as elusive, even where a rule was seemingly clear, because of the 'elusiveness of the facts on which decisions turn'.[109] Thus in a traffic accident case there are many facts which are completely irrelevant – the colour of the driver's hair, the clothes being worn, the make of car and so on – and there are others which are arrived at only through inference, that is to say through what Ivanier has called 'a hermeneutical process'.[110] Are these facts neutral in the normative sense or can the way they are perceived, constructed, by lawyers actually influence the normative conclusions of any litigation situation arising out of them? The traditional thesis is to say that in themselves facts are neutral and that the normative outcome is a result of applying to the facts a legal rule. Yet it has to be asked if this traditional division is an accurate model. If liability under article 1382 of the French Civil Code is triggered by the coming together of damage, fault and cause, one can certainly say that it is the *Code civil* article that provides the normative force; but this article says nothing about what constitutes 'damage', 'fault' and 'cause'. Thus, the mere finding that 'damage' has been incurred by a plaintiff will go some way towards establishing a solution in his or her favour.

The hermeneutical scheme is, in addition, of central importance in legal history. The medieval jurists gained their name, the Glossators, from the scheme of intelligibility that they applied to the newly discovered Roman texts. This was the age of *auctoritas* where texts had an absolute epistemological authority[111] and this meant that law as an intellectual discipline was, at least at first, only a matter of explaining these texts. Accordingly, the Glossators explained the *significance*

---

[107] This recourse to structuralism can be found in Ronald Dworkin's theory of law as well. Thus the judge 'must construct a scheme of abstract and concrete principles that provides a coherent justification for all common law precedents and, so far as these are to be justified on principle, constitutional and statutory provisions as well': R Dworkin, *Taking Rights Seriously* (London, Duckworth, 1977) 116–17. In saying therefore that Dworkin's theory is founded primarily on a hermeneutical scheme of intelligibility, this is not to imply that other schemes are excluded. As will be seen, an actional scheme can also be seen to underpin Dworkin's view of law.

[108] T Ivainer, *L'interprétation des faits en droit* (LGDJ, 1988) 22.

[109] J Frank, *Law and the Modern Mind* (London, Stevens, 1949) ix.

[110] For example, the discovery of 'fault' in a set of facts.

[111] W Ullmann, *The Growth of Papal Government in the Middle Ages,* 2nd edn (London, Methuen, 1962) 359–60.

of Roman legal terms in the margins of the Roman texts themselves;[112] that is to say the original Roman law was subjected to a vertical logic in which the Roman source was the signifier and the gloss explained the signified.[113] Hermeneutics thus explains why the gloss proved as important as the actual ancient statements in medieval legal thinking. Bearing in mind that the actual Roman texts were formulated within a society that was far removed from the actual feudal society of medieval Europe and that the texts employed complex expressions and concepts that were unknown to a feudal society, the Glossators were doing more than just interpreting the Roman sources. They were trying to explain what they meant and thus doing more than merely 'interpreting' them.[114]

In fact, the whole of the history of continental legal thought can be seen largely in terms of a history of methods. The medieval hermeneutical (and as we shall see dialectical) methods gave way to the structural (systems) thinking of the Enlightenment jurists[115] which, in more modern times, yielded to a return to what can be described as the 'new hermeneutics'.[116] The history of law can, to an extent, be seen as a struggle between various schemes and methods of analysis.[117] The importance of the French Humanist School of the sixteenth century is that it brought to bear on the Roman texts not just a different kind of hermeneutical analysis, historical methods, but to an extent a new scheme of intelligibility itself, namely a structural analysis which emphasised the coherence of Roman law as a system.[118]

Mention must of course be made of the importance of the hermeneutical scheme in comparative legal studies. During much of the twentieth century the 'basic methodological principle of all comparative law [was] that of *functionalism*';[119] however at the end of the century this 'basic principle' was challenged by Pierre Legrand who proposed, instead, what he called a 'deconstructive hermeneutical' approach.[120] Legrand sees legal rules, the traditional object of comparison, as nothing more than signifiers of a deeper *mentalité* and that the job of the comparatist is to comprehend these deep mental

---

[112] M Boulet-Sautel and J-L Harouel, 'Glose et exégèse' in Alland and Rials, *Dictionnaire de la culture juridique* (2003) 765–66.

[113] M Bellomo, *The Common Legal Past of Europe 1000–1800* (The Catholic University of America Press, 1995, translated by LG Cochrane) 129–35.

[114] *cf* D Maingueneau, L'interprétation des textes littéraires et des textes juridiques in P Amselek (ed) *Interprétation et droit* (Bruylant/Presses Universitaires d'Aix-Marseille, 1995) 61–62; P Legrand, La comparaison des droits expliquée à mes étudiants in P Legrand (ed), *Comparer les droits, résolument* (Paris, Presses Universitaires de France, 2009) 209, 216–17.

[115] J-L Thireau, Humaniste (Jurisprudence) in Alland and Rials, *Dictionnaire de la culture juridique* (2003) 795, 798–99.

[116] P Ricoeur, Le problème de la liberté de l'interprète en herméneutique générale et en herméneutique juridique in Amselek, *Interprétation et droit* (1995).

[117] A struggle that is still going on today: see generally, eg Troper, *La philosophie du droit* (2003). See also Maingueneau, 'L'interprétation des textes littéraires et des textes juridiques' (1995) 67.

[118] See generally D Kelley, *Foundations of Modern Historical Scholarship* (New York, Columbia University Press, 1970).

[119] Zweigert and Kötz, *An Introduction to Comparative Law* (1998) 34.

[120] See generally Legrand, *Le droit compare* (2009).

structures.[121] Even superficially similar rules – say those transplanted from one system into another – may have quite a different cultural and mentality significance in the new system from the significance they had in the old system. Legrand is sometimes seen as advocating what can be labelled as a cultural method in comparative legal studies (cultural paradigm); and while there is no doubt that the whole thrust of his thesis is one that emphasises the cultural and mentality context in which law operates,[122] he is very specific that his scheme of intelligibility is hermeneutical. In other words, he is advocating a vertical logic in which a legal rule (B) is nothing more than a signifier of a *mentalité* (A). This scheme contrasts strongly with functionalism which puts the emphasis on the rules themselves; rules are to be understood in terms of what they do. Equally, Legrand's hermeneutical analysis contrasts with a structural approach which, again, puts the stress on the conceptual structure of law and the way it interacts as a system. The importance of Professor Legrand's intervention, then, is that it is not restricted to his indepth social and historic (cultural) approach; he is indicating how methodology in comparative legal studies is inherently both epistemological and theory-orientated.[123]

VI. POSITIVISM (CAUSALITY) VERSUS DIALECTICS

Yet, hermeneutics is not the only scheme to challenge positivism and causality. As Professor Bergel has observed, logic has only a limited role in legal reasoning and while it 'remains, . . . the general support of reasoning . . . the choice of premises presupposes each time a debate'.[124] Legal argument is based, in other words, just as much upon a dialectical scheme. 'Each principle [of law] presupposes the coexistence of the contrary principle' and this 'dualism is sometimes to be found in history: all individualist regimes conceal within them an element of collectivism and any collectivism carries within it the seeds of individualism'. Accordingly, the 'state of the law is only ever a step in the continuing alternating relationship between the individual and society and, more generally, one of a mass of possible equilibrium points between the different imperatives in cause'.[125]

This observation is interesting in the way that it illustrates how the deductive method, when it does operate, functions only when closely interconnected with the 'influence of dialectics', that is to say with a scheme of intelligibility that can be differentiated, according to Berthelot, from causality and hermeneutics. This scheme is based on the idea that one phenomenon (B) is the result of an internal

---

[121] See generally P Legrand, European Legal Systems are not Converging (1996) 45 *International and Comparative Law Quarterly* 52.
[122] *Extra culturam nihil datur*: Legrand (n 6) 84. See generally Legrand, 'La comparaison des droits expliquée à mes étudiants' (2009).
[123] See Legrand (n 114).
[124] J-L Bergel, *Théorie générale du droit*, 4th edn (Paris, Dalloz, 2003) 295.
[125] ibid.

contradiction within another phenomenon (A). Thus, the phenomenon B will be understood only by the discovery of the internal tension or contradiction within phenomenon A, with the result that B can be said to emerge from A & non A (thus the formula will be expressed as A & non-A→B). As a method *dialectia* is associated with medieval scholasticism which was developed as a device for dealing with apparent contradictions in texts; these contradictions were believed only to be apparent since 'the unity of the human mind, being a divine creation, could not contradict itself in fundamental matters'.[126]

This idea of knowledge as dichotomy embedded itself at various levels in the law. And thus, in addition to the duality of concepts and categories (public and private, property and obligations, movable and immovable property and so on), the dialectical method finds important expression in Western legal systems in the maxim *audi alteram partem* (hear the other side) which translates, in the civil law, into the procedural principle of contradiction; that is to say judgement 'shall not be given against a party who has not been heard or summoned'.[127] The legal process, in other words, is based on the idea that the just solution (B) will emerge out of the formula A [for] & non A [against]. In reality, of course, it is a question of argumentation, the judge having ultimately to choose the one he or she finds the most convincing. Yet, the point needs to be made that this remains a different approach than the causal scheme, at least ideologically if not epistemologically, since a causal approach suggests that the solution to a case does not arise out of argumentation but out of the logical force of a rule acting as major premise (if p then q).

Dialectics thus becomes a means of distinguishing legal reasoning based upon an axiomatic approach from the kind of casuistic reasoning to be found in a system where precedent is (or was) central.[128] It is the means of distinguishing one apparently similar case from another. For example, one might take the case of *Donoghue v Stevenson*,[129] where a woman was injured by a defective bottle of ginger-beer bought for her in a café by her friend, and compare it with *Lockett v A & M Charles Ltd*,[130] in which a wife suffered food poisoning from a meal in a restaurant bought for her by her husband. In the first case it was assumed that the injured consumer would have no action against the seller because she had not bought the ginger-beer herself (privity of contract), while in the second case it was held that there was a contractual relationship between victim and seller (collateral contract). Why the difference? Contrasting the two cases using a *sic et non* method, one can isolate differences such as between café and restaurant, between friendship and marriage, between female purchaser and male purchaser and so on. Used in this way, the dialectical scheme of analysis becomes one that

---

[126] W Ullmann, *Medieval Political Thought* (London, Penguin, 1975) 121.
[127] *Nouveau Code de Procédure Civile* art 16.
[128] See generally AR Jonsen and S Toulmin, *The Abuse of Casuistry* (Berkeley, University of California Press, 1988).
[129] *Donoghue v Stevenson* [1932] AC 562.
[130] *Lockett v A & M Charles Ltd* [1938] 4 All ER 170.

can be seen in opposition to say structuralism (system of axioms) where the tendency is to put the emphasis on holist or universalist vision.[131]

This may seem paradoxical in that the dialectical scheme in social science is generally associated with an organic view of society. As Pheby explains, it is important to remember that a dialectical understanding of society is based not on an atomistic vision, that is to say on a vision of society consisting of individual actors or agents (as envisaged, one might add, by the actional scheme); it is based on the 'organic processes in their totality and implicit within this approach is a rejection of . . . naïve inductivism and instrumentalism'. For such piecemeal 'inductive facts of experience are likely to mislead us into accepting surface phenomena'.[132] Marx, developing a materialistic version of Hegel's dialectical method, accordingly saw production and consumption in terms of two opposites functioning within a whole;[133] and it is these types of 'conflicts and contradictions that are the very nature of the capitalist system' with the result that there will be an 'ultimate negation and replacement by another, opposite, form of society – socialism'.[134] Pheby goes on to illustrate how this dialectical vision is very different from a causal approach. 'By adopting a dialectical approach', he says, 'we are committed to analysing the economy as an organism, a totality'. We are, in other words, 'inhabiting a world of action, reaction and interaction'.[135]

Yet the problem is one of scope of the organic totality rather than one of paradox. Marx and Hegel were seeing dialectical oppositions within society as a whole, whereas the jurist who compares two decisions – or the comparatist who compares a French case with an English one – is creating an organic structure at a very much lower level of abstraction. The same is true of the critic who restricts herself to comparing two paintings, two novels or two films. Casuistic reasoning – that is to say reasoning from single cases – is a form of reasoning that is conducted within islands of isolated factual circumstances; when the single case is compared with another single case the two form a dialectical whole.[136]

VII. POSITIVISM VERSUS ACTIONALISM AND OBJECTIFICATION

This kind of casuistic reasoning equally has recourse to the actional scheme. Perhaps the most obvious actional construction in law is the 'reasonable man' and his counterpart in French law, the *bon père de famille*. However, such 'actors'

---

[131] See for example the dissenting judgments in *White v Jones* [1995] 2 AC 207.
[132] J Pheby, *Methodology and Economics: A Critical Introduction* (Basingstoke, Macmillan, 1988) 118.
[133] ibid 119.
[134] ibid 121.
[135] ibid 122.
[136] See further Y Thomas, L'extrême et l'ordinaire: Remarques sur le cas médiéval de la communauté disparue in J-C Passeron and J Revel (eds), *Penser par cas* (Éditions de l'école des hautes études en sciences sociales, 2005) 45.

appear in various manifestations; there is, for example, the 'reasonable businessman'[137] or, again, the 'reasonable bystander'.[138] These are hypothetical 'individuals' constructed by the court in order to test a proposition or fact.[139]

In one sense, of course, the whole discipline of law is founded upon the individual; and so in criminal law one cannot normally be liable unless the individual act and individual intention come together in an actor.[140] However, the importance of the actional scheme is particularly well illustrated in the area of causation. Here one immediately thinks of the causal scheme when analysing a set of facts to determine whether or not a defendant is to be liable for damage. And, indeed, the emphasis in English law was once on the causal relationship between wrongful act and subsequent damage.[141] However, in 1961, the test for remoteness of damage was changed by the Privy Council: a wrongdoer would only be liable for damage that was reasonable foreseeable.[142] This decision in effect replaced a causal analysis – that is to say the scheme of intelligibility that puts the emphasis on the causal relationship between one phenomenon (A) and another (B) – with a scheme that put the emphasis on the *actor*. What was in the actor's mind? This methodological change had practical consequences in that a wrongdoer might no longer be liable for damage directly caused if that damage was deemed unforeseeable from the position of the defendant actor. In fact much of the law of tort might be said, at least by some, to be plagued by an undue emphasis on the actor and thus activities such as driving or supplying a public service is never seen for what it is, namely a communitarian *activity* which produces a statistically predictable number of accident victims every year. It should come as no surprise, therefore, that the 'reasonable man' has been described as having in law a role analogous to that of the *homo œconomicus* in economics.[143]

The actional scheme might be said to make an appearance, once again, at the level of legal theory. We have seen how Ronald Dworkin has asserted a thesis that law is in essence an interpretative (hermeneutical) exercise. However, he has also argued that judges do not have discretion in hard cases; there is always a right answer to every problem.[144] He admits that this is an idealist position and thus constructs a mythical judge, Hercules, to illustrate how the search for the right answer ought to be conducted. Hercules, he says, 'must construct a scheme of abstract and concrete principles that provides a coherent justification for all common law precedents and, so far as these are to be justified on principle, constitutional and statutory provisions as well.'[145] Such a judge can certainly be seen as an 'actor', just as the focal point in the humanities is the author; and

---

[137] *Darbishire v Warran* [1963] 1 WLR 1067.
[138] Samuel, *Epistemology and Method in Law* (2003) 204.
[139] See also ibid 203–07.
[140] See, eg the French *Code pénal* art 121.
[141] *Re Polemis* [1921] 3 KB 560.
[142] *The Wagon Mound (no 1)* [1961] AC 388.
[143] AP Herbert, *Uncommon Law* (London, Methuen, 1935; reprint 1977) 1, 2–3.
[144] Dworkin, *Taking Rights Seriously* (1977) 81–130.
[145] ibid 116–17.

so law, like literature, can be considered as the work of individuals, as the work of 'actors'. In one way this emphasis on the legal actor brings Dworkin close to those Realists who asserted that law is what the officials of law – the 'actors' – do.[146] However, while the Realists combined this actional scheme with functionalism, Dworkin, in contrast, specifically rejects this approach; the judicial task is to determine rights not policy.[147] Dworkin, in other words, combines the actional scheme with a hermeneutical and a structural (coherence) approach.

Interestingly, it is this recourse to the actional approach that perhaps exposes a gap in Berthelot's six schemes. Berthelot's inventory of schemes is limited to six and he himself poses the question whether the list is complete,[148] perhaps responding to Granger who asserts that it can doubtless be extended.[149] The test that Berthelot sets is not just one of internal coherence but also whether or not a scheme asserted can be reduced, in terms of its fundamental logical relations, to one of the others; and he argues that not one of his six schemes can be so reduced. There is, however, possibly a gap in the list of schemes in that while the actional scheme puts the emphasis, as we have seen, on the actor or agent in society, there does not appear to be a scheme that takes the 'object' as a focus of attention. Yet, if all the world is a stage, then there must be not just 'actors' but equally 'props'; and even the bare stage can be regarded as a negative prop so to speak. The point is of particular importance to economists, whose 'actors' are endowed of course with 'interests',[150] and to jurists whose world, as Gaius asserted, consists not just of *personae* (legal subjects) but equally *res* (legal objects). It can therefore legitimately be asked if the actional scheme adequately accounts for what might be called the 'objectification' – or perhaps 'commodification' – of society, that is to say the social construction of objects both tangible and intangible.

Many objects are of course tangible in the sense that they have a physical existence and so, at first sight, it might seem that a social science interpretative and explanatory scheme is unnecessary. Objects thrust themselves upon the observer in a direct manner and can be understood using the causal or, in social science, the structural scheme. However, the same can be said of the person, that is to say the actor or agent, but such an object is still the basis of an interpretative explanatory scheme. One might object, of course, in saying that objects do not have *intentions* and desires and that it is these rationalised intentions, or reasons, that are the object of a scheme of intelligibility. Yet, many 'objects' have, so it has been argued, a role in the construction of the social[151] and, moreover, many 'things' or 'commodities' are not physical at all; intangible property is at least

---

[146] K Llewellyn, *The Bramble Bush* (New York, Oceana, 1951) 12.
[147] Dworkin (n 107) 82–100.
[148] J-M Berthelot, *Les vertus de l'incertitude* (Paris, Presses Universitaires de France, 1996) 81.
[149] Granger, G-G Granger, *La science et les sciences* 2nd edn (Paris, Presses Universitaires de France, 1995) 92.
[150] A Leroux and A Marciano, *La philosophie économique* (Paris, Presses Universitaires de France, 1998) 15–18.
[151] B Blandin, *La construction du social par les objets* (Paris, Presses Universitaires de France, 2002).

as important, if not more so, as physical things. Accordingly, economists and lawyers – and arguably sociologists – do regard property as the focal point of fundamental logical relations and Bernard Blandin even argues that objects 'are mediators between the subject and the world, and between subjects, but they can do this only on condition of being initially 'mediators one to another' and vice versa.'[152] It would appear, therefore, that the epistemologist might have need of a scheme of intelligibility that gives expression to these relations.

Certainly there is no denying the central importance of the *res* in legal studies and it has been said that the French Civil Code depicts individuals only in terms of their relations with property.[153] Yet, where an 'object' reading of facts is of central importance is with respect to the question of just what amounts to 'property'. Sometimes this question is directly posed and thus in several cases the problem has arisen as to whether a debt amounts to a 'thing' capable of being claimed as a property right. The case of *In re Campbell* concerned a bankrupt who, before the bankruptcy, had made an application to the Criminal Injuries Compensation Board in respect of serious injuries incurred by her as a result of a criminal assault.[154] She was finally awarded the compensation and the question arose as to whether the entitlement to the award that was eventually made to her was or represented property which was vested in the trustee in bankruptcy when she was made bankrupt. The judge observed that treating 'the matter purely as a matter of construction I am quite unable to accept that the word "property," when it is used in that definition of property, is intended to describe anything other than an existing item.[155] He went on to hold that this situation was analogous to a lottery ticket and the prize money; before the draw the ticket could not be considered as property representing the prize money.

What legal reasoning is doing in this kind of case is to construct social reality: it is formulating what 'exists' and what does not exist. Furthermore, this problem of ownership and object can impact upon the actor in as much as the question arises from time to time as to whether a person, or at least body parts of a person, can amount to things (commodities) capable of being owned. In Roman law the issue arose directly in respect of slavery where the law regarded some persons, that is to say slaves, as 'things' capable of being owned. However, the Romans also asserted that a human did not own parts of his or her body and thus in personal injury cases one could not regard the invasion of the body as an invasion of a thing.[156] In modern legal systems, the accident victim can get compensation for the loss of a limb and thus, to an extent, parts of the body are now treated as assets capable of being valued economically.[157]

---

[152] ibid 12.
[153] J-L Halpérin, *Histoire du droit privé français depuis 1804* (Paris, Presses Universitaires de France, 1996) 25.
[154] *In re Campbell* [1997] Ch 14.
[155] ibid 18.
[156] D.9.2.13pr.
[157] T Weir, *An Introduction to Tort Law*, 2nd edn (Oxford, Oxford University Press, 2006) 210.

Yet the problem of treating the body, or parts of the body, as an artefact can still arise. In one recent criminal case the question to be decided was whether a person who had his hand inside a jacket, forcing it out so as to give the impression that he has a gun could be convicted of possessing an imitation firearm. The House of Lords held that he could not because, according to Lord Bingham, what 'is possessed must under the definition be a thing' and a 'person's hand or fingers are not a thing'. If they were, he continued, 'the court could, theoretically, make an order depriving the offender of his rights to them and they could be taken into the possession of the police'.[158] Fingers are part of a person and as such cannot be treated as a separate object. However, despite this decision, it would probably be wrong to assume that body parts can never treated by the law as commodities; one can imagine situations where the appropriation of a body part might amount to theft and (or) to the tort of conversion. One can talk, equally, of selling one's blood. Whether or not, then, a person is liable in criminal or civil law might well depend upon the scheme of intelligibility applied by the judge to the facts.

Merely applying an actional or a structural scheme to social reality is, accordingly, not comprehensive enough to provide an ontological analysis of social reality, especially from an economic perspective. Emphasis also needs to be put on objects with which humans relate. What constitutes such an object? What makes it object-like? What is the relationship between objects and interests? When does an interest become an object, that is to say a thing with which a legal relation (*dominium, possessio*) with a human can be constructed? Have not jurists created a scheme of intelligibility within the details of their law of property or indeed within the *jus rerum* in general?[159] Can one own a flock of sheep or does one own only each individual animal?[160] A boat owner gradually replaces, over a long period, each rotten plank of the boat; when he has replaced every single plank does he still have the same boat?[161] This kind of object scheme is certainly of value to comparatists when comparing two very different social cultures and this in turn should suggest that it has an epistemological importance in social science thinking in general. It is certainly a scheme that relates to the holism versus individualism paradigm.[162]

Of course, nothing that has been said so far about the possibility of a seventh scheme should be taken as suggesting that it is uncontroversial. Had he lived, Professor Berthelot might well have disputed the arguments set out above; he may well have argued, for example, that social theory is about persons and not things. However, the point here is not to be controversial at the level of method. The point of raising the possibility of extending the schemes of intelligibility is to illustrate how law as a knowledge discipline could make its own distinc-

---

[158] *R v Bentham* [2005] 1 WLR 1057 [8].
[159] See, eg D.41.3.30.
[160] D.41.3.30.2.
[161] D.5.1.76; D.46.3.98.8; D.44.2.7.pr.
[162] See D.41.3.30pr.

tive contribution to the epistemology in social sciences debate. It need not be, in other words, just a discipline obsessed with norms and texts, using methods that are not its own; nor need it be the passive user of social science schemes of intelligibility. The discipline can be epistemologically active in its own right. Law has generated − and can continue to generate − its own model(s) through which one can problematise the forms of interaction between actants. In short, jurisprudence may well have been subverted by other social science disciplines, as Kelley has asserted,[163] but, at the level of schemes of intelligibility, law as a discipline is still capable of providing an epistemological lead. It is not a discipline conceptually and epistemologically cut off from sociological, economic, psychological and political thinking and thus is capable of operating within an enquiry paradigm.

Of course, for the most part, the majority of lawyers will not be interested in such a paradigm shift for understandable professional reasons. However for many jurists working in the world of research and scholarship there are different priorities. If schemes of intelligibility are a way of understanding social reality, the latter will, to some extent, be nothing more than the grilles de lecture used to understand it. The question is, then, whether law just makes use of schemes borrowed from outside its discipline or whether it can actively contribute, as a discipline, to the schemes. Does law have its own contribution to make to the 'social construction of reality'? The possibility of a seventh scheme suggests that law is not, so to speak, epistemologically passive.

VIII. PARADIGM AUTHORITARIANISM VERSUS COMPARATIVE STUDIES

Examining legal reasoning from the position of a social science epistemologist appears, then, remarkably fruitful. First because, as we saw with Annelise Riles' comments, the internal (doctrinal) and external (social science view) dichotomy is rendered meaningless. The kind of analysis undertaken by lawyers of what amount to 'property' or 'damage' is as much a (re)construction of social reality as any scholarly work by an anthropologist or economist.

Secondly, it is interesting because it confirms Berthelot's more general point about epistemological plurality in the social sciences. Facts studied in the social sciences cannot be so easily transformed into simple objects capable of being modelled into abstract schemes, allowing themselves logically and mathematically to be manipulated to produce reliable knowledge.[164] Human acts and facts are too complex to model in a way that makes accurate and relatively detailed prediction possible. And so, for example, it was and remains impossible to predict the political, economic and social outcomes resulting from an event like the military invasion of Iraq. As Granger asserts, the problem is how such social

---

[163] D Kelley, *The Human Measure: Social Thought in the Western Legal Tradition* (Cambridge, Mass, Harvard University Press, 1990) 279.
[164] Granger, above, 85.

facts can be conceptualised; and the difficulty with the social sciences is that the models employed can only very partially represent a phenomenon.[165] Much will depend, he says, on the 'scheme of intelligibility' employed, here making reference to Berthelot's work.[166]

Yet law ought to be central here in that it is a discipline whose concepts are supposed to make sense of social fact. And not just in a way that allows the law to be applied but also in a way that permits the solutions to legal problems to be predicted. However, it is, perhaps, this predictability dimension that results in causality being brought into the ideology of the law (if p, then q) and this causality is in turn assured both by the unitary model of positivism and by the epistemic validating element of coherence.[167] The epistemological truth is of course different because the 'rule is only a path, a bridge towards the law; it is not the law which is discovered when reality is met'.[168] And so the concepts of law would appear at best to capture social reality in only a partial way. What is left out, says Atias, is legal reasoning and argumentation whereby a 'margin of manoeuvrability is thus reintroduced between the rule of law and the solution which is attached to it.'[169] It is in this margin of manoeuvrability that Berthelot's schemes come into play.[170] However, in coming into play, these schemes import into law the epistemological and methodological pluralism to be found more generally in the social sciences. The 'diversity of theories, currents, approaches and debates is the rule' and 'within the disciplines, researchers group themselves according to particular orientations and models'. However, nothing 'prevents them, having exhausted the joys of one paradigm, to explore another one'.[171]

This diversity of approach is in some ways formally evident within the discipline of law. For example it becomes evident in the different schools of jurisprudence and so while positivism might remain a dominant model,[172] natural law theory, realism, critical legal studies and feminist jurisprudence bear witness to other approaches. Yet this evidence must not be over-estimated. The dominant legal theorists are still completely wedded to the idea that the ontological and epistemological foundation of law is the rule or the norm and that the work of the legal theorist is to provide a theoretical underpinning as to what counts as the legitimate sources of these rules and (or) norms.[173] As for the doctrinal

---

[165] ibid 85–86.
[166] ibid 90–92.
[167] Jones, *Historical Introduction* (1940) 206.
[168] Atias (n 40) 101.
[169] ibid 103.
[170] Samuel (2009) (n 2).
[171] Berthelot (n 21) 381.
[172] See, eg L Alexander and E Sherwin, *Demystifying Legal Reasoning* (Cambridge, Cambridge University Press, 2008).
[173] See, eg R Susskind, *Expert Systems in Law* (Oxford, Oxford University Press, 1987) 78–79; Alexander and Sherwin, *Demystifying Legal Reasoning* (2008). Even a sophisticated work on legal reasoning such as W Twining and D Miers, *How To Do Things With Rules,* 5th edn (London, Butterworths, 2010) is premised on the assumption that the ontological foundation of law is a body of rules.

academic lawyer, his or her work is 'to reveal an intelligible order or meaning in the law' so as to reduce the 'large and possibly confusing mass of legal information to a relatively tight and coherent theory which is thought to lie behind it or justify it'.[174] In other words, the authority paradigm is not only alive and well, but also still trying to imposing itself on legal scholarship in the common law tradition.[175] Doctrinalists fear for the security of their discipline.[176]

It is this fear that perhaps drives comparatists such as Professor Fauvarque-Cosson to reject interdisciplinarity in comparative legal studies. As Professor Hedley notes, private lawyers faced with threats 'tend to look inward, returning to traditional ideas both as to theories of liability and as to legal methodology, spurning modern developments, whether legal or political'.[177] In short, they tend to take refuge within the authority paradigm. The problem with this paradigm is that it restricts the vision of lawyers to understand in any sophisticated way their own methods and the epistemological implications that attach to them. This in turn leads to a discipline that becomes moribund when compared with disciplines outside law. Does a modern doctrinal lawyer, epistemologically speaking, actually know more about law as a discipline than say Ulpian, Bartolus, Domat or Savigny knew? In the natural sciences, Newton, despite his enormous contribution to knowledge, would, if brought back to life today, not be able to recognise the models now employed by his successors. A Post-Glossator, in contrast, would have few problems in understanding a law lecture in a common law faculty and Domat would probably have little difficulty with the French agrégation.[178]

Perhaps, then, Professor Van Hoecke's observation should be reversed. The comparatist does not so much need a better understanding of the methods employed by lawyers and jurists within domestic legal systems; what the comparatist needs is an ability to convince these lawyers and jurists within domestic legal systems that they are using methods that have been seriously analysed and reflected upon outside the discipline of law. And that this reflection, if only they knew it, has two consequences. First, it makes their work on legal method written within the authority paradigm look trite and unsophisticated.[179] Secondly, if domestic methods as governed by the authority paradigm are to be the tools of comparative law, it will result in nothing more than superficial scientific reductionism. Comparative law will remain a subject obsessed with common denominators and harmonisation projects, with what comparatists in other disciplines

---

[174] Hedley, 'The Shock of the Old' (2008) 206. Professor Hedley's critique of this doctrinal approach is well worth reading.
[175] See further Samuel (n 9).
[176] See, eg A Beever and C Rickett, 'Interpretive Legal Theory and the Academic Lawyer' (2005) 68 *Modern Law Review* 320; *cf* Hedley (n 61) 219–20.
[177] Hedley (n 61) 221.
[178] See on this JA Brundage, *The Medieval Origins of the Legal Profession* (Chicago, University of Chicago Press, 2008) 257–62.
[179] This point is developed to some extent in G Samuel, Can Gaius Really be Compared to Darwin? (2000).

call the problem of universal myths. It need not be like this. An interdisciplinary approach might well reveal, as indeed Annelise Riles has suggested, that law as a discipline has some interesting contributions to make to social science epistemology in general. Equally, of course, such an approach can reveal the shortcomings of legal reasoning and assertion.[180]

---

[180] In particular, the tendency of UK judges to make assertions about social policy unsupported by any empirical research. See further Samuel (2009) (n 2).

11

Comparative Law, Legal Linguistics and Methodology of Legal Doctrine

JAAKKO HUSA

I. INTRODUCTION

WITHIN LEGAL SCIENCES comparative law is part of general legal studies. This means that it differs from the doctrinal study of law which is central to continental European and Nordic systems. While the doctrinal study of law (German *Rechtsdogmatik*) interprets and systematises valid law, epistemological premises of other legal disciplines distance themselves from valid law. It is assumed in this contribution that legal doctrine is a scholarly discipline in its own right, thus, legal doctrine itself is not studied.[1]

Methodological freedom within doctrinal study of law has been nationally and territorially limited as to what kind of argumentation is allowed and on which jurisprudential view of legal sources and valid argumentation is to be based.[2] In the field of general legal studies, naturally there are also methodological and epistemic rules that are observed. However, the rules of general legal studies are not limited to the same extent to a particular view of argumentation and legal sources, nor to a specific interpretation of the ontology of law. In German legal sciences, such general legal studies are tellingly referred to as *Grundlagenfächer*, ie non-doctrinal basic research of law (*Grundlagenforschung*) whose core contents are *Rechtsgeschichte* (legal history), *Rechtstheorie* (legal theory) and *Rechtsvergleichung* (comparative law).[3] These fields are partly committed to the same epistemic premises as the doctrinal study of law; they complete the picture conveyed by doctrinal studies and enrich the methodology of legal study, without losing the internal legal perspective, unlike the sociology of law.

Comparative legal science (or comparative law for short), just like the doctrinal study of law, often engages in studying valid law and therefore differs

---

[1] The idea of legal doctrine as a discipline in its own right also emerges from Mark Van Hoecke (in chapter one of this volume).
[2] So, a legal system as a whole which is not merely the subject of research but also a conceptual framework for legal doctrine as stated by Pauline Westerman (in chapter five of this volume).
[3] See, eg O Behrends et al (eds), *Elementa iuris* (Nomos Verlag, Baden-Baden, 2009).

from such general legal studies as legal history and legal theory.[4] Comparative law, however, does not rely on the interpretation of law within one system only; instead a conceptual framework has to be built where several systems are simultaneously studied, side by side. In these comparisons the basic epistemic viewpoint of law is not completely identical with that of national doctrinal studies of law where the perspective is *internal*.[5]

Most general legal studies have certain common features but there are also differences. The normative perspective of an internal player is usually lacking in general studies, but the mutual dissimilarity of general studies ensures that too close a likeness is prevented. Several newcomers to the field of general studies, such as law and economics, can be beneficial for comparative law as well as to doctrinal study.[6] From the point of view of comparative law, one of the most interesting new fields is comparative legal linguistics which, in the family of legal studies, lies very close to comparative law.[7] It is often very difficult to tell these two apart.[8] The similarity between comparative legal linguistics and comparative law is easy to understand because legal texts in different systems are in different languages. On the other hand, it has to be remembered that problems with legal language are not only caused by non-national factors, but can be internal as well: also legal doctrine operates with legal language and is epistemically bound to it.

It would be wrong to claim that comparative law has only recently taken an interest in legal language. It is true to say that since the 1990s the theory of comparative law has contained an increasing amount of debate regarding the fact that the language of law and command of several languages is of a particularly great importance to comparative law. This point has been made with particular vigour in Anglo-American discussion where the use of English translations is threatening to become the dominant practice when old emigrant comparatists whose roots were in continental Europe have passed away.[9] Many significant comparatists have mastered several languages, and also in the twenty-first century it is considered a relevant requirement that a mature comparatist is capable of referring to sources in several languages. Alan Watson is quite right when he writes on the dangers involved in comparative law and says: 'too frequently

---

[4] Much ink has been spilled concerning the question of whether 'comparative law' and 'comparative legal science' mean the same thing, see P Arminjon, B Nolde, M Wolff, *Traité de droit comparé* (Paris, Librairie générale de droit et de jurisprudence, 1950) vol I, 23–40 and M Bogdan, *Comparative Law* (Stockholm, Kluwer/Norstedts, 1994) 17. In this text, these concepts are used as synonyms. In fact, 'comparative law' also covers the much later term 'comparative legal studies', at least for the purpose of the present argument.

[5] Legal doctrine and comparative law may also benefit each other, so differences should not be exaggerated. See, eg H Kötz, 'Rechtsvergleichung und Rechtsdogmatik' (1990) 54 *RabelsZ* 203.

[6] See U Mattei, *Comparative Law and Economics* (Michigan, University of Michigan Press, 1997).

[7] HES Mattila, *Comparative Legal Linguistics* (Aldershot, Ashgate, 2006).

[8] Here I base the argument on the experience gained from writing a large monograph about the law and legal language of one system (ie Greek), see J Husa, *Kreikan oikeus ja oikeuskieli* (*Greek Law and Legal Language*) (Suomalainen lakimiesyhdistys, Helsinki, 2007) 1–12. On a general level, see Bogdan, *Comparative Law* (1994) 16–17.

[9] See, eg VG Curran, 'Cultural Immersion: Difference and Categories in US Comparative Law' (1998) 46 *American Journal of Comparative Law* 43, especially 66–78.

linguistic deficiencies interpose a formidable barrier between the scholar and his subject'.[10] What this barrier is like is pondered in this contribution.

This contribution studies the relationship between comparative law and legal language from the point of view of mainstream theory, so that there is a methodological undertone with which the present argument is seen in relation to the European doctrinal study of law. It has long been common in comparative studies to apply so-called functional comparative law, the concept that the influential classic by Konrad Zweigert and Hein Kötz has made well-known, having been translated into several languages.[11] Functionalism has been both criticised and defended in discussions that have continued for decades and still do not show any signs of calming down. This is easy to understand if one agrees with Ralf Michaels: 'For its proponents it is the most, perhaps the only fruitful method; to its opponents it represents everything bad about comparative law.'[12]

The argument of this chapter neither supports nor opposes any particular branch of comparative law; instead attention is paid to the relation between the basic ideas of functional comparative law and comparative legal linguistics, legal translation and doctrinal study of law.[13] In an era when law is turning global, transnational or at least European, it is important to realise that legal translation, as well as interpretation and systematisation of supranational law in national systems means that comparison and legal linguistics become factors that also have an impact on national methodology. In the following, the point of view is methodological (in a non-normative sense) to the extent that the aim is to show how close to each other the theoretical premises of comparative legal linguistics and comparative law are. The point of view taken means practically that questions that are for instance related to whether it is possible or even necessary that there should be, in Europe, a common legal meta-language or at least a common technical legal language are not discussed.[14]

Section II., following this introduction, returns to the source of comparative law represented by Zweigert and Kötz; there we find the arch-functionalist Ernst

---

[10] A Watson, *Legal Transplants: An Approach to Comparative Law*, 2nd edn (Athens/London, University of Georgia Press, 1993) 11.

[11] Here an English translation is used: *An Introduction to Comparative Law*, 3rd edn (Oxford, Oxford University Press, 1998). Zweigert and Kötz are not shy about the fact that the core of their methodology comes directly from Rabel (see 36). [German version: *Einführung in die Rechtsvergleichung auf dem Gebiete des Privatrechts*, 3rd edn (Tübingen, JBC Mohr Siebeck, 1996)].

[12] R Michaels, 'The Functional Method of Comparative Law', in M Reimann and R Zimmermann (eds), *The Oxford Handbook of Comparative Law* (Oxford, Oxford University Press, 2006) 339–82, 340. See also R Hyland, *Gift: A Study in Comparative Law* (Oxford, Oxford University Press, 2009) 63–113 (claims that there is no functionalism in comparative law but rather 'purposivism').

[13] Today the methodological attitudes are softening and functionalism is recognised as a legitimate method; but merely as one of a number of possible methods. See VV Palmer, 'From Lerotholi to Lando: Some Examples of Comparative Law Methodology' (2004) 4 *Global Jurist Frontiers* issue 2, article 1. (www.bepress.com/gj/frontiers/vol4/iss2/art1). Also, in legal linguistics, there are obviously different schools and approaches, see Mattila, Comparative Legal Linguistics (2006) 8–14.

[14] See, eg AL Kjær, 'A Common Legal Language in Europe?' in M Van Hoecke (ed), *Epistemology and Methodology of Comparative Law* (Oxford, Hart Publishing, 2004) 377–98. See also M Van Hoecke and M Warrington, 'Legal Culture, Legal Paradigm and Legal Culture: Towards a New Model for Comparative Law' (1998) 47 *International and Comparative Law Quarterly* 495, especially 534–35.

Rabel. In section III., methodological core concepts of functional comparative law are discussed. In section IV., certain observations are made concerning methodological relationships between comparative law and legal linguistics. The final section, section V., deals with theoretic-methodological links between functionalism and legal linguistics and their possible relevance from the point of view of the modern doctrinal study of law.

II. BACKGROUND OF FUNCTIONALISM

While excavating the pedigree of comparative law, it is difficult to pinpoint any single person. Nevertheless, Rabel (1874–1955) is considered the founder of German comparative law, but in addition to that he specialised in international private law and Roman-Byzantine legal history in particular. His name is perpetuated in an esteemed German periodical *Rabels Zeitschrift für ausländisches und internationales Privatrecht* (RabelsZ) that was first founded in 1927. The periodical that is published by Mohr Siebeck Verlag and comes out four times a year is now dedicated to comparative law and both foreign and international private law. In addition to these, special fields covered by the periodical are supranational integration and European law in general. The periodical publishes articles in English and German.[15] Rabel, who established the periodical, is widely considered the father of comparative law.[16] In spite of that his name does not evoke much applause within present-day European legal circles. Here, it is justified to ask, who then was this Austrian-German legal scholar?

Rabel was born in Austria to a Viennese family of a successful solicitor. He grew up in a liberal atmosphere, and his habilitation dissertation was written at the University of Leipzig at the beginning of the 1900s.[17] He was a professor at his Alma Mater in the years 1904–06 after which he was a professor of various branches of legal disciplines in Germany: Basel (1906–10); Kiel (1910–11); Göttingen (1911–16); Munich (1916–26); and finally in Berlin (1926–37). Rabel had to move to the United States from Berlin after a short stop in Belgium because the political situation in Germany had turned intolerable for him. He was a Roman Catholic, but his ancestors were Jewish, which meant that it was not possible for him to make an academic career in Germany while it was ruled by the Nazis.[18] This emigrant background is characteristic to many other significant legal scholars of whom the best known is probably Austrian Hans Kelsen.

---

[15] For more information, see the webpages of the publisher (www.mohr.de).

[16] In the words of Rodolfo Sacco: 'Following Rabel, the comparatists began to pose questions that had to be grappled with in functional terms.' R Sacco, 'One Hundred Years of Comparative Law' (2001) 75 *Tulane Law Review* 1159, 1167.

[17] E Rabel, Die Haftung des Verkäufers wegen Mangels im Rechte. vol 1. Geschichtliche Studien über den Haftungserfolg (Walter de Gruyter, Leipzig, 1902).

[18] For more details about biographical information and production, see M Rheinstein, 'In Memoriam of Ernst Rabel' (1956) 4 *American Journal of Comparative Law* 185, and G Kegel, 'Ernst Rabel – Werk und Person' (1990) 54 *RabelsZ* 1. For his connections with legal history, see R Zimmermann, 'In der Schule von Ludwig Mitteis – Ernst Rabels rechtshistorische Ursprünge' (2001) 65 *RabelsZ* 1.

In the United States, Rabel was later on a professor in the law school both in Ann Arbor (Michigan) and Harvard. Before he left Germany, he had founded and been the first head in the Emperor Wilhelm Institute (*Kaiser Wilhelm Institut für ausländisches und internationales Privatrecht*) that specialised in foreign and international private law under his leadership. This highly-esteemed institute now operates in Hamburg under the name Max Plank. Rabel's contribution is now upheld in the highest esteem in Germany where he is considered to be the founder of systematic comparative law on whose theoretical basic concepts the study of comparative law still relies today.[19] Although the basic form of functionalism can apparently be traced back to Rabel, it is not clear if there are grounds to hold him responsible for the branch of comparative law that emphasises praxis, judicial harmonisation and similarities and leaves less scope for the cultural context and differences.

Rabel's work is considerable in volume and he wrote in several languages. In the *Gesammelte Aufsätze* series there are texts in German, English, French, Italian and Spanish which are the major languages of his publications. In the field of international private law his extensive work *The Conflict of Laws: A Comparative Study* (1945) is without doubt the classic in the field while *Law of the Sale of Goods* was for a long time a kind of theoretical model for supranational undertakings to harmonise law.[20] His scholarly production is collected in the four volumes of the *Gesammelte Aufsätze* series, edited thoroughly and comprehensively (as is usual in Germany). From the point of view of comparative law, the most interesting of them is Volume III where articles particularly on comparative law and legal integration from the years 1919–54 have been gathered.[21] Rabel's work began to get international renown at an early stage due to internationally active researchers who became the big names of comparative law later in the 1900s.[22] Notwithstanding, sometimes functionalism has been attributed to scholars who came a bit later than Rabel.[23] In turn, Rabel himself confessed to having been influenced during his studies by a leading legal

---

[19] In comparative law there are, of course, other schools, but normally it is admitted that functionalism has a special position. Béatrice Jaluzot distinguishes the following approaches: evolutionism, conceptualism, functionalism, factualism and culturalism/contextualism, see B Jaluzot, 'Méthodologie du droit comparé' (2005) 56 *Revue internationale de droit comparé* 29, 38ff. For an up-to-date formulation of functionalism see, eg JC Reitz, 'How to Do Comparative Law' (1998) 46 *American Journal of Comparative Law* 617.

[20] Originally, Das Recht des Warenkaufs. Eine rechtsvergleichende Darstellung, 2 vols (Tübingen/Berlin, 1936/1957).

[21] HG Leser (ed), *Ernst Rabel Gesammelte Aufsätze vol 3 Arbeiten zur Rechtsvergleichung und zur Rechtsvereinheitlichung* (Tübingen, Mohr Siebeck, 1967).

[22] In specific we may mention Max Rheinstein (1869–1977) and his early article which later became one of the classical texts on the field, 'Comparative Law and Conflict of Laws in Germany' (1935) 2 *University of Chicago Law Review* 232.

[23] Efstathios K Banakas traces functionalism to Max Rheinstein and in his article published 1937–38 ('Teaching Comparative Law', originally in the *University of Chicago Law Review*). E Banakas, 'The Method of Comparative Law and the Question of Legal Culture Today' (1994) 3 *Tilburg Foreign Law Review* 113, 118. ('First proposed by Max Rheinstein in 1937, functionality is now accepted as the orthodox, methodological principle of all meaningful comparative law.')

historian Ludwig Mitteis (1859–1921) who was interested in the functions of Roman law.[24]

It is, however, not surprising that this first formulator of functionalism has not always been esteemed. In fact, Rabel never formulated any comprehensive and systematic methodology. In spite of that his theoretical core ideas about comparative law have later commonly been referred to as functional or functionalist comparative law. The terminology used makes one think about connections with other disciplines. However, there seems to be no actual equivalence to the way this concept is used in other disciplines, for example, the way it is used to describe different systems in structural sociology, anthropology or biology. Due to this, concrete links to the same concept in other disciplines are mostly limited to the concept itself.[25] In the same breath one has to register the general kinship of Rabel's functionalism to the functional analysis that is part of Niklas Luhmann's system-theoretic macro-sociology.[26] This is one of the factors which connects functionalism and the social-scientific study of law. In spite of this somewhat distant social-scientific link, Rabel's functionalism is more closely related to the doctrinal study of law than to the sociology of law, as far as attitudes and spirit are concerned. This is hardly surprising because Rabel's background is in international private law, not in any of the social sciences.

From the point of view of comparative law, it can be stated that a functional approach continues to be the basis of mainstream methodology, although it has increasingly met with stronger criticism from supporters of several different theories.[27] From the point of view of legal linguistics, the functional theory of comparative law is interesting because it contains an analysed explanation of the significance of language to a comparatist who approaches it in the epistemic sense from the outside, ie having an external view.[28] It is also an unsophisticated basic theory in the respect that like other later comparative law theories of the 1900s it is derived from the scope of conflict of laws and mainly concentrated on private law. The transformation from conflict of laws and private law started to be practically corrected slowly starting as late as the 1990s and the 2000s

---

[24] D Gerber, 'Sculpting the Agenda of Comparative Law: Ernst Rabel and the Façade of Language' in A Riles (ed), *Rethinking the Masters of Comparative Law* (Oxford, Hart Publishing, 2001) 190–208, 192.

[25] Functionalism as a social theory, see, eg R Cotterrell, *The Sociology of Law*, 2nd edn (London, Butterworths, 1992) 93–95. Recently, however, there have been ideas, according to which functionalism should be developed toward a more strictly scientific and rational method and, by doing so, making it closer to the functionalism of other disciplines. See Michaels, 'The Functional Method of Comparative Law' (2006).

[26] See, eg N Luhmann, *Social Systems* (Stanford, Stanford University Press, 1995) 52–58. Luhmann was also interested in functional equivalents, but he was in other respects more systematic, holistic, theoretical, and causal-relations stressing than jurist Rabel who was interested in separate concrete legal problems (contract, marriage, sale of movables, etc).

[27] For a critique and the (possible) ability of functionalism to answer this critique, see J Husa, 'Farewell to Functionalism or Methodological Tolerance?' (2003) 67 *RabelsZ* 419.

[28] Originally this idea grew out of reading *David J* Gerber's writing (Gerber, 'Sculpting the Agenda of Comparative Law' (2001)). Gerber is probably the first who described Rabel's methodological relation to language in a clear form and described language as 'the façade of law'.

in the various sectors of public law in particular.[29] In the doctrinal study of domestic law, however, functionalism has had a surprisingly small role, although presumably it would perhaps fit particularly well together with the sociological approach of law. Importantly, the point of view taken by Rabel's functionalism differs from the social-scientific one; it recognises the *internal normative dimension* of law better than sociology does.[30]

III. FROM RABEL TO ZWEIGERT AND KÖTZ

Rabel's work is also impressive in its thematic coverage, and it is not practical to try to describe his ideas in general or to attempt to otherwise create a comprehensive picture of his extensive view of comparative law. Instead, it is worth concentrating on a few key ideas in his writing about the methods of comparative law. A good starting point could be *Die Fachgebiete des Kaiser-Wilhem-Instituts für ausländisches und internationales Privatrecht* (originally from 1937), a text in *Gesammelte Aufsätze* III where the field of research of the Institute is outlined from a professional viewpoint.[31] At the beginning of the text, the development of the theory of comparative law from the early 1900s is run through in the light of names, such as Raymond Saleilles, Edouard Lambert, Josef Kohler, Frederick Pollock, Roscoe Pound and John Henry Wigmore. When Rabel exegetically kind of compressed the parts of earlier writers' thinking which he found useful and synthesised the core of his own comparative method out of them, he summed up as follows:

> Mit einem Wort: wir vergleichen nicht starre Daten und isolierte Paragraphen, wir vergleichen viehlmer, welche Lösungen sich aus der Gesamtheit des ganzen vollen Rechtserlebens in den einen und in dem anderen Staat in den gleichen Lebensfragen ergeben. Indem dieses umfassende Untersuchungsprogramm *die Funktion der Rechtsinstitute* (emphasis added) an die erste Stelle setz [. . .].[32]

The research programme that had been outlined for the Institute and the core of Rabel's own comparatist identity is crystallised in the above quotation. Even if it is, in our eyes, not terribly original, it is formulated in style and is the first rough methodological guideline of comparative law concentrating on functions. Its principle components are basically unaltered compared to the way they are still formulated by Zweigert and Kötz and many other mainstream researchers in the 2000s. The core ideas are clear. Instead of concentrating on studying

---

[29] Obviously, this does not hinder functionalism from working in other areas of law, see, eg in administrative law, J Schwarze, *European Administrative Law* (London, Sweet & Maxwell, 1992) 82f and in constitutional law, F Venter, *Constitutional Comparison* (Cape Town, Juta/Kluwer, 2000) 19f. See even A Harding and P Leyland, 'Comparative Law in Constitutional Contexts' in E Örücü and D Nelken (eds), *Comparative Law: A Handbook* (Oxford, Hart Publishing, 2007) 313–38, especially 324–26.
[30] The standard view on legal sociology holds that: 'The sociologist remains a relatively uncommited observer' (Cotterrell, *The Sociology of Law* (1992) 5).
[31] Above Leser, *Ernst Rabel Gesammelte Aufsätze* vol 3 (1967) 180–234.
[32] ibid 187.

particular material and isolated provisions, emphasis should be on the comparison of those specific solutions that each state makes in situations that are practically identical. In such a study programme, a research method is used that gives preference to the functions of the institutions and norms under study. While the function is given priority, the comparatist is not restricted by the linguistic expressions and interpretations of the national systems they are studying.[33]

A. Relevance of Doctrine

From the present day point of view, it is easy to regard Rabel's methodology as rough and general, as a kind of rule of thumb, which in fact it is.[34] However, how should we conceive it today? Somehow, social and natural sciences have made the doctrinal internal methods that jurists have developed seem 'non-scientific'. Functionalism is no exception to this: consider functionalism in biology or sociology and underdevelopment of comparative law simply sticks out. On the other hand, the power of Rabel's rough functionalism might be in its apparent simplicity; on a general level it is possible to surpass difficult theoretical and practical problems that result from the plausible and systematic study of legal systems foreign to the comparatist with a flexible methodological rule that is easy to operate and remember. The rationale of following the method-rule is revealed in real terms only if one actually attempts to conduct research on comparative law and comes up with a number of questions: where to find reliable information on foreign law; how should the features of foreign law be understood (legal systematics, concept of legal rule, status of the courts of law and legislators, the extent of codification of law, concept of legal source, etc); and are the legal texts (statutes, argumentation of cases, judicial decisions, jurisprudential writing) reliable; does actual practice differ from the written law; and so on. It is easy to realise that in fact the national doctrinal study of law to a great extent ponders over similar problems. In other words, comparatists should at least try to reach the first doctrinal base of foreign law, even though deeper theoretical understanding might be unattainable.[35]

Another important text which was published earlier is *Aufgabe und Notwendigkeit der Rechtsvergleichung* where comparative law, its role and methodology are outlined.[36] In this text three main categories of comparative

---

[33] Gerber (n 24) 199 says that this approach has later been named as the 'function/context method', even though this formulation is rather coming from the followers of Rabel than from himself. Although this may be true, Rabel nevertheless had already used, by this early stage specifically, an expression 'die Funktion der Rechtsinstitute'.

[34] About functionalism, its critique and possible future-views (in critical tone), see M Graziadei, 'The Functionalist Heritage' in P Legrand and R Munday (eds), *Comparative Legal Studies: Traditions and Transitions* (Cambridge, Cambridge University Press, 2003) 100–27.

[35] The idea of different bases, in conceiving the law, comes from Roger Brownsword (in chapter eight of this volume).

[36] Above Leser (n 21) 1–21 (originally published *Rheinische Zeitschrift für Zivil- und Proceßrecht* 1924, 279–301).

law are separated: the dogmatic or systematic comparison, legal-historical comparison and legal-philosophical/legal-theoretical comparison. To some extent Rabel dissociates from all of these and ends up emphasising that single rules of law should not be compared completely out of context of the legal system.[37] He also wants to keep separate the actual contents of the rule of law and their purely linguistic formulation, which we without difficulty find from statutes or recognise in judgements. He strongly emphasises the fact that merely comparing texts is not proper comparative law at all; texts on their own are like the skeleton without muscles, practice, and nerves, ie the prevailing understanding of the doctrinal study of law.[38]

The same basic message applies *equally well* to national doctrinal study of law as to supranational legal study with national normative interest of knowledge.[39] Rabel took it for granted that nobody involved in the doctrinal study of law could ignore legal praxis or prevailing doctrinal writing, therefore he could not allow such an approach to any comparatists engaged in serious research either. He stressed the functions of law and its dependence on its own cultural contexts. Functions were for him like a lesson about everyday life that the comparatist has to grasp:

> Zu erfassen aber haben wir aus diesen Quellen das Leben, die Funktionen der Rechtsgestaltungen. Denn das Recht ist . . . eine Kulturerscheinung, es kann nicht unabhängig gedacht werden von seinen Ursachen und Wirkungen.[40]

Language is the form that law – one's own as well as foreign – takes. The comparatist has to strip the law of that camouflage and to attempt to find general reasons that have led to the adoption of the particular functions in each system. This presumes that the comparatist is not blind to legal praxis – the comparatist must not make the mistaken presumption that the surface gives a reliable picture of the law. However, it is not a question of actual legal realism in either its American or Scandinavian sense.[41] The intention is to get under the skin of law. First, the basic thinking (*Grundgedanken*) under the surface layer of law has to be identified and, then, reconstructed. It is not identical with what the legislator has intended, nor is it the formal realisation (*formalen Rechstelement*) of the rule of law or the legal system. It is a question of study that attempts to clarify the basic way of thinking in valid law (thinking *like* a lawyer); in other

---

[37] 'Der einzelne Rechtssatz ist erst im Zusammenhang der ganzen Rechtsordnung zu beurteilen' (ibid 3).
[38] 'Ein Gesetz ist ohne die zugehörige Rechtsprechung nur wie ein Skelett ohne Muskel. Und die Nerven sind die herrschenden Lehrmeinungen' (ibid 4). The *context* rises in an important role; it reveals itself in small-scale functions ie legal problem-solving – to understand the working of law one must take into account the whole context of law, see Gerber (n 24) 200–01. See also Bogdan (n 4) 54–56.
[39] Of 'interest of knowledge', see for more details J Habermas, *Knowledge and Human Interest* (Boston, Beacon Press, 1972) [translation from original *Erkenntnis und Interesse*, 1968].
[40] Above Leser (n 21) 4.
[41] See generally GS Alexander, 'Comparing the Two Legal Realisms – American and Scandinavian' (2002) 50 *American Journal of Comparative Law* 131.

words, how it solves the legal problem that the society has met. In this respect the comparative study of law has to be separated from the surface-level criticism of valid law and the approach that is openly legal-political.[42] Yet, this distinction remains blurry.

B. Relevance of Context

A challenge that is always involved in comparison – and in national doctrinal study – is presented by the need to understand the written material, to master legal language and in general to master an unfamiliar information environment. Simply, all this offers several chances to be mistaken. A particularly important role is taken by the overall command of foreign legal linguistics and cultures (*Auslandskunde*) and the value brought by that understanding to the professional self-esteem of a jurist which runs parallel to a diplomat or businessman's need to understand foreign cultures.

> [. . .] der Bildungswert des römischen, englischen, französischen Rechts entspricht dabei ziemlich genau dem der lateinischen, englischen, französischen Sprache. Aber erst die Vergleichung mit dem eigenen Recht ist für den Juristen dasselbe, wie dir Auslandskunde für den Diplomaten oder Kaufmann.[43]

Here, too, it can be seen that the basic idea is not strange to the study of national law either: in recent years certain approaches that are related to the mastery of 'unfamiliar scholarly culture' have become increasingly popular, such as law and economics and law and politics. And, there are even more avant-garde approaches like evolutionary analysis and behavioural economics.[44]

It has to be mentioned that in Rabel's opinion, comparative law and international private law were very closely related disciplines. Therefore, many of the methodological principles which he presented for the purposes of comparative law were, in his opinion, also applicable to international private law. This is based on the fact that Rabel was basically a Universalist who believed that there was a common core under all legal systems: 'Hidden behind apparent dissimilarity, there are fundamental likenesses, suggesting international cooperation, though of course not necessarily unification'. Thus he saw that the norms which regulated conflicts between legal rules in international private law had been 'derived from a national source like other legal rules, have special functions and purposes requiring a method of international scope'.[45] Such international private law is not very far from comparative law – Rabel was a dedicated inter-

---

[42] Above Leser (n 21) 7f. Gerber (n 24) 192 assumes that the sensitivity toward language has its origins in Rabel's childhood in the linguistically pluralistic environment in Vienna.
[43] Above Leser (n 21) 19.
[44] See the contributions by Bart Du Laing and Julie De Coninck in this volume.
[45] E Rabel, *The Conflict of Laws: a Comparative Study* (Chicago, University of Michigan Press, 1945), the quotes in the text at 59 and at 11. *cf* Zweigert and Kötz, *An Introduction to Comparative Law* (1998) 35.

nationalist.[46] To a great extent, this explains why it is difficult for those who in principle criticise harmonisation of law to accept many fundamental features of the methodology that Rabel represented.

Rabel's functionalism that is based on pragmatic professionalism of the jurist has certain more general theoretical consequences. In an epistemological sense, the comparatist is simultaneously inside and outside the law: when comparing individual national systems, the comparatist is bound to valid law and pertaining interpretations of legal sources, while as an outside observer they study different systems in a parallel arrangement from a measuring point/observation frame that is independent of the system in question (*tertium comparationis*).[47] Such functionalism can be characterised as rough legal *problem-functionalism* that concentrates on the micro level of law and leaves large social structures – which are essential for different functionalist sectors of sociology – more or less aside. As such, problem-functionalism is mainly a crude rule of thumb that is characterised by a downright lack of theoretical background.[48] The macro-level concept of law and society that is at the background is not analytically presented at any stage but instead remains an inexplicit presumption just like in the national doctrinal study of law.[49]

The basic functionalist theory of comparative law has certain obvious limitations.[50] Limitations have made some fervent proponents of functionalism reassess the limitations to its practicality, but this has not meant renouncing the leading ideas of legal problem-functionalism.[51] One of them is related to strong universalism.[52] It is obvious to the reader of Rabel's texts that when writing of different systems, he was, in his mind, mainly making the division between the Roman-Germanic law and common law. His mind was epistemologically imprisoned by this great divide. This also has an impact on the fact that he supported universalism and believed in the idea of basically similar legal systems. Other legal traditions are, from his practical point of view, in an unequal position,

---

[46] *cf* Gerber (n 24) 196f.

[47] *cf* O Kahn-Freund, *Comparative Law as an Academic Subject* (Oxford, Clarendon Press, 1965) 9.

[48] *cf* W Twining, 'Comparative Law and Legal Theory: The Country and Western Tradition' in I Edge (ed), *Comparative Law in Global Perspective* (London, Transnational Publishers, 2000) 21–76, especially 54–58. See also Husa, 'Farewell to Functionalism or Methodological Tolerance?' (2003) 423.

[49] However, even these ideas may be developed further in an attempt to create more rational and scientific comparative law, see L-J Constantinesco, *Traité de droit comparé,* vol 2 (Paris, Librairie générale de droit et de jurisprudence, 1974) 22–38.

[50] I have dealt with those on another occasion, see J Husa, 'Methodology of Comparative Law Today: From Paradoxes to Flexibility?' (2006) 58 *Revue internationale de droit comparé* 1095, 1099ff.

[51] Efstathios K Banakas clearly supported functionalism in his article 'Some Thoughts on the Method of Comparative Law: the Concept of Law Revisited' (1980) 32 *Revue hellénique de droit internationale* 155, especially 156–63, but some 15 years later he regards his earlier thinking as being too limited in its ability to take into account the cultural level of law (Banakas, 'The Method of Comparative Law and the Question of Legal Culture Today' (1994) 115–18 and 152–53).

[52] I am not quite sure if this general unspecified legal-ethical universalism leads automatically to obsession with common denominators and various harmonisation projects, as Geoffrey Samuel seems to be suggesting (in chapter 10 of this volume).

although inequality is not expressly emphasised in his general texts on comparative law.[53]

For Rabel, issues such as the pluralism of present-day comparative law and growing concern towards other legal cultures were not as important as they are now seen to be in comparative law. This involves a risk. If the assumption of the function of legal rules and institutions turns mechanical, law is in a danger of being reduced into functions that are utilitaristically defined and assumed to be identical in all societies. That would mean disregard of the cultural and symbolic dimensions of law, although it is well-known that law often has considerable symbolic functions.[54] At its most profound, law can be connected with an entire nation's national cultural identity.[55] This also concerns legal linguistics: it is obvious that in Central Europe it would often be more natural to use German or even French as lingua franca instead of the dominant English which lacks proper civil law terminology.

In the present discussion, the universalism of functionalism and the criticism against the presumption of similarity (*praesumptio similitudinis*) has resulted in post-modern extremism, according to which comparison should concentrate entirely on the differences between systems.[56] Carried to the extreme, this criticism is useless in the sense that in the end it results in argumentation, according to which it is impossible to understand foreign law and that different legal cultures are incommensurable. This utmost criticism has, however, been denounced for valid reasons.[57] Criticism has also led to responses where the functionalist research tradition has been defended, as well as the sense of the comparative study of legal rules in general.[58] There has also been reaction to criticism on a more general theoretical level where functionalism has not been excluded from among the methods used, even if its limitations are acknowledged openly.[59]

---

[53] In *Das Recht des Warenkaufs* (1936) 20–26, Rabel divided the legal families of the world (*Rechtsfamilie, Rechtskreis*) in the following manner (probably in some implicit order of importance): 1) Middle-European law, 2) Romanistic law, 3) Anglo-American law, 4) Nordic law, 5) Islamic/Religious law, and 6) Roman-Byzantine (Greek) law.

[54] A MacDonald, 'Hundred Headless Europe: Comparison, Constitution and Culture' in A Harding and E Örücü (eds), *Comparative Law in the 21st Century* (London, British Institute of International and Comparative Law, 2002) 193–210, especially 197.

[55] See, eg, concerning the Greek law, Husa, *Kreikan oikeus ja oikeuskieli* (*Greek Law and Legal Language*) (2007) 207–31. See also Mattila (n 7) 58–64.

[56] See, eg P Legrand, *Le droit comparé* (Paris, Presses Universitaires de France, 1999) 32–49.

[57] HP Glenn, 'Are Legal Traditions Incommensurable?' (2001) 49 *American Journal of Comparative Law* 133.

[58] M Bogdan, 'On the Value and Method of Rule-Comparison in Comparative Law' in H-P Mansel et al, *Festschrift für Erik Jayme* (München, Selliers, 2004) 1234f. One of Bogdan's central observations is that similarities or differences are *results* of research, not methodological choices made in advance.

[59] See A Peters and H Schwenke, 'Comparative Law beyond Post-Modernism' (2000) 49 *International and Comparative Law Quarterly* 800. See also Husa (n 27).

C. Paradigm?

The most widely known formulation of Rabel's idea is not directly from his own writings. It became a paradigm thanks to other writers. Due to the authoritative fundamental work of German comparatists Zweigert (1911–96) and Kötz (1935–), Rabel's methodological rule of thumb has, in spite of its deficiencies and partially justified criticism, become the dominant method in comparative law. They do not hesitate when they characterise the methodology of comparative law as follows: 'The basic methodological principle of all comparative law is that of *functionality* . . . the legal system of every society faces essentially the same problems, and solves these problems by quite different means though very often with similar results.'[60]

Overall they follow, seemingly obediently, Rabel. Zweigert and Kötz consider Rabel's demands on the command of foreign languages and cultures hard but legitimate. They too think that a comparatist ought to do their utmost to learn foreign languages and get to know foreign cultures, particularly when the comparatist moves away from the scope of their own legal family and ventures to the area of another legal culture. To be able to avoid the problems caused by the strange legal language, and simultaneously also concomitant misinterpretation of unfamiliar law, the comparatist has to rely on the basic principle of functionalism and to try to find from the strange system the rules which are functionally in accordance with the rules of their own system.[61] The surface layer of legal language has to be penetrated if the aim is to reach the level of legal problem-functionalism. Esin Örücü sums up the key question of such functionalism as follows: 'How is a special social or legal problem encountered both in society A and society B resolved by their respective (legal or other) systems?'[62] That is: what are the special legal rules/institutions in each system studied that have been formed as an answer to the assumed problem.[63] When this kind of research is conducted in practice, translating legal language sensitively ought to be in a vital position.[64]

So, if one follows this stream, function is a common question to all systems compared, independent of the system; a conceptual construction that enables a

---

[60] Zweigert and Kötz, *An Introduction to Comparative Law* (1998) 34. Characterisation has not remained the only one. We may consider an influential text within the English-speaking world, an article by Walter J Kamba, in which practically the same methodological rule is presented, see Kamba, 'Comparative Law: A Theoretical Framework' (1974) 23 *International and Comparative Law Quarterly* 485, 517. See even Bogdan (n 4) 58–67.
[61] Zweigert and Kötz (n 11) 36f.
[62] E Örücü, *Enigma of Comparative Law: Variations on a Theme for the Twenty-First Century* (Leiden, Martinus Nijhoff, 2004) 25.
[63] Husa (n 27) 428–31. Clearly, not all the comparatists accept these goals of comparative study: there has never been any kind of consensus which would be equivalent with the nationally defined understanding of doctrinal study of law, see HP Glenn, 'Aims of Comparative Law' in J Smits (ed), *Elgar Encyclopedia of Comparative Law* (Cheltenham, Edward Elgar, 2006) 57–65.
[64] See, eg, E Örücü, 'A Project: Comparative Law in Action' in E Örücü and D Nelken (eds), *Comparative Law: A Handbook* (Oxford, Hart Publishing, 2007) 435–49, 441 ('direct translations or synonyms did not suffice . . . Functional equivalents were sought').

meaningful and disciplined comparison of different systems. What is not asked is how we interpret 'the expression Y of article X in the civil law book in systems 1, 2 and 3', instead the question could be 'in what way should the circumstances change in systems 1, 2 and 3 for the contracting party to have the right to withdraw from a legally valid contract concerning matter X "or" what should the legal intent be for a legally binding contract of type Z to be made in a situation Y in systems 1, 2 and 3'. A concrete example of functionalist comparative law is research where rules concerning the authoritative interpretation of constitutional law are studied. In this study, the Finnish Parliamentary Committee for Constitutional Law and the Norwegian Supreme Court are compared on the level of their functions (maintenance of norm hierarchy at the highest authoritative level). In the study, the structure, duties and argumentation of the organs are compared, and the fact that in the state organisation they are distinctively dissimilar bodies is ignored: one is a layman-body of the Parliament elected on political grounds and the other a precedent court consisting of professional top judges.[65] From the point of view of translation, it has to be mentioned that by no means is functional translation always sufficient; often also the terrain of legal functionalism needs to be trespassed.[66] And yet, functionalism appears as a possible starting point, especially if the point of view of comparative legal linguistics is assumed: the growing number of legal languages means more difficulties.

D. Knowing the Context

To begin with, a functional researcher cannot rely solely on valid statute texts, neither can the researcher merely depend on the legal praxis of supreme courts, nor on the dominant views in jurisprudential writing; the researcher has to acquaint his or herself with, say, trade methods and business practices, as well as prevalent customs of a particular country. These are very high epistemological requirements if they are genuinely fulfilled. By studying all these, such an overall picture of law can be formed that it can be considered as reliable a picture as the comparatist coming from another system can reconstruct. If these demands are related to legal language, it becomes obvious that the entire methodical rule has been built to free the comparatist from legal language; legal language is the *façade* of law.[67] It is not a question of linguistic-philosophic distrust of language,

---

[65] See V-P Hautamäki, 'Authoritative Interpretation of the Constitution: A Comparison of Argumentation in Finland and Norway' (2002) 6 *Electronic Journal of Comparative Law* (www.ejcl.org/63/art63-.html). Gerber (n 24) 206–07 makes a remark according to which it is typical for problem-functionalism to look at such easily detectable everyday problems (eg marriage, contracts) which are further from public law related questions.

[66] See G-R de Groot, 'Legal Translation' in J Smits (ed), *Elgar Encyclopedia of Comparative Law* (Cheltenham, Edward Elgar, 2006) 423–33, 425 (saying that there must also be 'a similar and structural embedding').

[67] I have not defined clearly in the text what is meant by 'legal language'. However, this concept is used roughly in the same manner as in Mattila (n 7) 3–4.

but rather of the fact that one should not form their understanding of law on the basis of any one source, least of all on a mere statutory text or judicial decision.[68] *This epistemic point of view is very close to that of a legal doctrine*: interpretation and systematisation are based on several sources that are bundled by legal argumentation whose mutual weight is outlined by means of the doctrine on sources of law.

It is simultaneously a question of relation to the limits of law which takes the comparatist further than the national doctrinal researcher: the comparatist cannot stop where, according to the self-understanding of each national system, the borderline exists between law and some other walk of life (politics, economy, religion, culture).[69] When the demand not to stop, where one in the national understanding should stop, is carried out, the real extent of the required command of legal language is revealed. In Watson's words: 'What in other contexts would be regarded as a good knowledge of a foreign language may not be adequate for the comparatist.'[70] With European integration, the requirement of language skills has been extended to several EU relevant sectors of national legal science; they are not a matter that only concerns the small and eccentric group of comparatists. The doctrinal study of law also benefits from comparative law and comparative legal linguistics, particularly when an EU relevant matter is concerned.[71] The same applies to the European Court of Human Rights.

IV. LEGAL LANGUAGES AND FUNCTIONALISM

It is easy to notice that as far as comparative legal linguistics is concerned, legal translation in particular is in many ways closest to comparative law. Legal translation is in fact one of the most important issues in comparative law.[72] In legal translation the aim is that the legal content of a legal document is correctly transmitted to the foreign reader. This is anything but easy, even with only two languages. In practice this presumes that legal terms that represent legal concepts are in the legal sense correctly translated. From the legal linguistic point of view, the basic situation in translation is often similar to that of comparative law: the

---

[68] These methodological ideas are being tested in the *Trento Common Core* project which Ugo Mattei and Mauro Bussani are directing. The methodology of this project has gained influence from Robert Schlesinger's (1909–96) thinking. See, eg, N Kasirer, 'The Common Core of European Private Law in Boxes and Bundles' (2002) 2 *Global Jurist Frontiers* 1, 2 (www.bepress.com/gj/frontiers/vol2/iss1/art2).

[69] *cf* Watson, *Legal Transplants: An Approach to Comparative Law* (1993) 23. Transnational jurists of this sort, crossing many borders, like Rabel himself, can at best act as a mediator between different areas of life (different languages, states, law, business, politics, *cf* Gerber (n 24) 202).

[70] Watson (n 10) 1.

[71] *cf* VG Curran, 'Comparative Law and Language' in M Reimann and R Zimmermann (eds), *Oxford Handbook of Comparative Law* (Oxford, Oxford University Press, 2006) 675–707, especially 700–04.

[72] de Groot, 'Legal Translation' (2006) 423. See also Constantinesco, *Traité de droit compare* (1974) 68–70.

search for the situational equivalence. In such a case the translator searches the unfamiliar system for a legal institution or rule that, to as great an extent as possible, has the same function in a similar situational context.[73] In connection with legal translation this means formulation of terminological counterparts, which often has to be resorted to in the European Union; then the best policy in most cases is to translate: 'functionally, according to the circumstances and needs of communication'.[74] For the nationally binding interpretation of the EU law as well as for national doctrinal study of law, this opens up new dimensions in the form of expanding contexts of interpretation: ever more often it is possible to check how a matter is understood and interpreted in other Member States.[75]

On a general level, functional comparative law and legal translation could partly be seen as the same thing. The differences arise from the dissimilarity of interests of knowledge. The comparatist compares functions adopted in different systems to solve the same legal problem and seeks for similarities and differences. Ultimately they aim at solving what causes similarities and differences by looking for explanations in history, economy, politics, culture, even geography.[76] The translator tries to translate unfamiliar law in 'a legally correct manner'. In both, it is a question of the same thing, ie a serious attempt to understand *foreign* law. While for a translator, a strange legal system and legal culture are essential contexts for good-quality translation, for a comparatist understanding the language of a foreign legal system is one prerequisite for research.[77] Here it is possible to notice yet another connection with the national doctrinal study of law: when law becomes more trans-national, the same methodological demands spread to national legal study. In particular, the expansion of methodological demands applies to comparative law used in courts of law.[78]

In particular, the emergence of supranational legal structures (EU law, European Human Rights) is providing a methodological challenge to *both*

---

[73] *cf* Mattila (n 7) 265–67. It is not possible in this context to look deeper into this but obviously this reminds us of the language-philosophy of Ludwig Wittgenstein. His core-idea was already at the basis of *Tractatus* § 3.262 (at 20): 'Was in den Zeichen nicht zum Ausdruck kommt, das zeigt ihre Anwendung. Was die Zeichen versuchen, das spricht ihre Anwendung aus'. According to this a word has the meaning that is *given* to it by its users. This creates a kind of game of language. See *Philosophische Untersuchungen* in *Werkausgabe Band 1. Tractatus logico-philosophicus, Tagebücher 1914–1916, Philosophische Untersuchungen* (Frankfurt am Main, Suhrkamp, 1984). Wittgenstein also uses the concept of language-game (*Sprachspiele*) in several aphorisms. Legal language (national and non-national) is, from this point of view, a kind of a language-game.

[74] Mattila (n 7) 121. *cf* de Groot (n 66) 424–25 ('the translator needs to find an equivalent in the target language legal system for the term of the source language legal system').

[75] Clearly, 'description and systematising of law within (national) legal doctrine are inescapably becoming a cross-border activity' like argue Van Hoecke and M Warrington, 'Legal Culture, Legal Paradigm and Legal Culture' (1998) 527.

[76] See Bogdan (n 4) 66–77. Finally, the purpose is to study the relation between society and law and the role of law in societies as an organised way to solve certain societal needs of human communities (eg administration, economy, inheritance, etc), see Kahn-Freund, *Comparative Law as an Academic Subject* (1965) 31.

[77] *cf* Mattila (n 7) 19–21. See also Gerber (n 24) 208.

[78] See, eg J Smits, 'Comparative Law and its Influence on National Legal Systems' in M Reimann and R Zimmermann, *Oxford Handbook of Comparative Law* (Oxford, Oxford University Press, 2006) 513–38.

national legal doctrine and comparative law.[79] For non-national courts, the usability of comparative law is evident: to know how to deal with different national systems the European Court of Justice (ECJ) must first know how these systems function. A telling example of this is a (national) doctrine of sources of law related case in which the ECJ regarded it to be sufficient that certain parts of the Directive (2004/48/EC) were included in the *travaux préparatoires*, provided that the *travaux* was regularly consulted by the judiciary while interpreting the law.[80] However, to enter into this conclusion, some form of comparative study must be done. The same works for the European Court of Human Rights which relies, on some occasions, on comparative law arguments as, for example, in a case in which even a comparative study of legislation concerning State secrets in the Member States of the Council of Europe was explicitly cited (in the report certain types of classified information appeared to be punishable in all systems, but with a wide variety of approaches being adopted).[81] Comparative legal interpretation also has an important role in these sorts of comparisons: different language versions (more than two) are normally studied in parallel.

An example of the necessity of comparative law is presented by the expression 'civil rights and obligations' ('droits et obligations *de caractére civil*' in French) in article 6(1) of the European Convention on Human Rights. The expression is problematic because in different Member States it has different formulations that reflect the Member State's own legal culture rather than the contents of the European Convention on Human Rights. A good example of this is the German translation: '*zivilrechtliche* Ansprüche und Verpflichtungen' where the expression differs from the one used in English and French. In Italian the probatory French version is imitated ('dei suoi diritti e dei suoi doveri di *carattere civile*'); it seems to be in regular use in translations into many other languages, such as Greek ('των δικαιωμάτων και υποχρεώσεών του αστικής φύσεως') and Spanish ('derechos y obligaciones de *carácter civil*') as well as Swedish ('*civila* rättigheter och skyldigheter').[82] In practice the European Court of Human Rights has to give the expression a legally well defined meaning in its judgments, which means that it has to practice practical comparative law when it constructs a common content for different language versions.[83] Within the European Union the situation is even more complicated; after all there are 27 Member States and 23 official languages. The ECJ has for some time emphasised that it is precisely

---

[79] This is easy to see, eg, in the area of European constitutional law: we have simultaneously a kind-of constitutional court concerning human rights in Strasbourg, the EC/EU constitutional court in Luxembourg, and plurality of national supreme and constitutional courts interacting. Clearly, the legal hierarchies overlap and demand legal information from various sources, and not just in one's own national language. See, eg J Husa, '"We the Judges . . ." – European Constitutional Ius Commune' (2009) *Tilburg Institute of Comparative and Transnational Law. Working Papers Series* (papers.ssrn.com/sol3/papers.cfm?abstract_id=1334607).
[80] See *Commission of the European Communities v Kingdom of Sweden* [2002] ECR I–4147 [24].
[81] See *Stoll v Switzerland* (App no 69698/01) ECHR 10 December 2007 [44].
[82] Emphasis added to all of the quotes.
[83] See ECtHR cases *Pellegrin v France* 31 EHRR 651 and *Vilho Eskelinen v Finland* (App no 63235/00) ECHR 19 April 2007.

because of this that a uniform interpretation of the concepts of Community law must be established.[84] Therefore, it is not surprising that occasionally the ECJ has to engage in comparative legal linguistics in its decision-making process.[85] Linguistic knowledge-threshold must be somehow overcome and resolved, and the comparative approach is certainly useful in this. Yet, this kind of comparison is not the same as the one meant in academic debates.

In legal translation the principle of functionality is not so readily opposed as in comparative law, for the simple reason that it is not necessary in translation to make far-fetched assumptions about the similarity of the legal systems as later functional comparative law is accused of doing.[86] Usually the translator need not give a detailed explanation on the general (legal) level as to why he or she has chosen particular functionalist equivalents when translating. On the other hand, if we have comparative legal linguists who are doing translation they are not likely to succeed if they do not know the contexts of legal language. The same can be expressed in Vivianne Grosswald Curran's way: 'For comparative law, language knowledge not only is part of foreign legal systems under examinations; it is the most efficient shortcut to understanding how to understand.'[87] From the point of view of legal theory, this is also important because legal doctrine is relevant for comparative law: 'because it is a privileged forum where paradigmatic theories, as, for instance, a theory of legal sources, are made explicit'.[88]

The fact that legal linguistics and comparative law are so close explains why some linguistically oriented comparatists have completely switched over to legal translation and legal linguistics. It is often merely a question of different emphasis and research background. Their similarity, however, is not entirely beneficial to comparative law as Bernhard Grossfeld, a comparatist who takes an interest in legal language, has pointed out: 'Legal linguistics is an essential concomitant of comparative law, one which does not make it any easier.'[89] The reason for this is simple, as Richard Hyland says: 'A legal concept is not just a word. It is an element of theoretical construction.'[90] So, the rationale of this chapter boils down to this: what is the significance of all this from the point of view of legal doctrine? Indeed, is there any?

---

[84] See case *Hautpzollamt Mainz v CA Kupferberg & Cie KG a.A.* [1982] ECR 3641 [45].
[85] See, eg, case C-375/97 General Motors Corp v Yplon SA [1999] ECR I-5421 ([22]: 'That nuance, which does not entail any real contradiction, is due to the greater neutrality of the terms used in the German, Dutch and Swedish versions. Despite that nuance, it cannot be denied that, in the context of a uniform interpretation of Community law, a knowledge threshold requirement emerges from a comparison of all the language versions of the Directive.')
[86] A tiny specification is in order here: in functionalistic thinking one does not believe that there are *genuinely* similar legal solutions, but rather that roughly similar societal-human needs (caused by social, economic, cultural, and political pressures and factors) may create legal solutions which *resemble* each other in certain basic respects. See Kahn-Freund(n 47) 10.
[87] Above n 9, 682.
[88] Van Hoecke and Warrington, above n 14, 532.
[89] B Grossfeld, *The Strength and Weakness of Comparative Law* (Oxford, Clarendon Press, 1990) 103.
[90] Hyland, *Gift: A Study in Comparative Law* (2009) 124.

V. CONCLUSION

To begin with, it is a fascinating finding that the old-time functionalist approach, which critics usually consider to be rough and unconcerned with language, does in fact assume a reasonably organised and theoretically developed view of legal language. Matters stressed by today's comparative legal linguistics in the context of translating several legal languages also point out that functionalism, after all, may not be a relic. This is not to be seen as a pure defence of so-called functionalism in comparative law. Rather, the aim is to highlight certain elements of it which may still be useful and rational.[91] Furthermore, globalisation and Europeanisation as well as the transnationalisation of law in general, make functionalism a relevant method *also* in national legal study which might mean that functionalism could even be separated from comparative law. While legal sources are increasingly non-national, crude problem-functionalism may in the future have a more important role in the doctrinal study of law, particularly in Europe.

From the point of view of the method used in legal doctrine, the approaches taken in crude rule-of-thumb functionalism and comparative legal linguistics do not threaten the national legal *Anschauungen*, instead they illuminate the ways in which law, that is epistemically free of territorial and linguistic restrictions, can be outlined without losing the normative-legal framework. The viewpoint that concentrates on the functionalism of legal language, as long as it keeps away from linguistics or the 'law and' approaches, offers the *third way*, an alternative to the traditional legal doctrine and social scientific paradigm: to stay within national legal doctrine or to take up the social scientific paradigm are not the only methodological approaches in an increasingly trans-national world. It is easy to see that methodologically the approach that comparative law's crude functionalism offers is much *closer* to the hermeneutical and argumentative method than the model following positive sciences which are offered by empirical social sciences.[92] It is precisely here that pre-Zweigert-and-Kötz functionalism, developed in early comparative law, gets its opportunity within legal doctrine: it is more closely related than empirical sciences to the classical doctrinal approach to law. In short, it works inside a language-game(s). This contributes to retaining a firm contact with the legal mentality of national doctrine, the theory of legal sources, legal argumentation and the understanding shared by the jurists about

---

[91] Clearly, such an idea according to which there should be a methodological premise of similarity is excluded in the view of this author when it comes to the methodology of comparative law; similarity or dissimilarity is an outcome of research, not a proper methodological or epistemological premise. This same point is also made by John Bell in his contribution to this volume. See also Bogdan, 'On the Value and Method of Rule-Comparison in Comparative Law' (2004) 1240.

[92] A similar kind of idea has been presented concerning the sociology of law. Namely, the term 'juridical sociology' has been suggested to refer to a field which: 'is not branch of sociology but a study of society through law, and of law in society' (Cotterrell (n 25) 8).

legal reality and its nature.[93] To put it differently, if a lawyer cannot recognise what is presented as law from his or her own system by the comparatist, then something has gone badly wrong in the process of comparison.[94]

When the study of law assumes an external view of social sciences, it easily loses its special normative nature and becomes a 'law and' method which is also further away from the methodological starting points of old-time functional comparative law and legal linguistics. The comparative functionalist study of law and legal language are *Grundlagenforschung* at its best but the shrinking of the scope of national law makes them equally important auxiliary approaches for the doctrinal study of law. In other words, the doctrinal study of law *in itself* is less and less national, which means that in the interpreting and systematisation of law, several legal systems and languages that are parallel and on different levels have to be dealt with. Legal pluralism can be met with methodological pluralism. So, European comparison may be even a strong basis for the construction of domestic normative doctrinal argument.[95] To conclude, this binds together functional comparative law, study of legal language and normatively oriented doctrinal study of law in their capacity to take part in the continual construction of a normative legal system. Thus, the epistemological separation between external and internal viewpoints loses much of its earlier significance.

---

[93] Legal doctrine, if seen in this manner, 'is not just describing and reconstructing legal reality; rather it is also to a certain extent playing a part in the continual construction of the legal system itself' as Van Hoecke and Warrington (n 14) 523 put it.

[94] This point is clearly spelled out by John Bell (chapter nine in this volume).

[95] But see Reitz, 'How to Do Comparative Law' (1998) 624f (from an American point of view).

12

Doing What Doesn't Come Naturally. On the Distinctiveness of Comparative Law[1]

MAURICE ADAMS[2]

I. 'DOING' LAW IS IMMUTABLY COMPARATIVE...

COMPARISON IS INSEPARABLY connected with doing research in the humanities and social sciences.[3] Nearly any claim we make as lawyers, as well as every distinction we draw, will implicitly or explicitly be set against another situation. A legal arrangement can only be qualified as satisfactory or good because there is another arrangement by which it can be measured; such an arrangement is never good in and of itself. When judges are looking for principles to help decide an unprecedented or unregulated situation, they tend to rely on analogical reasoning, ie they apply a rule for a comparable situation, be it a real or hypothetical one, to the situation at hand. Also, ordering and classifying cases in a specific field or legal domain – call it the pursuit of coherence – is very much a comparative activity: it is an exercise which can only be done because there are a number of cases that can be situated against each other. Comparing, in other words, is a fundamental principle of legal research;[4] it even provides the inevitable and inescapable frame of reference for scientific activity. 'Thinking

---

[1] For the purposes of this contribution, I use the phrases 'comparative law' and 'comparative legal research' as synonyms.

[2] This contribution grew out of a comment I made as a designated discussant at the Tilburg colloquium of which this book is the product. The accompanying discursive style is maintained here. Dick Broeren of Tilburg Law School was most helpful in preparing the text. I benefited from the comments of the participants and from John Griffiths (University of Groningen).

[3] On this, see for example B Bix, 'Law as an Autonomous Discipline' in P Cane and M Tushnet (eds), *The Oxford Handbook of Legal Studies* (Oxford, Oxford University Press, 2003) 975–87 and Ch McCrudden, 'Legal Research and the Social Sciences' (2006) 122 *Law Quarterly Review* 623–50. The discussion on whether legal scholarship can and should only be considered part of what are usually called the 'humanities' or also of the social sciences goes, in my opinion, to the heart of what the Tilburg colloquium was about.

[4] Also in this vein, VV Palmer, 'From Lerotholi to Lando: Some Examples of Comparative Law Methodology' (2005) 53 *American Journal of Comparative Law* 262.

without comparison is unthinkable. And, in the absence of comparison, so is all scientific thought and scientific research.'[5] It could therefore be argued that there really is nothing very special about doing comparative law. To be sure, *legal* research has some distinctive features, but comparativeness is not one of them; that quality is part and parcel of all research.

From this it follows (almost naturally, it would seem) that it makes perfect sense to assert, as John Bell does in his contribution to this volume, that:

> [I]n major respects, comparative law is an instance of the more general form of legal research [which is according to Bell hermeneutic, interpretive and institutional, MA]. The way in which it attempts to reconstruct both the foreign and the researcher's own legal systems is similar to general legal research on either of those systems.[6]

II. ... 'AND YET IT MOVES!'

If all of this is true, why deliberate on the question of whether there is something special about doing comparative legal research? Why not simply refer to what doing legal research amounts to, and then add a few words of warning on the choice of countries, the dangers of translation, and so on?

The reason for this is of course that the foregoing cannot fully account for what happens in what is generally termed 'comparative law'. As I will explain there is indeed something special or distinctive about doing this kind of research – and Bell is very much aware of it. For why else would the phrase 'comparative law' proudly carry the term 'comparative' in its banner? If it does not want to be dismissed as a pleonasm – 'Thinking about the law is by definition comparative, silly!' – research of this kind should at the very least pose some specific challenges other than the problems lawyers and legal researchers routinely face.[7]

One of the main reasons why there is something special or distinctive about doing comparative legal research, something that calls for a specific approach and specific methods, is that legal comparatists must, among other things, immerse themselves in a foreign and therefore strange legal system. Such an 'involved' activity does not come naturally because legal comparatists have to deal with one or more legal systems whose 'language' (metaphorically understood) they do not speak, ie systems with different institutions and unexpressed codes, their

---

[5] GE Swanson, 'Frameworks for Comparative Research' in I Vallier (ed), *Comparative Methods in Sociology* (Berkeley, University of California Press, 1971) 141. Also quoted by Palmer 'From Lerotholi to Lando' (2005) 261. The anthropologist Clifford Geertz formulated the same view somewhat more subtly: 'Santayana's famous dictum that one compares only when one is unable to get to the heart of the matter seems to me ... the precise reverse of the truth; it is through comparison, and of incomparables, that whatever heart we can actually get to is to be reached.' C Geertz, *Local Knowledge* (New York, Basic Books, 1983) 233. More direct is J Hall, *Comparative Law and Social Theory* (Baton Rouge, Louisiana State University Press, 1963) 9: '[T]o be sapiens is to be a comparatist.'

[6] See J Bell's contribution in chapter nine, 'Legal Research and the Distinctiveness of Comparative Law'.

[7] Palmer (n 4) 262–63, *cf* PJ Glenn, 'Aims of Comparative Law' in JM Smits (ed), *Elgar Encyclopedia of Comparative Law* (Cheltenham, Edward Elgar, 2006) 59.

own histories, ideologies and self-images, systems they have not normally been trained, educated or disciplined in, and with which they are therefore not naturally or intimately connected. This process of trying to understand foreign legal systems (or some of their elements) with an eye to subsequent comparison, manifests particular problems because it goes far beyond mere fact-finding and the regular (ie national) way of legal interpretation, where lawyers engage the just mentioned social context as an almost natural given when determining the meaning of the law. The problems the law addresses and the solutions which it intends to provide are very much connected to the socio-cultural environment that gave rise to them. This environment should be actively and consciously engaged for meaningful comparison to become possible.

Thus anyone, for example, who wants to know what the Belgian rules on euthanasia mean,[8] will find that this is to a large degree determined by the institutional structure and legal culture in which they are embedded. A good example of this is the debate about the alleged existence of a *right* to euthanasia. Article 14 of the Belgian Euthanasia Act clearly provides that a medical doctor may refuse to perform euthanasia on grounds of conscience. This suggests that there is no such thing as a right to euthanasia in the sense that a patient can demand euthanasia from a specific doctor. Yet opinions differ among lawyers and doctors on the meaning of this provision.

Proponents of an enforceable right to euthanasia argue that because the Belgian Euthanasia Act explicitly requires that euthanasia be performed by a doctor, it must be considered 'normal medical behaviour'. Since it is 'normal medical behaviour', doctors are under an obligation to perform it if the extensive conditions listed in the Belgian Euthanasia Act are met.[9]

Opponents of such a right to euthanasia, on the other hand, rely heavily on a reconstruction of the legal context in which the Euthanasia Act should be placed, situating the supposedly applicable legal norms in the wider context of health care legislation.[10] From a legal point of view, the opinion that euthanasia is 'normal medical behaviour' cannot be correct, so the opponents argue, because under Belgian law medical behaviour that for non-doctors would constitute a criminal act can only be legally justified under the Royal Decree concerning the practice of health care professionals. This Decree provides, among other things, that a doctor has an obligation to treat a patient when there is a *medical indication* for the treatment – subject to the consent of the patient, of course. This legal justification (and the doctor's connected obligation) does not, however, cover behaviour of physicians for which there is, apart from exceptions, no medical indication, such as abortion, removal of an organ for transplantation, non-therapeutic medical

---

[8] As was among many other things the case in J Griffiths, H Weyers and M Adams, *Euthanasia and Law in Europe* (Oxford, Hart Publishing, 2008).
[9] See for this and other arguments, E De Keyser, 'Euthanasie: een medische handeling?' (2003) *Nieuw Juridisch Weekblad* 1067–73.
[10] H Nys, 'Euthanasie is geen medische handeling' (1999) 4 *Acta Hospitalia* 71–72 and H Nys, 'Euthanasie in de Caritasziekenhuizen: een juridische verheldering' (2002) *Ethische Perspectieven* 29–31.

research and euthanasia. In other words, so these opponents argue, to justify these medical activities explicit legalisation is required. It is the Euthanasia Act itself that creates a specific legal justification for euthanasia, but not a right to it. To the opponents the distinction between medically-indicated treatment and medical behaviour that is legal but not medically indicated clearly implies that euthanasia cannot be considered 'normal medical behaviour'.[11] As a result there cannot be an enforceable right to it.

Differences of opinion continue to date, but the key to understanding this matter lies in the political and societal context, and ultimately revolves around the mainly ideological question of whether Catholic hospitals may prohibit doctors in their employ from performing euthanasia: if euthanasia is not an enforceable right, they might do so. The answer to this question is not merely academic, since about 80 per cent of the hospitals in Flanders (the region that accounts for more than half of Belgium in terms of number of inhabitants and geographical size) are associated with Catholic organisations. Awareness of this political and societal context is the natural habitat of Belgian lawyers – indeed, of the population at large – when interpreting the legal norms; they will have no difficulty in recognising and understanding the interests at stake. Nevertheless, in legal literature the matter is translated into (some would say 'disguised as') an almost exclusively legal dispute. That single fact makes the issue even more difficult for outsiders to understand. Not only do they have to grasp all the political and societal interests concerned, merely identifying them or even establishing that these are relevant issues at all is extremely difficult for them.

What especially complicates matters for a comparatist is that in the Netherlands the idea that euthanasia cannot be considered a form of 'normal medical behaviour' has been discussed in similar terms (and there is general consensus that it is *not*), but for quite a different purpose. The Dutch discussion has focussed not on the matter of the existence of an enforceable right (for which there is little support) but rather on the question whether a criminal control regime for euthanasia is necessary and wise, or whether control could be left, at least in first instance, to the profession itself (as is largely the case for 'normal medical behaviour'). Here the discussion has not been so much ideologically inspired (at any rate far less so than in Belgium) as it has been policy driven: what form of control can best meet the need for safety and public confidence, once euthanasia is made legal?[12] So what we see is two countries using similar legal arguments in a seemingly similar debate but with quite different implications and a completely different cultural and political drive behind the debates.

As this example shows, of the many challenges that confront the comparatist the question as to the meaning of foreign legal 'facts' – how should they be interpreted and understood, or their existence explained? – is prominent. How

---

[11] The distinction was accepted by the Belgian Council of State in its advice on the pending euthanasia Bill. *Parliamentary Proceedings, Senate* (1999–2000) 2-244/21.
[12] See J Griffiths, H Weyers and A Bood, *Euthanasia and Law in the Netherlands* (Amsterdam, Amsterdam University Press, 1998) 285–98.

can one uncover, in a foreign legal system, the 'truth' behind the legal rules and other legally relevant facts that first catch the eye of a researcher? In a sense, this is easier if the legal facts concerned are exotic and plainly require further attention. It is especially when they seem familiar or even self-evident that the comparative researcher can be lead to draw 'obvious' but in fact superficial or misleading conclusions as far as similarities and differences are concerned.

In any case, trying to answer questions of this type raises very specific problems regarding the qualification of features of foreign law in a way not normally required for doing research within the boundaries of the home legal system. It is this situation that begs the question how to do research in such a way that reliable knowledge of the legal or legally relevant phenomena of one or more foreign legal systems can be acquired. In short, how can researchers engage in and understand the self-evidencies of another legal system so that meaningful comparison becomes possible, ie comparison which can identify real similarities and differences, relate them to each other and explain them? It is this problematic, and the methodological problems it poses, which I believe justifies calling comparative law a discipline in its own right. That is not to say that these are the only problems of doing comparative legal research, but I believe that it is this feature that makes comparative law particularly specific or distinctive.

The foregoing implies that these problems of doing comparative legal research are particularly manifest when comparatists attempt to focus on the stage of information gathering and juxtaposing the findings (presenting the materials found), ie the stage which must precede the process of explicit comparison. Here, comparatists should try to 'simply' gather as much information as possible about a foreign legal system and present it as best they can in the way it is understood by those internal to the legal system, ie those who are working from within and who experience the rules and institutions as daily realities and as reasons for action.

This preliminary phase of comparative legal research of course sets the stage for the subsequent explicit comparison. To avoid misunderstandings, I am not implying that this information gathering and reconstruction phase is utterly devoid of comparison.[13] To the contrary, even 'just' studying a foreign legal system will unavoidably, albeit implicitly and maybe even unconsciously, cause jurists to refer to and reflect on their native legal system.[14] Comparison

---

[13] It is, by the way, also not the false dichotomy of 'objective description/juxtaposition' versus 'subjective analysis' I am talking about. Far from it, indeed, because every description is always a personal interpretation as well.

[14] This point of view is in line with how some comparatists perceive their own activities, judging at least from how they talk and write about them. An example of this is the debate on the use of foreign law by national judges, an activity which might also be called *Auslandrechtkunde* since it usually is not geared towards explicit comparison as such. Even so, the literature on this topic often speaks of judges doing *comparative* law. For example, T Koopmans, 'Comparative Law and the Courts' (1996) 45 *International and Comparative Law Quarterly* 545–56; G Canivet, M Andenas and D Fairgrieve (eds), *Comparative Law Before the Courts* (London, British Institute of International and Comparative Law, 2004); B Markesinis and J Fedtke, 'The Judge as Comparatist' (2005) 80 *Tulane Law Review* 11–168, and A Barak, *The Judge in a Democracy* (Princeton, Princeton University Press, 2006) 198–204. Yet, it

in this sense may also steer the choices the comparatist makes when attempting to describe the foreign object of research. This is due to the fact that when this interference occurs, it inevitably does so with the 'home' system in mind as a frame of reference. It is this very propensity which can be highly hazardous because it may all too easily result in the other legal system being described or analysed within a framework which is characteristic of the researcher's own legal system (ethnocentrism!). The lack of acknowledgement and consideration of this fact often brings on misguided, misleading or erroneous conclusions, steering the research into the direction of the search for similarities rather than similarities *and* differences.[15] Be this as it may, the point here is that while explicit comparison is evidently not without potential pitfalls, it is the informational phase where methodological problems come to the fore in a prominent manner.[16]

At this point, it would not be incorrect to say that I do not necessarily disagree with Bell in the sense that comparative legal research can indeed be seen as an instance of general legal research; it is institutional and interpretative too. However, these qualities do not make it less *distinctive*, because, as I have argued, the juxtaposition and interpretation of foreign material calls for making *explicit* and trying to understand the institutional and socio-cultural context of the law. The trouble of being able to do this is always very prominent and demanding in comparative legal research.

To do justice to John Bell – whom I have, admittedly, quoted selectively above – I must refer to him again here. After having concluded that comparative law is an instance of general legal research, he also writes:

> [T]here are peculiar challenges in comparative legal research. The first is to understand the full institutional setting out of which the legal issues and solutions arise: the organisation of the legal system, its legal concepts, presuppositions and mental map of the relationships between legal institutions, its legal procedures, and the broader social and cultural context and assumptions. In one's own system, much of this is tacit knowledge. In relation to a foreign system, the researcher needs to acquire more explicit knowledge, and also has to make the tacit knowledge of his or her own system more explicit. Second, the hermeneutic approach requires the comparatist to adopt the internal point of view of the systems compared, but not necessarily to believe either of them is right, fair or just. Third, the comparatist is not reporting an internal point of view that comes as clearly packaged, even if he or she makes use of questionnaires

is also true that the judge who looks abroad for techniques to address a home legal question will surely, and at the very least implicitly, reflect in a comparative manner on what he or she finds.

[15] A mistake Zweigert's and Kötz's version of so-called functionalist comparative legal research has many times been accused of, and rightly so. See for this critique most prominently G Frankenberg, 'Critical Comparisons: Re-thinking Comparative Law' (1985) 26 *Harvard International Law Journal* 411–55. To be sure, the problem seems to me not to be functionalism as such. For important nuances of functionalism, see J Husa, 'Farewell to Functionalism or Methodological Tolerance?' (2003) 67 *Rabels Zeitschrift für ausländisches und internationales Privatrecht* 419–47, and also Husa's contribution to this volume. Also J De Coninck, 'The Functional Method of Comparative Law: *Quo Vadis?*' (2010) 74 *Rabels Zeitschrift für ausländisches und internationales Privatrecht* 318 50.

[16] *cf* N Jansen, 'Comparative Law and Comparative Knowledge' in M Reimann and R Zimmermann (eds), *The Oxford Handbook of Comparative Law* (Oxford, Oxford University Press, 2006) 306.

addressed to national lawyers. The comparatist has to interpret the systems to enable a dialogue between them. Each law is something that has to be reconstructed in order to provide intelligible results to people from another legal system. Finally, there is presentation in language and ideas that will be understood by lawyers in the home legal system. At each stage the potential for going wrong is great, not least in the institutional and interpretative features. However, that is why there is strength in the rigour of comparative research.[17]

Here it becomes fully clear that one of the main challenges that thrust itself at the comparatist is indeed to make explicit the broader social and cultural context and assumptions of a foreign legal system or legal concepts, as they are understood by the people working from within the system. It is exactly this endeavour that doesn't come naturally to comparative lawyers.

III. EXPLANATORY COMPARATIVE LAW AND INTERDISCIPLINARITY

Samuel, in his contribution to this volume, claims that the traditional interpretative method that lawyers use is hardly conducive to progress in the legal domain.

Does a modern doctrinal lawyer, epistemologically speaking, actually know more about law as a discipline than say Ulpian, Bartolus, Domat or Savigny knew? In the natural sciences, Newton, despite his enormous contribution to knowledge, would, if brought back to life today, not be able to recognise the models now employed by his successors. A Post-Glossator, in contrast, would have few problems in understanding a law lecture in a common law faculty and Domat would probably have little difficulty with the French *agrégation*.[18]

What is the added value of using the traditional approach in comparative law, as Samuel identifies it? The answer to him is clear: '[I]f domestic methods as governed by the [traditional] authority paradigm are to be the tools of comparative law, it will result in nothing more than superficial scientific reductionism.'[19] 'This [authority paradigm] is one where the primary scheme of intelligibility is hermeneutics operating in respect of a text (legislation, court judgment) whose authority is never put into question.'[20] More specifically, Samuel seems to find fault with the type of research that focuses exclusively on legal concepts and on issues of legal coherence and consistency (internal logic), ie legal research that filters out the inevitable normative and other dimensions that are reflected in the law and legal choices. Samuel is scathing about the chances of scientific progress when mere interpretative doctrinal research methods are used, and *ipso facto* about the

---

[17] See J Bell's contribution in chapter nine, 'Legal Research and the Distinctiveness of Comparative Law'.
[18] See G Samuel's contribution in chapter 10, 'Does One Need an Understanding of Methodology in Law Before One Can Understand Methodology in Comparative Law?'.
[19] ibid.
[20] ibid.

shallowness of comparative legal analysis based on these methods. Ultimately, Samuel's contribution is an ardent plea for interdisciplinarity and external perspectives in legal research, comparative or otherwise.

In a way, law has never been a fully autonomous discipline and legal research is ever interdisciplinary. The regulation of social order through the interpretation of a variety of authoritative texts has always, albeit often unconsciously, gone through the sluice of the techniques and content of other disciplines.[21] Legal interpretation will thus bring into play certain of the lawyers' conceptions and ideologies of social reality, and comparative law, as I argued in the previous section, asks for heightening these conceptions and ideologies. Neither Bell nor Samuel denies this, although the latter holds a plea for a type of research that builds explicitly on the external perspectives of the social sciences, an approach which contrasts with the more interpretative approaches Bell stresses. The reason for doing so is that Samuel wants to come up with a type of research that increases knowledge about law as a social reality. For Samuel interdisciplinarity is an aim in itself because it can better enhance our knowledge of social reality, at least when compared to doctrinal legal research. Comparative law for him is a kind of social laboratory.

I tend to agree with Samuel about the shallowness of rigid rule-centred (comparative) legal research, ie research that only describes and systematises legal rules of different legal systems vis-à-vis each other (but really, how much of that still exists?). The problem with this type of comparative legal research is that it contributes little to progress or innovation. (Which, of course, is not to say that it is easy to do this type of traditional research; it, too, can be intellectually demanding.) As an academic discipline comparative law should, I believe, also strive for progress and innovation. External legal perspectives have a role to play in this, but not necessarily so. Let me expand on this a little more.

To me, all scientific work begins with a question, either of a 'what'/'how' (facts) or of a 'why' (theory) sort. Research questions always go before research methods and without specifying the question no sensible discussion of any specific methodology is possible. I believe that trying to find a methodology for doing comparative legal research (or trying to decide what counts as similarities or differences, or trying to overcome a gap between goals and methods, and so forth) in the abstract, not connected to some kind of concrete question is like chasing a will-o'-the-wisp. This is also the main reason why it is impossible to speak of *the* methodology of comparative law: trying to find a methodology for something that is not a question – such as 'comparative law' – is not of any service. Comparative law is a collection of methods that may be helpful in seeking answers to a variety of questions about law.

---

[21] KM Sullivan, 'Interdisciplinarity' (2002) 100 *Michigan Law Review* 1220–21. Sullivan adds that this does not make law less of a discipline in its own right. 'If you have any doubt that legal method is distinctive, try reading a non-lawyer's attempt to state the holding of a judicial opinion' (p 1219).

Given all this, I would for the purposes of comparative legal research, rather than differentiate between external and internal perspectives on the law, make a distinction between what I would call *descriptive* comparative law and *explanatory* comparative law.[22] The former typically asks traditional legal questions: what is the law in at least two jurisdictions and how do they compare? The applicable legal norms in the different jurisdictions have to be identified and described with an eye to their subsequent systematisation and the identification of similarities and differences. All of this can be done with typical or traditional legal research means. The explanatory type of comparative law, however, aims not only to identify and describe legal differences and similarities between different jurisdictions and relate them to each other, but also wants to account for or explain them. It is here that progress can be made. Despite their differences, I think it is in this latter approach that Bell and Samuel find each other because both seem to hold a plea for this type of comparative legal research, which readily calls for an interdisciplinary approach.

If all this is indeed true, to me the most material question would be: how much or what type of interdisciplinarity or externality is needed for answering explanatory questions about the law? In his contribution, however, Samuel pays scant attention to this. What does it mean to include interdisciplinary and/or external perspectives? From a practical point of view, this issue is relevant because depending on the mode or intensity of interdisciplinarity or externality, lawyers may experience fewer or more difficulties while doing research.

The answer will of course depend on the aim of the research: the aforementioned explanations can be given from many different perspectives (economic, sociological, historical, etc).[23] Even so, some general observations can be made. Van Klink and Taekema have made an interesting and helpful classification of interdisciplinary legal research into four types, based on the extensiveness of the input from the other, non-legal discipline.[24] In the *first type* of interdisciplinary research they identify, the non-legal discipline is used merely heuristically

---

[22] The distinction is merely analytic, since knowledge collected in the context of research is in a way *always* descriptive. Yet depending on the research question, descriptive information can be obtained which can also be used to *explain* situations. On this B van Fraassen, *The Scientific Image* (Oxford, Clarendon Press, 1980) 157. Thus, the question 'How did bigger States arise after 1775?' will yield descriptive knowledge that does not easily serve the purpose of explanation. The question, 'How can it be explained that bigger States arose after 1775?' will more likely generate a description that can also function as an explanatory theory. I am grateful to my late colleague H Oost for referring me to Van Fraassen and discussing the example with me.

[23] *cf* D Nelken, 'Comparative Law and Comparative Legal Studies' in E Örücü and D Nelken (eds), *Comparative Law. A Handbook* (Oxford, Hart Publishing, 2007) 16: 'To go from classification to theoretical understanding and explanation requires greater engagement with other disciplines. Comparative law cannot do its work alone. But it might be more exact to say that it never did. What is at stake ... is the possible replacement or supplementation of legal, historical and philosophical scholarship with concepts and methods taken, for example, from economics, political science, sociology, or anthropology.'

[24] B van Klink and S Taekema, 'A Dynamic Model of Interdisciplinarity: Limits and Possibilities of Interdisciplinary Research into Law' 16ff. Available on SSRN:papers.ssrn.com/sol3/papers.cfm?abstract_id=1142847 (last accessed on 12 December 2009).

and possibly arbitrarily. The perspective of the research as such remains firmly within the legal framework, and the other discipline has no argumentative force of its own and is not necessary to answer the research question. It is, moreover, the legal discipline itself that provides the problem definition and research question, but in answering it the researcher also looks at other disciplines for material. In the *second type* of interdisciplinary legal research, the other discipline is not just used additionally but also constructively. Again, it is the legal researcher that provides for the problem definition and the research question – the legal perspective is dominant – but in order to be able to answer the research question, the input of another discipline is necessary. If, for example, a researcher wants to know why in jurisdiction X constitutional review by the judiciary is introduced and designed in a specific way, and why it is not introduced in jurisdiction Y, he or she has to rely on knowledge generated in political science. The *third type* is coined 'multidisciplinary research'. Two or more disciplines, including the legal, are being used as equally important perspectives. As a result, the legal perspective no longer prevails, and each of the disciplines provides a definition of the central problem to be researched. The core of such research is a study in which the transfer of knowledge is not one-way but at least two-way: each of the disciplines involved is both source and target domain. This type of interdisciplinarity asks for a fuller command of the disciplines being drawn on. In the research project on the regulation of euthanasia, for example, one of the things we wanted to find out was the social working[25] of the rules on euthanasia, and we analysed this comparatively with an eye to trying to explain this. This contribution is not the place to go into the theoretical difficulties of a simplistic instrumentalist approach to the 'effectiveness' of law, one that treats legal rules as direct (potential) causes of behaviour.[26] However, looking at the place that euthanasia law plays in the social practice of euthanasia does afford a wonderful opportunity to consider how complex the relationship between rules and behaviour can be. From the perspective of the idea of the social working of legal rules, it is obvious that it is not enough to look at what the rules are and how they came to be that way; it is also essential to take stock of what happens to them on the 'shop floor' of everyday life. How, when and why do people use the rules? Do the rules make a difference in social interaction? If so, what is it? To what can this difference be attributed and how does this come about? Comparison here provides an essential angle to test hypotheses and theories. To be able to answer questions like this, we, for example, had to rely heavily (though not exclusively) on empirical social-scientific research done by others and funded by the Dutch and Belgian government and research authorities. In other words, we did not have to do the original empirical work ourselves, although being competent – as, importantly,

---

[25] See J Griffiths, 'The Social Working of Legal Rules' (2003) 48 *Journal of Legal Pluralism and Unofficial Law* 1–84.
[26] See AL Stinchcombe, *Constructing Social Theories* (New York, Harcourt, Brace & World, 1968) for an unusually careful analysis and discussion of the circumstances in which such an approach may be appropriate.

one of us was – in the ins and outs of this type of research used was necessary to be able to judge and use the available materials. Two disciplines, including the legal, were thus being used as equally important perspectives; the legal perspective no longer dominated the scene, and the social-scientific analysis necessarily built on the more legally oriented part of the research project. The *fourth type* of interdisciplinarity Van Klink and Taekema identify fully integrates two or more research perspectives. It starts with an integrated problem definition and research question and ends with conclusions that are justified for all the disciplines that are being used in the research project.

Of course, each of these approaches has its challenges, opportunities and limitations. The more extensive the input from the non-legal discipline, the more potential problems there will be for the legal scholar; not just in integrating the different disciplines (the problems will be multiplied), but also in terms of ability: the researcher has to be knowledgeable in more than one discipline, and possibly even able and versatile in doing non-legal research himself.[27] But in any case, in order to be able *to account for* or *explain* the similarities and differences between legal systems, an interdisciplinary approach might well be indispensable. And depending on the aim of the research an external approach might even be used. On *pragmatic grounds* I would argue in favour of moderate types of interdisciplinarity or externality, one of them being to prevent the (comparative) legal researcher from becoming a 'jack of all trades (and a master of none)'. This is not a plea for excluding strong interdisciplinary or external perspectives altogether, but realistically that might well require group work.

To sum up, I believe it to be required for explanatory purposes to deliberately step out of the legal domain, but not necessarily to such an extent that the comparatist has to become fully versatile in another academic discipline. If the aim of comparative legal scholarship is to explain, then even measured forms of interdisciplinarity can generate information that helps answering explanatory questions.

IV. TO CONCLUDE

Engaging in comparative law can be considered distinctive because comparative legal researchers have to be able to reconstruct the meaning of legal rules that are foreign to them. That capacity does not come naturally, at least not in the same way as doing research in the context of the home legal system does; trying to reconstruct the meaning of foreign law calls for actively engaging its socio-cultural

---

[27] Moreover, we have to realise that Van Klink's and Taekema's division of interdisciplinary perspectives is an analytic one; there seem to be other 'in between' positions or classifications that are feasible. As a dynamic and analytic tool their division nevertheless provides a helpful yardstick to qualify and classify research projects, including comparative ones. See for another classification eg M Siems, 'The Taxonomy of Interdisciplinary Legal Research: Finding the Way Out of the Desert' (2009) 7 *Journal of Commonwealth Law and Legal Education* 5–17.

context and, depending on the aim of the research at hand, for a lesser or greater degree of interdisciplinarity and/or external perspectives. What to me seems to be particularly material in the context of comparative legal research, is the type of information that will be needed in 2011 and beyond, as well as the type of questions we should ask to gather this information. In my view, comparative law should, more than it has done before, self-consciously and explicitly encompass explanatory angles to supplement the customary perspective lawyers are used to. This does not mean that comparative legal researchers need to be fully versatile in other disciplines besides their own, at least not in terms of being able to do the type of research that is typical of these other disciplines. But they must at least be able to build on these other disciplines. In this way, in an increasingly interdependent era which makes ever greater demands on our ability to explain and understand the (legal) world with which we are confronted, comparative law can be of tangible benefit. As a result, comparative law might be even more 'distinctive'.

13

Promises and Pitfalls of Interdisciplinary Legal Research: The Case of Evolutionary Analysis in Law

BART DU LAING*

What is more, we have just argued that the Darwinian work to date is at best seriously incomplete. We make no apology for this. Science is an error prone, one-step-at-a-time procedure, and the story shall remain incomplete for a long time if not forever. The only thing about the project that we care to assert with utter conviction is that the Darwinian approach is worth pursuing. Those who engage in the pursuit will take proper delight in remedying our generation's errors and omissions![1]

I. INTRODUCTION

I WOULD LIKE to begin my chapter with a quote I happened to find in Mark Van Hoecke's inaugural lecture, on a topic similar to the one at hand in this volume, delivered at Ghent University in February 2009. It is a quote from Christopher Columbus Langdell, from his 1886 Address to the Harvard Law School Association, and it goes like this:

[t]he library is the proper workshop of [law] professors and students alike; that is to us all that the laboratories of the university are to chemists and physicists, all that the museum of natural history is to the zoologists, all that the botanical garden is to the botanists.[2]

---

* I wish to thank Julie De Coninck for commenting on an earlier draft of this contribution.
[1] PJ Richerson and R Boyd, Not by Genes Alone: How Culture Transformed Human Evolution (Chicago, University of Chicago Press, 2005) 254
[2] CC Langdell, 'Address to the Harvard Law School Association' (1886), as quoted in M Van Hoecke, 'Hoe wetenschappelijk is de rechtswetenschap?' (2009) (Inaugural lecture Ghent University 5 February 2009, on file with the author). A modified version of this lecture has been published as M Van Hoecke, 'Hoe wetenschappelijk is de rechtswetenschap?' (2009) 46 *Tijdschrift voor Privaatrecht* 629ff.

The use of this quote at the beginning of a lecture questioning, but ultimately affirming the scientific nature of legal (doctrinal) research,[3] immediately struck me, because I had just been reading Ernst Mayr's collection of papers entitled *Toward a New Philosophy of Biology: Observations of an Evolutionist*.[4] As some readers undoubtedly will know, Ernst Mayr is considered to be one of the principal architects of the so-called Modern Evolutionary Synthesis, the synthesis of Mendelian genetics and (neo-)Darwinian evolutionary theory, a synthesis that is still widely regarded as biological orthodoxy – although things are perhaps slowly beginning to change in this respect.

In this collection, there is an essay called 'Museums and Biological Laboratories' that Mayr wrote in 1973 for the opening of the laboratory wing of the Museum of Comparative Zoology at Harvard University. While on the one hand clearly acknowledging the continued usefulness of the collections of museums of natural history for biological research, Mayr on the other hand points to the fact that many crucial biological questions cannot be answered simply by the study of preserved material.[5] He also shows us that this is far from being a new idea.

Indeed, Mayr also quotes the founder of the Museum, Louis Agassiz, namely from his 1857 'Essay on Classification', as follows: 'Without a thorough knowledge of the habits of animals', [Agassiz] said, 'it will never be possible to determine what species are and what not.' He goes on to say that we want to find out 'how far animals related by their structure are similar in their habits, and how far these habits are the expression of their structure'. He continues: 'How interesting it would be a comparative study of the mode of life of closely allied species.' Indeed, Agassiz proposes a programme of study which is virtually identical with that of the founders of ethology[6] more than 50 years later.[7]

So what we see here is that, some 30 years before Langdell gave his address, zoologists at least already clearly expressed an interest in the behaviour of live animals, rather than merely focusing on the remains of dead animals. In more recent times, this interest in the behaviour of live animals has led to the development of ever more research methods, like both laboratory and field experiments, mathematical modelling and quite advanced statistical methods, and the incorporation of molecular biology and behavioural genetics, to name but a few

---

[3] See also M Van Hoecke's chapter one of this volume, 'Legal Doctrine: Which Method(s) for What Kind of Discipline?'.

[4] E Mayr, *Toward a New Philosophy of Biology: Observations of an Evolutionist* (Cambridge, Harvard University Press, 1988).

[5] See E Mayr, 'Museums and Biological Laboratories' (1973) in *Toward a New Philosophy of Biology* (1988) 289, 290ff.

[6] Human ethology or human behavioural biology in its turn can be seen as a precursor to the contemporary evolutionary approaches to human behaviour that will be discussed in the next section. *cf* also KN Laland and GR Brown, *Sense and Nonsense: Evolutionary Perspectives on Human Behaviour* (Oxford, Oxford University Press, 2002) 55ff.

[7] L Agassiz, 'Essay on Classification' (1857) as quoted in Mayr (n 4) 292.

of them.[8] So while the collections of specimens in museums of natural history continue to serve some function in biological research, I believe it is fair to say that they have been superseded by other types of data collection and analysis.

The central question of this essay then becomes the following: Should, paraphrasing Langdell, the library remain the proper workshop of law professors, given that zoologists in the meantime have moved far beyond the museums of natural history that once indeed were their main working area? While the first part of this question is of course by no means novel, perhaps even to the point of having become anachronistic, I hope to be able to add some elements to this debate by addressing it from the viewpoint of the question's second part. More particularly, my interest in the dealings of zoologists past and present stems from the perspective I have adopted in my current research: that of evolutionary theory as applied to the human species.[9]

After a necessarily brief introduction on these contemporary evolutionary approaches to human behaviour and the ways in which these approaches have (or have not) been put to use in legal analyses (see section II. below), I will try to position what has been called Evolutionary Analysis in Law – or perhaps evolutionary analyses in law would be a better term – within some of the more recently proposed classificatory schemes regarding legal methodology and interdisciplinary legal research (see section III. below). This should not only allow me to touch upon some of the respective strengths and weaknesses of these taxonomies, but, in so doing, will also allow me to address methodological questions of a more theoretical nature as they arise when pursuing interdisciplinary research. Could contemporary evolutionary approaches to human behaviour be of assistance in overcoming some of the traditional social science dichotomies that are often reproduced in legal scholarship (see section III. A. below)? Should legal scholars engage themselves in recent attempts at unifying the life and social sciences? Or is 'methodological integration' more valuable than such 'theoretical integration' (see section III. B. below)? Finally, would all this amount to little more than one-way traffic – from the various behavioural sciences to legal research – or is there room for at least some measure of cross-fertilisation originating from within the legal sciences (see section III. C. below)?

---

[8] Not to mention the likely development of what is increasingly referred to as an Extended Evolutionary Synthesis, on which see eg M Pigliucci and GB Müller (eds), *Evolution: The Extended Synthesis* (Cambridge, MIT Press, 2010); M Pigliucci, 'Do We Need an Extended Evolutionary Synthesis?' (2007) 61 *Evolution* 2743ff.

[9] See eg B Du Laing, 'Equality in Exchange Revisited: From an Evolutionary (Genetic and Cultural) Point of View' in M Freeman and OR Goodenough (eds), *Law, Mind and Brain* (Farnham, Ashgate, 2009) 267ff; B Du Laing, 'Dual Inheritance Theory, Contract Law, and Institutional Change – Towards the Co-evolution of Behavior and Institutions' (2008) 9 *German Law Journal* 491ff; B Du Laing, 'Evolutionary Analysis in Law and the Theory and Practice of Legislation' (2007) 1 *Legisprudence: International Journal for the Study of Legislation* 327ff.

II. CONTEMPORARY EVOLUTIONARY APPROACHES TO HUMAN BEHAVIOUR AND EVOLUTIONARY ANALYSIS IN LAW

A. Contemporary Evolutionary Approaches to Human Behaviour

In order to be able to address these questions relating to the methodology of interdisciplinary legal research, however, I must first say a few words on the three different styles in the evolutionary analysis of human behaviour that are currently usually distinguished from one another. These three approaches are as follows:

- Evolutionary psychology, or the specific version of evolutionary psychology that is more and more often referred to as 'narrow' Evolutionary Psychology or Evolutionary Psychology *sensu stricto*.[10]
- Human behavioural ecology.
- Dual inheritance theory, sometimes called gene-culture co-evolutionary theory or simply cultural evolutionary theory.

I will, as briefly as possible, give the main characteristics of these three approaches as well as their main differences and refer the interested reader to the original sources cited in this section for more elaborate discussion.[11] Since such a brief – perhaps too brief – overview may suggest to some readers that these different approaches are in effect incompatible, I should emphasise at the outset that most commentators on this subject, while acknowledging or even emphasising theoretical disagreements, do appear cautiously optimistic as to the prospects of their eventual (re-)integration.

i. *Evolutionary Psychology*

Evolutionary psychology is the contemporary evolutionary approach to human behaviour that is currently presumably still the most popular and in any case the most visible in the popular press. Evolutionary Psychologists *sensu stricto*,[12]

---

[10] See eg R Dunbar and L Barrett, 'Evolutionary Psychology in the Round' in RIM Dunbar and L Barrett (eds), *The Oxford Handbook of Evolutionary Psychology* (Oxford, Oxford University Press, 2007) 3, 5; M Mameli, 'Evolution and Psychology in Philosophical Perspective' in RIM Dunbar and L Barrett (eds), *The Oxford Handbook of Evolutionary Psychology* (Oxford, Oxford University Press, 2007) 21, 25ff.

[11] Accessible overviews are provided in Laland and Brown, *Sense and Nonsense* (2002), EA Smith, 'Three Styles in the Evolutionary Analysis of Human Behavior' in L Cronk et al (eds), *Adaptation and Human Behavior: An Anthropological Perspective* (New York, Aldine De Gruyter, 2000) 27ff; R Sear et al, 'Synthesis in the Human Evolutionary Behavioural Sciences' (2007) 5 *Journal of Evolutionary Psychology* 3ff. See also the references cited in Du Laing, 'Dual Inheritance Theory' (2008) 492ff, on which this part of my chapter is largely based.

[12] For this approach, see eg JH Barkow et al (eds), *The Adapted Mind: Evolutionary Psychology and the Generation of Culture* (Oxford, Oxford University Press, 1992); DM Buss (ed), *The Handbook of Evolutionary Psychology* (Hoboken, Wiley, 2005); L Cosmides and J Tooby, 'Evolutionary Psychology, Moral Heuristics, and the Law' in G Gigerenzer and C Engel (eds), *Heuristics and the Law* (Cambridge, MIT Press, 2006) 175ff.

like John Tooby and Leda Cosmides, argue that the human brain is the result of evolution by way of natural selection having operated in the remote past – our 'environment of evolutionary adaptedness' or 'EEA'. Hence, they propose to explain human behaviour by appealing to specific genetically evolved psychological mechanisms that are adaptations to specific features of this EEA. They also emphasise that this adaptedness to ancestral environments will frequently lead to maladaptive behaviour in our current environments – the so-called adaptive lag hypothesis. Moreover, they claim that our human species-typical psychological mechanisms are characterised by so-called domain specificity and massive modularity – so that our brain consists of a great many modules that are highly specialised to perform certain specific tasks. More general purpose mechanisms, involving 'learning', 'culture' or 'rational choice', are regarded as insufficiently domain-specific and modular to serve as plausible outcomes of the process of natural selection. Unsurprisingly, evolutionary psychologists are highly sceptical of views of the human mind as a blank slate, engraved only by experience and culture, allowing for a nearly infinite malleability of the behaviour to which it gives rise – a view they derogatorily call the 'Standard Social Science Model'. Finally, the characteristics of evolutionary psychology's theoretical framework are reflected in their threefold division of the phenomenon of culture. The set of universal psychological mechanisms with which we are endowed and the resulting behavioural patterns are called 'metaculture'. Different behavioural patterns that are triggered by different environmental cues are called 'evoked culture'. 'Epidemiological culture' or 'transmitted culture' refers to what most people would recognise as comprising culture, namely a complex of shared beliefs, values, customs, etc.[13] Here I think it is fair to say that the quest for a 'metacultural' universal human nature appears high on the evolutionary psychologists' agenda.

ii. Human Behavioural Ecology

The second approach, human behavioural ecology,[14] essentially views human behaviour as consisting of adaptive responses to varying environments and variation in human behaviour as a result of ecological variation, eliciting different optimising responses. In so doing, human behavioural ecologists assume that humans display a high degree of 'phenotypic plasticity', that humans are capable of flexibly adapting their behaviour to particular environmental factors. Unlike evolutionary psychology, human behavioural ecology focuses on current circumstances and expects humans to be overall well adapted to the environments in which they currently live. Existing behavioural diversity is largely explained as

---

[13] On these last two types of 'culture' as apprehended in the evolutionary psychological framework, see most recently D Nettle, 'Beyond Nature versus Culture: Cultural Variation as an Evolved Characteristic' (2009) 15 *Journal of the Royal Anthropological Institute* 223ff.

[14] For this approach, see eg B Winterhalder and EA Smith, 'Analyzing Adaptive Strategies: Human Behavioral Ecology at Twenty-Five' (2000) 9 *Evolutionary Anthropology* 51ff; L Cronk et al (eds), *Adaptation and Human Behavior: An Anthropological Perspective* (Hawthorne, Aldine de Gruyter, 2000).

a consequence of differing contemporary socio-ecological environments that evoke different conditional behavioural strategies or decision-rules which dictate the most adaptive behaviour under the given ecological conditions ('In context X, engage in strategy A; in context Y, engage in strategy B').

iii. Dual Inheritance Theory or Gene-culture Co-evolutionary Theory

Third and finally, proponents of dual inheritance theory or gene-culture co-evolutionary theory,[15] like Robert Boyd and Peter Richerson, focus on transmitted culture. They are interested in finding out how genetic evolution could give rise to cultural capacities in a species like ours and how these cultural capacities then affect (cumulative) cultural evolution. Dual inheritance theorists consider culture to be a whole of ideas, values, knowledge and the like that is learned and socially transmitted between individuals. Since cultural information exhibits the characteristics required for evolution by way of natural selection – namely variation, retention and selection, they argue that Darwinian *methods* can in principle be used to analyse cultural evolution, important differences between biological evolution and cultural evolution notwithstanding. While cultural evolution, in their theoretical framework, can result from a wide array of possible forces (including, among others, random forces and natural selection on cultural variants), Boyd and Richerson and their collaborators have been primarily interested in modelling the evolution of so-called decision making forces, mainly cultural transmission biases. They plausibly argue that genetically evolved learning biases, leading people to preferentially acquire some cultural variants rather than others, can be important forces in cultural evolution. Such learning biases could include a frequency-based conformity bias and a model-based prestige bias, which, for instance, can both help to maintain stable variation between different cultural groups and their respective social norms. Finally, dual inheritance theorists also address the interactions between the cultural and the genetic system of inheritance. This aspect of their theoretical framework is often referred to as gene-culture co-evolutionary theory and aims at elucidating the complex feedback relationships between these two inheritance systems.

B. Evolutionary Analysis in Law

Now how have these contemporary evolutionary approaches to human behaviour been put to use in legal analyses? Well, to answer this question, we need to take a closer look at the work of Owen Jones, founder of the Society for Evolutionary

[15] For this approach, see eg PJ Richerson and R Boyd, *Not by Genes Alone: How Culture Transformed Human Evolution* (Chicago, University of Chicago Press, 2005); J Henrich and R McElreath, 'Dual-inheritance Theory: the Evolution of Human Cultural Capacities and Cultural Evolution' in RIM Dunbar and L Barrett (eds), *The Oxford Handbook of Evolutionary Psychology* (Oxford, Oxford University Press, 2007) 555ff. See also Du Laing, 'Equality in Exchange Revisited' (2009) 274ff.

Analysis in Law. His work can be regarded as both pioneering and representative for what is usually understood – by friends[16] and enemies[17] alike – to be 'evolutionary analysis in law'. According to Jones, 'effective law requires an effective behavioural model' and such an effective behavioural model should integrate social-science models with life-science models – 'including the effects of evolutionary processes on species-typical brain form and function'.[18] As I have argued at length elsewhere,[19] I think it is very important to realise that Jones's views on the subject are heavily influenced by a very specific school of thought within the existing variety of contemporary evolutionary approaches to human behaviour – namely John Tooby and Leda Cosmides's specific 'narrow' version of evolutionary psychology. To show this, I will briefly compare some of the basic features of their framework I have just outlined with some aspects of Jones's work.

The striking resemblances between John Tooby and Leda Cosmides's Evolutionary Psychology *sensu stricto* and Owen Jones's influential approach to Evolutionary Analysis in Law are summarised in the table below.

John Tooby & Leda Cosmides's Evolutionary Psychology	Owen Jones's Evolutionary Analysis in Law
Environment of evolutionary adaptedness and adaptive lag hypothesis.	Time-shifted rationality and law of law's leverage.
Domain specificity and massive modularity.	(Implicit throughout.)
Focus on 'metaculture'.	Bio-legal history.

All of the key elements of the 'narrow' evolutionary psychological theoretical framework mentioned in the left column indeed reappear in Jones's work on Evolutionary Analysis in Law.

Owen Jones includes the adaptive lag hypothesis in his framework, under the heading of 'time-shifted rationality'. By this is meant that once adaptive behaviour may appear irrational in present environments. Understanding why this is so may consequently help to improve legislation aimed at counteracting this seemingly irrational behaviour. Closely related is a device called the 'law of law's leverage', which stresses evolutionary psychology's potential in distinguishing flexible, and hence legally modifiable, behavioural patterns from others which are less flexible and thus more resistant to legal influence.[20]

---

[16] For example DJ Herring, 'Legal Scholarship, Humility, and the Scientific Method' (2007) 25 *Quarterly Law Review* 867ff.
[17] Most notably B Leiter and M Weisberg, 'Why Evolutionary Biology Is (So Far) Irrelevant to Legal Regulation' (2010) 29 *Law and Philosophy* 31ff.
[18] OD Jones, 'Law, Evolution and the Brain: Applications and Open Questions' (2004) 359 *Philosophical Transactions of the Royal Society of London B: Biological Sciences* 1697, 1699.
[19] See Du Laing, 'Evolutionary Analysis in Law and the Theory and Practice of Legislation' (2007) 329ff.
[20] See OD Jones, 'Time-Shifted Rationality and the Law of Law's Leverage: Behavioral Economics Meets Behavioral Biology' (2001) 95 *Northwestern University Law Review* 1141ff.

Evolutionary psychology's claims regarding the domain specificity of human psychological mechanisms and the massive modularity of the brains that contain them are also, at the very least implicitly, present throughout this type of legal research.[21]

Finally, as regards the third feature, we can take a look at what Jones calls 'bio-legal history'. The concept of bio-legal history refers to the assertion that 'the legal features of any legal system will reflect ... specific features of evolved, species-typical, human brain design'.[22] So here again, there is a strong focus on what Tooby and Cosmides would probably prefer to call metaculture, or, if one wishes, on human universals. Evolutionary psychology apparently would be capable of providing us with 'natural legal histories' of some of the universal or at least recurring features of existing legal systems.[23]

III. TAXONOMISING EVOLUTIONARY ANALYSES IN LAW: THREE QUESTIONS

Now that I hope to have given the reader an idea about the richness and variety of the research field designated here as contemporary evolutionary approaches to human behaviour and culture, I want to try to position *both* evolutionary analysis in law as it is usually conceived of *and* possible alternative approaches to evolutionary analysis in law within some of the more recently proposed classificatory schemes regarding legal methodology and interdisciplinary legal research – not accidentally in two cases by authors who are also contributing to this collection. My main objective is to provide a few often rather speculative thoughts on the following three questions, some of which appear to be only rarely discussed in the legal literature.

Could contemporary evolutionary approaches to human behaviour be of assistance in overcoming some of the traditional social science dichotomies that are often unquestioningly reproduced in legal scholarship (see section III. A. below)? In addressing this first question, I will engage Geoffrey Samuel's ongoing work in epistemology and methodology of law. The second set of questions ties in with Matthias Siems's concerns of developing a workable taxonomy

---

[21] See eg OD Jones and TH Goldsmith, 'Law and Behavioral Biology' (2005) 105 *Columbia Law Review* 405, 447f.

[22] OD Jones, 'Proprioception, Non-Law, and Biolegal History' (2001) 53 *Florida Law Review* 831, 858.

[23] So here we are not all that far removed from the nineteenth century approaches to law and legal phenomena Mark Van Hoecke mentions – in a somewhat critical manner for that matter – in the introduction to his contribution (see M Van Hoecke, 'Legal Doctrine: Which Method(s) for What Kind of Discipline?' in chapter one of this volume). I am referring here to the work of Albert Hermann Post in legal ethnology, which indeed, to say the least, did not leave a big mark on subsequent legal research. However, I believe it is also worth remembering that – methodologically speaking – Post was one of the first researchers to work with relatively 'modern' looking surveys to gather data, thereby, to at least some extent, attempting to leave the confines of the library (see on Post's questionnaires and their significance, A Lyall, 'Early German Legal Anthropology: Albert Hermann Post and His Questionnaire' (2008) 52 Journal of African Law 114ff).

of interdisciplinary legal research. Should legal scholars engage themselves in recent attempts at unifying the life and social sciences? Or is 'methodological integration' more valuable than such 'theoretical integration' (see section III. B. below)? Finally, in addressing a concern expressed by Christopher McCrudden, would all this amount to little more than one-way traffic, from the various social and behavioural sciences towards legal research, or is there room for at least some measure of cross-fertilisation originating from within legal research itself (see section III. C. below)?

A. Overcoming Traditional Social Science Dichotomies?

In positioning various approaches to evolutionary analysis in law, one could indeed refer to the sets of differing paradigms and schemes of intelligibility Geoffrey Samuel addresses briefly in his contribution to this book in chapter 10 and more elaborately elsewhere,[24] especially individualism/collectivism and/ or reductionism/holism, nature (genes)/culture (nurture), and perhaps I could add to this universality/diversity. In addition, 'narrow' evolutionary psychology, and its counterpart in legal research, does seem to fall quite neatly within these categories. At least by its many critics, it is usually described as being individualist and reductionist. Evolutionary psychology, as we saw, focuses on universality and on the nature end of the nature/nurture continuum.[25]

However, the same does not hold for other contemporary evolutionary approaches to human behaviour and their possible applications in legal research. As to individualism/collectivism, I cannot resist the urge to give a somewhat longish quotation from two prominent dual inheritance theorists whose work I think provides an excellent starting point to approach legal phenomena from an evolutionary point of view, namely Peter Richerson and Robert Boyd:

> The social sciences have long been bedevilled by the 'micro-macro problem'. If, like economists, you start with a theory based on individual behavior, how can you ever get to a proper account of society-scale phenomena like social institutions? If you start with collective institutions, like many sociologists and anthropologists do, how do you make room for individuals? A distinguished sociologist once astounded us with the claim that it had been *proved* that you had to pick one or the other and that it was a logical certainty that the two approaches could never be unified. Actually, Darwinian

---

[24] See G Samuel, 'Does One Need an Understanding of Methodology in Law Before One Can Understand Methodology in Comparative Law?' in chapter 10 of this volume. See also G Samuel, 'Taking Methods Seriously (Part One)' (2007) 2 *Journal of Comparative Law* 94ff; G Samuel, 'Taking Methods Seriously (Part Two)' (2007) 2 *Journal of Comparative Law* 210ff.

[25] For some reactions by evolutionary psychologists to such (and other) allegations, see eg EH Hagen, 'Controversial Issues in Evolutionary Psychology' in DM Buss (ed), *The Handbook of Evolutionary Psychology* (Hoboken, Wiley, 2005) 145ff; R Kurzban and MG Haselton, 'Making Hay Out of Straw? Real and Imagined Controversies in Evolutionary Psychology' in JH Barkow (ed), *Missing the Revolution: Darwinism for Social Scientists* (Oxford, Oxford University Press, 2006) 149ff.

concepts provide a neat account of the relations between individual and collective phenomena. Darwinian tools were *invented* to integrate levels. The basic biological theory includes genes, individuals, and populations.[26]

While admittedly unlikely to conclusively 'solve' this perennial 'micro-macro problem',[27] multi-level evolutionary approaches of this kind do appear to be able to steer away from reductionism, while at the same time retaining a rather healthy distance from unfettered holism. Furthermore, some combination of evolutionary psychology (*sensu lato*) and dual inheritance theory could prove to shed more light or at least cast a different kind of light on the relationship between universality and diversity (as regards legal and other phenomena).[28] Evidently, these approaches constitute an interesting way to try to bridge the nature/culture (or nurture) divide. Put differently, again referring to Samuel's work on methodology and epistemology of (comparative) law, most if not all gene-culture co-evolutionary theorists whose work I have studied[29] would not regard as somehow mutually exclusive (1) the view that 'social phenomena are considered to be a continuity of natural phenomena, and accordingly should be subjected to the same mechanisms' (Samuel's 'naturalist paradigm') and (2) the view according to which 'social phenomena are regarded as being a matter of cultural norms and values formed within particular groups or societies which, through the mediation of socialisation, enculturation or inculcation, define the sense of the behaviour patterns or social practices' (the apparently, by necessity, opposite 'culturalist paradigm').[30]

An example I have been working on to make these promises evolutionary theory seems to hold more concrete with regard to law, concerns comparative law and its theory.[31] Let me first quote from an article by Geoffrey Samuel, where he is referring to the different schemes of intelligibility identified by the French social theorist Jean-Michel Berthelot, in relation to different approaches to comparative legal research:

> The functional method, along with the causative and actional schemes, lead inexorably towards a comparative methodology based on a *praesumptio similitudinis*, 'a

---

[26] Richerson and Boyd, *Not by Genes Alone* (2005) 246f.

[27] Perhaps it is useful to repeat at this point that further on in their book, Richerson and Boyd (ibid 254) are careful to stress that the only thing about their project they 'care to assert with utter conviction is that the Darwinian approach is worth pursuing'.

[28] *cf* also PM Hejl, 'Konstruktivismus und Universalien – eine Verbindung contre nature?' in PM Hejl (ed), *Universalien und Konstruktivismus* (Frankfurt, Suhrkamp, 2001) 7ff.

[29] Apart from the authors already cited, *cf* also, eg WH Durham, 'Cultural Variation in Time and Space: The Case for a Populational Theory of Culture' in RG Fox and BJ King (eds), *Anthropology Beyond Culture* (Oxford, Berg, 2002) 193ff; MW Feldman, 'Dissent with Modification: Cultural Evolution and Social Niche Construction' in MJ Brown (ed), *Explaining Culture Scientifically* (Seattle, University of Washington Press, 2008) 55ff.

[30] Samuel, 'Taking Methods Seriously (Part One)' (2007) 113f.

[31] See B Du Laing, 'Evolutionair sociaal constructivisme, recht en rechtsvergelijking' (2007) 36 *Rechtsfilosofie & Rechtstheorie [Journal for Legal Philosophy and Jurisprudence]* 34ff; J De Coninck and B Du Laing, 'Comparative Law, Behavioural Economics and Contemporary Evolutionary Functionalism' (2009) (working paper available at ssrn.com/abstract=1445287).

presumption that the practical results are similar'. The deep hermeneutical approach, not surprisingly, will lead to quite the opposite methodological presumption.[32]

For this reason, certain versions of the latter approach are, as is well-known, also sometimes referred to as 'difference theory'. Such 'difference theoretical' approaches to comparative law could be related to Owen Jones's concept of bio-legal history, designating the not altogether unlikely possibility that the legal features of any legal system will, to some extent, reflect specific features of evolved, species-typical, human brain design, and, still according to Jones, providing 'ample support for believing that bio-legal histories connect the world's disparate legal systems together'.[33] As we saw, this view is heavily influenced by evolutionary psychology, an evolutionary approach to human behaviour, which, focusing on universal human cognitive adaptations, is currently lacking a convincing approach to culture and cultural diversity. Much the same approach is taken in Raffaele Caterina's article on comparative law and the cognitive revolution, questioning as he does the position according to which comparative lawyers should deliberately seek 'astonishment' and 'purposefully privilege the identification of differences'.[34]

To me, however, it appears rather less useful to simply point to an opposite point of view originating in or at least backed up by another discipline, thus effectively reproducing existing dichotomies, without being able to address at least some of the genuine concerns of the existing approach one is criticising.[35] An evolutionary theory of culture like the one outlined by Robert Boyd and Peter Richerson, stresses that culture is *neither* supra-organic *nor* the handmaiden of the genes. It seeks to give cultural evolution its due weight without divorcing culture from evolutionary biology, thus providing a plausible – *and necessary* – link between genetic and cultural evolution. A combination of two inherently compatible contemporary evolutionary approaches to human behaviour and culture could very well be able to account at least in part for *both* legal universality *and* legal diversity within an encompassing theoretical framework.[36]

Or, to put it differently still, not everyone is convinced of the merits of what Berthelot refers to as 'the logic of confrontation' between differing schemes of intelligibility existing in the social sciences.[37] Some integration between them, as well as with other types of sciences, whilst retaining a degree of pluralism – in the sense of a plurality of models working together, rather than against each other – could very well appear to be useful, and evolutionary theory is not that

---

[32] G Samuel, 'Epistemology and Comparative Law: Contributions from the Sciences and Social Sciences' in M Van Hoecke (ed), *Epistemology and Methodology of Comparative Law* (Oxford, Hart, 2004) 35, 64.

[33] Jones and Goldsmith, 'Law and Behavioral Biology' (2005) 474f.

[34] R Caterina, 'Comparative Law and the Cognitive Revolution' (2004) 78 *Tulane Law Review* 1501, 1546.

[35] *cf* also A De Block and B Du Laing, 'Paving the Way for an Evolutionary Social Constructivism' (2007) 2 *Biological Theory* 337ff.

[36] See also Du Laing (2009) (n 9) 286ff.

[37] *cf* Samuel, 'Epistemology and Comparative Law' (2004) 76.

unlikely a candidate as it may seem to build some bridges between, as things stand, often not communicating disciplines.[38] Anyhow, quite a few people nowadays seem optimistic about this endeavour, and I have chosen to share, for the time being, some of their ultimately perhaps unwarranted enthusiasm. So, to conclude for this section, I do believe that at least some contemporary evolutionary approaches to human behaviour could contribute to some bridge-building between various strands of thought within the social sciences that are traditionally thought of as being incompatible.

B. Theoretical Integration versus Methodological Integration?

This brings me to the second point I want to make with regard to the taxonomy of interdisciplinary legal research. Should legal scholars engage themselves in recent attempts at unifying the life and social sciences? The main recent attempt I am thinking of here is Herbert Gintis's proposal for an integration or even a unification of the various behavioural sciences: psychology, economics, sociology, anthropology and biology. Closely related to the foregoing are indeed Gintis's observations on the fragmentation of this set of scientific disciplines:

> In particular, psychology, economics, anthropology, biology, and sociology should have concordant explanations of law-abiding behavior, charitable giving, political corruption, voting behavior, and other complex behaviors that do not fit nicely within disciplinary boundaries. They do not have such explanations presently.[39]

According to Gintis, such cross-disciplinary incoherence can be partially explained by the fact that these distinct disciplines traditionally dealt largely with distinct phenomena. However, at least in the areas where the interests of the various behavioural disciplines overlap, he argues, their models should be consistent and preferably even synergic. Recent theoretical and empirical developments are said to have created the conditions for achieving this ambitious goal. The fact that the theoretical tools and data gathering techniques to be deployed in this task transcend disciplinary boundaries, should moreover render such an integration easier to attain. In any case, the theoretical framework Gintis proposes as a unifying bridge incorporates gene-culture co-evolutionary theory as one of the, if not the most important, integrating principles of behavioural science.

Gintis is far from being alone in deploring the current state of affairs in the social and behavioural sciences. Actually, most evolutionary theoretically

---

[38] Of course, attempting to build bridges between them in a way always presupposes pre-existing conflicting approaches.

[39] H Gintis, 'A framework for the unification of the behavioral sciences' (2007) 30 *Behavioral and Brain Sciences* 1, 1. See also H Gintis, 'Towards a Unity of the Human Behavioral Sciences' in S Rahman et al (eds), *Logic, Epistemology, and the Unity of Science* (Dordrecht, Kluwer, 2004) 25ff.

inspired social scientists, as well as biologists working on human behaviour and culture, seem to regret the existence of relatively small archipelagos of knowledge within the social sciences that remain disconnected from one another.[40] When I go to evolutionary social science conferences,[41] I see people from different social science disciplines working on the same topics, bringing their respective different research methods to bear on these topics. However, they do so from a shared theoretical perspective, allowing for communication between the different disciplines, as well as allowing for inter-comparability of research results.

Nevertheless, quite a few legal scholars commentating on interdisciplinary legal research seem to suggest that the interdisciplinary component in this type of legal research and the scientific integration it entails mainly if not merely involves incorporating methodological tools from other disciplines, rather than developing a shared theoretical framework. For instance, this appears to be the case for Mathias Siems's recently proposed taxonomy of interdisciplinary legal research.[42] While, in distinguishing in the first place between interdisciplinary research addressing legal questions and interdisciplinary research addressing non-legal questions, it could perhaps be argued that Siems is hinting at what I would call 'theoretical integration', it quickly becomes clear, at least to this reader, that the level of 'advancement' of the different types of interdisciplinary legal research under consideration is, in his taxonomy, quite closely tied to the extent to which they integrate scientific *methods* into legal thinking. The term 'methods' used here seems to designate primarily if not exclusively the more 'practical' aspects of conducting scientific research (statistical methods, experimental methods) and should in my view, following Banakar and Travers,[43] be contrasted with the larger notion of 'methodology', incorporating the idea of an inextricable link between the theoretical framework and the 'practical' methods used.[44] Since the terms 'methods' and 'methodology' are, however, often used interchangeably in legal research addressing interdisciplinarity, I prefer to refer

---

[40] cf also, eg DS Wilson, *Darwin's Cathedral: Evolution, Religion, and the Nature of Society* (Chicago, University of Chicago Press, 2002) 65f and 83ff; JH Barkow, 'Introduction: Sometimes the Bus Does Wait' in *Missing the Revolution: Darwinism for Social Scientists* (Oxford, Oxford University Press, 2006) 29ff.

[41] Like the ones annually organised by the European Human Behaviour and Evolution Association (www.ehbea.com).

[42] See MM Siems, 'The Taxonomy of Interdisciplinary Legal Research: Finding the Way out of the Desert' (2009) 7 *Journal of Commonwealth Law and Legal Education* 5ff.

[43] cf R Banakar and M Travers, 'Law, Sociology and Method' in R Banakar and M Travers (eds), *Theory and Method in Socio-Legal Research* (Oxford, Hart, 2005) 1, 19f; R Banakar and M Travers, 'Method Versus Methodology' in R Banakar and M Travers (eds), *Theory and Method in Socio-Legal Research* (Oxford, Hart, 2005) 28, 28. See also J De Coninck, 'The Functional Method of Comparative Law: Quo Vadis?' (2010) 74 *Rabels Zeitschrift für ausländisches und internationales Privatrecht* 318ff.

[44] cf also B van Klink and S Taekema, 'A Dynamic Model of Interdisciplinarity. Limits and Possibilities of Interdisciplinary Research into Law' (2008) (working paper available at ssrn.com/abstract=1142847) 17ff (distinguishing between concepts, methods, object, problem awareness and self-image of disciplines in order to classify different types of interdisciplinary legal research).

to this distinction as one between 'theoretical integration' and 'methodological integration'.[45]

Is such 'methodological integration', however, necessarily more valuable for legal research than the 'theoretical integration' envisaged by people like Gintis, an integration that (also) takes place at the level of the underlying and encompassing theoretical framework used to generate hypotheses? I for one believe the time has come for legal scholars to get more involved in such endeavours than currently seems to be the case. This would allow the time gap to be closed between theoretical (and, for that matter, the usually ensuing method(olog)ical) advances in other disciplines and their incorporation in legal research – up till now still a notoriously slow process. Moreover, this would force legal researchers to cooperate with researchers from other disciplines in developing a shared theoretical language.

C. One-way Traffic?

While 'law' was not entirely absent from Herbert Gintis's views on the current state of the behavioural sciences sketched in the previous section, it remains telling that 'law-abiding behavior' merely featured as one of the *explananda* to be explained by the (other?)[46] social and behavioural sciences. Moreover, this tacit assessment seems to be quite expressly acknowledged in Owen Jones's reaction to Gintis's target paper,[47] and consequently condoned by Gintis in his stating that 'some, including Jones, elaborated on a theme only implicit in my analysis, that unification could foster more powerful *intra-disciplinary* explanatory frameworks'.[48] This may very well eventually be(come) the case.

In his frequently cited article on legal research and the social sciences, Christopher McCrudden, however, also addresses the question as to whether or not legal research has anything to offer to the external approaches it tries to make use of.[49] Well, one could of course ask much the same question with regard to contemporary evolutionary approaches to human behaviour and legal research. Now I will not dwell on this topic for too long, but I would like to point out that the same point has been raised by Oliver Goodenough, a legal scholar working

---

[45] Or perhaps a distinction between 'theoretical-methodological integration' and 'practical-methodological integration' could also be used, whereby the former would often appear to incorporate the latter.

[46] *cf* on this question also G Samuel, 'Is Law Really a Social Science? A View from Comparative Law' (2008) 67 *Cambridge Law Journal* 288ff; G Samuel, 'Interdisciplinarity and the Authority Paradigm: Should Law Be Taken Seriously by Scientists and Social Scientists?' (2009) 36 *Journal of Law and Society* 431ff.

[47] OD Jones, 'Implications for Law of a Unified Behavioral Science' (2007) 30 *Behavioral and Brain Sciences* 30, 30f.

[48] H Gintis, 'Unifying the Behavioral Sciences II' (2007) 30 *Behavioral and Brain Sciences* 45, 45 (my emphasis).

[49] See C McCrudden, 'Legal Research and the Social Sciences' (2006) 122 *Law Quarterly Review* 632, 645ff.

within the frame of the Gruter Institute for Law and Behavioral Research, in an attempt to look at legal data to help understand the existence and source of certain kinds of specifically human behaviour. According to Goodenough, 'in the study of animal behaviour there is always a role for both fieldwork and lab experimentation, and in human zoology the law represents a rich, if somewhat idiosyncratic, pool of data on the wild behaviour of Homo sapiens'.[50]

Unfortunately, while to some extent interpretable as constituting 'two-way traffic' between law and the social and behavioural sciences, merely being able to provide the latter with data would not seem to secure a firm position for legal scholarship in years to come, perhaps even culminating in the 'world without law professors' Mathias Siems vividly evokes in his chapter in this volume.[51] However, perhaps it is only fair, in a publication aimed at a legal audience, to also look at what a non-legal scholar has to say about this topic. My non-legal scholar of choice in this essay then appears to have become Herbert Gintis who, in his Amazon Review of Eric Posner's book on law and social norms, starts with the following, in my view, quite apt remarks:

> Legal scholars are a special breed of academic. While firmly ensconced in academia, they have no formal training in any scientific discipline, and can be completely ignorant of mathematical formulations of social theory, of statistical hypothesis testing, and the received wisdom of the various disciplines in the social sciences. Moreover, they publish long, weighty, footnote-laden papers in law review journals that, rather than being peer-reviewed, are reviewed by law students with doubtless less expertise in the behavioral sciences than the professors whose work they judge. As such, we do not generally expect the social sciences research of legal scholars to be of great interest to researchers in the various behavioral disciplines.[52]

These observations seem to be highly congruent with Samuel's less than promising diagnosis of traditional (doctrinal) legal scholarship.[53] However, somewhat surprisingly, Gintis himself ultimately begs to differ, for reasons that are, to my knowledge, rarely if at all explicitly discussed in legal writings on the issue.[54] Gintis indeed continues to say that:

> However, the same conditions that deprive legal scholars from the rigors of the scientific disciplines allow them to develop exciting transdisciplinary ideas with a speculative freedom that is simply not open to an economist, psychologist, or other member of the standard disciplines. Moreover, the behavioral disciplines are less 'scientific' than they prefer to consider themselves, because they disagree in the fundamentals – a

---

[50] OR Goodenough, 'Law and the Biology of Commitment' in RM Nesse (ed), *Evolution and the Capacity for Commitment* (New York, Russell Sage Foundation, 2001) 262, 272.

[51] See MM Siems' chapter four of this volume, 'A World Without Law Professors'.

[52] H Gintis, 'Reputation is not Enough' (2008) (Amazon review of Eric A Posner, *Law and Social Norms* (Cambridge, Harvard University Press, 2002) available at www.amazon.com/review/R2BUZGGWB03POC).

[53] See eg Samuel 'Interdisciplinarity and the Authority Paradigm' (2009) 456.

[54] But *cf*, albeit from an entirely different theoretical perspective than Gintis's and mine, Peter Goodrich's remarks on the virtues of 'indiscipline' in P Goodrich, 'Intellection and Indiscipline' (2009) 36 *Journal of Law and Society* 460, 470ff.

situation that would never be tolerated in the natural sciences. So, we perhaps have much to learn from the legal scholars.[55]

So it would seem that, to borrow one final time Geoffrey Samuel's terminology, once legal scholars have managed to leave behind their usual 'authority paradigm',[56] they are at a competitive advantage to social and behavioural scientists as regards their capacity of transgressing remaining disciplinary boundaries. Or perhaps there is just more than a grain of truth to the saying that the grass always appears somewhat greener on the other side of the road. Whichever of these is true, presumably they both are, this allows me to end my contribution on a positive note: the very least we as legal researchers could do, is to use the speculative freedom, for the time being still at our disposal, to try to develop exciting theoretical transdisciplinary ideas.

---

[55] Gintis, 'Reputation is not Enough' (2008).
[56] See Samuel (2009) (n 46) 455ff.

14

Behavioural Economics and Legal Research

JULIE DE CONINCK

I. INTRODUCTION

THIS CHAPTER IS concerned with the use of behavioural economics in legal research or, in other words, with the field of 'behavioural law and economics'. This, of course, raises the primary question of what behavioural economics has to do with legal research.

If one takes the view that law aims to regulate human behaviour, one would expect legal scholars to take a natural interest in how people actually behave. Nevertheless, much legal scholarship typically relies on mere intuitions about human behaviour.[1] This state of affairs is, while probably not entirely avoidable, problematic insofar as such intuitions based on personal experience are partial, highly subjective and therefore far from necessarily correct.[2] From this perspective, behavioural economics, with its pronounced interest in *actual* human behaviour and, in particular, the approach known as behavioural law and economics, that is concerned with the possible implications of the empirical findings and theoretical insights of behavioural economics for legal issues, seem to hold considerable potential for providing legal scholarship with an empirically-based account of human behaviour. Or, as Donald Langevoort formulates it,

> [n]early all interesting legal issues require accurate predictions about human behavior to be resolved satisfactorily. Judges, policy-makers, and academics invoke mental modes of individual and social behavior whenever they estimate the desirability of alternative rules, policies, or procedures. Contemporary legal scholarship has come to recognize that if these predictions are naive and intuitive, without any strong empirical grounding, they are susceptible to error and ideological bias. Something more rigorous

---

[1] See, eg A Tor, 'The Methodology of the Behavioral Analysis of Law' (2008) 4 *Haifa Law Review* 237, 238 (available at ssrn.com/abstract=1266169).

[2] See, eg J Lüdemann, 'Die Grenzen des homo oeconomicus und die Rechtswissenschaft' in C Engel et al (eds), *Recht und Verhalten* (Tübingen, Mohr, 2007) 7, 29f.

is thus expected when normative claims are advanced, and the place of the social sciences has expanded in legal discourse to satisfy this expectation.[3]

At the same time, the findings of behavioural economics are often invoked against another type of legal scholarship, that is, law and economics scholarship. Although this branch of legal scholarship clearly does have an explicit model of human behaviour, as well as a theory on how people respond to legal rules, it is argued that it relies on overly stylised behavioural assumptions that, when tested empirically, frequently appear at odds with the way in which individuals actually behave. Behavioural law and economics could therefore be regarded as an approach that offers a fruitful middle ground between mere intuitive and strongly idealised behavioural assumptions.[4]

In discussing the use of behavioural economics in legal research, this chapter devotes particular attention to a distinctive difficulty for the field of behavioural law and economics, that is, the difficulty of translating the findings of behavioural economics to particularised legal settings. This problem is discussed largely through an example related to contract law (see section III.B. below). Also, the question of whether behavioural law and economics is in need of a normative theory of its own is briefly considered, although admittedly more as an afterthought (see section III.C. below). Before addressing these issues, however, it seems apposite to depict some of the main features of the fields of behavioural economics (see section II. below) and of behavioural law and economics (see section III.A. below) in somewhat more detail.

II. BEHAVIOURAL ECONOMICS

A. What is Behavioural Economics?

Without offering a strict definition, behavioural economics can be described through its concern with improving the explanatory and predictive power of traditional neoclassical economics (see section C. below) by providing it with psychologically more realistic assumptions on human judgement and decision making (see section B. below), based on well-documented empirical findings that are obtained through a variety of methods (see section D. below).

Behavioural economics has amassed compelling empirical evidence on human behaviour, indicating that individuals do not always behave according to the behavioural norms or predictions of neoclassical, rational choice-based economics. Quite the contrary, in their actual behaviour, a considerable percentage of people violate, in a systematic and predictable way,[5] some of the axiomatic

---

[3] DC Langevoort, 'Behavioral Theories of Judgment and Decision Making in Legal Scholarship: A Literature Review' (1998) 51 *Vanderbilt Law Review* 1499, 1499 (fn omitted).

[4] eg Tor, 'The Methodology of the Behavioral Analysis of Law' (2008) 242.

[5] This consideration carries particular weight, since it implies that these deviations are not simply random and thus unpredictable 'noise' (see, eg RH Thaler, 'The Psychology and Economics

or working assumptions of neoclassical economics.[6] Indeed, what makes behavioural economics of particular interest is that it does not content itself with stating that real people are much more complex than the model-man of traditional economics, but that it also collects *empirical* evidence showing *in what ways* people are more complex.[7]

B. Topics and Themes

The research area of behavioural economics is typically divided into research on judgement and choice: how do individuals come to hold certain beliefs and how do they select among alternative options, taking into account the judgements they may have made?[8] Within this research area, the main findings of behavioural economics are often roughly described as challenging three types of assumptions typically made in traditional economic models, namely the assumptions of full rationality, total self-control and exclusive self-interest.[9]

As regards the assumption of full rationality, it appears that, when making probabilistic judgements, individuals do not always conform to the postulates of neoclassical economic theory. Rather than making assessments according to the laws of probability, people frequently rely on simplifying heuristics or rules of thumb. For instance, people tend to assess the likelihood of an event by the rate or ease with which they can imagine or recall such events, seem to be quite insensitive to sample size and insufficiently adjust from often arbitrary initial guesses. While these heuristics usually work quite well, they can sometimes lead to errors, typically referred to as 'biases'.[10] Moreover, individuals do not invariantly act as

Conference Handbook: Comments on Simon, on Einhorn and Hogart, and on Tversky and Kahneman' (1986) 59 *Journal of Business* 279, 280f, who submits the term 'quasi rational' (rather than irrational) to denote behaviour that deviates in such a systematic manner from the rationality axioms of standard economic theory).

[6] Thus the findings of behavioural economics are not to be taken as evidence that all people display all of the involved behavioural inclinations under all circumstances.

[7] *cf* Lüdemann, 'Die Grenzen des homo oeconomicus und die Rechtswissenschaft' (2007) 21.

[8] See, eg CF Camerer and G Loewenstein, 'Behavioral Economics: Past, Present, Future' in CF Camerer et al (eds), *Advances in Behavioral Economics* (New York, Russell Sage Foundation, 2004) 3, 9.

[9] eg P Diamond and H Vartiainen, 'Introduction' in P Diamond and H Vartianen (eds), *Behavioral Economics and Its Applications* (Princeton, Princeton University Press, 2007) 1, 2; S Mullainathan and RH Thaler, 'Behavioral Economics' in NJ Smelser and PB Baltes (eds), *International Encyclopedia of the Social & Behavioral Sciences* (Amsterdam, Elsevier, 2001) vol 2, 1094, 1095 (speaking of the 'three bounds on human nature'). *cf* also M Rabin, 'A Perspective on Psychology and Economics' (2002) 46 *European Economic Review* 657, 658.

[10] See notably A Tversky and D Kahneman, 'Judgment under Uncertainty: Heuristics and Biases' (1974) 185 *Science* 1124. A good deal of the research conducted in this area tends to focus on the biases resulting from the use of heuristics (so-called 'heuristics-and-biases' research). Others, however, object that this tendency to equate heuristics and biases underestimates the ecological rationality of heuristics (eg G Gigerenzer, 'Heuristics' in G Gigerenzer and C Engel (eds), *Heuristics and the Law* (Cambridge, MIT Press, 2006) 17; G Gigerenzer and H Brighton, 'Homo Heuristicus: Why Biased Minds Make Better Inferences' (2009) 1 *Topics in Cognitive Science* 107). For a recent (over)view of these divergent views on rationality, see J Rieskamp et al, 'Bounded Rationality.

narrowly self-interested utility maximizers who make choices or decisions in view of a set of relatively well-defined, stable and coherent (pre-established) preferences. Often, people's preferences appear to be constructed, rather than just revealed, by the way a particular decision problem is framed, by the procedure used to elicit preferences or by the presence of other, seemingly irrelevant, alternative options.[11]

Frequently, individuals' preferences appear to be time-inconsistent, as people make choices they regret after the fact and struggle with problems of self-control.[12] Finally, people seem to exhibit other-regarding preferences to a greater extent than is routinely assumed or accounted for in traditional economic models.[13]

In sum, in the words of Richard Thaler, 'Humans are dumber, nicer, and weaker than *Homo Economicus*'.[14]

C. Relation to Neoclassical Economics

In studying these limitations of traditional economic theory, behavioural economists do not, however, envisage a wholesale rejection of neoclassical economics. To the contrary, behavioural economists are interested in *strengthening* traditional economic theory. Insofar as some of the foundational or usually relied upon working assumptions of neoclassical economic theory may reflect an inaccurate view of human judgement and decision making, models based on these assumptions can yield erroneous predictions. By increasing the psychological realism of its assumptions, behavioural economists thus hope to enhance the predictive (as well as the explanatory) power of traditional economics.[15] In so doing, so-called 'second wave' behavioural economics is pushing beyond merely compiling evidence of behavioural 'anomalies', but also aspires to develop convincing theoretical accounts of these observed behavioural patterns and,

Two Interpretations from Psychology' in M Altman (ed), *Handbook of Contemporary Behavioral Economics. Foundations and Developments* (Armonk, New York, Sharpe, 2006) 218.

[11] See notably A Tversky and D Kahneman, 'The Framing of Decisions and the Psychology of Choice' (1981) 211 *Science* 453; A Tversky and D Kahneman, 'Rational Choice and the Framing of Decisions' in D Kahneman and A Tversky (eds), *Choices, Values, and Frames* (Cambridge, Cambridge University Press, 2000) 209; A Tversky and I Simonson, 'Context-dependent Preferences' (1993) 39 *Management Science* 1179.

[12] eg RH Thaler and HM Shefrin, 'An Economic Theory of Self-Control' (1981) 89 *Journal of Political Economy* 392; M Rabin, 'Psychology and Economics' (1998) 36 *Journal of Economic Literature* 11, 38–41.

[13] For a recent overview, see E Fehr and KM Schmidt, 'The Economics of Fairness, Reciprocity and Altruism – Experimental Evidence and New Theories' in S-C Kolm and J Mercier Ythier (eds), *Handbook of the Economics of Giving, Altruism and Reciprocity. Foundations* (Amsterdam, Elsevier, 2006) vol 1, 615.

[14] RH Thaler, 'Doing Economics without *Homo Economicus*' in SG Medema and WJ Samuels (eds), *Foundations of Research in Economics: How Do Economists Do Economics?* (Cheltenham, Edward Elgar, 1996) 227, 227.

[15] M Altman, 'Introduction' in Altman (ed), *Handbook of Contemporary Behavioral Economics* (Armonk, New York, Sharpe, 2006) xvi-xvii; Camerer and Loewenstein, 'Behavioral Economics: Past, Present, Future' (2004) 3. *cf* also Rabin, 'A Perspective on Psychology and Economics' (2002) 658f.

especially, to construct and test (the predictive power of) enriched economic models of behaviour based thereon.[16]

D. Methods: Eclectic

Behavioural economists like to describe themselves as 'methodological eclectics. They define themselves not on the basis of the research methods they employ but rather on their application of psychological insights to economics.'[17] While a comprehensive review of these various methods is evidently beyond the scope of this chapter, a short remark on the use of experiments seems in order. Laboratory experiments are an important source of evidence for behavioural economists and continue to be heralded for their ability to control the conditions to which the subjects are exposed. Laboratory experiments are said to allow for specifically testing the variables of interest, while carefully controlling for other possibly intervening variables, so that the observed effect can be fairly confidently attributed to the variable under consideration. However, an oft-heard criticism pertains to the generalisability of experimental findings or their 'real-world' or 'external' validity. To the extent that this kind of criticism seems justified,[18] the methodological eclecticism of behavioural economics appears as an important strength in that the experimentally obtained evidence is frequently combined with empirical studies using (more) naturally occurring data, such as surveys, field studies and field experiments.[19] In this respect, the complementary nature of (laboratory) experimentation, field observation[20] and theory[21] should be stressed.

[16] See, eg Camerer and Loewenstein (n 8) 7; Rabin (n 9) 658. To what extent behavioural economics succeeds in this effort, remains debated though. Compare eg Camerer and Loewenstein (n 8) 41f with D Fudenberg, 'Advancing Beyond Advances in Behavioral Economics' (2006) 44 *Journal of Economic Literature* 694, 697ff.

[17] Camerer and Loewenstein (n 8) 8.

[18] See however, eg RA Weber and CF Camerer, '"Behavioral Experiments" in Economics' (2006) 9 *Experimental Economics* 187.

[19] For a recent survey of field evidence confirming deviations from standard economic theory observed in laboratory experiments, see, eg S DellaVigna, 'Psychology and Economics: Evidence from the Field' (2009) 47 *Journal of Economic Literature* 315.

[20] Compare eg A Falk and JJ Heckman, 'Lab Experiments Are a Major Source of Knowledge in the Social Sciences' (2009) 326 *Science* 535 (primarily defending the importance of laboratory experiments, while pointing to the complementary nature of field data, survey data and experiments, both lab and field, as well as standard econometric methods, and asserting that the issue of generalisability of results is universal to all of them) with GW Harrison and JA List, 'Field experiments' (2004) 42 *Journal of Economic Literature* 1009 (primarily stressing the value of (different types of) field experiments in relation to issues of generalisability, but likewise regarding field and laboratory experiments as complementary).

[21] *cf* C Camerer and E Talley, 'Experimental Study of Law' in AM Polinsky and S Shavell (eds), *Handbook of Law and Economics* (Amsterdam, Elsevier, 2007) vol 2, 1619, 1623–28 (succinctly discussing issues of control, generalisability, different experimental conventions in psychology and economics, as well as the complementary nature of experiments, field observation and theory); SD Levitt and JA List, 'What Do Laboratory Experiments Measuring Social Preferences Reveal About the Real World?' (2007) 21 *Journal of Economic Perspectives* 153, 170. *Adde* JW Lucas, 'Theory-Testing, Generalization, and the Problem of External Validity' (2003) 21 *Sociological Theory* 236.

III. BEHAVIOURAL LAW AND ECONOMICS

A. What is Behavioural Law and Economics?

i. In General

As Christine Jolls, Cass Sunstein and Richard Thaler describe it, 'The task of behavioral law and economics, simply stated, is to explore the implications of *actual* (not hypothesized) human behavior for the law.'[22] Behavioural law and economics scholars are thus interested in the potential significance of the findings of behavioural economics for legal analysis, in extrapolating from and applying (experimental, field and other) evidence and insights generated by behavioural economics to legal issues. For these purposes, behavioural economics' empirically-based understandings of human behaviour are regarded as instructive not only with respect to the behaviour of individuals as addressees of legal rules, but they are deemed relevant to illuminate the behaviour of all actors involved in the legal system, such as judges, juries, lawyers and legislators.[23]

ii. Relation to Neoclassical (Law and) Economics

Not unlike behavioural economists, behavioural law and economics scholars frequently define their research agenda in relation to neoclassical economics and more in particular to neoclassical, rational actor-based law and economics.[24] In a similar vein, they often declare that behavioural law and economics is not intended to undermine traditional law and economics, but rather to strengthen its underlying assumptions in order to improve its predictive power.[25] Not

---

[22] C Jolls et al, 'A Behavioral Approach to Law and Economics' (1998) 50 *Stanford Law Review* 1471, 1476.

[23] See, eg Langevoort (n 3) 1508–19.

[24] As Engel observes, by its adherence to neoclassical economics, behavioural law and economics could, at least theoretically, be distinguished from the related approach known as (new) law and psychology, that has its roots in psychology, rather than economics (C Engel, comment to Christine Jolls, 'Behavioral Law and Economics' in Diamond and Vartiainen (eds), *Behavioral Economics and Its Applications* (Princeton, Princeton University Press, 2007) 148–53. See somewhat differently, M Englerth, 'Behavioral Law and Economics – eine kritische Einführung' in Engel et al (eds), *Recht und Verhalten* (Tübingen, Mohr, 2007) 60, 98f and 102ff). Others, however, have argued that in reality economics does not figure in any meaningful way in behavioural law and economics analyses (eg T Rostain, 'Educating *Homo Economicus*: Cautionary Notes on the New Behavioral Law and Economics Movement' (2000) 34 *Law & Society Review* 973, 975, 981ff and 988f) and tend to equate behavioural law and economics with law and psychology (ibid 983. *cf* also RA Posner, 'Rational Choice, Behavioral Economics, and the Law' (1998) 50 *Stanford Law Review* 1551, 1558).

[25] eg C Jolls, 'Behavioral Law and Economics' in Diamond and Vartiainen (eds), *Behavioral Economics and Its Applications* (Princeton, Princeton University Press, 2007) 115, 116; Jolls et al, 'A Behavioral Approach to Law and Economics' (1998) 1474; RB Korobkin and TS Ulen, 'Law and Behavioral Science: Removing the Rationality Assumption from Law and Economics' (2000) 88 *California Law Review* 1051, 1074f and 1144; TS Ulen, 'The Growing Pains of Behavioral Law and Economics' (1998) 51 *Vanderbilt Law Review* 1747, 1748.

surprisingly then, many of the topics studied by behavioural law and economics scholars bear on topics or assumptions that have a long pedigree in law and economics scholarship.[26]

iii. Topics and Themes

As a rule, behavioural law and economics scholars are not the methodological eclectics behavioural economists affirm to be. To a large extent, they draw upon the empirical findings and theoretical insights of behavioural economics, rather than on its methods.[27] Behaviourally informed legal scholarship generally hypothesises about the applicability of the findings of behavioural economics to legal settings and avails itself of these understandings of human behaviour as a means to understand the law and as arguments to support some prescriptive proposition or normative claim.

On a descriptive level, some scholars invoke the findings of behavioural economics as a way to illuminate the content of the law, interpreting existing legal rules or doctrines as responding to or accounting for certain behavioural phenomena.[28]

Most behavioural law and economics scholarship is particularly interested in evaluating existing or proposed legal rules in view of how individuals actually behave. Taking into account understandings of how people actually behave can indeed cast a different light on how or whether a particular rule will achieve its intended goals. In this spirit, it is frequently claimed that rules or prescriptions that would seem efficient or effective from a law and economics perspective (based on idealised assumptions on human behaviour) may very well turn out to be inefficient when dealing with real people.[29]

Finally, many behavioural law and economics scholars seem to regard the findings of behavioural economics as supportive of paternalistic interventions. The gist of the argument is that if people are prone to predictable cognitive errors, if

---

[26] A, if not the, most famous example, the endowment effect and its relation to the Coase Theorem, is discussed below, see text to nn 43–49.

[27] See, eg G Mitchell, 'Taking Behavioralism too Seriously? The Unwarranted Pessimism of the New Behavioral Analysis of Law' (2002) 43 *William and Mary Law Review* 1907, 1915, fn 12 ('Most of these legal scholars simply apply findings from behavioral decision research to legal issues and do not conduct their own behavioral studies ... Thus, the work tends to be more theoretical and speculative than empirical in nature'); less pejoratively, C Engel and U Schweizer, 'Experimental Law and Economics' (2004) 163 *Journal of Institutional and Theoretical Economics* 1, 1.

[28] See, eg Jolls et al (n 22) 1508ff; RC Ellickson, 'Bringing Culture and Human Frailty to Rational Actors: A Critique of Classical Law and Economics' (1989) *Chicago-Kent Law Review* 23, 35–39. *cf* also C Camerer et al, 'Regulation for Conservatives: Behavioral Economics and the Case for "Asymmetric Paternalism"' (2003) 151 *University of Pennsylvania Law Review* 1211, 1223 and 1232ff. But see also I Ayres, comment to Christine Jolls, 'Behavioral Law and Economics' in Diamond and Vartiainen (eds), *Behavioral Economics and Its Applications* (Princeton, Princeton University Press, 2007) 145, 146f.

[29] See, eg Jolls et al (n 22) 1522ff; CR Sunstein, 'Behavioral Analysis of Law' (1997) 64 *University of Chicago Law Review* 1175, 1177; TS Ulen, 'Cognitive Imperfections and the Economic Analysis of Law' (1989) *Hamline Law Review* 385, 400ff.

their preferences are constructed so as to become susceptible to manipulation, if they make choices they later regret, then the traditional law and economics' aversion toward legal intervention may be called into question. This theme is also emerging within the behavioural economics literature itself. While this so-called 'anti-anti-paternalism' defended by early behavioural (law and) economics scholars remained a fairly moderate claim,[30] recent proposals tend to be more explicitly in favour of paternalistic interventions. In so doing, most behaviourally informed scholars adhere to a kind of 'light paternalism'[31] that is not too restrictive on individual choices and mostly accounts for the fact that the judgement or decision making errors they intend to correct are not universally displayed by all individuals to the same degree,[32] such as, most famously, 'asymmetric paternalism',[33] striving for large benefits for boundedly rational individuals, while imposing little or no costs on fully rational individuals, or 'libertarian paternalism',[34] endorsing legislative intervention that steers people toward choices that leave them better off, yet without coercion.[35] In particular in the area of judgement errors, suggestions are made to deploy the law as a means to 'debias' individuals, so as to reduce or eliminate such biases, if possible, rather than to positively interfere with the choices people make.[36]

---

[30] eg D Laibson and R Zeckhauser, 'Amos Tversky and the Ascent of Behavioral Economics' (1998) 16 *Journal of Risk and Uncertainty* 7, 29 (noting that 'Tversky's work at least admits to the possibility that well-implemented government interventions could have normative merit, a possibility ruled out by the mainstream rational choice model when there are no externalities'); Jolls et al (n 22) 1541; Sunstein, 'Behavioral Analysis of Law' (1997) 1178.

[31] G Loewenstein and E Haisly, 'The Economist as Therapist: Methodological Ramifications of "Light" Paternalism' in A Caplin and A Schotter (eds), *The Foundations of Positive and Normative Economics* (Oxford, Oxford University Press, 2008) 210.

[32] Compare JJ Rachlinski, 'Cognitive Errors, Individual Differences, and Paternalism' (2006) 73 *University of Chicago Law Review* 207 (complaining that paternalistic arguments often fail to account for individual variation in the commission of cognitive errors in judgement).

[33] Camerer et al, 'Regulation for Conservatives' (2003).

[34] CR Sunstein and RH Thaler, 'Libertarian Paternalism is Not an Oxymoron' (2003) 70 *University of Chicago Law Review* 1159, a proposal further developed to a set of methods of choice architecture for policy-makers in RH Thaler and CR Sunstein, *Nudge* (London, Penguin, 2009). See, however, critically as to its libertarian nature, O Amir and O Lobel, 'Stumble, Predict, Nudge: How Behavioral Economics Informs Law and Policy' (2008) 108 *Columbia Law Review* 2098, 2120ff; G Mitchell, 'Libertarian Paternalism is an Oxymoron' (2005) 99 *Northwestern University Law Review* 1245.

[35] See also the recommendations by R Korobkin, 'The Problems with Heuristics for Law' in Gigerenzer and Engel (eds), *Heuristics and the Law* (Cambridge, MIT Press, 2006) 45, especially 58; JJ Rachlinski, 'The Uncertain Psychological Case for Paternalism' (2003) 97 *Northwestern University Law Review* 1165, especially 1219ff.

[36] See notably C Jolls and CR Sunstein, 'Debiasing through Law' (2006) 35 *Journal of Legal Studies* 199. Compare, tentatively, Laibson and Zeckhauser, 'Amos Tversky and the Ascent of Behavioral Economics' (1998) 29.

B. Lost in Translation?

i. In General

As mentioned above, behavioural law and economics scholars typically hypothesise about the relevance of the insights on human behaviour generated by behavioural economists to some legal setting in order to evaluate existing or proposed legal rules in view of these behavioural patterns.

However, as Russell Korobkin and Thomas Ulen have observed,

> [i]n the early stages of the movement, legal scholars have been able, by and large, to make important strides by hypothesizing that empirical and experimental findings published by social science researchers apply to actors subject to legal commands. To progress beyond the current initial stage of scholarship, legal scholars will have to conduct more empirical and experimental work of their own to test whether these hypotheses are in fact true in the particularized setting they study.[37]

Indeed, as a rule, research in behavioural economics is not tailored to suit the particular interests of legal scholars.[38] As a consequence, the findings of behavioural economists are not necessarily readily usable for legal scholars, especially since contextual factors have been shown to exert an important influence on decision making. Therefore, as regards the evidence on human behaviour obtained in laboratory settings, the high degree of decontextualisation that is often strived for in laboratory experiments[39] raises the question as to whether the studied behavioural patterns will play out in the same way in legal settings that are rife with context.[40] Similarly, empirical evidence obtained in a given field setting does not as such readily carry over to particularised legal settings. Hypothesising about their applicability in specific legal contexts by mere extrapolation of the experimental/empirical findings of behavioural economics can therefore be hazardous, notably in the absence of more refined theories on when, why and subject to what conditions the behaviour in question is likely to occur.[41]

---

[37] Korobkin and Ulen, 'Law and Behavioral Science' (2000) 1058 (fn omitted). Similar calls for more research to better align the findings of behavioural economics to issues of legal interest have also been addressed at legally minded behavioural/experimental economists (cf Camerer and Talley, 'Experimental Study of Law' (2007)).

[38] Engel and Schweizer, 'Experimental Law and Economics' (2004) 2 (observing that 'not so rarely, in its discipline of origin, the evidence has been generated for a purpose that is only tangential to its use in legal decision-making').

[39] See, eg Harrison and List, 'Field experiments' (2004) 1028f and 1050; G Loewenstein, 'Experimental Economics from the Vantage-Point of Behavioural Economics' (1999) 109 *The Economic Journal* 25, 29ff.

[40] cf C Engel, 'Verhaltenswissenschaftliche Analyse: eine Gebrauchsanweisung für Juristen' in Engel et al (eds), *Recht und Verhalten* (Tübingen, Mohr, 2007) 363, 374. Adde RJ Oxoby, 'Experiments and Behavioral Economics' in Altman (ed), *Handbook of Contemporary Behavioral Economics* 441, 445f.

[41] I believe the following statements by Engel to nicely summarise these issues: 'Das Herzstück der Verhaltenswissenschaft sind empirische Befunde. Man muss diese Befunde richtig deuten und ihre Tragweite richtig einschätzen . . . Oft fehlen empirische Ergebnisse gerade dort, wo man als Jurist besonders auf sie angewiesen wäre . . . Dann kann man sich nur noch mit Hypothesen

In the next section, these problems are illustrated, focusing on a particular example related to contract law, that is, the study by Russell Korobkin on 'the status quo bias and contract default rules'.[42]

ii. Example: The Status Quo Bias and Contract Default Rules

In this study, Korobkin is concerned with the question whether the status quo bias and related findings of behavioural economics are also operative in the context of contract default rules, ie terms that will govern the parties' contract by operation of law if the parties do not contract around them.

a. Potentially Relevant Behavioural Findings

The behavioural findings that are of potential interest to the study are the related findings on the endowment effect and the status quo bias.

The endowment effect or 'willingness-to-pay (WTP) – willingness-to-accept (WTA) disparity' pertains to the observation that people frequently are willing to pay significantly less to obtain a particular object than they demand for accepting to give up that same object.[43] This finding is usually taken to suggest that people value goods more highly when they are part of their endowment than when they are not part of their endowment – hence the label 'endowment effect'.[44] This finding runs counter to the neoclassical (or even intuitive)[45] assumption that, absent wealth or income effects, the maximum amount an individual is willing to pay to obtain a particular good should be approximately the same as the minimum amount the individual would demand in order to give up that same good.

Not only does the endowment effect appear to be one of the most robust phenomena observed by behavioural economists,[46] but it bears additional sig-

---

helfen. Dafür bräuchte man durchdachte Theorie. Leider fehlt sie oft . . . Auch dort, wo man auf empirische Resultate oder theoretische Modelle zurückgreifen kann, sollte man im Auge behalten, dass sie mit einem ganz anderen Erkenntnisinteresse gewonnen worden sind. Deshalb versteht sich die Integration verhaltenswissenschaftlicher Ergebnisse oder Einsichten in das Recht nicht von selbst' (Engel, 'Verhaltenswissenschaftliche Analyse: eine Gebrauchsanweisung für Juristen' (2007) 364 (fn omitted)). See also, for an extensive discussion of these – and related – problems, Tor (n 1) 274ff.

[42] R Korobkin, 'The Status Quo Bias and Contract Default Rules' (1998) 83 *Cornell Law Review* 608.

[43] See the seminal article by D Kahneman et al, 'Experimental Tests of the Endowment Effect and the Coase Theorem' (1990) 98 *Journal of Political Economy* 1325.

[44] But see also the objection to this labelling by CR Plott and K Zeiler, 'The Willingness to Pay – Willingness to Accept Gap, the "Endowment Effect," Subject Misconceptions, and Experimental Procedures for Eliciting Valuations' (2005) 95 *American Economic Review* 530, 530, fn 1.

[45] *cf* L Van Boven et al, 'Egocentric Empathy Gaps between Owners and Buyers: Misperceptions of the Endowment Effect' (2000) 79 *Journal of Personality and Social Psychology* 66 (whose experiments suggest that people do not anticipate the WTA/WTP gap).

[46] The effect has been noted in countless studies. See, eg the overviews by JK Horowitz and KE McConnell, 'A Review of WTA / WTP Studies' (2002) 44 *Journal of Environmental Economics & Management* 426; S Sayman and A Öncüler, 'Effects of Study Design Characteristics on the WTA – WTP Disparity: A Meta Analytical Framework' (2005) 26 *Journal of Economic Psychology* 289; JL Knetsch and F-F Tang, 'The Context, or Reference, Dependence of Economic Values' in Altman

nificance for legal analysis insofar as it challenges a centrepiece of law and economics, the Coase Theorem,[47] which holds that, in the absence of transaction costs, the initial allocation of an alienable entitlement should not matter for its final distribution, since people will bargain for it, so that the entitlement will end up with the person who values it the most – thus resulting in an efficient allocation.[48] However, if the initial allocation of an entitlement affects people's preferences for it, the 'invariance claim' of the Coase Theorem, as well as the host of legal prescriptions that rely upon it may need re-examination.[49]

The endowment effect is often connected to the so-called status quo bias. The status quo bias refers to the experimental finding that in choosing among alternatives, individuals display a strong tendency to remain at the status quo.[50] From this status quo bias, it has been conjectured that, in cases where there is no status quo, people may be inclined to exhibit a preference for the option that is (framed as) the default choice.[51] This 'stickiness of the default option' has indeed been observed in real-life situations.

An oft-cited example of such a 'natural experiment' relates to the different default options adopted by the states of New Jersey and Pennsylvania when they changed their automobile insurance legislation. Both states offered drivers a choice between a cheaper insurance policy with limited rights to sue and a more expensive insurance policy with more expansive rights. New Jersey set the limited rights-policy as default, while in Pennsylvania the more extended rights-policy was the default choice. As reported by Eric Johnson et al, at the time of their study, only 20 per cent of New Jersey drivers chose to adopt the extended-rights policy, while approximately 75 per cent of Pennsylvanian drivers retained the extended-rights policy; a finding these researchers also replicated experimentally.[52]

(ed), *Handbook of Contemporary Behavioral Economics* 423. But see also Plott and Zeiler, 'The Willingness to Pay' (2005) and responses by eg S Gächter et al, 'Individual-Level Loss Aversion in Riskless and Risky Choices' (2007) CeDEx Discussion Paper No. 2007-02, www.nottingham.ac.uk/economics/cedex/papers/2007-02.pdf (accessed 20 December 2009); JL Knetsch and W-W Wong, 'The Endowment Effect and the Reference State: Evidence and Manipulations' (2009) 71 *Journal of Economic Behavior & Organization* 407.

[47] *cf* P Brest, 'Amos Tversky's Contributions to Legal Scholarship: Remarks at the BDRM Session in Honor of Amos Tversky, June 16, 2006' (2006) 1 *Judgement and Decision Making* 174, 174f; Langevoort (n 3) 1504 (referring to the endowment effect as providing 'the most distinctive legal contribution of the behavioral literature').

[48] After RH Coase, 'The Problem of Social Cost' (1960) 3 *Journal of Law & Economics* 1, 2–15.

[49] See, eg E Hoffman and ML Spitzer, 'Willingness to Pay vs. Willingness to Accept: Legal and Economic Implications' (1993) 71 *Washington University Law Quarterly* 59, 63ff; R Korobkin, 'The Endowment Effect and Legal Analysis' (2003) 97 *Northwestern University Law Review* 1227, 1231f. See also the early critique by M Kelman, 'Consumption Theory, Production Theory, and Ideology in the Coase Theorem' (1979) 52 *Southern California Law Review* 669, 678ff.

[50] See notably W Samuelson and R Zeckhauser, 'Status Quo Bias in Decision Making' (1988) 1 *Journal of Risk and Uncertainty* 7, 12ff (also referring to field observations consistent with this tendency at 26ff).

[51] *cf* CF Camerer, 'Prospect Theory in the Wild' in Kahneman and Tversky (eds), *Choices, Values, and Frames* (Cambridge, Cambridge University Press, 2000) 288, 294.

[52] EJ Johnson et al, 'Framing, Probability Distortions, and Insurance Decisions' (1993) 7 *Journal of Risk and Uncertainty* 35, 46ff.

Another famous observation that is typically referred to as confirming the stickiness of default options, is the study by Eric Johnson and Daniel Goldstein on the percentage of people registered as an organ donor as a function of the default rule across 11 European countries.[53] Comparing the part of the population enrolled as organ donors in countries where people are organ donors unless they register not to be (presumed-consent countries) and in countries where people are not organ donors unless they register to be (explicit-consent countries), these scholars observed a registration rate as a donor of almost 98 per cent in the presumed-consent countries, compared to only about 15 per cent in the explicit-consent countries.

These findings on the endowment effect, the status quo bias and the stickiness of default options are often linked as they are generally all understood to represent instances of loss aversion.[54] Building on the notion that people evaluate their options in decision problems as changes relative to a reference point, loss aversion expresses the idea that people are more averse to changes that are coded as losses relative to the reference point than they are positively attracted by equal-sized changes that are coded as gains, or simply stated, that losses loom larger than corresponding gains.[55] As Camerer observes, the endowment effect, the status quo bias and the stickiness of default options can all be seen as consistent with aversion to losses relative to a reference point: endowing someone with a good, making one option the status quo or default rule seems to establish a reference point people move away from only reluctantly.[56]

b. Applicability to Contract Default Rules?

However, do these effects also operate in the context of contract default rules? As Korobkin himself notes, the behavioural evidence mentioned above is potentially, but not necessarily, relevant with respect to contract default rules.[57] There are two related reasons for this.

First, as an *empirical* matter, while these effects appear to be quite robust, they are also highly context-dependent. For instance, as regards the endowment effect, both its magnitude and its occurrence have been found to depend on a multitude of different factors,[58] and while many factors thus seem to have an

---

[53] EJ Johnson and D Goldstein, 'Do Defaults Save Lives?' (2003) 302 *Science* 1338.
[54] This is not to say that the loss aversion-account has gone unchallenged. See, for instance, n 61 below.
[55] See notably D Kahneman and A Tversky, 'Prospect Theory: An Analysis of Decision under Risk' (1979) 47 *Econometrica* 263, 279; RH Thaler, 'Toward a Positive Theory of Consumer Choice' in RH Thaler (ed), *Quasi Rational Economics* (New York, Russell Sage Foundation, 1991) 3, 5ff; A Tversky and D Kahneman, 'Loss Aversion in Riskless Choice: A Reference-Dependent Model' (1991) 106 *Journal of Quarterly Economics* 1039, 1047.
[56] Camerer, 'Prospect Theory in the Wild' (2000) 295. See also D Kahneman et al, 'Anomalies: The Endowment Effect, Loss Aversion, and Status Quo Bias' (1991) 5 *Journal of Economic Perspectives* 193; K Sontheimer, 'Behavioral Versus Neoclassical Economics' in Altman (ed), *Handbook of Contemporary Behavioral Economics* 237, 247f.
[57] *cf* Korobkin, 'The Status Quo Bias and Contract Default Rules' (1998) 612.
[58] The effect has been found to vary as a function of the type of good involved, source and duration of the endowment, subjects' emotions and intentions, market experience or learning opportunities etc. See, eg Sayman and Öncüler, 'Effects of Study Design Characteristics on the WTA – WTP

influence, they are often not decisive in themselves.[59] Given the bearing of contextual factors on these effects, simply hypothesising that the findings obtained within so to say 'context-free' laboratory environments will equally hold in the specific case of contract default rules seems too hasty a conclusion. The same is true for field evidence obtained in quite different contexts: simply assuming the unqualified applicability of these findings to contract default rules is arguably a precipitant conclusion.

Second, on a *theoretical* level, the aforementioned findings are, as said, usually explained or described as instances of loss aversion. However, even though loss aversion is often presented as one of the most successful explanatory constructs within behavioural economics,[60] it does not allow for predicting under what circumstances these effects are likely to occur or to vary.[61] Put differently, the loss aversion-account does not seem a strong enough theoretical tool to confidently hypothesise about the pertinence of these effects in the context of contractual default rules.

c. Experiments

Korobkin tries to deal with this difficulty by conducting experiments of his own.

In addressing this question, the author is more specifically interested in whether contracting parties' preferences for contract terms depend on the content of the legal default terms.[62] The idea (or hypothesis) is that contracting parties may place a higher value on a contract term if they perceive that term to represent the status quo. Therefore, the legal default term may appear to parties to represent the status quo of allocation of rights and responsibilities – causing them to value it more highly. On the other hand, before parties enter into the contract, a party does not yet derive any benefits from the default term, which

---

Disparity' (2005); N Novemsky and D Kahneman, 'The Boundaries of Loss Aversion' (2005) 24 *Journal of Marketing Research* 119, 120 and 123ff; N Novemsky and D Kahneman, 'How Do Intentions Affect Loss Aversion?' (2005) 24 *Journal of Marketing Research* 139. See also TC Brown and R Gregory, 'Why the WTA – WTP Disparity Matters' (1999) 28 *Ecological Economics* 323, 326ff.

[59] For instance, while physical possession of the good seems to be a salient factor (J Reb and T Connolly, 'Possession, Feelings of Ownership and the Endowment Effect' (2007) 2 *Judgment and Decision Making* 107), the effect has also been observed when the good in question is not amenable to physical possession.

[60] See, eg L Brenner et al, 'On the Psychology of Loss Aversion: Possession, Valence, and Reversals of the Endowment Effect' (2007) 43 *Journal of Consumer Research* 369, 369; C Camerer, 'Three Cheers – Psychological, Theoretical, Empirical – for Loss Aversion' (2005) 42 *Journal of Marketing Research* 129.

[61] See, eg OD Jones and SF Brosnan, 'Law, Biology, and Property: A New Theory of the Endowment Effect' (2008) *William and Mary Law Review* 1935, 1951ff. This criticism builds on the observation that loss aversion seems to be used both as a description and as an explanation of the phenomena under study and that its underlying mechanisms are still poorly understood. *cf* D Gal, 'A Psychological Law of Inertia and the Illusion of Loss Aversion' (2006) 1 *Judgment and Decision Making* 23, 24; N Novemsky and D Kahneman, 'The Boundaries of Loss Aversion' (2005) 120; A Lanteri and A Carabelli, 'Lost in Aversion. Loss Aversion, the Endowment Effect, and (Little) Realisticness' (2008) www.luis.it/iarep2008/programme/papers/21.pdf (accessed 20 December 2009).

[62] Contrary to the 'preference exogeneity assumption' of traditional law and economics literature on contract default rules (*cf* Korobkin (n 42) 613ff, especially 623–25).

may support the alternative view that parties' valuations of such terms will not be affected by their perception of a term as the status quo.[63]

To test his hypothesis,[64] Korobkin conducted a series of experiments with first-year law students who were asked to play the role of a lawyer providing advice on the hypothetical negotiation of a shipping contract on behalf of their client, the delivery company. The students were presented with two different scenarios, where the primary difference was the content of the default term that would govern the contract if the parties did not explicitly agree to an alternative term.

In the first scenario, two terms were possible for dealing with damages for loss or delay of the packages: the client would be liable either only for reasonably foreseeable damages or for all consequential damages. Half of the subjects were told that the limited-liability rule was the legal default rule and were asked to state the minimum amount they would recommend their client to demand in order to accept (WTA) to include a full-liability rule into the contract. The other half of the subjects were informed that the full-liability rule was the legal default term and were asked to state the maximum amount they would advise their client to pay (WTP) so as to have a limited-liability rule adopted in the contract.

In the second scenario, two terms were possible for dealing with unforeseen circumstances that would make delivery impossible or impracticable: their client would either be excused from performing or liable for damages. Similarly, half of the subjects were told that excuse for impossibility was the legal default rule and were asked to advise their client as to the minimum amount to demand in order to accept liability (WTA) in such cases. The other half of the subjects were told that liability was the legal default rule and had to advise their client as to the maximum amount to pay (WTP) in order to obtain a rule of impossibility excuse in the contract.

In both experiments, subjects tended to favour the legal default rule, replicating the WTA/WTP disparity with respect to contract default rules. Subjects presented with a limited-liability default rule were reluctant to advise their client to contract around it, advising a minimum WTA of, on average, $6.96 per package handled to do so, whereas subjects confronted with a full-liability default rule recommended their client, on average, to pay a maximum of $4.46 per package to obtain a limited-damage rule. Similarly, when the legal default rule accepted impossibility or impracticability as a valid excuse for non-performance, subjects advised their client to demand a minimum of $302.000 to accept a term including

---

[63] Korobkin (n 42) 631. As for this alternative hypothesis, the fact that the legal default term does not yet procure a vested right may not be decisive as such, since the perceived reference state is not necessarily the current or actual endowment (*cf* eg B Köszegi and M Rabin, 'A Model of Reference-Dependent Preferences' (2006) 121 *Quarterly Journal of Economics* 1133).

[64] This obviously requires subjects to be informed about the content of the default term (and the alternative) (*cf* Korobkin (n 42) 635), which is not necessarily the case in the 'real-world' examples mentioned above (text to nn 52–53), where, other than arguably somewhat higher transaction costs, ignorance as to the content of the default option may explain at least part of the stickiness of the default option.

additional liability, whereas confronted with the opposite default rule, subjects recommended their client to pay no more than $78.000 to have an impossibility excuse provision included in the contract.[65]

In these two scenarios, the legal default terms were clearly in favour of one or the other party. In a third scenario, it was further investigated whether the content of legal default terms that are not obviously in favour of one particular party would also affect parties' preferences for those terms. In this scenario, the term in question dealt with the payment of the attorneys' fee in the event of any litigation (each party pays his or her own attorney or the losing party pays all fees). Here, the majority of the subjects preferred whichever term that was set as the legal default term – suggesting that in addition to its apparent influence on the *magnitude* of the value placed on a favoured term (as observed in the first two scenarios), the content of a legal default rule can also affect *whether* a party prefers a certain term over another.[66]

These results suggest that the content of the legal default terms *can* indeed affect contracting parties' preferences for contract terms. However, in these experiments, the subjects were presented with a rather straightforward binary choice between two terms and the default rule was explicitly presented as the reference point. However, this does not mean that the legal default rule *necessarily* acts as a reference point for contracting parties. More specifically, the legal default term is not necessarily made explicit,[67] nor is it the only conceivable reference point.

As for the latter possibility in particular, it seems plausible that terms embedded in standard form contracts are more likely to act as a reference point for contracting parties than the legal default rules on that subject. Acknowledging this issue,[68] Korobkin also performed follow-up experiments where the original consequential damages scenario was altered so that subjects negotiating the shipping contract were informed of both the legal default rule and the term in the standard form contract.

Subjects were told that the contracting parties had agreed to use a standard form contract, typical of the industry, as a basis for their negotiations. Half of

---

[65] See Korobkin (n 42) 637–44.

[66] ibid 644–47.

[67] As observed (above n 64), subjects were not only asked to focus only on the choice between the legal default rule and one alternative, but they were also explicitly informed about the content of the default rule. However, 'unsophisticated' contracting parties are not necessarily aware of (various) default rules, in which case their content will probably not affect parties' preferences. See Korobkin, 'The Endowment Effect and Legal Analysis' (2003) 1275; CR Sunstein, 'Switching the Default Rule' (2002) 77 *New York University Law Review* 106, 110 and 118f – both referring to the likely salience of social norms.

[68] See especially Korobkin (n 49) 1274. Initially, the author considered these follow-up experiments primarily as a way of testing his 'inertia hypothesis', the idea that parties would tend to favour the contract terms that would result from inertia (see R Korobkin, 'Inertia and Preference in Contract Negotiation: The Psychological Power of Default Rules and Form Terms' (1998) 51 *Vanderbilt Law Review* 1583, 1605; R Korobkin, 'Behavioral Economics, Contract Formation, and Contract Law' in CR Sunstein (ed), *Behavioral Law and Economics* (Cambridge, Cambridge University Press, 2000) 116, 123).

the subjects were informed that the form contract contained a limited-liability term, whereas the legal default rule was one of full liability. The other subjects were told that the form contract provided full liability, whereas the legal default term was one of limited liability. Subjects belonging to the first condition demanded, on average, a minimum amount of $7.24 per package, before recommending their client to agree to having the limited liability term removed from the form contract, whereas subjects in the second condition recommended their client to offer, on average, a maximum discount of $4.08 per package for obtaining the removal of the full liability term from the form contract. These findings seem to indicate that standard form contract terms are indeed more likely to act as a reference point, influencing contracting parties' preferences, than legal default terms.[69]

How are we to interpret these experiments? Taken together, these results suggest[70] that the endowment effect can also operate in contractual settings and influence contracting parties' preferences for certain contract terms. They also suggest that the reference point from which parties will tend to evaluate changes, are not invariably *legal* default terms.[71]

iii. Conclusions

The point of mentioning this research is not to lament about its relative indeterminate results,[72] but that more studies can be useful to better evaluate the potential significance or insignificance of certain behavioural findings in more concrete legal settings. However, this should not be mistaken for a plea to test every single proposition in a particular legal setting. To the contrary, such experiments should be complementary to the development of more refined theories on the boundary conditions of the behavioural phenomena and on their applicability in legal settings.[73] In this sense, rather than considering experiments as a way to obtain definite and irrefutable proof of a singular proposition, they can help corroborate the plausibility of hypotheses on the applicability of behavioural findings in legal contexts. Put somewhat differently, whether and how

---

[69] Korobkin, 'Inertia and Preference' (1998) 1606f. Compare, on the impact of standard form terms, also the survey reported by LA DiMatteo, 'Penalties as Rational Response to Bargaining Irrationality' (2006) *Michigan State Law Review* 883, 896f.

[70] As Korobkin himself recognises, it would be exaggerated to view a single set of experiments as incontrovertible evidence in support of a point (Korobkin (n 42) 612). And of course, as with many experiments, one can think of possible objections to question the internal or external validity of the experiments (see, eg the concerns mentioned by Korobkin himself (ibid 662–64)).

[71] *cf* Korobkin (n 49) 1275 (proffering that 'the content of contract law probably substantively affects the content of contracts, but not all the time').

[72] Although the observation that sometimes an untested idea can appear more convincing to legal scholars than the same idea supported by an experimental test, certainly holds a grain of truth (*cf* the criticism by R Hollander-Blumoff, 'Legal Research on Negotiation' (2005) 10 *International Negotiation* 149, 156).

[73] Compare also W Güth and G von Wangenheim, 'Fairness Crowded Out by Law: An Experimental Study on Withdrawal Rights. Comment' (2007) 163 *Journal of Institutional and Theoretical Economics* 102, 105; Camerer and Talley (n 21) 1634.

a behavioural account can be used for the purpose of legal analysis will arguably always, to some extent, remain a matter of 'plausibility' in the light of the existing empirical and theoretical knowledge, which is never truly complete and always indeterminate to some degree.[74] This does not, in my view, detract from the value of the enterprise of behavioural law and economics. It does, however, call for caution both as regards descriptive claims and prescriptive recommendations based thereon.[75]

C. Afterthought: An Independent Normative Theory for Behavioural Law and Economics?

As mentioned above,[76] many behavioural law and economics scholars are prone to claim that in many instances a better understanding of actual human behaviour, notably the findings on bounded rationality and bounded self-control, points to the desirability of (light) paternalistic interventions.

However, contrary to what might perhaps be inferred from the apparent rampancy of such 'paternalistic tendencies', or from the fact that behavioural law and economics scholars seem to regard such propositions as part of their 'normative work', behavioural law and economics as a field has not (yet) developed a normative theory of its own. The various proposed paternalistic interventions do not follow per se from the findings of behavioural economics on human behaviour,[77] but they rest on additional normative arguments that are external to the field. Indeed, the normative goal to be pursued does not somehow logically follow from behavioural (law and) economics itself.[78] This is also evidenced by the different uses that are made of the findings of behavioural economics: to examine the efficiency of legal rules, to advance traditional goals of justice or fairness or otherwise determined social ends, etc.[79]

It may appear surprising[80] that some legal scholars seem to regard this absence of an independent normative theory of behavioural law and economics and the

---

[74] Compare R Korobkin, 'Possibility and Plausibility in Law and Economics' (2005) 32 *Florida State Law Review* 781; Korobkin, 'The Problems with Heuristics for Law' (2006) 54ff (observing that, for all its difficulties, however, simply reverting to the assumption that individuals act in accordance to rational choice theory is 'an approach resembling a drunk looking for his lost keys under a lamp post because that is where the light is best' (at 56)).
[75] *cf* also Rostain, 'Educating *Homo Economicus*' (2000).
[76] Text to nn 30–36.
[77] As Englerth observes, statements to the contrary would be confusing the occasion (*Anlass*) for intervention with its justification (*Legitimation*) (M Englerth, 'Vom Wert des Rauchens und der Rückkehr der Idioten – Paternalismus als Antwort auf beschränkte Rationalität?' in Engel et al (eds), *Recht und Verhalten* (Tübingen, Mohr, 2007) 231, 241f).
[78] ibid, especially 236f, 240f, 242, 254f and 256.
[79] Tor (n 1) 314f. See also DA Kysar et al, 'Group Report: Are Heuristics a Problem or a Solution?' in Gigerenzer and Engel (eds), *Heuristics and the Law* (Cambridge, MIT Press, 2006) 104, 123.
[80] See also Englerth, 'Vom Wert des Rauchens und der Rückkehr der Idioten' (2007) 256 ('Es wäre merkwürdig, wollte man ausgerechnet einem juristischen Ansatz vorwerfen, dass er Wertungsfragen aufwirft. Wertungen sind und bleiben ein Kerngeschäft des Juristen').

resulting indeterminate policy conclusions that can be derived from its findings[81] as problematic.[82] As such, for instance, Samuel Issacharoff has expressed his *concern* that 'empiricism does not readily generate normative conclusions',[83] and that any normative conclusions must be derived externally from broader economic and policy considerations.[84]

Nevertheless, it seems doubtful that behavioural law and economics scholars would be well-advised to take such remarks as an invitation to develop an independent normative theory on the basis of the empirical findings of behavioural economics themselves. To the contrary, its relative open-endedness may very well be regarded as a strength, especially as compared to law and economics with its (more or less) exclusive adherence to social welfare.[85] I would venture that its 'normative neutrality',[86] turning it into a useful tool for legal scholars of varied normative persuasions,[87] is an advantage behavioural law and economics scholars should not be eager to give up. Moreover, 'strategically' it does not seem wise to give in to the rhetoric of an explicitly normative behavioural law and economics, in view of the deep-seated fear of traditional legal scholarship of any hint at transgressing the sacred is/ought distinction and the vehement attacks at the so-called naturalist fallacy. Whatever we may think about the validity of such arguments – or about their appositeness to the issue of a normative behavioural law and economics for that matter – it remains the case that they are very often invoked in legal scholarship. It may therefore be feared that attempts at developing an independent normative theory for behavioural law and economics, linking behavioural findings too directly to normative conclusions will fall prey to such standard negative reactions and run the risk of making the field as a whole suspect.

This does, evidently, not mean that in making behaviourally informed prescriptions, individual behavioural law and economics scholars should not render their normative arguments (more) explicit – rather than making it seem as if

---

[81] Behavioural (law and) economics may also complicate policy conclusions in other ways, for instance by revealing the impossibility of determining people's 'true' preferences (and thus undermining proposed interventions to help people choose 'what they really want'). See summarily CA Hill, 'Anti-Anti-Anti-Paternalism' (2007) 2 *New York University Journal of Law & Liberty* 444, especially 445–48. To the extent that such problems make the need for (external) normative arguments explicit, these issues can be thought as related (*cf* eg DA Farber, 'Toward a New Legal Realism' (2001) 68 *University of Chicago Law Review* 279, 300–02).

[82] In a similar vein, Laibson and Zeckhauser consider the fact that Tversky's written work leaves 'major unanswered questions' about the normative implications of his findings to be a shortcoming (Laibson and Zeckhauser (n 30) 29f).

[83] S Issacharoff, 'The Difficult Path from Observation to Prescription' (2002) 77 *New York University Law Review* 36, 39.

[84] ibid 40, 42, 44f and 46.

[85] See notably L Kaplow and S Shavell, *Fairness Versus Welfare* (Cambridge, Harvard University Press, 2002) 3 and 15ff. Consider also more broadly A Bernstein, 'Whatever Happened to Law and Economics?' (2005) 64 *Maryland Law Review* 303, 311ff and 325f; M Tunick, 'Efficiency, Practices, and the Moral Point of View: Limits of Economic Interpretations of Law' in MD White (ed), *Theoretical Foundations of Law and Economics* (Cambridge, Cambridge University Press, 2009) 77.

[86] *cf* Tor (n 1) 314.

[87] ibid 316.

their prescriptions would follow directly or logically from certain behavioural findings.[88] Nor does this preclude from developing empirically based welfare – or other – *criteria*, as some have suggested could be forthcoming from the emerging 'happiness-research'.[89]

IV. CLOSING REMARKS

While research in behavioural economics seems to have a lot to offer legal scholarship, it is important to acknowledge the (current) limitations of behavioural law and economics and to resist the temptation to oversell its merits. Although it is certainly not an attractive strategy for individual scholars to constantly point to the limits of their analyses and proposals,[90] neglecting the difficulties of translating sometimes highly context-dependent and little understood behavioural patterns into legal settings and making very broad prescriptive conclusions that seem insufficiently supported by empirical findings and/or theoretical insights, does not appear to further the field as a whole in the (mid-)long run.[91] Indeed, the field is still relatively young and although it has had some successes, it also has the potential to wither. It may be feared that it will wither if it keeps over-promising and under-delivering.

---

[88] Compare also Rostain (n 24) 1002 and 1003 (deploring the 'crowding out of normative debates').
[89] *cf* eg Englerth (n 77) 243f and 255. See on this issue, G Loewenstein and PA Ubel, 'Hedonic Adaptation and the Role of Decision and Experience Utility in Public Policy' (2008) 92 *Journal of Public Economics* 1795.
[90] Compare, albeit in a different context, Lüdemann (n 2) 23f ('Wer dennoch auf die Nachbarwissenschaft zurückgreift und im gleichen Atemzug selbst Zweifel an der Aussagekraft der verwendeten Modelle äussert, der handelt zwar intellektuell redlich, setzt aber im konkreten Kontext zugleich die Überzeugungskraft seines Arguments aufs Spiel').
[91] *cf* Engel (n 40) 364.

15

Theory and Object in Law: the Case for Legal Scholarship as Indirect Speech

BERT VAN ROERMUND

MY CONTRIBUTION TO the methodology debate in law hails from the philosophy of science.[1] It aims at giving an account of the relationship between law as a positive, normative order (including the various (and sometimes diverging!) practices of drafting, enacting, executing, applying and obeying norms) on the one hand; and law as a scholarly discipline devoted to theory-building on such a normative order, on the other. In doing so, it joins the concerns of other contributions to this volume, notably those by Westerman, Mackor and Vranken. In a way therefore, it revisits the famous distinction made by Kelsen between norms (*Rechtsnormen*) and statements on norms (*Rechtssätze*). However, I propose a novel version of this account (preserving the correct intuition behind the Kelsenian distinction), to wit that statements on norms are propositions on the validity of norms within a certain legal order, cast in the mould of indirect speech. This creates special problems for the truth conditions of these propositions, of which I hope to solve at least some. If my view holds, it offers an alternative to Westerman's thesis that scholarship in law is predetermined by the categories and the arguments of the legal order under scrutiny. It also teases out an ambiguity in Mackor's solution, inviting her to clarify that a theory of law is

---

[1] Methodology is somewhat more than method. A method is a road to the solution of a set of problems, and to the extent that the road is already laid out, it is a default way to solve these kinds of problems, with all the profits and pitfalls that are proper to default solutions. You can run a sophisticated algorithm to detect whether certain brush strokes are really Van Gogh's cf I Berezhnoy, Digital Analysis of Painting (Doct Diss TICC, Tilburg, Tilburg University, 2009). Or in a more practical mode you may gradually develop a standardised 10-step plan to treat children with eating and feedings disturbances. cf DM Seys, JHM Rensen and MHJ Obbink (eds), Behandelingsstrategieën bij jonge kinderen met voedsel- en eetproblemen (Houten – Diegem Bohn Stafleu Van Loghem, 2000). These are methods. The methodology of a certain discipline, on the other hand, gives an account of why this road is appropriate in terms of primarily two sets of reasons: (i) successful methods used in best practices by professionals; and (ii) the conceptual framework of a philosophy of (the relevant) science. Thus, methodology in the case of law is a back-and-forth between actual practice in legal scholarship and rather abstract philosophy. I come from the latter angle, trying to understand what lawyers do and hoping that they will make the opposite move.

not a meta-language about the object-language of the legal order. By contrast, it joins sides with Vranken's comments on the topic, framing these within a more abstract, and therefore more pertinent, epistemological framework. These three stakes, therefore, govern the structure of my contribution.

I. LEGAL SCHOLARSHIP PRE-DETERMINED BY THE LAW IT INVESTIGATES?

On the final count, Westerman encourages legal scholars to continue doing what they have always done, to wit doctrinal law; only they could do with an update and apply some more rigorous techniques of empirical research to get their facts (or effects) right. She thinks that what legal scholars do, and can do, is largely determined by the categories and the reasonings inherent to the object they are investigating: law, or rather some specific legal order, as it struggles with the ever changing facts of socio-political life. This order emerges and re-emerges without a premeditated plan or method, let alone a methodology, much like, after some tinkering, order re-emerged in her mother's cupboard, according to parameters of integrity and continuity.[2]

I want to take issue with this – rather Savignyian[3] – thesis, that scholarship on law ('legal science' if you wish) is predetermined by the categories and the reasonings in law. My alternative thesis is that the two are certainly related (as legal scholarship is a hermeneutic enterprise), but in a much more complicated way than Westerman suggests. Legal scholarship is indeed supposed to offer a theory of a legal order, but not necessarily in the terms of that legal order.

Let us start at the common place, where Westerman and I agree. Legal scholars are well advised to improve on their scientific knowledge of how facts are construed. Here is an example, derived from Van Fraassen.[4] Let me slightly change the context and the story for our purposes. Suppose a city considers reorganising a department of civil servants due to its sub-standard performance. A group of civil servants in that department brings charges against the city, claiming that lighting and ventilation condition in their workplaces harm their wellbeing, hence their ability to perform according to standard (let's call that their productivity), hence their individual chances of tenure, or promotion, or getting fired in a reorganisation. Here, I continue with Van Fraassen:

---

[2] *cf* Westerman in chapter five of this volume.
[3] Westerman's picture of things reminds me of Von Savigny's theses on the relationship between politisches und technisches Recht (cf FC von Savigny, Vom Beruf unserer Zeit für Gesetzgebung und Rechtswissenschaft, 1814 edn (Reprogr Nachdr der Ausg Heidelberg, Hildesheim, Olm, 1967); and of the quite non-historical thesis of law being already an order in actual fact. See G Haverkate, Gewissheitsverluste im juristischen Denken, zur politischen Funktion der juristischen Methode, Schriften zur Rechtstheorie 73 (Berlin, Duncker & Humblot, 1975, [1977]) ; and Marx already on the first page of K Marx, 'Das philosophische Manifest der historischen Rechtsschule' in Marx Werke, Bd I: Frühe Schriften (Darmstadt, Wissenschaftliche Buchgesellschaft, 1842 [1971]).
[4] B Van Fraassen, Scientific Representation: Paradoxes of Perspective (Oxford, Clarendon Press, 2008) 48 ff.

The city hired a statistician who showed conclusively by means of sampling that the productivity among workers in ill-lit and ill-ventilated spaces was no less than among workers in general (or in better lit, better ventilated spaces) – the productivity level was the same in both groups. So the complaint was concluded to be baseless.

Then the civil servants asked for an opinion by another scientist:

> (...) (T)he second statistician broke the data down by looking separately at women and at men. She showed clearly that among women, the productivity was less for workers in the ill-lit and ill-ventilated spaces than elsewhere. She also showed that among men, the productivity was less for workers in ill-lit and ill-ventilated spaces than elsewhere! So relevance of working conditions did not show up until there was a subdivision by this third factor (gender). How is this possible? That is precisely Simpson's paradox; correlations can be washed out, or on the other hand brought to light, by averaging in different ways. Here is the solution to the puzzle: under all conditions the women *were more productive* than men working under the same conditions, but the women *were predominantly working in poor conditions*.

For those who want to check, I also quote Van Fraassen:

> To make this concrete, imagine a very small situation, involving only 4 men and 7 women. Under good conditions the women produce 8 items per hour and the men 4. Under bad conditions the women produce 4 items per hour and the men 2. But two men and two women work in good conditions, with two men and five women assigned to bad working conditions. In the bad workplace, the production is 2(2) + 5(4) = 24 items per hour. In the good workplace, the production is 2(4) + 2(8) = 24 as well, precisely the same.[5]

	BAD	GOOD
F	5 × 4 items = 20	2 × 8 items = 16
M	2 × 2 items = 4	2 × 4 items = 8
Total	24	24

I propose to extend Van Fraassen's example by one legal turn. The city dismisses this reasoning by saying that the whole statistical exercise shows only one thing: if men would just work harder, there would be no issue of good and bad working conditions in the first place, as the department would perform according to expectations. These working conditions are not just good or bad, they are 'good enough' for all practical purposes, if only men would be less lazy in general. The city admits that the present situation is possibly harmful for female workers in particular, it promises to take measures to improve male performance and postpone reorganisation, but it denies that it is liable. So according to the municipality, there is no (relevant) correlation between production and working conditions, whereas the civil servants say there is.

---
[5] ibid fn 354.

Here I pause and ask Westerman what it means here that 'the legal system functions as a theoretical framework that selects the facts and highlights them as legally relevant ones'?[6] It is only trivial to say that there are no legal rules on averaging in, for instance, the Dutch, the German, or the French legal system, as far as I know. Indeed the whole concept of averaging is unknown in law, and no judge would hold a defendant liable by dint of not having his statistics right. What is more important, however, is this: the legal order does not give us any explicit ruling on which statement of fact is the more appropriate one considering the rules it upholds. And yet, although statistics will not be part of the law's language, it may be part of the language that says what the law says. Scholars with sufficient knowledge of the Dutch legal order, for instance, will be able to predict that officials will have much more sympathy for the second way of averaging than for the first. It is also clear why: this has to do with equal opportunities, non-discrimination, etc, ie with norms that *are* explicitly promoted by law. The connection is there, however, not by virtue of the authority of the legal order, but by virtue of what legal scholars find pertinent in that legal order. So Westerman is right in claiming that legal scholarship feeds on the categories of the legal order, but not in the sense that these pre-determine the categories of legal scholarship.

Now let us suppose – for a second example – that this case goes to court, where there are three judges who will decide by majority vote in chambers. The rule they have to apply in this case is that if the working conditions are of unequal quality, and if unequal conditions bring harm to individual civil servants by affecting their productivity, the city is liable for having these bad working spaces renovated before a certain date. We can easily see that these judges may get into what contemporary literature on judgment aggregation calls a discursive dilemma.[7]

	Judge A	Judge B	Judge C
Bad working conditions?	+	+	-
Harm done?	+	-	+
City liable?	+	-	-

How should these votes be counted? What is majority vote in this case? If we go by the conclusions, the majority vote will be that the city is not liable. However, if we go by the premises, we see that the majority of judges think that there *are* bad working conditions, and that there *is* harm done. Should they not, as a collective body, infer that the city is liable? I pause again and ask: what would it mean to say in this context that the legal system functions as an order that imposes itself on this dilemma? The law does not speak about discursive dilem-

---

[6] *cf* See Westerman's contribution in chapter five of this volume.
[7] On the relevance of discursive dilemmas, see, eg P Pettit, *A Theory of Freedom. From the Psychology to the Politcs of Agency* (Oxford, Oxford University Press, 2000) and references offered there.

mas. It is not at all clear in this case how the categories of legal scholarship on judgment aggregation have their bearing on the categories or principles of the legal order. First, discursive dilemmas are a relative recent discovery. Apart from being exciting in their own right, they may provide a nice explanation for the fact that judges in chambers do not vote that much, but intuitively hover, while dialoging, between a conclusion oriented and a premise oriented strategy of aggregating judgments until they sense that their judgment can claim to be valid law. However, second, and more importantly, while the judges will not be able to explain their practice in terms of logic, the legal scholar will. The legal scholar will be able to spell out the horns of the dilemma in terms of logic, and submit how these relate again to issues of law. This relation, although informed by the categories of law, is not in any more sense pre-determined by the legal order he or she is investigating. I think that, again, this is because his or her language as a scholar says what the law says, though not always, or necessarily, in the language of the law.

Now let us push our example one step further again. Suppose the judges reappear in the courtroom and say to the plaintiff and the defendant:

> Look, we are not done yet. We got into a vehement debate on the concept of harm, and this will take time. That is because we are not just officials, but learned officials. We took a degree from Groningen, where we were taught that we should 'build our theoretical framework from the very concepts, criteria and categories of the legal system'. We had no doubt that the concept of harm is such a concept of the legal system. But we were unable to build anything from there as we had to admit that the legal system does not tell us what harm is. We pretend as if we do know on a daily basis, but the law is silent about it. You remember the Jeffrey-decision by our Hoge Raad, which caused a great deal of upheaval among private law scholars fighting which concept of harm was at the bottom of Dutch private law, indeed putting their academic job on the line.[8] Now before giving you our decision, we will first take some post-academic courses from Tilburg Law School, where they require students to read Joel Feinberg's trilogy on harm for starters.[9] Feinberg seems to define harm as (wrongful) set-backs to interests, which is very elucidating for understanding what we as officials of the law are doing, although these are not the concepts or the categories of the law. In fact these professors there teach a lot of concepts which are not the concepts of the law, one of them being 'corrective justice' . . .

Suppose these judges say all that, and suppose you see the connection with the discursive dilemma they went already through without recognising it, and with the various modes of averaging they had no idea about. Then the general question becomes: what is the conceptual relation between the language of a legal order and the language of a theory of that legal order?

---

[8] CE Drion, 'Kroniek van het vermogensrecht' (1999) Nederlands Juristenblad 74, 1454–63, 1455.
[9] J Feinberg, The Moral Limits of the Criminal Law; I Harm to Others; II Offense to Others; III Harm to Self; IV Harmless Wrongdoing (New York/Oxford, Oxford University Press, 1984–88). Feinberg's statement on harm is in the first chapter of the first volume, p 36.

II. THEORETICAL LANGUAGE AS META-LANGUAGE?

This is also a central question in Anne Ruth Mackor's contribution,[10] as it takes its cue from Kelsen's distinction – conceptually coercive, in my view – between norms and norm statements.[11] The former are rooted in prescriptions (and I would like to add: intentions, singular and plural), which can be either valid or invalid. The latter are assertions on the validity of norms in relation to a certain legal order, which can be either true or false. The former are the utterances which officials of, and (in general) participants in, a legal order issue, the latter are the statements which legal scholars exchange in their debates. The question is how the relationship between the language of the law and the language of legal scholarship (as a language of theory) should be accounted for? Mackor, following Kelsen, submits that norm statements (or contentions, as she calls them) describe norms, ie describe prescriptions singling out those that are valid from the rest. This is an account I join. My problem comes with the various modes 'description' can take. Even if we take 'validity' as the angle from which we describe norms (rather than, say, efficiency), there are different ways by which we may relate the content of norms, all of them arguably describing the same norm. So again, how do norm statements in legal scholarship take up norms? What is description here?

My answer[12] is this: the perfect model for a discourse which says what is said, though not necessarily in the terms in which it is said, is called indirect speech. Let me first polish the negative side of this medal. First, a theory of some legal order is not a quotation machine, taking in legal norms as explicitly stated by some legal authority and stamping them 'valid' or 'invalid'. Although it does pass valid/invalid judgments on norm claims, it modifies the content of these claims with often great liberty. A legal scholar may surely decide to stick to quoting a legal authority issuing norms. However, the scholar will usually do so for political rather than epistemological reasons. On the contrary, as the history of the learned law shows, legal scholarship proved its value, if at all, in glosses, commentaries, re-statements, etc regarding the content of the law. In comparative law, in particular, it is not highly regarded when the only thing a scholar can do is to quote explicitly stated regulations of a foreign legal order and add a valid/invalid stamp. Second, nor is a theory of some legal order a meta-language that takes the language of a legal order as its object. In this a theory in law is unlike a theory in natural science. The latter *would* be a meta-language deciding which of the claims on natural states of affairs made in an object language were true. A theory of law is also unlike a theory of syntax which would conceive of

---

[10] See Mackor's contribution in chapter three of this volume.
[11] I am in agreement with much of what Mackor writes and I thank her for an incisive exchange on the topic both during the workshop, of which this volume is the upshot, and by email afterwards.
[12] Defended earlier in Bert Van Roermund, Wetten en weten. 'Theorie van het recht': een wijsgerige kritiek (Diss Tilburg) (Leuven-Zwolle, Acco, 1983).

a grammar as an algorithm deciding, in a finite number of steps, which sentences in a natural language are well-formed, and which not. What is the difference? For the meta-object distinction to make sense it is necessary that the object language is a so-called transparent context, ie a context into which we are allowed to quantify. For a natural scientist it makes sense to assess whether it is true that the morning star is identical with the evening star since the natural scientist can reduce both expressions to the claim that there is at least one object that if it is at position P_a at t_1 it must be at P_b at t_2.[13] For a grammarian it is possible to decide that the sentence 'If Paris is in Europe, then the moon is a green cheese', though semantically puzzling, is a well-formed sentence in English. That is because his or her criteria for grammaticality in English, though phrased in scientific language, directly describe the tacit linguistic competence of most native speakers.

Let's turn the medal now and look at the positive side of what it means that legal scholarship is in indirect speech. A legal order by virtue of being an order posited by authority is not a transparent realm for those who venture to describe it. They describe the norms of a legal order introducing them with the prefix 'The legislator rules that . . .', or 'According to the law of New Jersey one should . . .', or 'The German *Bundesverfassungsgericht* decided that . . .' These 'that' clauses and their equivalents announce a realm of thought that is not directly accessible to the speaker of the main clause. It is governed by the position of another speaker, and therefore by how he or she sees the world around him or her. Now, this *would* reduce legal scholarship to the quotation machine after all, were it not for the possibility of indirect speech. In indirect speech you can say what someone else is saying, and negotiate to what extent you use the conceptual and referential devices of your subject or your own. Philosophers will say that legal scholars are studying opaque contexts all the time, and that they are playing with the terms in that opaque context, bringing them in or out of these contexts, to rephrase them in their own terms and projecting them back into the legal system to see if they are absorbed.

There are rules for the game legal scholars are playing. The basic principle is that you should never quantify into opaque contexts. For instance, if the legislator rules that assisting suicide is forbidden, and you believe that assisting suicide is euthanasia,[14] you cannot conclude that the legislator rules that euthanasia is forbidden. That is because euthanasia is your term, not the legislator's. By hypothesis, it is not (necessarily) part of the legislator's belief content. However, you can try to sort things out by saying 'What we prefer to call euthanasia is forbidden by the legislator.' Then you bring 'euthanasia' from the opaque context governed by the prefix 'The legislator says that . . .' to the transparent context of your account of the world. In other words, you use 'euthanasia' *de re* rather than *de dicto*; and you can plug that translation back into the system to see how it

---

[13] Formats like 'There is at least one x such that . . .' and 'For all x it is the case that . . .' are called 'quantification' is first order predicate logic.
[14] By the way: euthanasia is another fine example of a concept that the law not only does not use but utterly refuses to use, at least in The Netherlands.

reacts. You don't have to pretend, as Westerman advises us to do, that you derive your categories from the legal system.

A more difficult rule of the game is that we should make a distinction between propositional opacity and referential opacity: we as speakers (ie as legal scholars) may either be shielded off from what a rulemaker rules (content) or from what he or she is ruling about (referent). Suppose we utter the norm statement: 'According to the Dutch High Court decision of date t, professional retailers should inform private customers about the risks of their products.' Suppose 'professional retailers' is our referential device, not the High Court's. Then it is us who determine what the norm is about. The High Court may have used another device in its decision, such as, for instance, 'a company like C'. The generalisation is the scholar's. However, it is also possible to take the duty imposed by the Court out of the opaque context of the decision as phrased by the Court. Then we as legal scholars re-formulate the duty in our words, leaving it to the domain of the High Court's speech to whom exactly it is to be attributed.

Why should we make this distinction? Because, and this is a third rule of the game, there is a trade-off between propositional and referential opacity. You cannot have it both ways at any given point in your hermeneutic exercise: if you lift referential opacity you will be left with propositional opacity, and if you lift propositional opacity, you will be left with referential opacity.[15] So if you wish to say what the High Court said, and if you want to rephrase the duty imposed by the Court, you are stuck with the referential device of the Court. Inversely, if you choose to rephrase the referential device, you are stuck with the propositional content of the Court's ruling. Of course you may lift both if you wish; but then you cut the link with whatever the Court decided and you can no longer claim that you are saying what the Court said. Legal scholarship uses the hybrid form of indirect speech, as it is, in point of fact, a theory of validity building on *meaning*.[16]

III. SOME IMPLICATIONS

These are only the first logical features of indirect speech. There would be a lot more to detect if we were to enter the level of semantics and pragmatics of indirect speech, especially from a phenomenological angle.[17] However, already

---

[15] All of this can be found in HN Castañeda, Thinking, Language and Experience (Minneapolis, University of Minnesota Press, 1989) 88ff.

[16] This is, in my view, the precise sense of calling legal scholarship 'hermeneutic'. This has little to do with legal scholarship (or doctrine) being about texts. Texts are only phenomena of norms, while other phenomena of norms are pictures, gestures, technological constraints (road bumps, for instance), etc. Legal scholarship is primarily about norms qua contents (of acts of will, as Kelsen saw), not about their appearances (although that is an area of knowledge in its own right). This was recognised in the early tradition of legal scholarship and its emphasis on dogma / doxa. cf M Herberger, Dogmatik, Zur Geschichte von Begriff und Methode in Medizin und Jurisprudenz (Frankfurt a.M., Ius Commune, 12, Klostermann, 1981).

[17] cf for instance, B Waldenfels, Vielstimmigkeit der Rede. Studien zur Phänomenologie des Fremden, vol 4 (Frankfurt aM, Suhrkamp, 1999) passim.

here we are able to see that my account of things has major consequences, in particular with regard to what 'coherence' can amount to as a criterion for truth in legal scholarship. We should be careful to distinguish coherence of the legal order under description as a criterion for truth telling about that legal order, on the one hand, and the unity a legal order claims in the effort of organising final discretion, on the other. The former is construed by legal scholarship from various data, one of which is the way final discretion is provided in the legal system(s) under investigation. The latter is an institution arranged to give form and substance to a necessary presupposition of law, to wit that it is all geared towards ending or preventing conflict in a certain community by offering an authoritative decision. The difference is crucial, not in the last place for methodology. For instance, if a judge appeals to 'the foresight of a reasonable man', the judge appeals to a criterion that functions within the overall purpose of the law to provide authoritative decisions to its subjects. Thus, it has to be fleshed out by authoritative assessments. It would make no sense at all to back up the judge's decision by measuring what the 'average' citizen is able to foresee by sending out questionnaires, holding interviews, doing psychological tests, or setting up sociological experiments. Obviously, having knowledge of the outcomes of such scientific exercises would help the judge greatly in making a sound decision. However, the judge should be careful not to transform the conflict before him or her into a fight between scientists, as it would make things worse.

However, social science research does make sense for the legal scholar because he or she has other fish to fry. It is the legal scholar's business to rephrase the norms of a legal order with an eye on their coherence from a much wider angle than the institutional role of the judge. The coherence criterion he or she works with tests a specific legal order against coherence from a variety of viewpoints. It is characteristic of his or her business, in particular, to apply epistemic rather than political criteria of coherence. For instance, the legal scholar will not only determine the place of a decision in a series of similar decisions of tort law, but also compare it with decisions in other areas of law (for instance contract law, criminal law, administrative law, constitutional law). The legal scholar may widen the scope of his or her research to other jurisdictions. Although these will often be neighbouring jurisdictions due to the political stakes of the legal order, there is no compelling epistemological reason why the legal scholar should not engage in comparison with more exotic ones. It is quite predictable that, under the influence of political developments, the state of the art comparative law of the future will be much more inclined to include Chinese, Indian, or Brasilian law, and put less emphasis on civil law versus common law, European law versus US law, etc. In a similar vein, legal scholars find reason to map the systematic character of law on to a much more incisive, sophisticated, and substantiated account of facts than the past required. Their statements will formulate what the law requires in order to remain fit to provide authoritative decisions in cases of actual or potential conflict. However, this is precisely the reason, both why they are not necessarily bound by what a legal order says about itself, and why they do not have to dress up as if they are.

Finally, I submit that my account of the relationship between law and legal scholarship squares nicely with Vranken's objections to Westerman's view.[18] Legal researchers select their own perspective on 'the system' of law, they track the dynamics of that system in relation to its ever changing environment, they are concerned with progress, and they relate this, on the final count, to issues of social justice as a matter of political morality rather than systematicity. These objections cannot easily be countered by saying that they prove the point of the law's categories and principles dominating legal scholarship. Of course legal scholarship is subservient to what a legal order is all about in society. However, precisely to render that service it often has to cut loose from established categories and principles. For these categories and principles are provisional articulations of what law is about.

---

[18] See Westerman's contribution in chapter five of this volume.

Index

academic articles, 80
academic lawyers, 77, 79, 128, 130
academic scholarship, 119, 123, 127
academic world, 119
academic writing, 165
actional scheme, 191, 196, 200–2, 250
alternative forms of regulating behaviour, 106
American Realism, 6, 153
analogical comparison, 183
analysis in law, 243, 248
analytical questions, 155
anthropological enquiry, 159
argumentation, 4–5, 7, 12, 15, 31, 38, 65, 194, 199, 206, 209
argumentative discipline, 4, 5, 82
assumption, 10, 21, 28, 34–5, 37, 39, 41, 44, 101, 119, 142, 145, 147, 206, 220, 259, 262, 266, 269, 273
authoritative, 1, 11–12, 22, 24–5, 35, 42, 159–61, 221–2, 236, 285
authoritative sources, 11
authoritative texts, 22, 24, 35, 42, 236
authority paradigm, 160, 164, 179, 207, 235, 254–6
autonomous law, 87
autonomous legal methodology, 156
autonomous system, 87
axiomatic discipline, 6, 9
axioms, 20, 25, 26, 96–7, 99, 103, 200, 259

behavioural economics, 218, 242, 247, 249, 252, 254–66, 268, 272–5
Bell, John, 26, 74, 76, 123, 155–6, 158, 160–6, 168, 170–2, 174, 176, 186, 227–8, 230, 234–5
Berthelot, Jean-Michel, 131, 177–8, 180, 182, 187, 202, 204–6, 250–1
Beyleveld, Deryck, 134, 145
binding precedent, 11
bio-legal history, 248, 251
Boyd, Robert, 241, 246, 249–51
Bubloz, Y., 183

business practice, 142–3, 222
calculability, 148
Carbonnier, Jean, 129
cartesian ideal, 97
case notes, 80
casebooks, 79
casuistic reasoning, 199–200

categorisation of reality, 192
causal explanation, 53–4
causal hierarchy, 193
causal scheme, 188–9, 191–4, 199, 201
causality, 50–1, 53, 188, 191, 194, 198, 206
causation, 51, 173, 201
choice of values, 26
civil law, 16, 74–5, 78, 80, 128–9, 183, 186, 199, 204, 220, 222, 285
Coase theorem, 263, 266–7
code, 16–17, 36, 90, 115–16, 126–8, 142, 148, 166, 183–5, 195–6, 199, 203, 230, 268
coherence, 9, 15, 33–5, 56, 59, 64–5, 89, 93, 104, 107, 109, 112, 117–19, 128, 134, 155, 193, 197, 202, 206, 229, 235, 252, 285
 – criteria of, 285
coherence of the legal system, 82, 112, 118–19
coherent order, 91
coherent picture of law, 105, 108, 110
coherentism, 33–4, 41
commentaries, 80, 156, 282
Common Law, 13, 73, 75, 78, 80, 139, 145, 179, 183–5, 195–6, 201, 207, 219, 235, 285
Common Law of contract, 139
common legal meta-language, 211
common legal tradition in Europe, 183
comparative approaches, 183
comparative law, 78, 82, 84, 117, 123–4, 130–1, 155, 157–9, 164, 167, 169–70, 173, 175, 177–84, 186–7, 197, 207, 209–24, 226–8, 230, 233–7, 239–40, 250–1, 282, 285
comparative lawyers, 157–8, 167–70, 172, 185, 187, 235, 251
comparative legal linguistics, 210–11, 222–3, 226–7
comparative legal research, 82, 91, 120, 123, 131, 158, 174–5, 229–30, 233–4, 236–7, 239–40, 250
comparative legal studies, 131, 173, 177–8, 181–4, 186, 197–8, 207, 210, 216, 237
comparative researcher, 5, 7, 108, 187–9, 192, 246, 249, 251
comparison, 28, 72, 89, 92, 131, 162, 167, 169, 172, 175, 178, 180–4, 187, 197, 210–11, 215–18, 220, 222–3, 225–31, 233–4, 238, 285
complexity, 73–4, 76, 137, 148, 161–2, 164, 186, 189
comprehensive view, 113
concept formation, 26

288 Index

conceptual framework, 87, 162, 209–10, 277
conceptual structure, 170, 198
concours d'agrégation, 125, 129–30
congruence, 138
conservative, 93–4, 147, 263–4
consistency, 34–5, 56, 64, 93, 112, 117–19, 235
consumer lawyers, 151
consumer protection, 17, 138, 151
contextualisation, 170, 265
continental European perspective, 74
contract, 17, 75, 81, 84, 98, 100, 103, 105, 114–6, 133–48, 150–6, 157, 161–3, 173, 181, 184, 186, 199, 214, 258, 266, 268–72, 285
corrective and distributive justice, 98
correctness of arguments, 7
critical rationalism, 25
cultural contextualisation, 170
cultural evolution, 244, 246, 250–1
cultural matrix, 124
cultural method in comparative legal studies, 198
cultural paradigm, 198
cultural phenomenon, 191
culturalist paradigm, 191, 250
culture, 79, 93, 113, 130, 141, 161, 163, 168–72, 174, 191–2, 197, 204, 211, 213, 218–221, 223–5, 231, 241, 244–250, 252–3, 263

deduction, 188, 190, 194
deductive arguments, 31
deductive justification, 32
deductive techniques, 179
deductivism, 128
democracy, 43, 151, 233
description, 4, 13–4, 17–9, 21, 23–4, 28–9, 43, 47–8, 52, 54, 56, 59–60, 62–70, 80, 83, 88, 101, 105, 113, 114, 117–8, 128, 142, 158, 168, 185, 224, 233, 237, 269, 282, 285,
descriptive, 3, 10, 13, 18, 47, 52–3, 58–70, 86, 110, 113, 127, 152, 155–8, 166–7, 175, 178, 237, 263, 273
descriptive disciplines, 10
descriptive research, 18
dialectical oppositions, 185, 200
dialectics, 26, 35, 186, 198–9
distributive Justice, 88, 98–100, 102–4, 124–6
doctrinal analysis, 87, 108
doctrinal approach, 118–19, 207, 227
doctrinal construction, 127
doctrinal issues, 134
doctrinal legal research, 8, 14, 79–82, 84, 86, 91, 93, 101, 111, 113–21, 175, 235–6, 242
doctrinalists, 207
dogmatism, 128–29, 131
Dworkin, Ronald, 4, 21, 41–2, 64, 92, 99, 104, 152, 164–5, 175, 195–6, 201–2

economic perspective, 204, 261, 268
economical, 7–8, 87, 95, 114, 203
effectiveness of rules, 108–9
empirical data, 1–2, 6–7, 11, 13, 22
empirical discipline, 3, 5–6, 113
empirical discovery of principle, 128
empirical legal doctrine, 6, 108
empirical legal studies, 83, 120
empirical orientation, 88, 105, 109–10
empirical outlook, 107, 109
empirical research, 1–2, 6–7, 113, 119–20, 180, 184–5, 208, 278
empirical social science, 3, 5, 110, 155, 175, 227
empirical verification, 5, 7
empirical-hermeneutical discipline, 3
empiricism, 25, 128, 187, 274
England, 72–3, 75, 120, 160–1
English contract law, 81, 141, 156
Enlightenment jurists, 197
epidemiological culture, 245
epistemological orientation of the comparatist, 182
epistemological pluralism, 189
epistemological regime, 189
epistemological studies, 129
epistemological validity of law, 193
epistemology, 29, 34, 37, 80, 82–3, 131, 162, 177–8, 180, 187–8, 190, 193, 201, 205, 208, 211, 248, 250–2
ethics, 10, 35, 46, 51–2, 83, 131, 137, 173
equality
 – formal, 102, 105–6
 – material, 102
European Convention on Human Rights, 225
European Court of Human Rights, 223, 225
European Court of Justice, 225
European Human Rights case, 164
European legal harmonisation, 183
European legal history, 184
European legal systems, 13, 75, 178, 198
European private law, 113–14, 117, 151, 153, 223
European societies, 185
europeanisation, 118–19, 129, 171, 174, 178, 218
euthanasia, 15, 63, 231–32, 238, 283
evaluative inquiries, 133
evoked culture, 255
evolutionary analysis in law, 241, 243–9, 251, 253, 255
evolutionary psychology, 244–51
Ewald, W., 159, 169–70
experimentation, 55, 188, 255, 261
explanation, 8, 11, 13, 20, 28, 38, 45, 47–50, 52, 56, 58, 69, 71, 91, 131, 169, 173, 175, 188–9, 192–3, 214, 224, 226, 237, 252, 269, 281
explanatory capacity of a theory, 15

explanatory disciplines, 8–9, 45–6, 49–51, 58, 69
explanatory legal doctrine, 20
exploratory inquiries, 18
external approach,119, 239, 254
external perspective, 109, 119, 124, 131, 236–7, 239–40
external theory, 94
extra-legal, 54, 62–3, 67, 69
extra-legal criteria, 62, 67, 69

fairness, 93, 156, 260, 272–4
Fauvarque-Cosson, Bénédicte, 178–82, 207
fiction, 52, 66, 100, 127
field research, 6
foreign law, 158, 171, 179, 213, 216, 220, 224, 233, 239
formal logic, 9,23
forms of justification, 30–1
foundationalism, 34,
French Humanist School, 197
French legal doctrine, 4, 17, 101, 123–31, 179–80
French legal heritage, 124
function of law, 161
functional approach, 181, 195, 214
functional method in comparative law, 178
functional objective, 184
functionalism, 181, 186, 191, 196–8, 202, 211–16, 219–23, 227, 234 ,250

gaps, 5, 64, 66, 70, 266
general clauses, 106–7
general laws, 50
general legal norms, 50, 53–6
general principles, 11, 15, 155, 173
Gény, François, 127–8
globalisation of the law, 129
Germany, 7, 9, 71–2, 75, 80–1, 101–4, 212–13
Gintis, Herbert, 252, 254–5
good faith, 134–5, 141, 143, 151, 156, 185–6
Gordley, James, 97, 174
Griffith, John, 135, 229, 231–2, 238
Grossfeld, Bernhard, 226
Grosswald Curran, Vivianne , 226
Grotius, Hugo, 88, 95–6, 98–102, 104
Grundnorm, 193

H(appiness)–standard, 43
hard cases, 21, 38, 46, 50, 56, 68, 70, 201
harmonisation, 151, 157, 180, 183–4, 186, 207, 213, 219
harmonisation projects, 184, 186, 207, 219
Hart, Herbert, 193
Heidmann, Ute, 180–1
hermeneutic, 3–6, 8, 11, 17, 19, 22, 29, 35, 44, 64, 68, 72, 112–13, 127, 158–9, 161, 166–74, 176, 179, 181–2, 186, 189–98, 201–2, 227, 230, 234–5, 251, 278, 284

hermeneutic element in legal research, 11
hermeneutic perspective, 168, 172
hermeneutic point of view, 159, 166, 172, 174
hermeneutical approach, 189, 194, 197, 251
hermeneutical functionalism, 196
hermeneutical legal scholar, 112
hermeneutical process, 196
hermeneutical scheme, 191, 195–7
hermeneutical structuralism, 196
historical discipline, 6
historical research, 6
history of law, 297
history of legal science, 193
holistic approach, 190
Holmes, Oliver Wendell , 6,76
homo oeconomicus, 191, 201, 257, 259
humanities, 50, 71, 85, 201, 229
Hyland, Richard, 211, 226
hypotheses, 1, 3, 11–12, 14–15, 17–18, 23, 25, 40, 66–7, 83, 136, 174, 238, 254, 265, 272

ideological approach, 147
ideological frame, 137
ideologies, 134, 136, 181, 231, 236
imperfect rights, 98–100, 102
implicit theories, 34
imputation, 10, 50–3
imputative explanations, 54
independent theoretical perspective, 89, 94
independent third, 89
indirect speech, 277, 282–4
individualism/collectivism, 249
innovation, 93–4, 113, 119–20, 134, 149, 188, 236
institutional character of law, 161– 2
institutional fact, 26, 59–60, 69, 161–2
institutional features of the law, 169
institutional knowledge, 158
intention of the legislator, 165
interdisciplinarity, 5, 128, 130–1, 178–9, 187, 207, 235–40, 253–5
interdisciplinary approaches,178,
interdisciplinary legal research, ix, 84, 237–9, 241, 243–4, 248–9, 252–3
internal coherence, 109, 128, 134, 155, 202
internal point of view, 159–61, 166, 168, 174, 176, 234
interpretation, 1, 3–5, 7–18, 22, 24–5, 28, 38, 42–3, 46, 56–60, 62–70, 81, 89–90, 92, 96, 108, 111, 124, 127, 135, 137, 156, 158, 162, 164–7, 171, 175, 190, 195–7, 209–11, 216, 219–26, 231, 233–4, 236, 260, 274
interpretation and culture, 171
interpretative analysis, 171
interpretative character of facts, 165
interpretative character of law, 158, 164

intersubjective consensus, 10, 18
intra-legal criteria, 62, 67–9

Jamin, Christophe, 125–6, 128
Jestaz, Philippe, 124–7, 129, 179–81
Jones, Owen, 246–7, 251, 254
judges, 6, 10, 12, 14, 79–81, 93, 108, 112–13, 119, 123, 126–7, 136, 139, 141, 162,183, 201, 208, 222, 225, 229, 233, 257, 262, 280–1
judicial decision, 6, 10, 12, 28, 50, 54, 61, 100, 108, 115, 136, 165, 216 ,223
jurisprudence,2, 7–8, 14, 28–9, 45, 64, 72–3, 78, 101, 124, 126–8, 145, 152–3, 170, 192, 197, 205, 210, 219, 250
justification
 – of a belief, 31
 – of behaviour, 30
 – forms of, 30–1
 – nature of, 30–1, 33
 – methodological, 120–1
 – theories of, 33–4
justificatory argument, 30, 32–3, 145

Kahn-Freund, Otto, 169, 219, 224, 226
Kelsen, Hans, 10, 46–8, 51–58, 64– 66, 99, 160, 168, 193–4, 212, 277, 282, 284
Kennedy, Duncan, 105–6
knowledge, 8, 15, 19–30, 37–8, 40–1,43–6, 49–50, 58–9, 65–6, 72–5, 79, 84, 90–2, 97, 116–17, 119–20, 124–6, 128–31, 156, 158–60, 167, 169,175–6, 179–80, 184, 188–9, 192–5, 199, 204–5, 207, 217, 220, 223–4, 226, 230, 234–9, 242, 246, 253, 255, 261, 273, 275, 278, 280, 284–5
Korobkin, Russell, 120, 262, 264–73
Kötz, Hein, 145, 157, 171, 174–5, 178, 197, 210–11, 215–16, 218, 221, 227, 234

Lakatos, Imre, 66
language, 23, 30, 130, 140, 151, 157, 170–3, 176, 185–6, 210–1, 213–15, 217– 28, 230,235, 254, 278, 280–4
Lasser , Mitchel, 124, 127, 168
Latour, Bruno, 130
law and economics, 2, 77, 82, 84, 119–20, 210, 218, 257–8, 261–5, 267, 269, 271, 273–5
law and finance, 72, 77, 82
law and literature, 120, 195
law and religion, 77, 82, 160
law in books, 73
law in context, 18, 72, 74, 77, 170
law professors, 71–86, 180–1, 241, 243, 255
law schools, 13, 71–4, 76–80, 82–5, 88, 120, 130–1, 143, 213, 229, 241, 281
lawmakers, 80, 84, 107, 195
legal anthropology, 2, 248

legal argument, 4, 5, 25–6, 38, 99, 166, 170, 198, 223, 227, 232
legal certainty, 19, 28, 42, 44, 116
legal concept, 2, 8–9, 14–15, 89, 155, 163–4, 175, 181, 223, 226, 234–5
legal cultures, 161, 163, 171, 220
legal doctrine, 1– 15, 17–8, 20, 22, 25–6, 29, 35, 45–70, 80, 88, 91, 93–5, 97–8, 100–1, 104, 108–10, 113, 128, 133, 152, 209–10, 223–7, 242, 248
 see also doctrinal legal research
legal dogmatism, 129
legal education, 72–81, 83–6, 126, 188, 239, 253
legal facts, 26, 59, 164, 233
legal families, 220
legal field, 13, 128–9
legal history, 77, 82, 156, 180, 183–4, 196, 209–10, 212, 247–8, 251
legal idealist position, 134
legal justification, 31, 169, 231–2
legal knowledge, 19, 24, 73, 91, 124–6, 128–31, 158, 194–5
legal material, 42, 57, 65, 169
legal mentality, 124, 227
legal method, 24–5, 29, 42, 92, 195, 207, 236,
legal normativists, 58–60, 62, 69
legal offence, 103
legal order, 49, 53, 56, 66–7, 93–4, 97, 108, 277–8, 280–3, 285–6
legal philosophy, 7–8, 45, 77–8, 82, 157, 250
legal practice, 2–5, 18, 64, 68, 79, 82, 152
legal practitioners, 2–3, 18, 47, 49, 65, 77, 85–8, 90, 152
legal principles, 2, 5, 7, 14, 17, 25, 65, 81, 89, 93–4
legal psychology, 2
legal reaction, 103
legal reality, 2, 47, 109, 228
legal reasoning, 7, 9, 25, 28, 31, 42, 44, 48, 82, 93, 99, 125 –6 , 128, 131, 155, 166, 178, 183, 186–7, 194–5, 198–9, 203, 205–6, 208
legal research, 3, 9, 11, 17–9, 22, 26, 45, 71–2, 78–80, 82–93, 101, 112–4, 116, 118, 120–3, 131, 133–4, 155–61, 163–5, 167, 169, 171–5, 177, 179, 229–30, 233–41, 243–4, 248–50, 252–9, 261, 265, 267, 269, 271, 273, 275, 286
legal rules, 2, 4, 8, 13–4, 42, 72, 76, 78, 84, 107, 115, 156–9, 162–3, 165, 170, 172, 197, 218, 220–1, 233, 236, 238–9, 258, 262–3, 265, 273, 280
legal scholars, 3, 4, 6, 10–1, 15, 18, 46–9, 53–6, 58, 60, 62–7, 70–1, 73, 79– 80, 83, 85, 87, 89–91, 94, 106, 111–2, 117, 120, 126–7, 152, 187, 212, 243, 249, 252–7, 263, 265, 272–4, 278, 280, 282–5

legal scholarship, 1–5, 8, 11, 14, 17, 71, 79, 81–3, 85, 90– 108–9, 111–4, 118–20, 123–4, 126–8, 177, 179, 182, 186–8, 193, 207, 229, 239, 243, 247–8, 255, 257–8, 263, 267, 274–5, 277–8, 280–6
legal science, 1–2, 4, 9, 19–29, 31, 33, 35, 37, 39–44, 54–5, 82, 88, 94–5, 102, 104, 109–10, 113, 118, 137, 180, 182–3, 193, 209–10, 223, 243, 278
legal scientists, 43
legal sociology, 2, 6, 8, 77, 82, 205
legal structures, 169, 224
legal syllogism, 162
legal system, 1, 10–8, 24, 47, 56–7, 73, 75, 77–80, 87, 89–95, 97, 104–5, 110, 112–9, 123–5, 155–61, 163–78, 181, 186–7, 195, 198–9, 203, 207, 209, 216–9, 221, 224, 226, 228, 230, 231, 233–6, 239, 248, 251, 262, 280, 281, 263, 284–5
legal tradition, 123–4, 183, 205, 219–20
legal training, 72–8
legal translation, 211, 224–6
legislative lawyers, 112
Legrand, Pierre, 75, 131, 158, 168, 171, 173–5, 178,184, 185, 186, 197–8, 216, 220
Llewellyn, Karl, 133, 135, 164, 202
Locke, John, 98, 150, 199
logic, 6, 8–10, 23, 26–7, 30, 32, 38, 41, 68, 128, 162,170, 186, 197–8, 235, 251–2, 281, 283
 – dialectical, 186
 – internal, 8, 10, 128, 235
logical discipline, 9
logical positivism, 60
logical system, 23
Luhmann, Niklas, 111, 114–5

MacCormick, Neil, 4, 26, 31, 48, 158, 61–2, 166
Mackor, Anne Ruth, 20–1, 24–6, 44–5, 47–8, 91, 277, 282
maintenance of the legal system, 24
McCrudden, Christopher, 155, 157, 159, 165–6, 249, 254
mental map, 162, 169, 175, 234
metaculture, 245, 247–8
meta-language, 211, 278, 282
meta-object, 283
method for legal science, 19–20, 22, 28–9, 40, 43–4
methodological justification, 120–1
methodological pluralism, 206, 228
methodology, 3–4, 11, 15, 17–8–9, 24, 45, 66, 82, 87–8, 95, 104, 108, 112–3, 115, 117–21, 123,133–5, 152–3, 156, 172–4, 177–9, 181–3, 185, 187, 188–91,193,195, 197–201, 203, 207, 209,211, 214, 216, 219, 221, 223, 227, 229, 235–6, 243–4, 248–51, 253, 257–8, 278, 285

methodology of enquiry, 172–4
methodology of social sciences, 87
methods, 2–4, 6, 14, 19, 22–4, 41–2, 44, 56, 60, 71, 82–3, 89, 117, 121, 124–6, 129, 152, 155, 177–8, 182, 186, 188, 190–1, 194–5, 197, 205, 207, 211, 215–6, 220, 223, 230, 235–7, 242, 246, 249–50, 253, 258, 261, 263–4, 277
micro-macro problem, 249–50
Michaels, Ralf, 178,181, 211, 214
mind-independent reality, 29–30
misrepresentation, 143–4, 186
monist view on science, 3
Moore, Underhill, 153
morality, 28, 41–2
multidisciplinary research, 119, 238

national cultural identity, 220
national culture, 93, 171
natural law, 2, 7, 67, 88, 95–6, 98–101, 128, 134, 206
natural lawyers, 96–7, 102–3
naturalist paradigm, 191, 250
nature /culture, 250
nature of the law, 19, 24–5, 29, 43
neoclassical economics, 258, 260, 262, 268
neutrality, 105, 109, 226, 274
Nonet, Philip, 105–06
nonmonotonicity, 32–3
non-normative legal doctrine 20, 26, 45, 47, 49, 51, 53, 55, 57, 59, 61, 63, 65, 67, 69
normative discipline, 4, 10, 45–6, 54, 69
normative legal science, 4, 19–21, 23, 25, 27, 29, 31, 33, 35, 37, 39–44, 82
normative neutrality, 274
normative questions, 29, 41, 157–8
normative science, 19–20, 29–30, 39–40, 43
normative theory, 258, 273–4
normative positions, 113
normativity, 59, 68, 90, 92, 95, 109, 113, 155–6, 158, 175
norm-contention, 65, 67, 69
norm-description, 64–5, 68
norm-recommendations, 60, 62, 67–70

objective, 7, 8, 18, 37–8, 46, 51, 62, 67–8, 96, 151, 157, 159, 168, 174, 183–4, 189, 233, 248
objective external world, 38
objective reality, 8, 18, 189
objectivism, 188
objectivity, 18, 61, 81, 109, 168
objectivity in legal research, 18
objects of justification, 30
ontological realism, 21
ontologicalisation of concepts, 181
order, 1, 7, 13, 18, 22, 29, 31, 47, 49, 53, 55–6, 59, 64, 66–7, 71–2, 76–7, 81–2, 84,

order (*cont.*):
  88–94, 96–102, 105–8, 110, 115–6, 123, 128–9, 144, 148, 156, 161, 163, 172–3, 176–7, 179, 187, 190, 193–4, 201, 204, 207, 220, 226, 235–6, 238–9, 244, 253, 261–2, 265–6, 270, 277–8, 280–3, 285–6,
ordering reality, 15
original contract, 100
ought-conclusion, 30
ought-sentence, 30

paradigm, 162, 191, 266
paradigm orientations, 191
paradigmatic, 14–5, 98, 116, 226
paradigmatic change, 116
paradigmatic framework, 14–5
paradigmatic theories, 14, 226
paternalism, 134, 163, 264
penalties, 100, 272
phenomenological angle, 284
philosophers, 24, 47, 82, 83, 283
philosophy, 7, 8 , 10, 13, 20, 23, 38, 45, 77–8, 82, 85, 94, 99, 131, 133–4, 137, 155, 157, 175, 224, 242, 247, 250, 277
piece of knowledge, 21–2
political decisions, 110
political developments, 285
positive morality, 51
positive sciences, 1, 4–5, 227
positive law, 19, 28–9, 42–3, 46, 56–7, 62–3, 65–7, 88, 96, 100, 180
positivism, 60, 130, 188–9, 192–4, 198, 200, 206
Posner, Eric, 79, 81–4, 113, 255, 262
post-modernism, 220
practical orientation, 90, 101, 108, 113
practical reason, 45–8, 59, 67, 69, 148–50, 157, 160
practitioners, 2–3, 18, 47, 49, 65, 71–7, 80, 82, 85–6, 90, 152
predictability, 148, 206
prediction, 193, 205
presumption of similarity, 180, 220
private law, 13, 97, 99–102, 104–5, 113–4, 116–7, 123, 126, 151, 153, 162, 184–5, 188, 212–4, 218, 223, 281
procedural character of law, 163
procedural context, 164–70
procedural law, 25, 114
proof, 21, 23, 26, 115, 181, 272
property, 16, 99–101, 116, 129, 163, 169, 181, 184, 199, 203–5, 269
proportionality principle, 65, 107
psychological, 6, 7, 8, 10, 57–8, 205, 245, 247–8, 260–1, 264, 269, 271, 285
public law, 102, 104, 169, 171, 174, 184, 215, 222
punishment, 61, 65, 103, 149

Rabel, Ernst, 211–21, 223
rational abstraction, 97
rational perspective, 36
rationalist optimism, 97
rationality, 23, 34, 36, 127, 134–5, 137–8, 247, 259, 262, 273
Rawls, John, 24–5
Raz, Joseph, 35, 160
real position, 35–6
realist movements, 6
realist scholarship, 185
reasonable expectations, 135, 146–7, 153
reasoning methods, 190
reconstructive work, 94
reductionism, 179–80, 182, 188, 207, 236, 249–50
regulatory impact assessment, 107
relationship between teaching and research, 72, 86
relevance, 12, 35, 52, 103, 127, 149, 163, 196, 212, 216, 218, 265, 279–80
representation of the law, 165
research assessment, 1, 3, 120
research hypotheses, 12
research question, 12–3, 22–3, 118, 120–1, 173, 237–9
Richerson, Peter, 310, 315, 316, 320–2
Riles, Annelise, 186–7, 205, 208, 214
role of law, 72, 77, 100, 157–8, 224
Roman law, 16, 129, 183, 192, 197, 203, 214
Roman legal doctrine, 1
Roman texts, 196–7
Ross, Alf, 5–6
rule of law, 105, 136, 147, 150, 160, 206, 217
rule of recognition, 193

Sacco, Rodolfo, 165, 212
Samuel, Geoffrey, 5, 81, 83, 93, 95, 123, 131, 159–60, 162–3, 165, 169, 177–182, 184–8, 190, 192–6, 198, 200–2, 204, 206–9, 219, 235–7, 249, 251, 254–6, 274
Scandinavian Realism, 6
scepticism about rules, 106
schemes of intelligibility, 177–8, 186, 189, 191–2, 195, 204–5, 249–51,
science, 2–3, 7, 9, 19–20, 22–4, 28–9, 38, 40, 43–4, 73, 88, 110, 129, 131, 155, 193, 202, 237
  – conception of, 1
  – nature of, 2, 20
sciences of the spirit, 189
scientific, 1, 3, 5, 9,–15, 17–8, 21, 23–4, 37, 40, 46, 49–51, 54–5, 60–3, 66, 68–9, 81, 90, 109–10, 113, 120, 156, 159, 179, 182, 185, 188, 194, 207, 214–6, 219, 227, 229–30, 235–9, 242, 247, 252–3, 255, 278, 283, 285
scientific observation, 13
scientific theory, 14

scientific discipline, 1, 17, 23, 255
scientific inquiry, 11
scientific knowledge, 23,37, 49–50, 90, 278
scientific method, 5, 21, 40, 113, 247
scientific production, 18
scientific reductionism, 179, 182, 207, 235
scientific structure, 185
scientists, 2, 5, 20, 38, 41, 43, 49, 52–3, 55–6, 61–2, 64, 68–70, 91, 106, 111, 131, 179, 249, 253–54, 256, 285
self-referential legal research, 84
set of rules, 29, 88
shared understanding, 15
shared world view, 15
Smits, Jan, 4, 19, 26, 28, 29, 44, 82, 221–2, 230
social and cultural context, 175, 234–5
social construction of reality, 161, 205
social context, 170, 231
social fact, 25–8, 44, 59, 62–4, 66–7, 70, 185, 191, 206
social needs, 102
social reality, 27, 59, 66, 181, 190, 192, 203–6, 236
social science, 2–3, 5, 8, 50, 58, 61–2, 71, 83–5, 87, 91, 95, 110, 113, 119, 128–31,133–4, 155, 157, 159–60, 175, 178–80, 182, 184, 186–92, 194, 200 ,202, 203–6, 208, 214, 227–8, 229, 236, 243, 245, 247–9, 251–5, 258, 261, 265, 285
social science research, 131, 192, 285
social scientist, 24
social welfare, 274
societal context, 232
socio-cultural environment, 231
socio-legal scholars, 187
sociological, 7, 8, 10, 87, 94, 143, 169, 205, 215, 237, 261, 285
sociology, 2, 6, 8, 10, 19, 22, 42, 44, 77, 82, 95, 109, 128, 133, 177, 180, 191, 209, 214–6, 219, 227, 230, 237
socio-psychological, 7
Soeteman, Arend, 26, 46, 53–4, 59, 68–9
soundness assumption, 34–5
sources of law, 8, 11, 15, 45–6, 127–8, 171
standards, 25, 28, 34, 41, 62–3, 65, 67, 69, 82, 88, 106, 115–6, 133, 149, 151, 155, 159–60, 172
structuralism, 186, 191, 196, 200
subjectivity, 10, 40
supreme courts, 12, 222
syllogism, 6, 128, 162, 188
systematisation, 17–8, 20–1, 28, 45–6, 48–50, 58, 65, 114, 211, 223, 228, 237
systematising activity, 45

taxonomy, 84, 184–5, 239, 248, 252–3
teaching, 71–8, 86, 130, 213
tertium comparationis, 219

testable hypotheses, 14–15
text analysis, 6
textbooks, 75, 80–1, 128, 156
't Hooft, Gerard, 47
theology, 3, 7, 51–2
theorems, 20, 23–6
theoretical assumptions, 3
theoretical framework, 13, 87–8, 90–1, 93–5, 109–14, 117–8, 120, 221, 245–7, 251, 253–4, 280–1
theoretical inquiries, 133
theoretical integration, 243, 249, 252–3
theory in law, 15, 282
theory in natural science, 282
Tijssen, Hervé, 118–9
topoi, 5
traditional, 5–6, 19, 23, 25, 42, 44, 80, 84, 88, 102, 104, 108, 110, 123, 125, 126, 130, 147, 149, 179, 184, 188, 196–7, 207, 227, 235–7, 243, 248–9, 255, 258–60, 262, 264, 269, 273–4
transactional practice, 148
translation, 57, 111, 172, 186, 211, 217, 222–6, 230, 265, 283
transmitted culture, 245–6
transnationalisation, 227
Treaty of Amsterdam, 107
types of legal research, 71,248, 253,

underlying ethic, 135, 139
underlying legal principles, 89
underlying values, 8, 56, 136
understanding, 8, 11, 15, 35, 44, 47, 49–50, 58, 77, 81, 83, 91, 94, 101, 103, 108–11, 123, 133–7, 144–7, 152–3, 155, 159, 163, 172–3, 177–9, 182, 184, 188–9, 191, 195, 200, 205, 207, 216–8, 221, 223–4, 226–7, 232, 235, 237, 247, 249, 273, 281
understanding of rules, 108
United States, 7, 72, 74, 83, 85, 104, 212–3
universal, 38, 96–7, 100, 134, 180, 208, 245, 248, 251, 261
universalisation, 180
universalist, 200, 218
universality/diversity, 249

valid legal norm, 193
validity, 1, 11–2, 14–5, 17,48, 50, 53–7, 60, 63, 66, 69, 75, 96, 103, 115, 155, 171, 185, 193, 261–2, 272, 274, 277, 282, 284
values, 8, 10, 15–6, 18, 30–1, 41, 56, 58, 62–3, 65–7, 69, 74, 101, 128, 133–4, 136, 157, 191,245–6, 259, 266–7
van Fraassen, Bas, 237, 278–9
Van Hoecke, Mark, 22, 29, 45–6, 48, 50, 57–8, 71, 78, 82, 113, 123, 133, 152, 157, 177–8, 209, 211, 224, 226, 228, 241, 248, 251

Van Quickenborne, Marc, 8, 50, 55
variety of viewpoints, 285
von Jhering, Rudolf, 88, 95, 101–5
vulgarisation, 18

Watson, Alan, 79, 170, 210–1, 223
Westerman, Pauline, 24, 45, 87, 96, 98–100, 106, 111–3, 115–6, 119, 156, 209, 277–8, 280, 284

Western legal systems, 199
Western tradition, 193, 219
will of the legislator, 97, 110
Wissink, Marc, 111–2
world view, 15–6

Zweigert, Konrad, 92, 96, 123, 157, 171, 174, 179, 197, 211, 215, 219, 221, 227